www.wadsworth.com

wadsworth.com is the World Wide Web site for Wadsworth and is your direct source to dozens of online resources.

At *wadsworth.com* you can find out about supplements, demonstration software, and student resources. You can also send email to many of our authors and preview new publications and exciting new technologies.

wadsworth.com
Changing the way the world learns®

Logic and Controversy

Logic and Controversy

Maurice F. Stanley

University of North Carolina, Wilmington

WADSWORTH

THOMSON LEARNING

Australia • Canada • Mexico • Singapore • Spain • United Kingdom • United States

WADSWORTH

THOMSON LEARNING™

Publisher: *Eve Howard*
Philosophy Editor: *Peter Adams*
Assistant Editor: *Kara Kindstrom*
Editorial Assistant: *Anna Lustig*
Development Consultant: *Jake Warde*
Marketing Manager: *Dave Garrison*
Project Manager, Editorial Production: *Erica Silverstein*
Print/Media Buyer: *Robert King*

Permissions Editor: *Joohee Lee*
Copy Editor: *Betty Duncan*
Illustrator: *Dale Gray*
Cover Designer: *Yvo Riezebos Design*
Cover Image: *EyeWire*
Text and Cover Printer: *The Maple-Vail Book Manufacturing Group*
Compositor: *Shepherd, Inc*

For more information about our products, contact us at:
Thomson Learning Academic Resource Center
1-800-423-0563
For permission to use material from this text,
contact us by:
Phone: 1-800-730-2214
Fax: 1-800-730-2215
Web: http://www.thomsonrights.com

Library of Congress Cataloging-in-Publication Data

Stanley, Maurice
　Logic and controversy / by Maurice F. Stanley
　　p. cm.
　Includes index.
　ISBN 0-534-57378-9
　　1. Logic. I. Title.

BC71 .S734 2001
160—dc21   2001045343

Wadsworth/Thomson Learning
10 Davis Drive
Belmont, CA 94002-3098
USA

Asia
Thomson Learning
60 Albert Street, #15-01
Albert Complex
Singapore 189969

Australia
Nelson Thomson Learning
102 Dodds Street
South Melbourne, Victoria 3205
Australia

Canada
Nelson Thomson Learning
1120 Birchmount Road
Toronto, Ontario M1K 5G4
Canada

Europe/Middle East/Africa
Thomson Learning
Berkshire House
168-173 High Holborn
London WC1V 7AA
United Kingdom

Latin America
Thomson Learning
Seneca, 53
Colonia Polanco
11560 Mexico D.F.
Mexico

Spain
Paraninfo Thomson Learning
Calle/Magallanes, 25
28015 Madrid, Spain

In memory of my father
Claude L. Stanley
(1917–1998)

Contents

PART TWO   *Informal Logic*

CHAPTER THREE   **Informal Fallacies   52**

PART THREE   *Formal Logic*

CHAPTER FOUR   **The Syllogism   126**

CHAPTER FIVE   **Truth-Functional Logic   177**

CHAPTER SIX   **Quantifiers   236**

Preface

The purpose of this textbook is to enable students to apply the methods of critical analysis to some of the important and interesting issues of our time. The overall topics include those of critical thinking, which helps with the crucial task of finding arguments in their contexts; informal logic, which provides a sensitivity to the uses and abuses of language; and formal logic, from Artistotle's syllogism to the deductive proofs and quantifiers of modern symbolic logic.

Logic and Controversy pulls these disciplines together into a kind of toolkit to be used in the analysis of arguments. Some of the tools are meant for rough work, some for more precise work. In this book, the uses and applications of logic are given the prominent place, although I do include comments on theory in each chapter.

The logic courses I took as an undergraduate and as a graduate student were mostly highly formal and abstract, using examples and exercises that did not encourage me to think that logic could ever be useful in the analysis of interesting, timely issues. When I began teaching logic, I realized that the use of real-life examples and exercises served to both motivate the students to see the connections to everyday life and to help them more readily understand the concepts being discussed. So I began adding newspaper and magazine editorials, debates, and so on, focusing on contemporary issues. The students appreciated this approach and realized they were not only learning logic but also gaining new perspectives on the issues of the times. Having refined the course over several years, I then decided that I would write a logic text that served these purposes better, and the result is *Logic and Controversy*.

Major Features of this book include:
- A very complete treatment of the fallacies (thirty-eight fallacies defined, with examples, as opposed to only eighteen or so in most other standard texts)

- A unifying procedure (in Chapter 8) that pulls all these elements of critical analysis into a step-by-step analytic procedure to be used to analyze arguments in context—that is, whole editorials from newspapers, magazines, and the Internet

- A "rich trove of exercises," as one reviewer put it, that give the student ample practice in analytic techniques

Special pedagogical aids and high-interest features of *Logic and Controversy* include:

- An "Applications" section in each chapter, in which two or three complete editorials or essays on controversial issues are fully worked out using the techniques in that chapter

- A "quick list" of thirty-eight fallacies in Chapter 3 for easy reference

- A summary for each chapter, to keep the overall objective of critical analysis of arguments in the student's mind

- An overabundance of exercises for every section of every chapter and answers to selected exercises at the back of the book

- An appendix with logic puzzles and an appendix for the logic-class debate

Acknowledgments

For their reviews and comments, I want to express my thanks to Henry N. Carrier, Brevard Community College; Suzanne Cataldi, Southern Illinois University; Marthe Chandler, DePauw University; Sandra Edwards, University of Arkansas; Henry J. Folse, Jr., Loyola University, New Orleans; Barbara Forest, Southeastern Louisiana University; George Gale, University of Missouri, Kansas City; Milton Goldinger, University of Wisconsin, Oshkosh; Michael Harrington, University of Mississippi; Marcus Hester, Wake Forest University; Hugh Hunt, Kennesaw State College; Charles Kielkopf, Ohio State University; Erik Kraemer, University of Wisconsin, Lacrosse; David L. Morgan, University of Northern Iowa; H.S. Moorhead, Northeastern Illinois University; Emil Piscitelli, Northern Virginia Community College; Jan R. Sugalski, Santa Fe Community College; Paul Tang, California State University, Long Beach; Ed Teall, Central Michigan University; and Stephen Wall-Smith, Lincoln University.

Also, my thanks to these people at Wadsworth: Peter Adams, Philosophy editor; Jerry Holloway, Chalida Anusasananan, Erica Silverstein, and Joohee Lee.

Thanks to Betty Duncan, my copy editor, for the great improvements that she has made throughout the book.

Many thanks to the students here at the University of North Carolina at Wilmington who helped me work through the material in this book: Melanie Moore, Cate Powell, and Jeff Bradley. Special thanks to Jeff for his generous help with those aspects of the book that required computer expertise and also for the article he contributed to the book.

Thanks to Joe Wilson, my chairman in the Philosophy and Religion Department at UNC-Wilmington, for letting me teach a special course in spring 2000 to try out this approach to logic and critical thinking.

Thanks to Maynard Adams, UNC-Chapel Hill, a serious philosopher who has always encouraged me over many years since I was his student. He persuaded me that, though people disagree about values, values are real nonetheless.

Thanks to Bill Mander and The Bradley Society at Oxford University for letting me participate in their philosophy conference over the past few years, which has been inspirational to me. They enjoy arguing there, too!

Thanks to Glana, my wife, for an enormous amount of work on this project, for her patience (and her impatience), and for her sweet beauty and kindness during our life together.

Logic and Controversy

Introduction

Logic and critical thinking are about arguments. By argument, logicians do not mean a quarrel or otherwise angry dispute, but simply a statement backed up by reasons. Here is an example of an argument, in this sense:

> *If it quacks, it's a duck.*
>
> *It quacks.*
>
> *Therefore, it's a duck.*

Nothing much rides on this simple little argument, but other arguments are more complex and much more important—that you should get a certain job or a promotion; those of a prosecutor or defense attorney, upon which someone's life or freedom might depend; or those, like arguments for a comprehensive test ban treaty, on which the fate of nations and the lives of millions of people may hang.

Arguments are crucial to law, science, business, and politics and indeed to every rational human pursuit. Few of us can get through a day without being called upon to back up one of our statements or beliefs with some good reasons.

Our lives, then, are filled with arguments. The point of this book is to teach you about arguments—how to recognize them, how to take them apart (analyze them) to see if they are any good, and how to put them together (compose them)—especially in the context of serious issues.

In Chapters 1 and 2 we will learn some basic concepts of logic—argument, premise, conclusion, and suppressed premise—and apply them to such issues as the conviction of Dr. Jack Kevorkian and the Columbine High School killings.

In Chapter 3 we will take up informal fallacies, which are not only fun but also very useful in the critical analysis of essays and articles on such issues as abortion and capital punishment. Informal fallacies often show up in advertising, as well. This is a long chapter, but well worth the time; the list of fallacies is a great toolbox for the logical analyst.

Next we turn to symbolic logic and its deductive rigor: syllogism and Venn diagrams in Chapter 4 and truth-functional logic and deductive proofs in Chapter 5. We will apply this powerful logical machinery to such issues as assisted suicide, abortion, and human cloning.

Inductive arguments and ways of testing them for strength are the subject of Chapter 7. We will examine whether the death penalty is racially discriminatory, the dangers of AIDS, and the fascinating issue of whether we humans are alone in the universe.

Finally, Chapter 8 gathers the critical methods of the earlier chapters into a step-by-step procedure and applies it to the crucial issues of the Middle East peace process, animal rights, prayer in school, violence in the media, and others.

Logic can clarify these issues wonderfully, by showing which of the relevant arguments on either side are effectively reasoned and which are not. Logic is an important tool in both criticizing and constructing arguments. However, we will not solve these grand issues by means of logic alone. Although logic can tell us whether an argument is effectively reasoned, it cannot tell us if the statements on which it is based—the premises—are true or false. Knowing all the facts about even one of these issues is undoubtedly impossible.

Language, in which every argument is expressed, is not fixed and absolute in its meaning. For this reason you will not always agree with my analyses, so it is unrealistic to think that we can obtain the "right" answers to all these issues. People of intelligence and goodwill will disagree about what a word or a statement means or about how an argument should be paraphrased or symbolized. The "last word" is not easy to come by, and so even the most brilliant analysts must maintain humility and an open mind.

On the other hand, these factors do not mean that "anything goes." In virtue of living in the same world, speaking the same language, and having to a great extent the same values, we will agree on many issues.

CHAPTER ONE

Arguments

Every science has its theory, and every art has its principles—not that one cannot be a scientist or an artist, on some level at least, without knowing the underlying conceptual questions that arise with any discipline. In this book we focus on applications rather than theory. Still, you should be aware that the basic concepts of logic and critical thinking were developed by the inspiration and hard mental labor of generations of thinkers, all the way back to Aristotle.

Some logic students will be interested in the theory of logic and will not feel that they understand logic without being presented some underlying theory. For those students especially, we will consider some relevant issues of what logicians call philosophy of logic, philosophical logic, or logical theory. We will also offer some explanation in terms of logical theory of the main concepts that logicians use in practice.

In this chapter the central concepts are argument, premise, and conclusion; premises and conclusions are statements. Why do we choose statements rather than sentences or (as some logicians insist) propositions? For one thing, two or more sentences, in more than one language ("Snow is white" and "Schnee ist weiss") can mean the same thing; or the same sentence, uttered on different occasions, can mean two or more different things ("I'll see you here tomorrow"). So some philosophers of logic choose this "same meaning" and call it a statement, or proposition, but a statement (proposition) can mean either what is stated (a fact) or the act of stating—or what is proposed or the act of proposing.

I have chosen to use the term *statement;* it is natural, unlike *proposition,* and I want to stay within ordinary, natural language as far as this is possible. I have defined the term *statement* as "what is stated." The same statement may be made in many different languages, and we would ordinarily say that this "what is said" can be true or false, as propositions are. But statements are not thought of as platonic universals that have some mystical, otherworldly existence (such as do Plato's "Forms" or

3

"Ideas" or the medieval logicians' "universals"). We can talk all we like about statements without committing ourselves to the existence of universals. Ordinary language has a place for statements, as it does for ideas and blueprints, for example.

Whether we are committed by these terms to universals is hardly settled among philosophical logicians. Analogously, mathematics has not really settled the question of what sort of things numbers are, but mathematicians keep on doing their mathematical work. So, in a similar way, we will use the term *statement,* without being entirely complacent about it.

1.1 Arguments: Premises and Conclusions

Before we can bring the techniques of logic and critical thinking to bear on the great issues of our time, we must first get a firm hold on certain basic concepts. **Logic** is the study of arguments, and arguments are composed of **statements.** So we should begin with a clear idea of what a statement is. When I say "Joe is late" and you say "Joe is tardy" we are, by means of different sentences, making the same statement, to the effect that Joe hasn't shown up on time. The same statement can be expressed in many different ways, even in many different languages. Some logicians call these *propositions,* or *claims,* rather than *statements,* for philosophical reasons. Another important aspect of statements is that they must be either true or false—unlike questions, commands, exclamations, expressions of emotion, and so on.

Now we can define an argument: An **argument** is a set of statements of which one, the **conclusion,** is supposed to be supported by the others, which are called the **premises.** For example:

> *Caesar wept for the poor, so he was not ambitious, for uncaring people do not weep for the poor, and ambitious people are uncaring.*

The word "so" gives us a clue that the conclusion is "Caesar was not ambitious." The other statements are premises that are offered in support of that conclusion. Logicians rewrite such arguments in what is called **standard form**—premises first, conclusion last—like this:

> *Caesar wept for the poor.*
>
> *Uncaring people do not weep for the poor.*
>
> *Ambitious people are uncaring.*
>
> ∴ *Caesar was not ambitious.*

(*Note:* For *so* or *therefore,* the logician writes ∴.)

An argument may have any number of premises supporting its conclusion. For example:

Most Republicans are conservative, and George W. Bush is a conservative, so he probably favors prayer in school because all conservatives do.

We rewrite this in standard form:

Most Republicans are conservative.

George W. Bush is a Republican.

All conservatives favor prayer in school.

∴ *George W. Bush probably favors prayer in school.*

The conclusion is indicated by the word "so." (There are other such indicator words, which we will discuss in Chapter 2.) This is a different kind of argument from the one about Caesar, but it has the same elements: premises and conclusion.

Exercise 1.1   A. Find premise(s) and conclusion in each argument. Then write the argument in standard form. (Use ∴ for *therefore*.)

1. The new "flat tax" is a good idea. It amounts to a tax cut for everyone.

2. You should get on the Internet soon. Everybody who is anybody is going to be online. And you don't want to be out in the cold.

3. NATO officials were concerned about the deadly rocket strike on Sarajevo because such incidents shake Bosnians' confidence in the mission, which in turn endangers the fragile peace in the region.

4. Mrs. Jones is a serious liability for her husband, the mayor, for he cannot distance himself from her, and she is engulfed in a terrible scandal.

5. If we cut education, environment, and Medicare, the president will veto the tax cut. But, without a tax cut, Republican voters will be disappointed. If they are disappointed, they won't get out and vote. So if we cut education, environment, and Medicare, we'll lose the election.

6. Nobody knows how many people live in the United States because the census always undercounts urban minorities. So we don't know how much government benefits the cities really need.

7. A vicuna overcoat is $20,000. A vicuna scarf is only $750. I only have $5000 left on my charge card, so I guess I'll have to take the scarf.

8. Picabo Street was the first U.S. skier to win the World Cup downhill season title, so she deserved to be named 1995's Sportswoman of the Year.

9. The Suns probably won't lose Barkley to the Clippers. Barkley likes Phoenix, and he says that he's not going to go to a "bad team" and play. Anyway, he's already making $20 million per year.

10. Michelle Lewan can handle the pressure because she's a champion, and champions always do.

B. Find the premises and conclusion in the following letter to the editor.

Rich Are Taxed Big-Time; They Deserve Break[1]

In response to "Moderates suggest seeking a more prudent tax cut" (Feb. 14 Viewpoint):

David Broder parades the views of Washington Democrats without mentioning the most compelling story: tax inequality. Opponents of Bush's tax cut argue that the "wealthiest 1 percent receive most of the benefit" without mentioning that the same 1 percent pay 33.6 percent of all taxes while earning just 15.4 percent of all income (according to the Joint Committee on Taxation). Contrary to popular belief that the middle class bears the brunt of taxation, the top 5 percent of taxpayers pay 54 percent of all income taxes!

It is those wealthy taxpayers whom the Democrats love to hate who are footing the bill for the enormous surpluses the government is hoarding.

What a shame it would be to actually give them their own money back.

Jason Smith
Charlotte

C. According to the following article, what is Secretary of State Colin Powell's argument for backing Palestinian demands? State his premises and main conclusion.

---

1. *Source:* Letter to the Editor, *Charlotte (N.C.) Observer,* 17 February 2001. Reprinted with permission from the *Charlotte Observer.* Copyright owned by the *Charlotte Observer.*

Powell Backs Palestinian Demands[2]

Ramallah, West Bank (AP)—Secretary of State Colin Powell backed Palestinian demands that Israel ease its economic curbs on the West Bank and in Gaza.

Using Palestinian terminology after a two-hour meeting with leader Yasser Arafat, Powell said Sunday it was time "to lift the siege."

Earlier in the day in Jerusalem, Powell was evidently unable to persuade Israel's Prime Minister-elect Ariel Sharon to alleviate the economic pressure that has been applied to Palestinian-held areas in an effort to deter attacks on Israelis.

Powell said the economic pressure "does nothing to improve the security situation." He blamed both sides for violence and promised that when it subsided, President Bush would play "a leadership role" in trying to negotiate an agreement between Israel and the Palestinians.

For his part, Arafat insisted peacemaking must begin where it broke off last month. Outgoing Prime Minister Ehud Barak had offered the Palestinians most of the West Bank and control over parts of east Jerusalem.

Arafat rejected the offer and Barak called it dead after his landslide loss to Sharon. Arafat said "no government can basically erase the moves of previous governors."

Powell's meetings with Arafat at the Palestinian leader's headquarters on the West Bank came on the second day of a four-day visit to the Middle East, Persian Gulf and Europe.

Powell acknowledged that the bombing of Iraq by U.S. and British warplanes had stirred a surprising outcry in the Arab world, though Powell said he had no apologies to offer for retaliating for Iraqi harassment of U.S. overflights.

At a news conference after meeting with Sharon, Powell said the attack could have been coordinated better in order not to inflame Arab sentiment.

"Our action was a little more aggressive than usual and got a little more attention," Powell said. "But I have no apologies."

Three Iraqis were killed and 25 others were wounded in the Feb. 16 missile attack on air defense and radar sites south of Baghdad.

Powell, meanwhile, apparently made no headway with Sharon and, on Saturday night with outgoing Prime Minister Ehud Barak, on persuading Israel to ease its economic curbs.

Sharon said Arafat first must end violence against Israelis. "In order to ease the restrictions there are steps Chairman Arafat will have to take," he said.

---

2. *Source:* The Associated Press, 25 February 2001. Reprinted with permission.

Powell said he was "greatly disturbed" by the report on Israel's security he received Saturday night from Chief of Staff Shaul Mofaz.

"It is a very dangerous situation," Powell said. "This is the time to bring calm to the region and to bring about security cooperation."

Sharon, underscoring their apparent accord on the issue, said Israel required "full security" and that while he maintained "pipelines" for messages to the Palestinian

Authority there were no ongoing negotiations.

From here, Powell went to Ramallah on the West Bank for talks with Arafat.

Responding to reports Iraq may be nearing development of nuclear weapons, Powell said it was all the more important to prevent Saddam Hussein from acquiring weapons of mass destruction.

"Saddam Hussein is a threat to the nations of the region as well as Israel," he said.

1.2 Deductive and Inductive Arguments

Consider this argument:

> *All quarterbacks are fit.*
>
> *Bill is a quarterback.*
>
> ∴ *Bill is fit.*

This is a **deductive argument,** which means that the conclusion is supposed to follow with *certainty* from the premises. If the conclusion of such an argument *does* follow with certainty from the premises—in such a way that if the premises are true, the conclusion *must* be true—then the argument is called **valid.** The above argument is valid because if the premises are true, then the conclusion must be true.

Now consider this argument:

> *All senators are honest.*
>
> *Some senators are lawyers.*
>
> ∴ *All lawyers are honest.*

Even if both premises were true, the conclusion might still be false. All we can derive from these premises is that *some* lawyers are honest. So this argument is **invalid.**

So deductive arguments can be valid or invalid, depending upon whether the conclusion has to be true if the premises are true. Furthermore, one or more premises of a valid deductive argument might be false. If an argument is either invalid or has one or more false premises, the logician calls it **unsound. A sound** deductive argument is not only valid but also has true premises (and therefore a true conclusion).

It should be noted here that validity is a *formal* property of deductive arguments. Consider this simple argument:

> *All Dredds are heroes.*
>
> *All heroes are tough.*
>
> ∴ *All Dredds are tough.*

Obviously, if the premises were true, the conclusion would certainly be true, so this argument is valid. But it would still be valid if you replaced all the terms with other terms. Replace "Dredd" with "Mavis," "hero" with "Nuthead," and "tough" with "inorganic":

> *All Mavises are Nutheads.*
>
> *All Nutheads are inorganic.*
>
> ∴ *All Mavises are inorganic.*

This is still valid.

What's more, you could replace these terms with letters—like *P* and *Q*—and you would get an abstract form of this argument, which shows that validity does not depend upon the subject matter of an argument but on its form:

> *All M are B.*
>
> *All B are I.*
>
> ∴ *All M are I.*

We'll have more to say about validity in Chapters 4–6.

Valid, invalid, sound, and *unsound*—these terms apply only to deductive arguments. But consider the following argument:

> *Thelma's sister-in-law is usually honest and level headed.*
>
> *She says someone stole her purse.*
>
> ∴ *Someone probably did steal her purse.*

This is a fairly strong argument, if we take the premises to be true. If it were considered a deductive argument, it would not prove its conclusion with certainty;

but clearly it is not intended to do that. It only concludes that someone *probably* did what Thelma's sister-in-law said. This is what the logician calls an **inductive argument.** This one is **strong** if the premises are true because it lends a high degree of probability to its conclusion. But consider this argument:

It's safe to walk down my street alone at night.

∴ *It's probably safe to walk down any street alone at night.*

This is a **weak** inductive argument because it is based on only *one* observed case. (We will cover inductive arguments more thoroughly in Chapter 7.)

Now that we have introduced most of the basic technical vocabulary of logic, we next consider the more general task of critical thinking: going after arguments in the dense undergrowth that is their natural habitat.

Exercise 1.2 Write each argument in standard form (premises first, conclusion last; use ∴ for *therefore*). Indicate which arguments are deductive and which are inductive. (Don't worry about whether they are valid/invalid or strong/weak.)

1. If you like mysteries, you'll like *Murder, She Wrote.* You don't like cop shows, so you won't like *Murder, She Wrote.*

2. Most Democrats disapproved of Judge Thomas's nomination to the Supreme Court. Senator Kennedy is a Democrat, so he probably disapproved of Thomas's nomination.

3. If Mickey is a patriot, so is Donald. Donald is not a patriot, so neither is Mickey.

4. All Greeks are mortal. Socrates is mortal, so Socrates is Greek.

5. The Masters of the Universe are powerful beings. He-Man is a Master of the Universe, so he is a powerful being.

6. The Pope visited Louisiana, so he must have visited Baton Rouge because Baton Rouge is in Louisiana.

7. America is a rich country, so most Americans are probably rich.

8. Most college courses are useful, and logic is a college course, so it's probably useful, too.

9. Tom must be wealthy because Tom is a postal worker and all postal workers are wealthy.

10. Most TV shows are unrealistic, so *e.r.* is probably unrealistic because it's a TV show.

11. If John is a veteran, he's probably bitter because most veterans are bitter.

12. If Jim believes, Tammy does, too. Tammy believes, so Jim must believe, too.

13. If Jim is rich, so is Tammy. Jim is rich, so Tammy is, too.

14. Either Jim must leave or Tammy must leave. Tammy will not leave, so Jim must leave.

15. If Oral says something, it must be true. He said the Lord would "take him home" if he didn't get the money. He got the money, so the Lord did not "take him home."

16. Either Steve must divulge his tax returns or drop out of the race. He will not do so, so he must drop out of the race.

17. All Democrats are hopeful. Joe is a Democrat, so he's hopeful.

18. Either Custer knew about Sitting Bull's plan or he didn't. If he did, he should have avoided the massacre at Little Big Horn. If he didn't, he was woefully out of touch. Either way, Custer was inept.

19. Either Tawana was raped or she was not. If she was, she would bring formal charges. But she doesn't, so she was not raped.

20. Either Ollie North is a hero or he's a traitor. If he tried to undermine and break the law, he is no hero. So he's a traitor.

21. If Marilyn had taken an overdose of Nembutal, a residue of the capsule would have been in her intestine. There was not, so she must have been murdered.

22. NASA sent the *Challenger* up too soon, so NASA caused the deaths of the *Challenger* crew.

23. All Democrats are liberals. No liberals are morally upright, so no Democrats are morally upright.

24. *Dancing in the Dark* was staged, so Bruce Springsteen is a phony.

25. If *L.A. Confidential* is accurate in its portrayal of Los Angeles, that city is a vicious jungle. It was not accurate, so Los Angeles is not a vicious jungle.

1.3 Extended Arguments

Consider this bit of dialogue:

> *Your battery is dead. That's evident because your headlights won't burn. That means your car won't start, so we'll be late for the meeting.*

A careful reading, or in this case even a cursory reading, reveals that the context is a discussion about a car and a meeting. Furthermore, it is *argumentative,* an attempt to prove a point. It is not, however, just one simple argument; it is an **extended argument** in which one main conclusion is supported by a *series* of arguments. We can write these as follows:

> Your lights won't burn.
>
> ∴ Your battery is dead.

> Your battery is dead.
>
> ∴ Your car won't start.

> Your car won't start.
>
> main conclusion ∴ We'll be late for the meeting.

Each argument produces a conclusion that becomes the premise for the next argument. Making each subargument valid requires us to supply some suppressed premises. A **suppressed premise** (which we abbreviate supp →) is one that you must add to make an argument valid or strong and that seems to be assumed by the arguer.

> Your lights won't burn.
>
> supp → If your lights won't burn, then your battery is dead.
>
> ∴ Your battery is dead.

> Your battery is dead.
>
> supp → If your battery is dead, your car won't start.
>
> ∴ Your car won't start.

> Your car won't start.
>
> supp → If your car won't start, we'll be late for the meeting.
>
> ∴ We'll be late for the meeting.

This kind of extended argument is also called a **chain argument.**

Another kind of extended argument is represented by the following:

> *First, he took me to lunch, but he didn't talk about my work; he only wanted to discuss my political beliefs. Then he started writing me these stupid little notes and calling about how much he wanted me to vote Republican in the next election. Then he started whispering "Dubya needs your vote" and such whenever we passed in the hall. Finally, he told me that unless I promised him that I'd vote for George W. Bush, he would recommend that I be fired! To me, this all adds up to harassment.*

The context is that of a complaint about harassment on the job. The main conclusion is

My boss illegally (politically) harassed me and the arguments are these (with suppressed premises supplied):

He took me to lunch and talked about my political views.

supp → <u>*A boss's doing that is harassment.*</u>

∴ *He harassed me.*

He wrote notes and phoned to coerce me to vote a certain way.

supp → <u>*A boss's doing that is harassment.*</u>

∴ *He harassed me.*

He started whispering political things to me.

supp → <u>*A boss's doing that is harassment.*</u>

∴ *He harassed me.*

He told me that he'd recommend that I be fired if I didn't promise to vote a certain way.

supp → <u>*A boss's doing that is harassment.*</u>

∴ *He harassed me.*

All these conclusions add up to a charge of harassment. That each by itself would establish such a charge is not implausible, but taken all together they would, unless the boss could come up with a different interpretation or the speaker's assertions proved unsupportable. The proper analysis of this kind of **cumulative extended argument** requires us to see the main conclusion as supported in this case by four main premises, which are themselves the conclusions of four subarguments. The main premises are the following:

He harassed me by prying into my private political beliefs.

He harassed me by calling me about politics.

He harassed me by by bothering me about politics on the job.

He harassed me by threatening to fire me over it.

We then add a suppressed premise that would make the whole argument *deductively* valid:

supp → If all these actions happened, they add up to harassment.

This yields the conclusion, which is plausible. On the other hand, we could make the argument *inductive* by adding

supp → If all these actions happened, they very likely *add up to harassment.*

The proper premise to add would depend on our best judgment about how probable or certain the speaker intends the conclusion to be. This kind of consideration—whether the argument is intended as deductive or inductive—helps us in analyzing more complex arguments. Let's make one more point about extended arguments. Imagine that the employee in our preceding example expressed herself as follows:

> *You know how the miserable jerk started out? On only my second day of work, he invited me out to lunch. I thought he was going to praise my work, but the sorry weasel only wanted to ask me about my politics, who I intended to vote for, stuff like that! Was I burned!*
>
> *A week later, he started calling me at home, next he started writing me these goofy notes, and then he threatened to get me fired if I didn't vote for Bush! I don't think anyone should be treated that way. Your politics is your own business. I think it all adds up to harassment. The Constitution says we're free to vote as we please. I could kick him, messing up my job the way he did.*

This is practically the same extended argument as the previous one, only this one has spurious (to the logician), emotive embellishments. Cross out all the extra nonargumentative material—all statements that are neither premises nor conclusions—and you get pretty much what we had before. The argument still looks either valid or very strong.

The point of paraphrasing and reducing such passages to their bare premises and conclusions is not to deny the importance of emotions and attitudes but to bring out and clarify the features we want to examine critically.

How freely may we paraphrase an argument? We must try always to retain the basic meaning of the statements that constitute the premises or conclusions of the original argument, while ignoring the frills. We must never *falsify* the statements of the original. For example:

> *Brave Tom managed to remove from battle that wicked Jack Spratt, spawn of Satan, by firing a single, well-placed projectile from his ancient but reliable Colt .45 into Spratt's corpulent torso.*

We may paraphrase this as

> *Tom shot Jack*

unless the other material is somehow crucial to the argument we are trying to analyze.

Let's look now at a *real* extended argument, a speech given April 13, 1923, in Munich, Germany, by Adolf Hitler:

> It is evident that the stronger has the right before God and the world to enforce his will. History shows that the right as such does not mean a thing, unless it is backed up by great power. If one does not have the power to enforce his right, that right alone will profit him absolutely nothing. The stronger have always been victorious. The whole of nature is a continuous struggle between strength and weakness, an eternal victory of the strong over the weak. All nature would be full of decay if it were otherwise.   [Carl Cohen, ed., *Communism, Fascism, and Democracy* (New York: Random House, 1972), 385.]

Given this context, you must imagine this spoken with patriotic fervor and received with wild enthusiasm.

The main conclusion is

The strong have the right to enforce their will.

The subarguments (with suppressed premises supplied) are

> *In history, right is useless and meaningless without power.*

supp → *If so, right depends upon power.*

∴ *In history, right depends upon power.*

> *In nature, if the strong did not defeat the weak, nature would be full of decay.*

supp → *Nature is not full of decay.*

∴ *In nature, the strong always defeat the weak.*

These two conclusions then become the main premises for the extended argument:

> *In history, right depends upon power.*
>
> *In nature, the strong always defeat the weak.*

supp → *What is true in history and nature is right.*

∴ *The strong have the right to defeat the weak.*

Are the suppressed premises plausible? Is the main argument valid or strong? Again, there is no one absolutely correct way to think such a passage through. In the above analysis, for example, Hitler apparently means his audience to assume that not only is nature *not* full of decay but also *ought not* to be full of decay, which would make his speech a bit more persuasive. Nature, this view would hold, is "right" and "natural," and whatever the beasts of the wild do should be good enough for us. To me, that is dubious. Another question: Is whatever wins "the strong" or "the powerful"? The truth seems to be that the weak *can* win, sometimes at least, unless you define "the strong" as "whatever wins," which is a fallacy that we will discuss in Chapter 3.

Exercises 1.3   A. Find an extended argument in the following passage. Can you supply any suppressed premises?

> *The problem with the idea of animal rights is just this: Medical research cannot get by on computer simulation because a computer cannot mimic the complexity of life. So medical research must use living creatures. We cannot use human beings as guinea pigs (like the Nazis did). That means medical research must use animals. We must protect humans before animals.*

B. Can you find an extended argument in this letter to the editor? Can you supply any suppressed premises?

Home's in Cuba[3]

Editor: I just wanted to comment about the Cuban boy, Elian Gonzales. A lot of people feel this little boy should remain in the United States with his family here. I feel he should be reunited with his father and family in Cuba.

All children should be with their parents whenever possible. We should ask ourselves this question. "How would we feel if our little boy or girl was taken into another country and the family and government there did not let him come back to us?"

We would call that kidnapping. This is a serious crime and no one I know wants to lose a child this way.

It would be a shame for our wonderful country to be labeled as a country that helps in this type of crime. I hope the best interest of the child is put forth.

Wendy Carter
Wilmington

---

3. *Source:* Letter to the Editor, *Star-News* (Wilmington, N.C.), 23 January 2000. Reprinted with permission.

1.4 Explanations and Other Nonarguments

An argument tries to prove that some statement is true. An **explanation** assumes that some statement is true and tries to explain how it came to be true. Consider this dialogue:

A: *Why won't my car start?*

B: *Your car won't start because the battery is dead.*

B's statement is an explanation, not an argument. A already knows that his car won't start, and he wants to know why. B explains the *cause* of the car's failure to start. B is not trying to argue or prove anything; she's just explaining why the car won't start.

But consider this:

A: *Do you suppose my car will start?*

B: *No sir, the battery is dead, so it won't start.*

Here B *is* giving an argument, which looks like this, in standard form:

The battery is dead.

∴ *Your car won't start.*

There is a suppressed premise here: "A car with a dead battery won't start." So the complete argument is

The battery is dead.

supp → *A car with a dead battery won't start.*

∴ *Your car won't start.*

Sometimes explanations look like arguments. For example:

A: *Why do you believe in a Supreme Being?*

B: *My parents threatened to beat me if I didn't.*

This is an explanation of the cause of B's belief. But consider:

A: *Why do you believe in a Supreme Being?*

B: *I can't see how the universe could exist if it was not created by a Supreme Being.*

B's reply is an argument:

> *The universe could not exist unless it was created by a Supreme Being.*
>
> supp → *The universe exists.*
> _____
>
> ∴ *The universe was created by a Supreme Being.*

Sometimes it is hard to tell the difference, but an explanation tries to *explain* some agreed-upon fact—for example, a murder, an eclipse, the collapse of a building, or a dinosaur fossil—whereas an argument tries to *prove* that some statement should be accepted. The "why" that calls for an explanation is asking for a *cause;* the "why" that calls for an argument is asking for a *reason for believing* something.

Explanations can be offered, however, as part of an argument. For example:

> *We shot them both. We were just so terrified of them, and we believed that if we didn't kill them, they would kill us. It was the years and years of abuse that made us so scared that we killed them.*

This is an attempt to explain an action *and* to argue that the killings were justified. The unstated conclusion is obviously that the killers could not help themselves and therefore should not be punished. This is what we might call an attempt at justification of the action.

Other nonarguments look like arguments. Consider this dialogue:

> A: *What condition was Dr. Smith in, that day?*
>
> B: *Dr. Smith wasn't drunk . . . that particular day. I don't* think *he was. I know I've told him over and over that he should never drink before an operation. He told me that he was sober and that was good enough for me.*

Literally, B says that Dr. Smith was *not* drunk, but between the lines he says just the opposite. This is an example of **innuendo.** Here is another example of innuendo:

> *You're perfectly right to stand by him. You're his wife. A little talk? What does it mean? It's just gossip; you can't take it seriously, even if everybody says he's been involved with all those women. I'm proud of you, though everyone may call me a fool. You believe he's faithful, and that's the main thing.*

This person never *says* the husband is unfaithful, but strongly hints at it by means of innuendo.

Other nonarguments can be found in discourse of all kinds, from everyday conversations to articles in newspapers and news magazines, but many of these are traditionally grouped with the informal fallacies, which we will discuss in Chapter 3.

Exercise 1.4   Can you find an argument, an explanation, or an instance of innuendo in the following passage?

Recorders Detail Concorde's Woes[4]
by Suzanne Daley
N.Y. Times News Service

Paris—Flight recorders show that the pilots of the Air France Concorde that crashed on Tuesday had problems with both engines on the plane's left side and also reported that the pilots could not retract the landing gear, investigators said Thursday.

The recorders make clear that the plane was too far down the runway to abort the flight when air controllers told the pilot that they could see flames at the back of his plane.

The pilots responded that the No. 2 engine had stalled and shortly after takeoff, they reported that they could not store the landing gear.

But the flight recorders also show that the No. 1 engine had failed briefly as well during takeoff. And one minute into the flight, it failed again just before the plane rolled to the left and crashed into a small hotel on the outskirts of Paris.

Investigators said the plane was in the process of breaking up throughout its brief flight as debris was found along its path. They also noted that scraps of tire had been found on the runway.

But many questions remained about what triggered the crash: whether it was related to objects like parts of tires or wheels being sucked into an engine, last-minute repairs made to engine No. 2 before Air France flight 4590 took off from Charles de Gaulle airport or still some other reason.

French government investigators said their inquiry was still in its preliminary stages and far from determining what had caused the supersonic jet to crash, killing 113.

Some experts said Thursday that it was unlikely the repairs to the No. 2 engine's thrust reversers had anything to do with the kind of fire that seemed to engulf the left side of the plane as the plane's captain, Christian Marty, tried desperately to cut short the flight and land at the smaller, nearby airport, Le Bourget. The repair job, the experts said, would have had to have been badly botched, causing a rupture in a fuel line for instance, to create the kind of engine collapse that occurred.

Others speculate that it was more likely that something was sucked into the engine on takeoff.

---

4. *Source:* Copyright © 2000 by the New York Times Co. Reprinted with permission.

1.5 Summary

Logic and critical thinking are concerned with arguments. An argument is a set of statements, of which one—the conclusion—is supported by the others, the premises. A deductive argument is one whose conclusion is supposed to be supported *with certainty* by the premises. A valid deductive argument is one in which the premises do in fact support the conclusion with certainty. A sound deductive argument is valid and has all true premises. An inductive argument is one whose premises lend the conclusion some degree of probability. A strong inductive argument lends its conclusion a high degree of probability; a weak one does not. Explanations are not arguments. An argument tries to prove that some statement is true; an explanation assumes some statement is true and tries to give the cause of its being true.

Logic is mostly concerned with the validity or strength of individual arguments. Critical thinking is not only interested with what logic has to say about arguments but also (1) with finding those arguments in the context of issues, (2) with whether the premises of those arguments are actually true or plausible, (3) with providing suppressed premises, and (4) with judging among several essays or speeches representing diverse points of view on an issue.

In the following chapters, we will examine more precise critical techniques. At the end of each chapter, including this one, we work through an application of these techniques to some actual, controversial speech or essay.

1.6 Application

The Suicide Machine Read the following editorial.

Editorial from the *Chattanooga Times*[5]

Mrs. Janet Adkins' decision to take her life rather than suffer the inexorable onslaught of Alzheimer's disease is not unique in context of the right-to-die issue that increasingly confronts society. Choosing and seeking to die in the face of debilitating terminal illness has clearly become an alternative that many people consider. But Dr. Jack Kevorkian's active assistance of Mrs. Adkins' lethal injection, through the on-the-scenes use of this suicide device, bursts through accepted bounds.

The questions this maverick doctor poses to justify his intervention are not his to answer for individuals trapped by unconquerable disease. He says physicians must aid patients in such circumstances to die with dignity, lest they die through slow suffering or through their own otherwise messy or uncertain suicide efforts.

His assumption topples enormous philosophical and religious barriers, however. Would he be the one to judge whether a patient has accurately assessed his diagnosis, prognosis and competence to make such a decision? Should the healing profession be also at the center of a death profession? At what point on the continuum from life to death can an outsider say that it is all right now for life to end, and then assist in death?

Terminal patients may weigh privately when they want their lives to end, and certainly many contemplate just that point. They also may deserve to know how to overcome unbearable burdens of suffering which may be extended, on the other hand, by advancing medical technology. But the absence of a defined instrument for death seems a fair obstacle to restrict the suicide of cognizant, but depressed, terminally ill patients.

Dr. Kevorkian went several steps too far to defeat inherent restraints. First he publicized a home-made suicide device. His was a simple rack that allowed intravenous injection first of saline solution, then a lethal chemical at the patient's push of a button. Contacted by Mrs. Adkins, he agreed to see her and, after an evening dinner, to assist her with the use of his device. In Michigan, where the Oregon woman flew to meet Dr. Kevorkian, there is no legal statute prohibiting causing or assisting a suicide, so Michigan authorities are confused about what, if anything, they could or should do regarding Dr. Kevorkian's involvement.

Mrs. Adkins' history is that of a well-educated woman who lived life fully and whose determination to control her demise overcame her husband's and sons [sic] objections. It suggests that Dr. Kevorkian served her purposes as well as she served his. He promotes euthanasia and non-profit suicide clinics, however. And there are too many pitfalls on the road to sanctioned suicide, and too many distraught, would-be victims, to give his ideas loose rein.

---

5. *Source:* Editorial, *Chattanooga (Tenn.) Times,* 11 June 1990. Copyright © Chattanooga Times Free Press. Reprinted with permission.

We have discussed only the most basic concepts of logic and critical thinking, but let's analyze this editorial as far as we can, using the techniques we have learned so far.

The first step is to read the essay thoroughly and then identify the issue, what the essay is about. The main issue is whether Kevorkian's use of his suicide machine is morally acceptable. This essayist is evidently arguing that it is not. So we state the main conclusion:

Kevorkian's use of his suicide machine is morally unacceptable.

The next step is to ask *why* the arguer thinks this. What are his or her reasons or premises? One premise is

Kevorkian cannot judge the accuracy of a depressed patient's assessment of his or her prognosis.

Another premise is

Kevorkian's machine defeats a "fair obstacle" (the lack of an instrument of death) to suicide.

Neither premise by itself, nor even both together, will yield the arguer's conclusion. But, if the first premise is indeed true, we could get the conclusion by supplying an obvious suppressed premise:

Nobody who cannot judge the accuracy of the patient's medical self-assessment should be assisting in that patient's suicide.

This suppressed premise is very plausible, for obvious reasons, and so we can write the following argument and attribute it to the arguer:

Kevorkian cannot judge the accuracy of the patient's self-assessment.

supp → *Nobody who cannot judge the accuracy of the patient's self-assessment should be assisting in that patient's suicide.*

∴ *Kevorkian should not be assisting in that patient's suicide.*

Only a bit of paraphrasing is necessary to get the main conclusion.

The second of the arguer's explicit premises,

Kevorkian's machine defeats a "fair obstacle" to suicide

also needs us to supply a suppressed premise to the effect that

Whatever defeats a "fair obstacle" to suicide is morally unacceptable.

This yields the following:

Kevorkian's machine defeats a "fair obstacle" to suicide.

supp → <u>*Whatever defeats a "fair obstacle" to suicide is morally unacceptable.*</u>

∴ *Kevorkian's machine is morally unacceptable.*

Further questions, about rigorous tests for validity and such, must wait until later chapters, but we have greatly clarified this essay. The first premise and the argument it suggests are persuasive (to me), but Kevorkian could meet it by making sure to find out the patient's real prognosis. The second argument is murky: It suggests that there are rules to suicide.

Important: This has been *my* analysis and is by no means the only acceptable analysis. Critical thinking is not as pat as arithmetic, and there is often no *exactly* right answer. On the other hand, we can reach some agreement—the issue, the main conclusion, the main premises, the suppressed premises, and even the plausibility of the premises. (In later chapters we will discuss methods of testing the arguments involved for validity or strength.) You might very well state or paraphrase these elements differently, but if we try to be objective and fair and try to see the other person's side, we can often achieve a surprising level of agreement.

Being objective and fair and seeing the other person's side of an issue are not easy. It is more difficult than learning arithmetic or logic. It is evidently even more difficult than nuclear physics: Although we've had nuclear weapons for over fifty years, we still have war, terrorism, violent crime, and all the other ferocious offspring of irrationality.

In this application we have already taken a few steps into the undergrowth of controversy, where there is uncertainty and danger. Some of the issues we will discuss have been so resistant to clear thought that people have killed and been killed over them. However, as the philosopher Baruch Spinoza (1632–1677) said, "All things excellent are as difficult as they are rare."

Exercise 1.6   In the following essay,

1. Identify the issue.

2. Identify the main conclusion.

3. Find the premises that support the main conclusion.

4. Supply suppressed premises, if any.

After Others Fail, Oregon Offers Death with Dignity[6]

Our View: Patients deserve better than our current "underground" system of assisted suicide

Tim Shuck, 45, of Portland, Ore., is dying of AIDS.

"Eventually my brain is going to be mush," he told USA Today. "At that point, I don't want to continue to live."

What does Shuck want? A little help from a doctor so he can die with dignity.

And on Nov. 8, the voters of Oregon can make it legal for Shuck and other terminally ill patients to get such assistance.

It's the third time in recent years that a state's voters will decide whether to permit physician-assisted suicide. But unlike proposals in California and Washington, which failed and were opposed in this space, Oregon's doesn't put healers in the position of killing people.

Under Oregon's Measure 16, control of when to end life would be in the hands of patients, which is where it belongs. Doctors would provide prescriptions for drugs but not administer them. To prevent rash decisions, patients would face 15-day waiting periods and have to make a request three times, once in writing. Each patient also would have to get a second physician's opinion that agreed the patient was likely to die within six months. Either doctor could propose counseling for depression.

In that way, the proposal provides far better protection for patients than the pile of absurdities that make up today's laws.

No state legally allows assisted suicide.

Yet in Michigan, juries refused to convict Dr. Jack Kevorkian, who's assisted in 20 suicides. In New York, authorities dropped an investigation of Dr. Timothy Quill, who wrote about how he provided the painkillers that helped a leukemia patient commit suicide.

No doctor is likely to go to prison for thoughtfully helping a dying patient end his or her life. Few even come to prosecutors' attention because, unlike Kevorkian, they don't tell anyone what they're doing.

None of the 33 physicians who admitted in a New Hampshire poll that they assisted patients drew headlines for their actions. Why? Because they acted anonymously.

And if they hadn't helped, would they have prevented their patients' suicides?

Probably not. Every day, cancer and AIDS patients ask family and friends to help end their suffering. Or, as Shuck says he's prepared to do, they kill themselves.

The only difference is the suicides are more painful, with the victim sometimes left not dead but as a vegetable.

That makes no moral sense at all.

Terminally ill patients shouldn't have to beg friends and family to help kill them. They shouldn't have to blow their heads off to end their own suffering.

Oregon's proposal provides those individuals a better way to a death with dignity without turning doctors into killers.

---

6. *Source:* "After Others Fail, Oregon Offers Death with Dignity," *USA TODAY,* 25 October 1994. Copyright © 1994, USA TODAY. Reprinted with permission.

 *CHAPTER TWO*

The Context of Arguments: Critical Thinking

The discipline and art of critical thinking is both ancient and recent. We see Socrates (ca. 470–399 B.C.) using it with amazing skill in Plato's *Dialogues.* Indeed, at his trial Socrates asked his fellow Athenians to be sure to criticize and argue with his children, because he believed so strongly that criticism is a good and positive thing.

Argumentation cannot solve every problem, but it is a great improvement over violence and war. The great American logician W. V. O. Quine (1908–2000) believed that philosophy and logic should be pursued as part of science, part of the search for truth. In this, Quine was a pragmatist. In this text we take a broader view of truth than Quine does so that we can bring logic to bear on such serious issues as abortion, assisted suicide, the death penalty, the Middle East situation, human cloning, the Comprehensive Test Ban Treaty—issues that involve not only scientific facts but also ethical and religious values.

2.1 Disagreement and Controversy

People disagree about all sorts of things: whether animals have rights, what "sexual harassment" means, whether assisted suicide should be legal, whether black holes really exist, whether *Frankenstein* is scarier than *Dracula,* whether the United States should send troops into such-and-such a place—Somalia, Haiti, Bosnia, Kuwait, and so on.

Some such disagreements are trivial, and some are not. Some will vanish from the public forum, and some will not. What seemed important to an earlier generation might fail to interest us: whether to kiss on the first date, whether someone evaded the draft during the Vietnam War, whether Richard III really murdered the two princes.

A **controversy** (from the Latin *controversus,* meaning "disputed") is defined as "a protracted public debate." We will therefore try to avoid the ephemeral issues, which arise suddenly and fade quickly (though we don't always know which those are!), and concern ourselves with questions that are more lasting in virtue of involving significant principles.

Some disagreements are **factual:** whether North Korea has nuclear weapons, whether water boils at 212 degrees Fahrenheit, whether a certain person is a spy, whether a certain former football player stabbed his ex-wife to death. Other disagreements are **valuational** (about values): whether censorship is wrong, whether prayer has a place in public schools. Such disagreements often find their way into courts of law.

Still other disagreements have mostly to do with concepts and ideas: whether machines can think; whether, if $2x + 5 = 17$, x must $= 6$; whether a fetus is a person. Such disagreements are called **conceptual.**

And then there are **verbal** disagreements, over what a word or phrase means. Suppose I argue that since many people desire pornography, pornography must therefore be desirable! You might respond that I have implicitly used the word *desirable* in two different ways: as "capable of being desired" and as "worthy of being desired." This ambiguity is so central to the argument that pointing it out might settle the dispute.

Real controversies involve all these kinds of disagreement. The issue of the nature of sexual harassment, for example, is partly about how to use the word *harassment,* but it also involves more profound matters of right and wrong, about how we ought to treat one another.

The soul of controversy is argumentation: stating what you think and giving your reasons. The following editorial is an example of the kind of argumentation we find in contemporary controversies.

Abortion and the RICO Ruling[1]

The abortion wars obscured the true importance of an historic unanimous ruling this week by the U.S. Supreme Court.

The media stress is on the fact that abortion activists won the right to use the Racketeer Influenced and Corrupt Organization Act to put militant right-to-lifers out of business for blocking women's access to abortion clinics.

Largely overlooked is that this wasn't just a victory for abortion rights, but a dramatic (and

---

1. *Source:* "Abortion and the RICO Ruling," *Augusta (Ga.) Chronicle,* 27 January 1994. Reprinted with permission.

dangerous) broadening of the federal racketeering statute.

Operation Rescue and other anti-abortion groups face total ruin if activists on the other side prevail in court for jail terms and treble damages.

If this RICO ruling had been around in Martin Luther King Jr.'s day, civil disobedience convictions would have bankrupted the civil rights movement before it ever got off the ground!

This was not the intent when Congress approved RICO in 1970.

The law was supposed to be used as a weapon to bring down organized crime, and to a great extent it's succeeding. Many Mafia families have been successfully prosecuted.

But RICO has also been used and abused in contexts never envisioned by Congress, including civil disputes. Critics of the law were making some headway in Congress toward

narrowing it until the Clinton administration decided to appease its "pro-choice" constituency.

It urged the Court to expand RICO to put pro-life civil disobedience demonstrators in the same category as crime dons, calling for similar fines and lengthy jail sentences.

This isn't to say people who unlawfully block access to public establishments, for whatever reason, shouldn't be held accountable. That's why we have local and state laws.

But the use of federal RICO against protesters is totally inappropriate, unless one believes that stifling dissent is good law-enforcement.

Perhaps after this ruling wiser congressional heads will prevail and there will be renewed efforts to narrow RICO to ensure its use as originally intended—as a tool to fight organized crime.

After a close reading (or two), we can state the main conclusion:

RICO should not be used against protesters.

And why not? What premises does the writer give in support of this conclusion? One reason given is that

Such uses were not intended by Congress when it passed RICO.

Let's see how convincing the argument is when we put premise and conclusion together:

Such uses were not intended by Congress when it passed RICO.

Therefore, RICO should not be used against protesters.

Is this persuasive? Does something seem to be "missing"? How does the writer get from "not intended by Congress" to "should not be used against protesters"? The writer *must* be assuming the valuation,

> *No law should be used in a way not originally intended by Congress.*

This, as you will recall, is what the logician calls a **suppressed premise.**

Now that we have done a bit of critical thinking, we will be able to analyze—using the methods of this book—more complex pieces of argumentation much more closely. Will we be able to settle the big issues? Probably not. You and I don't know everything, and logic by itself can't tell us much about whether the premises of some argument are true. However, considering the truth of premises is an important part of critical thinking, so we will discuss some ways of verifying and challenging the statements that comprise the arguments we find in the context of contemporary controversies.

Exercise 2.1　A. What kinds of disagreement—factual, valuational, conceptual, or verbal—are represented in the following exchanges?

1. A: That's a duck.

   B: No, it's a goose.

2. A: Pornography is immoral.

   B: It's just another way to make a living.

3. A: Euthanasia is murder.

   B: Sometimes it's for the best.

4. A: Calvin Klein's ads are pornographic.

   B: They're not. They're works of art.

5. A: We should send troops to Bosnia.

   B: There's nothing in it for the United States.

6. A: Letting someone die isn't murder.

   B: It is if you're a doctor.

7. A: This is pumpkin pie.

   B: No, it's sweet potato pie.

8. A: Your plan means cutting Medicare benefits.

   B: No, it just cuts the rate of growth.

9. A: Dr. Ruth suggests a glass of champagne before sex.

   B: She doesn't know anything about sex.

10. A: It was Hillary who broke the law.

   B: It was Bill. He's just letting her take the heat.

B. Think of some controversy that has gained your attention in the past year. Write a brief, clear paragraph on it, stating your position and giving some reasons for your statement.

C. What is the conclusion of each passage? What premises are offered to support each conclusion?

1. Assisted suicide should not be legal because it is wrong to help someone take her or his own life.

2. Everyone has the right to die as he or she wishes; anyway, you can't punish the person who has actually committed suicide. So it would be wrong to punish someone who has only assisted a suicide.

3. No medical doctors should help patients commit suicide because that would conflict with their oath as doctors, which says, in part, "I will administer no deadly drug."

D. Can you add a suppressed premise (a statement assumed by the arguer) to passage C1?

2.2 Aims of Critical Thinking

To clarify and evaluate arguments, we use logic and critical thinking, but we first must find the arguments by digging into the murky undergrowth, the bewildering tangle of rhetoric and argumentation that is the natural habitat of controversy. We also use critical thinking to compare arguments and sets of arguments, to determine which side of some issue is most rationally persuasive. We use critical thinking to evaluate a term paper, a political speech, a newspaper or magazine editorial, an article in a learned journal, a book—all kinds of argumentative material.

   Criticism is a positive thing. Of course, it can be negative and even mean, if it is employed to low purposes—to embarrass or to one-up someone. But at its best, it is helpful, especially to those who can learn from it. It takes time, work, and care.

   Suppose you are working for a political candidate who shows you a speech she wrote hurriedly. She is very enthused about it, but when you read it you discover that she's made some foolish and illogical remarks. If you care about her, you'll show her what's wrong, rather than let her make the speech and damage herself. In that care lies the value of critical thinking.

The first step in critical thinking is to recognize the issue being discussed. Some logicians suggest that the issue be expressed as a *whether:*

whether abortion should be legal or illegal

whether animals have rights

whether the United States should send troops to Bosnia

whether one should vote for Al Gore

and so on.

The next aim of critical thinking is to find the arguments in a given speech or essay. We have discussed this briefly already, in Chapter 1. Here we expand on what was said there.

Finding arguments means finding premises and conclusions. Certain **indicator words** often serve as *clues* to premises and conclusions. The following words often indicate that *premises* follow:

since

for

for these reasons

because, because of this

The following words often indicate that a *conclusion* follows:

therefore

so

thus

consequently

for this reason, we conclude that

it follows that

this shows that

For example, in

Most senators are honest, because Joe is a senator and he's honest

the word "because" indicates that "Joe is a senator" and "he's honest" are the premises; this means, too, that "Most senators are honest" is the conclusion.

Similarly, in

Socrates is Greek, so he's mortal because all Greeks are mortal

the word "so" indicates that "he's mortal" is the conclusion; the other two statements are premises—the word "because" indicates that "all Greeks are mortal" is
a premise, and "Socrates is Greek" is needed for the argument to be valid.

But sometimes there are no such clues, no indicator words. For example:

Tom is probably here. Nancy is here, and wherever Nancy is, Tom probably is, too.

No indicators are here, no *therefores* or *becauses;* but a bit of mental trial and error
shows that the only plausible interpretation is that the first statement is supported
by the other two. In standard form,

Nancy is here.

Wherever Nancy is, Tom probably is, too.

∴ *Tom is probably here.*

It is hard to see any other argument here, at least not one with strength or
validity.

Like other aspects of the discipline of critical thinking, finding arguments
requires some practical insight that comes with experience. In any argumentative
essay, the main conclusion, once found, reduces the majority of the other statements in the essay to supportive status. So, in practice, finding arguments and their
premises and conclusions is not very difficult. Just jump in and do it. Telling arguments from rhetoric or from explanation is sometimes not easy. One approach the
logician and the critical thinker uses is **paraphrase,** putting the material "in our
own words." We ask ourselves: What is the *point* (the main conclusion) here and
what *reasons* (premises) are given? For example:

*Dr. Foster gives me a pain. I don't think there's intelligent life on other worlds. If
there were, we'd have heard from them by now. I'm going to drop astronomy and
major in English, and Foster can keep his "billions and billions" of stars and galaxies.
That's how I feel about the whole thing. Who does Foster think he is, anyway?*

After peeling away the expressions of attitude in this passage, we are left with this
(paraphrased) argument:

If there were (intelligent life on other worlds), we would have heard from them by now.

∴ *There is no life on other worlds.*

This argument is not persuasive as it stands. We obviously need to supply a suppressed premise to the effect that "We haven't heard from them (the life on other worlds) yet," which is undeniable (as far as I know). So now we have the following paraphrased argument:

> *If there were life on other worlds, we'd have heard from them by now.*
>
> supp → *We haven't heard from them.* _____
>
> ∴ *There is no life on other worlds.*

Look again at the essay on abortion protests and the RICO ruling in Section 2.1. From the single premise

> *Such a use of RICO would have crippled the Civil Rights movement*

it clearly does *not* follow that RICO should not be used against abortion protesters. So we ask: What must we *assume* to get that conclusion? If we add

> *Whatever would have crippled the Civil Rights movement is wrong*

we now have a complete argument that will prove the conclusion (if the premises are actually true):

> *Such abuse of RICO would have crippled the Civil Rights movement.*
>
> supp → *Whatever would have crippled the Civil Rights movement is wrong.* _____
>
> ∴ *Such a use of RICO is wrong.*

If the premises are true, the conclusion would certainly be true. This is now a valid argument.

There is another approach. Instead of "whatever would have," we could add a weaker statement: "Whatever would have crippled the Civil Rights movement is probably wrong." This would yield the following inductive argument:

> *Such abuse of RICO would have crippled the Civil Rights movement.*
>
> supp → *Whatever would have crippled the Civil Rights movement is probably wrong.*
>
> ∴ *Such a use of RICO is probably wrong.*

Notice that we paraphrased the preceding arguments somewhat, being careful not to change their original meaning, and we supplied only those suppressed premises that were necessary to make the argument valid, or strong, and which were themselves plausible. We would be justified in saying that the resulting arguments are what the arguers intended.

Whereas logic is mainly interested in formal properties of arguments—for instance validity—critical thinking is concerned with whether the premises of a given argument are actually true. Concerning the abortion–RICO argument, critical thinking would ask whether the RICO Act would have *actually* crippled the Civil Rights movement, given that the violence and gangsterism at that time were usually on the "establishment" side—police agencies and the national guards. In the life-on-other-worlds argument, critical thinking would ask whether the fact that we have not yet been contacted really means that *no* life exists on other worlds.

Critical thinking is also concerned with how arguments on one side of an issue stack up against arguments on the other side. One can imagine pro-choice advocates arguing that anti-abortion protesters "really are" gangsters of a special kind. One could then compare the arguments on either side, to see which are more persuasive.

As was said earlier, logicians and critical thinkers are only human, and our analyses are not the *only* analyses. People of goodwill often paraphrase and analyze differently from one another, and we must always keep an attitude of charity and humility as we evaluate the arguments of others. However insightful and penetrating our critical analyses, we might be wrong!

Exercise 2.2 A. Which of the following passages contain arguments? In the arguments that you identify, which statements are premises, and which are conclusions? Paraphrase and put in standard form.

1. I think Dr. Kevorkian is a great humanitarian; you'd better not say anything critical about him, or I'll punch your ugly face.

2. The old man was dreaming of the lions when it began to rain. He sat up, wiped his face with his bandana, and looked around. It was raining on him and on the ocean that lay before him, and he knew it was raining on the lonely churchyard where Thelma was buried.

3. The new health plan will not work because it will cost much more than it will save and because it will diminish our freedom of choice. So I will vote against it.

4. When will you learn not to trust everyone who tells you a sad story? They're just making a fool of you. You should learn to think for yourself.

5. This budget plan is a poor one. It just balances the budget on the backs of the old and the poor, and such a budget is a poor one. I intend to veto it.

6. The most likely suspect in a child murder is a close family member. Tom is the child's stepfather. So Tom probably did it.

7. Marcus Brutus: Well, to our work alive. What do you think
Of marching to Philippi presently?

Cassius: I do not think it good.

Marcus Brutus: Your reason?

Cassius: This it is:—'Tis better that the enemy seek us:
So shall he waste his means, weary his soldiers,
Doing himself offence; whilst we, lying still,
Are full of rest, defence, and nimbleness.   (Julius Caesar IV.iii)

B. In the following essay, find the arguments and write them in standard form (premises first, conclusion last):

It is disgusting to me to hear our involvement in Bosnia compared to Vietnam and Somalia. The pundits who make such arguments are way off base. We must not allow the war crimes and genocide to continue any longer, and without U.S. leadership, they will continue. So we must be involved. Besides this, we are committed to NATO and so must meet that responsibility by getting involved. America is too great a country to allow a few isolationists to frighten us. These characters should shut their mouths, that's how I feel about it! It really gets under my skin.

2.3 Uses of Language

Whereas logic is concerned with the assessment of individual arguments that have been somewhat artificially removed from the battlefield of controversy, critical thinking requires some serious attention to the context of arguments. To critically evaluate a real argument, we need to know what issue the argument figures into, along with who is presenting it, as well as when and where. Actual arguments, unlike the abstract, bodiless examples usually found in logic texts, occur in our ordinary lives, every day, whenever we need to persuade someone of something: We deserve a raise or a promotion; he should vote Republican; a blizzard is coming; AIDS is dangerous; abortion should be made illegal; terrorists should be treated with special brutality. Law, politics, science, business, and education—all serve as the contexts of serious argument.

The most fundamental context, without which there could be no argument at all, is language itself.

Language has many uses, and the logician must be able to distinguish among them. Some statements, for example, are meant to be purely **informative:**

The car is out of gas.

It's five o'clock.

Water boils at 212 degrees Fahrenheit.

The intent of such statements is to inform someone of something, to state a fact. The logician is most interested in this kind of statement, the kind found in most arguments. (Recall that an *argument* is a set of statements, one of which is supported by the others.)

Then there is **evaluative** language (also called **prescriptive** or **normative**), which says how something ought to be or what ought to be done. It is found in moral discourse, legal reasoning, and discussions of aesthetic values, as in

Cheating is wrong.

We should ban pornography.

The Pieta is beautiful.

Obviously, such language is essential to almost all controversies about government policy, legal disputes, critical evaluations of the arts, and so forth. Philosophers disagree about the *cognitive status* of evaluative language—that is, whether evaluative statements are really true or false or merely expressive of emotions and attitudes. Since "You ought not to abuse your children" seems more like a true statement than like an expression of some subjective attitude, in this text we consider evaluative language to be cognitive; where it occurs in examples and exercises, we treat it just as we do informative language. (This decision does not necessarily settle the philosophical issue about values.) Are values, rights, and the like "things" like stones and houses?

Other statements are meant as directions in which someone is told, directed, to do something:

Go shut the door!

Put out the cat!

Make a left turn onto Main Street.

The point of these sentences is **directive:** to issue a command or an imperative.
Some language has an **expressive** use:

What a pretty day!

Don't you just love Frost's poetry?

Wow!

These sentences are intended to express emotion, not to inform, evaluate, or direct.
They tell no facts, issue no commands, and make no evaluations but simply express
one's feelings, likes, and preferences. Some logicians call such language emotive.
Then there is **ceremonial** language:

Hello, how are you?

Fine, and you?

Do you take this man to be your lawfully wedded husband?

Such sentences are not really intended to ask about your health or to ask whether you
really take this man. They are ceremonies, rituals, we go through. Philosophers have
also noted another form of language similar to ceremonial, called **performative:**

I hereby sentence you to ten years.

When the judge says that, she is not just saying something but is also performing
the act of sentencing. The same goes for

I promise to pay you Monday.

Telling the difference between ceremonial and performative language is
sometimes difficult. When in doubt, choose ceremonial. Such language is very
important in human life—we use it to marry, to take office, to give our word, to
commit ourselves—but it is not meant to inform or evaluate (though philosophers might argue about that). Logicians thus mostly deal with the informative
and evaluative uses of language.

Just because a sentence is a question doesn't mean that it is a simple request
for information. For example:

Don't you think it's time for you to go?

This is not just a question but is actually a hint, a direction, that you should go.
In the same way,

Would you like some tea?

What time is it?

Aren't you chilly?

all are really requests, directions, for certain responses—to say whether you want tea, to tell the time, to turn up the thermostat. So most logicians classify all questions as directions. But, as we have seen, a question can also be expressive, as in

Isn't love wonderful?

or ceremonial, as in

Do you solemnly swear to uphold the Constitution?

or even informative:

Did you know that Bag o' Bones *was written by Stephen King?*

Are you aware that there is now a drug that can lower your cholesterol?

Can you believe that Shaquille O'Neal makes $84 million per year?

Finally, there is the **rhetorical question** to which no answer is expected or to which only one answer can be made:

Coach: What could be more important than winning?

Questions can serve almost any function. How do we tell what use is intended by a question or, for that matter, by any sentence? This is pretty much a matter of context and common sense. You ask: Is the real point of this sentence to *inform? To evaluate? To direct? To express* emotion? To function as part of a *ceremony?* To *perform* some action? It's all a matter of how it's meant, how it's intended—and that often depends upon its context.

Summary: Uses of Language

- Use **informative language** to inform, to state facts, and to say how things are. It is cognitive and true or false.

- Use **evaluate language** to say how something ought to be and to prescribe or set a value upon something. It is cognitive and true or false.

- Use **directive language** to issue a direction, a command, or an imperative.

- Use **expressive language** to express emotions and attitudes.

- Use **ceremonial language** to carry out ceremonies, rituals, and the like.

- Use **performative language** to perform certain acts—for example, sentencing and marriage.

Exercise 2.3   A. Classify the following sentences according to which uses of language they most likely illustrate: informative, evaluative, directive, expressive, ceremonial, or performative.

1. Oh!

2. The cat is black.

3. Please sit down.

4. The pizza is hot.

5. What day is this?

6. Congratulations!

7. Have a nice day!

8. Don't you think we should go to class?

9. It's 7 P.M.

10. I now pronounce you husband and wife.

11. Happy Birthday!

12. More coffee?

13. What a movie!

14. I can't stand anchovies on my pizza.

15. To be or not to be, that is the question.

16. I come to bury Caesar, not to praise him.

17. All the world's a stage, and all the men and women merely players.

18. Force equals mass times acceleration.

19. Are you ready for dinner?

20. When are you going to grow up?

21. A rose by any other name would smell as sweet.

22. Did you know that Edward Fitzgerald wrote *The Rubáiyat?*

23. Who is the star of *Murphy Brown?*

24. Don't you know that lying is wrong?

25. Did you know this is the nonsmoking section?

26. You'll have to get out and push.

27. I'd appreciate your not smoking.

28. Glad to meet you.

29. How's the family?

30. What time is it?

31. Better safe than sorry.

32. If you don't stop, I'll scream.

33. The Lord has spoken to me out of the whirlwind, saying he wants me to be president.

34. Praise the Lord!

35. Adultery is wrong.

36. I'm forty-three years old.

37. Art is long, life is short.

38. You'd better stop that this minute.

39. When I met you, time stood still.

40. Al Gore was behind in the polls.

41. He still hoped to win.

42. Israel has repudiated Arafat's proposals.

B. What uses of language can you find in the following passages?

1. Pornography is bad for our children, for it reduces people to little more than physical bodies and portrays them as incapable of sensitivity or intelligence. Pornography should be forbidden.

2. In the name of the Grand Dragon of the Glorious Order of the Unforgotten Memory of the Golden Aryan Chapel, I name you Grand Rattlesnake in Full Standing of the Old Mason-Dixon Nest of Vipers.

3. *Nairobi, Kenya*—A passenger burst into the cockpit of a British Airways Jet with 398 people aboard and grabbed the controls Friday, sending the plane into two violent nosedives that left people screaming and praying out loud. The plane landed safely after the crew and other passengers subdued the attacker, who officials said was bent on suicide.

4. Don't resolve to lose twenty pounds in a month, which is unrealistic. Rather, resolve that you are going to eat healthier or that you will exercise three times a week. You should establish small steps you can take in accomplishing the larger goals.

C. In the following passage from Shakespeare's *Hamlet,* can you find examples of some of the six uses of language presented in this chapter?

First Clown: A pestilence on him for a mad rogue! a' pour'd a flagon of Rhenish on my head once. This same skull, sir, was Yorick's skull, the king's jester.

Hamlet: This?

First Clown: E'en that.

Hamlet: Let me see.   [*Takes the skull.*]   Alas, poor Yorick!—I knew him, Horatio: a fellow of infinite jest, of most excellent fancy: he hath borne me on his back a thousand times; and now, how abhorred in my imagination it is! My gorge rises at it. Here hung those lips that I have kist I know not how oft. Where be your gibes now? your gambols? your songs? your flashes of merriment, that were wont to set the table on a roar? Not one now, to mock your own grinning? quite chop-faln? Now get you to my lady's chamber, and tell her, let her paint an inch thick, to this favour she must come; make her laugh at that.—Prithee, Horatio, tell me one thing.

Horatio: What's that, my lord?

Hamlet: Dost thou think Alexander lookt o' this fashion i' th' earth?

Horatio: E'en so.

Hamlet: And smelt so? Pah!   [*Puts down the skull.*]

Horatio: E'en so, my lord.

2.4   Challenging Premises

Once we are sure that we are dealing with an argument—rather than an explanation or some other nonargument—and are clear what the premises are and what the conclusion is, then as logicians we would ask whether the argument is deductive or inductive, and if it is deductive whether it is valid and so on. But as critical thinkers we can also ask—once the argument is set forth clearly—whether the premises are indeed *true.*

In challenging premises, we may ask:

- *Does the premise conflict with our own firsthand observations?* Consider the statement "*Pocahontas* is rated R." You and I know this is not plausible. I saw it and you probably did, too. Anyway, we both have seen lots of Disney movies, none of which was rated R.

On the other hand, memories can be distorted by bias, so we must always consider the possibility that we have seen things a certain way when they were not that way at all. For instance, a parent may see his child as a little angel when the opposite is true. Furthermore, if your experience happened when you were very sleepy, drunk, or distracted in some way, your observations might be unreliable.

- *Does the premise conflict with our general knowledge and common sense?* Consider the statement "Computers are useless." Common sense and general knowledge (and your own experience, probably) indicate that this is blatantly false. Or consider the statement "It's perfectly safe to pick up hitchhikers."

- *Does the premise conflict with what we can find out from an encyclopedia or other standard reference?* Consider the statement "Bats are rodents." If you look up the word *bat* in an encyclopedia or a standard zoology text, you will find that it is *not* a rodent.

- *Does it come from a biased or dubious source?* Consider the statement "The president is a congenital liar," said by a member of the opposition party. Or consider the statement "Barbara Walters abducted by UFO" as a headline on one of the tabloids. If this were reported by the *New York Times,* however, or *Time,* or *U.S. News and World Report,* it might be worth taking a bit more seriously. (Not that these sources can't be mistaken!)

Your own experience, education, and common sense will greatly help you in challenging dubious premises, but sometimes you will have to refer to authorities and people with expertise in the area under consideration. For example, if the subject is astronomy and you are not an astronomer, you will need to consult an astronomer—or an astronomy textbook or an encyclopedia. The expert or authority should be expert or authoritative in the relevant area. To consult and cite a prominent astronomer on a question about plumbing would be to commit a fallacy (which we will discuss in Chapter 3).

Exercise 2.4   A. Challenge the premises of the arguments in each passage.

1. The use of fetal tissue for medical research is wrong. Murdering an innocent baby to get its tissue, which is what this amounts to, is morally unacceptable. Moreover, it will turn women into mere incubators, wombs to be exploited for raw material. I am horrified by the whole business, and I intend to write my congressman condemning it.

2. Rodents give me the creeps, and bats are rodents, so bats give me the creeps. I hate the way they swoop down on your head and sink their little rat teeth into your neck and suck your blood. Shooee.

B. In the following essay, find the arguments, put them into standard form, and challenge the premises.

> *Only the death penalty is suitable punishment for a capital crime such as first-degree murder.*
>
> *But what about such crimes as those of John Wayne Gacy, Ted Bundy, Jeffrey Dahmer, and Timothy McVeigh, who blew up the Murrah Federal Building in Oklahoma City? Surely the death penalty is too lenient for them. The only way to prevent such crimes as theirs is to match those crimes with punishments as equally harsh.*
>
> *Someone like McVeigh should, after a speedy and businesslike trial, be executed, but before that he should be humiliated. We should stone them, beat them, spit on them.*
>
> *Terrorists want attention; they want to be thought of as heroes to their cause. That is all that motivates them. They want to be important "somebodies." They should therefore be reduced to nothing. That would surely deter other such monsters in human form. They should not be given comfortable lives in prison, painting clown pictures, writing their memoirs, and the like. They should be brutally killed, publicly. That would be just retribution, and it would match their crimes.*
>
> *Law-abiding American citizens will feel more secure, and the crime rate will go down. And any measure that can save one innocent person is justifiable.*

C. Can you challange the premises of this advertisement?

> A Timex watch ad: ". . . When our spotlight went dead one night on a remote Florida lake, I used my Indiglo watch to light our way back through the channel. Thankfully, the local residents, stunned by the blue glow, parted and let us pass."—Suzanne Michaels, Sanford, Florida   [This statement appears under a photo of a lake filled with alligators.]

2.5 Competing Arguments

Sam: *Reincarnation must be true. Under hypnosis I discovered that I was a soldier in the pharaoh's army. I remembered the awful terror of drowning when the waters of the Red Sea closed over me. I also found that I was Jesse James and I was shot in the back by a low character, Robert Ford. These experiences prove reincarnation.*

Pam: *Reincarnation cannot be true. If I dream, even under hypnosis, that I am Arnold Schwarzenegger, that does not mean I am Arnold Schwarzenegger.*

In the same way, my dreaming that I was Julius Caesar does not mean I was Julius Caesar. And if I am the reincarnation of Caesar, doesn't it follow that I should hurry to Rome, claim my throne, look for the reincarnation of Brutus, and on and on? Wouldn't it follow that historians should flock to me to find out the real truth *about Caesar? That is ridiculous, so reincarnation cannot be true.*

These two passages offer competing arguments about reincarnation. It would be easy to offer an opinion on which passage is more **cogent,** more logically persuasive; but we want to offer a reasoned, critical judgment, one that is informed by our critical discipline and supported by good reasons. So we analyze each one and then compare them.

Sam's main conclusion is

Reincarnation is true.

The argument is (briefly)

Under hypnosis I discovered my past lives.

If I had past lives, reincarnation is true.

∴ *Reincarnation is true.*

Pam's main conclusion is

Reincarnation is not true.

The main argument is

If any person is the reincarnation of Caesar, that person should go to Rome, claim his throne, find Brutus (or the reincarnation of Brutus), and on and on.

No person should do that (that is ridiculous).

∴ *No person is the reincarnation of Caesar.*

Which argument is more persuasive? Let's challenge the premises of each argument: Sam's first premise is very dubious. *Dreaming* of a jade Statue of Liberty is not *discovering* a real jade Statue of Liberty. Being under hypnosis must be like dreaming, a kind of unconscious mental activity. Sam's stance on reincarnation looks unpersuasive.

Pam's first premise seems true. If I discovered that I was the reincarnation of Shakespeare, I would surely try to write a sonnet or two—really good ones— or visit Stratford or do something Shakespearean. I'd give interviews to graduate students in English Lit. If I couldn't do such things, I'd be unlikely to tell anybody I was the reincarnation of Shakespeare. Even if I discovered I was the reincarnation of a long string of ordinary people of past times, I would surely have some convincing stories to tell about being a baker in the 1800s or a soldier in the pharaoh's army—with lots of verifiable statements.

From the perspective of critical thinking, Pam is more persuasive than Sam. Someone might object that this is just my opinion. But I've given my reasons, and an opinion backed up by reasons is a judgment, a conclusion, which carries more weight than a mere opinion.

Of course, reincarnation might turn out to be true (but Sam would *still* have to come up with a better argument). We have only given a critical evaluation of these two competing arguments, based on the principles of our discipline. We have not settled the issue of reincarnation.

Furthermore, our analysis is not necessarily the only possible analysis. Critical thinkers can disagree and still be competent practitioners of their discipline, just as competent astronomers can disagree on a point of astronomy. On the other hand, critical thinking is not just a "matter of opinion." A reasoned, critical judgment such as we have made on the preceding two passages carries more weight than an opinion not backed up by any reasons. We offer our judgment and support it with good reasons. We must also have humility and objectivity enough to remember that, even with all our good reasons, we might still be wrong.

Exercise 2.5   Give a brief critical evaluation of the following competing essays. Find the arguments, put them into standard form, and challenge the premises; then say which is more persuasive.

1. If there's one thing high school students need today, it is a sense of morality. Morality comes, more than anywhere else, from religion. Ninety-five percent of Americans believe in God, and those people would support school prayer; what is more democratic than majority rule? Common sense tells us that prayer in school is not an establishment of "state religion," as First Amendment activists charge. So we should allow prayer in schools.

2. Majority-rule prayer in school violates the rights of religious minorities. Those rights should be respected. It is a kind of tyranny of power, the power of the majority over the powerless minority. Majority-led prayer is comparable to suppression of religious dissent in Renaissance Europe, the persecution of the Christians by the Romans, and even the demands of King Nebuchadnezzar that the Israelites bow to his pagan gods. Religious values are incompatible with the coercion of high school students. Government-led prayer has no place in public schools.

2.6 Summary

Critical thinking is concerned with arguments in their natural contexts, in the disagreements and controversies people engage in. There are several kinds of disagreement: factual, valuational, conceptual, and verbal. Being able to distinguish the various uses of language—informative, evaluative, directive, expressive, ceremonial, and performative—in which disagreements are expressed is important.

After making sure that we understand what's at issue, state the main point, or conclusion, of the essay (which is often indicated by such words as *so* and *therefore*) and then the premises that support it (as we did with the *Augusta Chronicle* article, pages 26–27). If the resulting paraphrased argument is not persuasive, ask what suppressed premises we must add to make it persuasive; then ask whether these premises, both stated and suppressed, are actually true. Do they square with our own firsthand experience, our general knowledge, and standard authorities, or do they come from a biased source?

Sometimes we find two competing essays or speeches and we can compare them for persuasiveness by analyzing their arguments.

2.7 Applications

Essays on Bosnia   Consider these two competing passages:

PASSAGE 1

We should not send U.S. troops to Bosnia now. The history of Bosnia, a long period of ethnic hatred including a three-and-a-half-year war involving war crimes and genocide, makes it plain that the killing will resume when our troops leave. If so, our efforts will have been futile. Furthermore, if we wait, eventually the Bosnians will be wiped out. If the Bosnians are wiped out, we won't have to send troops at all. So we should not send troops now.

PASSAGE 2

We should send U.S. troops to Bosnia now. If we don't send troops, the crisis will worsen; if that happens, the rest of Europe will be dragged in. European history— that is, World Wars I and II—shows that if Europe is dragged in we will eventually have to get involved. If we have to get involved then, our losses will be disastrous. We must avoid such a disaster.

Our task here is to apply the critical techniques we have discussed so far to these two passages, to form a critical judgment about which is more persuasive.

The main conclusion of passage 1 is

We should not send troops now.

Two separate arguments support this conclusion:

Bosnian history shows that if we send troops the killing will resume when we leave.

If the killing resumes when our troops leave, our efforts will have been futile.

If sending troops now is futile, we should not send them now.

∴ *We should not send U.S. troops to Bosnia now.*

If we wait, all Bosnians will eventually be killed.

If the Bosnians are all killed, we won't have to send troops at all.

If waiting means we won't have to send troops at all, we should not send troops now.

∴ *We should not send troops now.*

The main conclusion of passage 2 is

We should send troops to Bosnia now.

This conclusion is supported by a *chain argument:*

If we don't send troops now, the crisis will worsen.

If the crisis worsens, the rest of Europe will be dragged in.

European history shows that if Europe is dragged in we will have to get involved eventually.

If we have to get involved eventually, our losses then will be disastrous.

We must avoid such a disaster.

∴ *We should send troops to Bosnia now.*

We will leave aside questions of validity and strength until we present rigorous techniques for symbolizing and testing such arguments. We can, however, challenge the premises of these arguments.

In the first of the two arguments of passage 1, we may ask: Is it true that Bosnian history shows that when our troops leave the killing will resume? The worst bitterness and killing has occurred in the few years since the breakup of the Soviet Union. This suggests that putting a structure in place, by means of NATO troops, might succeed where inaction cannot. *Not* sending troops means letting more Bosnians be killed.

The second argument of passage 1 is horrifying and ignores not only the thousands of Bosnians who will die but also the real possibility mentioned in passage 2: Before the genocide spends itself, the rest of Europe might be dragged in, risking another world war—perhaps nuclear war.

In passage 2 the chain of premises is no stronger than its weakest premise, which is that Europe will be dragged in. If Europe has remained neutral this long, it might not be pulled in at all. When the Bosnians are all killed, the crisis will be over, as passage 1 says.

Now, admitting that this is a very artificial and limited example, we want to determine which passage is more persuasive. Without being experts on Eastern Europe and given that we all have biases and that we have not included other highly relevant information, we begin by making a critical, reasoned judgment of each passage.

Premise (2) in passage 2, that without U.S. troops Europe will be dragged in, is not ridiculous or unthinkable. If that happened, Europe and the rest of the world would be facing the danger of nuclear holocaust. But it *might* not happen. On the other hand, it is not implausible that correcting the present crisis with U.S. troops would reduce the probability of the spread of war in the area.

The second argument of passage 1 is inhumane. The arguer seems willing to let genocide and war crimes proceed unchecked. That is monstrous. If passage 2 is right, we might avert a cataclysmic world war, in which enormous numbers of U.S. troops and countless others would die.

So passage 2 is more plausible than passage 1. In retrospect, in winter 1995 President Clinton sent U.S. troops to Bosnia, and at this writing the crisis has subsided. That does not mean it will not resurge again.

We are not experts. We might be wrong. Even presidents, secretaries of state, and military chiefs of staff cannot possibly know everything, or even everything important, about such situations as in Bosnia or the Middle East. However, their jobs demand that they inform themselves on such issues and to think reasonably and responsibly about them, before they decide what they must do. Imperfect human beings though they are, their decisions can mean life or death, happiness or misery, to vast numbers of people.

Columbine School Shootings Read the following editorial.

Editorial from the *Forum*[2]

For God's sake! Everyone, please, step back and take a few deep breaths.

The nation surely has had it up to its collective eyeballs with all the analysis—expert and otherwise—of what went wrong at Columbine High School in Littleton, Colo. Frankly, all we really know is this: Something went wrong. Kids killed kids with guns and bombs.

But thus far, the why of it all is little more than a morass of speculation, fueled mostly by special interests. Narrow conclusions are sprouting like noxious weeds from nearly every point on the political and ideological spectrum. Consider:

- It's guns, of course. There are too many guns. Guns are too easily available. Well maybe.

- It's bloody violence in music, video games and movies. Disaffected teens become desensitized to mayhem and death, so they kill easily. Well maybe.

- It's absent parents. It's divorce and single-parent families. It's parents being too busy to know what their kids are doing. Well maybe.

- It's the schools. Take prayer out of the schools, and see what happens. Take dress codes out of the schools, and see what happens. Take God out of the curriculum, and see what happens. Well maybe.

Or maybe not.

In fact, at this point, the only common denominator is maybe.

How dare stuffed shirt columnists, morning talk radio morons and shallow TV commentators presume to understand the dynamics in the families of the two teens who committed the horrible crime. How dare politicians use tragedy to advance their agendas. How dare holier-than-thou preachers and letter-writing religionists conclude the aberrant behavior of troubled kids was a message from God.

How dare any of us be so arrogant as to proclaim we know the mind of God.

Simple answers won't do, no matter how we long for them. Simple answers give comfort to simpletons and scoundrels, but get us no closer to the complex truth of Littleton.

---

2. *Source:* Editorial, *Forum* (Fargo, N.D.), 27 April 1999. Reprinted with permission.

The main conclusion is

Simple answers give comfort to simpletons and scoundrels but get us no closer to the truth about Littleton.

The premises are the following:

- "Too many guns, too easily available" is a simple answer, but only a speculation (a "maybe").
- "Violence in music, video games, and movies" is a simple answer, but only a speculation.
- "Too-busy, divorced parents" is a simple answer, but only a speculation.
- "Absence of God and prayer in schools" is a simple answer, but only a speculation.

These examples support a suppressed conclusion, which then becomes a premise for the main conclusion:

Such answers are simple and speculative.

The arguer then claims that

Simple answers give comfort to simpletons and scoundrels

and

Speculative answers get us no closer to the truth

which, all together, yield the main conclusion.

But we know that simple answers are sometimes right, even though they give comfort to simpletons and scoundrels; we also know that speculative answers, when backed up by knowledge—even statistics—*can* get us closer to the truth.

The harangue against morons, holier-than-thou preachers, and the like adds little, so we ignore it. But we will look at such tactics in Chapter 3.

Exercise 2.7 In the following speech by former secretary of state Madeleine K. Albright, find the main conclusion and premises (note indicator words). Can you challenge Albright's premises? What uses of language can you identify?

Senate Shouldn't Delay Passing Nuclear Test-Ban Treaty[3]
by Madeleine K. Albright

Three years ago last month, President Clinton became the first world leader to sign the Comprehensive Test Ban Treaty. Since then, 153 other world leaders have followed suit. Fifty-one nations, including most of our allies, have ratified the treaty.

Almost two years after the treaty was submitted to Congress for ratification, the Senate began hearings Wednesday. Senators will focus on the concrete benefits this treaty brings the United States. And when they do so, they should conclude that the treaty is an unalloyed benefit for America's national security and an important tool in blocking the threat of nuclear proliferation.

The simple truth is that because the U.S. has the world's most advanced nuclear capabilities, we have much to gain from freezing the picture by ending explosive testing forever. We already have the expertise gained from more than a thousand tests of our own. We have the ability to maintain a safe and reliable nuclear deterrent without further explosive tests. Indeed, we have not tested since 1992—when Republicans and Democrats in Congress together enacted a national moratorium.

We don't need explosive testing. Only would-be proliferators, rogue states and terrorist groups do. And there is no good reason to let them have it.

There are those who say the treaty is too risky because some countries might cheat. But what exactly would we be risking? With no treaty other countries can test without cheating, and without limits. The treaty will improve our ability to deter and detect clandestine nuclear-weapons activity. It will provide a global network of more than 300 sensors, and it commits every signatory to accept intrusive monitoring. The more countries that support and participate in the treaty, the harder it will be for others to cheat and the higher price they will pay if they do.

Of course, signatures on a piece of paper cannot by themselves end the threat of nuclear attack. We cannot rely on a treaty as our sole means of defense. But we know that strong global rules against proliferation make a difference. Those norms helped persuade countries from Argentina to Ukraine not to go nuclear. They rallied a global response when India and Pakistan defied international public opinion by testing.

---

3. Madeleine K. Albright, "Senate Shouldn't Delay Passing Nuclear Test-Ban Treaty," *Chicago Tribune,* 7 October 1999.

The treaty is the capstone of that legal framework. And as long as the United States fails to ratify the treaty, we cannot insist that India and Pakistan—or Russia and China—play by its rules. What is more, we are excluded from discussions about the treaty's future.

Around the world we face dangerous possibilities for proliferation that make it more important than ever to put explosive testing out of bounds for good. Imagine a nuclear standoff in the Persian Gulf or one involving a terrorist group with nuclear materials. If we reject this treaty we are telling the world—terrorists, rogue states, regional rivals—that nuclear weapons testing and technology are not just acceptable but essential. And that can only harm America's security.

We have the technical capability we need to monitor other nations' nuclear programs. The treaty would give us means for new intrusive monitoring around the world. And it will ensure a strong global response if tests ever do take place.

We have everything we ought to need to make this a simple, non-partisan, non-controversial vote. The treaty has the support of the chairman of the Joint Chiefs of Staff and his distinguished predecessors John Shalikashvili, Colin Powell, William Crowe and David Jones. The heads of America's nuclear weapons laboratories support it, as do many of the physicists who developed our nuclear deterrent.

And almost as long as there have been nuclear explosions, a test-ban treaty has been popular with Americans and sought by ordinary people everywhere.

People around the world do not want to live in a world in which nuclear testing is business as usual. They do not care for the threat of radiation in their air and water or in their children's bones. They do not want to make it easy or acceptable for nuclear weapons to spread further.

I urge the Senate to recognize that this universal wish is a sensible safeguard for our security

Madeleine K. Albright is the [former] U.S. Secretary of State.

Informal Fallacies

Some disagreement arises among logicians about the informal fallacies: how many there are, how to classify them, and how to understand them in some more basic theoretical way.

They are just there, it seems—we've been finding fallacies since the time of the Greek philosopher Aristotle (384–322 B.C.), who compiled the first list of fallacies, and since then the list has grown. In general, they are more or less easily recognizable ways that arguments can go wrong.

The purpose of logic is the evaluation of arguments in ordinary language. The purpose of the list of fallacies, which follows, is to make it easier to recognize bad arguments in their natural setting without using any sophisticated logical symbolism.

Formal logic ignores the context of language in which arguments are found, but informal logic jumps right into the dense jungle of argumentation. Because they are produced mostly by human beings, few real arguments are completely impersonal and objective; actual arguments in their natural habitat contain hidden presuppositions, lies, sophistries, tricks, and diversions. So even though informal logic is not as precise and rigorous as formal logic, if we want to grapple with real-world arguments, we can hardly do without it.

3.1 Fallacies

A **fallacy** is a bad argument that may seem to be correct but is rendered defective by an error in reasoning. In a fallacious argument, the reasons given do not adequately support the conclusion.

A **formal fallacy,** such as the fallacies of the syllogism (which we will discuss in Chapter 4), fails because of its structure or form. In this chapter we discuss

informal fallacies, arguments that (1) fail because of their content rather than their form and (2) cannot be detected by the techniques of formal logic.

These informal fallacies, logical mistakes that are common in ordinary discourse, have been classified and given names. Traditionally, informal fallacies have been divided into three or four main groups. In any such scheme, a certain amount of overlap occurs, and different logicians group them differently. So our approach cannot be mechanical. This part of logic and critical thinking is difficult, but success is very satisfying—so much so that we must try to restrain ourselves from finding fallacies that aren't there!

Remember the *logician's Golden Rule:* Always treat others' arguments as you would wish them to treat yours. Place the most reasonable interpretation on others' arguments and hope that they do the same to yours. Misunderstanding someone on purpose is in fact itself a fallacy (the straw man), which we discuss later in this chapter.

Learning the fallacies not only makes it easier to spot them in others' arguments but also makes it easier for us to avoid committing them in our own arguments.

Why are fallacies so wickedly persuasive? People often so strongly *want* to believe something that they are glad to find "reasons" to believe it; that's where fallacies come in. If a bully tells us something, we want to believe it if we can find any justification. If "beautiful people" say we ought to think a certain way—that a certain exercise machine or headache remedy is right for us, for example—we want to "go along." Anything that seems to confirm our prejudices and fantasies we are happy to embrace. If we want to think that there are good reasons to buy lots of things, advertisers will give us a million "good reasons" to work hard so that we can afford those things.

If you find yourself alone in thinking that a certain government policy is wrong, it is very human to be receptive to reasons for giving up that unpopular view. If one car maker tells you that you're smarter than others and therefore deserve "the best," why not lean back and soak it all in?

And if you believe something—that there are angels among us or demons from hell—you might not have patience with doubters, and you might very naturally come up with flimsy sophistries, secure in your belief that you "could" come up with good reasons if you had to.

Whether there are indeed angels among us, there certainly are flocks of fallacies and sophistries all around us, thick as flies around a rotten apple. Is that a false analogy?

It is hard to resist being swept by fallacious arguments into believing what we want to believe anyway. Pity, fear, prejudice, and greed are often so strong in us that clear thinking is next to impossible. It is often tempting to try to shore up a flimsy argument with slanted language and ambiguities that subtly shift attention from the real point, with cunning tricks that work like the magician's sleight of hand. Sometimes we use such tactics consciously, but perhaps more often we use them without fully realizing that we are.

We get away with it and are taken in by it ourselves, because it is always easier to consent uncritically and "go along" than it is to think critically. Besides that, it is always harder to spot fallacies in our own views than it is to find them in the views of others, especially when these views oppose ours.

Philosophers have now and then observed that logic is fundamentally a branch of ethics, and there is truth in this observation. Thinking critically, considering reasons, taking responsibility for our choices and actions, and trying always to be fair and objective are elements of one's moral character. A *person* in the full moral sense is one who, quite simply, thinks for herself or himself and is not bumped around through life like a ball on a pool table. People who always say "I couldn't help myself" or "I only believed and did as I was told" are not meeting their responsibilities as free, mature human beings.

The existentialist Jean-Paul Sartre (1905–1980) said: We are all free whether we like it or not; when we deny that we are free, we are lying to ourselves. One way we lie to ourselves is by letting ourselves be deceived by fallacies—others' and our own. Logicians have long recognized that there is no complete list of fallacies, because it would be impossible to identify *every* way an argument can go wrong. It should be noted that an argument can contain more than one fallacy and that an extended argument can contain several types of fallacies.

Some logicians classify *inconsistency* as a kind of fallacy of presumption, akin to special pleading (to be discussed later in this chapter). It seems to be a more important and general mistake, however, because when it occurs, it renders the whole argument or essay worthless. So we are setting it apart from the other informal fallacies and giving it its own separate treatment. The **fallacy of inconsistency** occurs when the premises of an argument, or a premise and the conclusion, contradict each other. For example:

> *Drinking is bad for my health, so I've given it up. I'll have a couple for lunch, of course, if I'm out with friends or business associates. You can't be a wet blanket. So I'm glad I've made this decision.*

Obviously, "I've given it up" and "I'll have a couple for lunch" contradict each other. It is important to note, however, that this fallacy does not produce an invalid argument. From "I've given it up," it follows that "I've given it up or I'm Mel Gibson"; from "I'll have a couple," it follows that "I have *not* given it up."

Then, from "I've given it up or I'm Mel Gibson" and "I have not given it up," it follows that I'm Mel Gibson! And this kind of argument can be used to prove "anything"—that I'm Mel Gibson and that I'm not, that the moon is made of provolone and that it's not, and on and on.

Logicians call this fallacy and its consequences "curious." From an inconsistency, everything follows, and so any argument containing a contradiction is valid but worthless. However, any argument containing such an inconsistency cannot be *sound,* even though it is valid.

This peculiar but important fallacy will be discussed again in connection with truth-functional logic in Chapter 5, where its paradoxical character will be made a little easier to understand.

Exercise 3.1   Find an inconsistency in each passage.

1. Our troops will be sent to keep the peace, and nothing more. Of course, they will be heavily armed so that if they are attacked they can respond with overwhelming force. But their responsibility will be to keep the peace. This will bring peace to Bosnia.

2. Once, at the beginning of our universe, there was a point with no size and infinite mass. Then this point exploded, creating the universe. Therefore, space and time began then. This is what our calculations indicate.

3. God is all good and all powerful. But there is evil in the world, which means that if God is all good he wants to destroy evil, but obviously he cannot. And it also means that if God is all powerful he is able to destroy evil, but he does not want to. So God is either not all good or not all powerful.

4. Intentionally killing a human being is murder. Murder is wrong and so it should be punished by execution. We should take the life of a person who takes a life.

3.2 Fallacies of Ambiguity

Fallacies of ambiguity are arguments, or statements that occur in arguments, that turn on the fact that many words, phrases, and sentences can be understood in more than one way. An argument that involves such an ambiguity might seem at first to be valid; on closer examination, however, it can be seen to depend on taking certain words in two different ways.

Amphiboly Amphiboly occurs when a sentence is put together in such a manner that it can be understood in two ways. This is a matter of *syntax,* or linguistic structure. For example:

Customer: What's this fly doing in my soup?

Waiter: Looks like it's drowning.

Clearly, the question really means *why* is this fly in my soup, but the waiter takes it to mean *what* the fly is doing. The implication of the question is plainly that the fly shouldn't be in the soup at all and that the waiter should therefore have an explanation. But the waiter takes the question in a different way and commits the fallacy of amphiboly.

Here are two more examples of amphiboly:

Roy came out twirling his gun and shot off his mouth.

Wife: I see Mr. Smith is cooking out on his new barbecue grill.

Husband: So his wife finally got fed up with his drinking!

The first sentence means Smith is cooking hamburgers or steaks or something. The second takes it to be saying that Smith himself is being cooked.

When we *disambiguate,* remove the ambiguity by spelling out literally what is meant, the misunderstanding (and the joke) disappears.

Consider the following examples:

For sale: German Shepherd. Will eat anything. Especially likes children.

So the dog prefers four-year-olds to puppy kibble? Who wants a dog that eats children? Any argument formulated on the basis of this misunderstanding would be bound to go wrong.

Wanted: Bicycle for small boy with training wheels.

The way this is put invites the comment: If he's got wheels already, why does he need a bicycle?

Wanted: Air rifle for child with pump action.

What kind of child has "pump action"?

Newspaper classified ads usually contain many examples of amphiboly. Most jokes (usually naughty) of the *double entendre* (French for "double meaning") variety are usually instances of this fallacy.

Equivocation **Equivocation** occurs when a word or phrase is used two different ways in the same argument. It is, unlike amphiboly, a matter of *semantics,* the "meaning" of the terms involved. For example:

Pornography is undesirable. But many people desire it, so it must not be undesirable.

The word "undesirable" means "unworthy of being desired" in the first sentence and "not capable of being desired" in the second.

Equivocation is very similar to amphiboly, but there is a difference. Amphiboly depends on taking a whole *sentence* the wrong way, whereas equivocation is a matter of taking a *word* or *phrase* the wrong way.

Here are two more examples:

I have a right to speak. What is right ought to be done. So I ought to speak.

Here "right" first means "not prohibited" and then is changed to mean "what ought to be." So equivocation on *right* occurs here.

The man walked down to the bank.

Here "bank" could mean a financial institution or a river bank.
    Our final example is from an advertisement:

A diet Coke ad: The Two Greatest Things on Ice: Katarina Witt and diet Coke.   [This statement appears beside a photograph of Katarina Witt, the ice skater, holding a diet Coke.]

Accent   The fallacy of **accent** depends upon stressing a word in a sentence and thereby changing the meaning of the whole sentence. For example:

All men are created equal.

This implies that the sentence does not include *women,* which was not necessarily the intention of the framers of the Declaration of Independence.
    And then there are the familiar street signs:

Slow	Slow
Children	Men
at	at
Play	Work

Read one way, they mean "slow down," for there are children at play or men at work. Read another way, they mean dull-witted children or men are about.
    And then there's this:

I hope you get everything you deserve

which can mean two opposite things, depending on the tone in which it's expressed. Even the simplest statement can vary in meaning, depending on which word is accented:

Fred was not drunk last night. (But Joyce was.)

Fred was not drunk last night. (No matter what the police say.)

Fred was not drunk last night. (But he was stoned.)

Fred was not drunk last night. (But he will be tonight).

Hypostatization **Hypostatization** occurs when an abstraction is turned into a real, concrete thing. The following four examples are all instances of *personification*, a special case of hypostatization.

> *Don't fool around with Mother Nature.*

This turns nature into a person—a person who'll get angry with you and retaliate if you try to improve on "her" work. But, of course, nature is not a person at all.

> *Uncle Sam wants you.*

As if the U.S. government is a person—a kindly but stern old guy who wants and expects you to join the army. There is no such person.

> *Hurricane Edna slaps at Carolina Coast.*

This suggests that Edna is a ferocious woman on the rampage, but hurricanes aren't angry at anyone.

> *Because I could not stop for death*
> *He kindly stopped for me.*

Death has no kindness or cruelty—it's not a "he" at all.

Finally, here's a more philosophical example:

> *How does the mind interact with the body?*

This takes the mind to be a kind of (physical) "thing," which it isn't. (Or is it? *Many* books have been written on this topic.)

Composition The fallacy of **composition** occurs when something that is true of each member of a collection is falsely applied to the whole collection taken as a totality; that is, it attempts to apply to a whole group what is true only of its parts or members. The next four examples illustrate:

> *Each member of the team is a good player, so the whole team will play well.*

This is not necessarily true, for it is possible that each player is good but they can't play well together.

> *One sheet of typing paper is very light in weight, so a ream of typing paper is light, too.*
>
> *Each grain of sand is tiny and light in weight, so a truck load of sand will also be tiny and light.*
>
> *The script is good, and the actors are good, so the show will be good.*

A slightly different version of this fallacy happens when the *distributive* and *collective* uses of a term are confused, as in

> *A giraffe eats more than a dog; therefore, all giraffes eat more than all dogs.*

Although a giraffe eats more than a dog, there are many more dogs than giraffes; that is, giraffes eat more than dogs distributively, but not collectively.
Here's another example:

> *The U.S. government spends more money on one ship than on one employee's lifetime salary. So the government spends more on ships than on employees' salaries.*

Just because any particular ship costs more than any individual's salary (distributively) that does not mean that all ships cost more than all salaries (collectively) because there are so many more employees than ships.

Division **Division** is the opposite of composition. Here, what is true about the whole is assumed to be true of its parts or members. For example:

> *A tidal wave is dangerous, so a glassful of water is dangerous, too.*

But a glassful of water won't carry you out to sea.

> *The whole car is heavy, so each of its parts must be heavy, too.*

Obviously this does not follow.

> *Wally works for a big, important corporation, so he must be a big, important person.*

This is a fallacy because what's true of the corporation need not be true of all its employees. And so is

> *America is a wealthy nation; therefore, all Americans are wealthy.*

And then there is the slightly different type of fallacy of division, in which what is true collectively is said to be true distributively, as in

> *Every third child in America grows up to be mentally ill, so you shouldn't have more than two children.*

Exercise 3.2   A. Which fallacy of ambiguity is committed in the following advertisements?

 1. A Lysol Disinfectant Spray ad: 24-hour home security.   [This statement is under a picture of a two-story house with porch lights on.]

2. A Toyota ad: Admit It. You Have to Be Pretty Well Built to Carry 2 Million People.   [This statement is above a picture of a single Toyota Camry.]

3. A Foot Shox Insoles ad: Kiss Your Aching Feet Goodbye.

B. Find which fallacy of ambiguity is committed in the following passages. In many, only a suggestion of a fallacy is given. Ask yourself: What fallacy would result if this passage is part of an argument?

1. A bus uses more fuel than a car, so all buses use more fuel than all cars.

2. Furniture ad: We stand behind every bed we sell.

3. None of the cuts by itself will kill him; so all of them together won't kill him.

4. Whatever runs has legs. This car runs, so it must have legs.

5. Laugh and the world laughs with you.

6. Justice is blind. So being innocent won't do you any good in court.

7. Wanted: Dresser suitable for lady with thick legs and large drawers.

8. No individual is indispensable, so we could do without everyone.

9. He turned and walked away with his dog, Tony, laughing and waving to us.

10. You can't be too honest.

11. America expects you to do your duty.

12. Goodwill toward *men*.

13. A cat eats more than a locust, so all cats eat more than all locusts.

14. The government is inefficient and wasteful. Toby is a government employee, so he must be inefficient and wasteful.

15. A nuclear weapon is more destructive than any other weapon, so nuclear weapons have destroyed more than all other weapons put together.

16. The nuthatch was discovered by Tilly Turnow in the woods, while hopping from branch to branch of an elm tree, singing happily.

17. God is love. Love is blind. So God is blind.

18. Every part of the human body has a function—so the whole human being must have a function, too.

19. The defendant says that the dead man chased him with a razor.

20. Ad for laundry: Ladies who drop their clothes off here will receive prompt attention.

21. Q: Do you serve shrimp here?

    A: We don't care how big you are, as long as you have money.

22. The buffalo is disappearing fast. So if you see one, you'd better look quickly.

23. The old bum walked along the tracks with his dog, Bosco, cursing and muttering under his breath.

24. No news is good news. Iranian threats are no news. So Iranian threats are good news.

25. You can't spend too much money to win an election.

26. Shirts and shoes required to eat inside.

27. The average family has 1.3 children. The Joneses are an average family, so they must have 1.3 children.

28. The language of America is English, so Chang Lee must speak English, since he's an American.

29. Pizza John's is a bigger company than Burger Sal's, so the employees of Pizza John's are bigger than those of Burger Sal's.

30. Since the Sun and the planets are spherical, the whole universe must also be spherical.

31. Shakespeare is truly immortal. So he must be a very old man by now.

32. A little knowledge is a dangerous thing, so a lot must be even worse.

33. Some dogs are retrievers. My dog is a retriever, so my dog is some dog!

34. Mrs. Hiram Leatherwood has recently had her appendix taken out and a new dishwasher put in.

35. If practice makes perfect, Karla must be perfect, for she's practiced law for three years.

36. He took the hood of a Pontiac, the frame of a Ford, and the wheels of a Toyota. You know what he got? Ten years!

37. The new minister gave his first sermon last Sunday. Extension of the cemetery has become necessary six months before expected.

38. Actions speak louder than words.

39. The American economy has held steady since 1980. Farming is a part of the American economy, so it must be holding steady, too.

40. All things are made of atoms. So hopes, dreams, and thoughts must be made of atoms, too.

41. The Democratic Party seems to favor high taxes and low morals.

42. "Economy Struggles in Grip of Inflation"

43. I hope you get everything you want.

44. I've never seen you looking better.

45. Swimsuits one-half off.

46. No single person in the crowd would start a riot, so they wouldn't do it all together.

47. Dr. A. J. Thomas gave a lecture on "Teaching the Illiterate." Over one hundred were present.

48. Whatever you want, that's what I want.

49. If you drop one grain of sand on the beach, there is no noise. So if you drop a truckload of sand on the beach, there won't be any noise, either.

50. Do you have Prince Albert in a can?

51. A fetus is human, and it's life; so it's human life.

52. Women live longer than men, on the average. So you will live longer than your husband.

53. All the actors in *Mississippi Burning* were excellent. So the whole movie was excellent.

54. The Constitution says the people have a right to bear arms. That means I can carry an AK-47.

55. The Chinese are an industrious people. Kam Fong is Chinese, so he must be industrious.

56. Congress repudiated the 51 percent pay increase. Senator Ross is a congressman, so he repudiated the 51 percent pay increase.

57. "Killer Ted Bundy Faces Grim Reaper"

58. "Death Claims Jeffrey Dahmer"

59. One out of every sixty-one children born in New York City has AIDS. So if you're pregnant, you should stay out of New York.

60. Colonel Oliver North believes that you can't go too far in the fight for freedom.

61. Germany is friendly with America, so all Germans are friendly with all Americans.

62. Tom: I'd like a second opinion.

    Doctor: Okay. You're ugly, too!

63. A: I just met a man with a wooden leg named Smith.

    B: Well, what was the name of his other leg?

64. No salary would be just compensation for your work.

65. Why are you afraid to tell the truth?

66. I fought a grizzly bear in my pajamas.

67. A dog eats more than an insect, so all dogs eat more than all insects.

68. IBM is a huge and powerful company. So George, who works for IBM, must be a huge and powerful man.

69. Ad: My mother's tampons? No way!

70. Are you awake or asleep?

71. The sweet bird of her youth had flown away.

72. The Senate voted against funds for the Contras, so Senator Thurmond voted against it.

73. A factory causes more pollution than a car, so all factories cause more pollution than all cars.

74. Wanted: Dog for small boy with short hair, long ears.

75. World opinion condemns Israel for their treatment of the Palestinians.

76. We can't be too cautious in dealing with the Bosnians.

77. The forest is dark and forbidding, so this maple tree is dark and forbidding.

78. You can't take human life too seriously.

79. That Old Man River just keeps rolling along.

80. You can't escape the long arm of the law.

81. Wanted: Exerciser for young couple in good condition.

82. Old Father Time is cruel.

83. Make him an offer he can't refuse.

84. Love walked into my life.

85. Her huge engine roaring, Clara boarded the jet for Chicago.

86. Many people admire Saddam, so he must be admirable.

87. You see this nail? Now, when I nod my head, you hit it with your hammer.

88. Tom: I've broken my leg in three places!

    Doctor: Well, you should stay out of those places!

89. My life is miserable. I want to share it with you.

90. Beauty is as beauty does.

91. That Lucky Old Sun just rolls around heaven all day.

92. For sale: Motorcycle for student that is cheap and reliable.

93. One Valium isn't dangerous, so a whole bottle full isn't dangerous, either.

94. Santa Claus knows if you've been bad.

95. One union member has little political power, so a whole union has little political power.

96. The ocean is blue, so a glass of ocean water must be blue, too.

97. Your next case of diarrhea may be your last.

98. He paints with his heart.

99. In this book he examines the mind of the South.

100. Are you behind our troops or not?

101. The grave beckoned.

102. Liberty is a grand lady.

103. The average American can't afford a house. So I can't afford a house.

104. Technology is a great success. So Tom, who's a technologist, is a great success.

105. Mary walked away with her cocker spaniel, Fluffy. John swore in his heart that he would someday make passionate love to her.

106. I was once engaged to a wonderful man, but when I found out he had a wooden leg I felt I had to break it off.

107. George: Gee, you're daffy! Did your nurse drop you on your head when you were a baby?

     Gracie: Oh, no. We were too poor to have a nurse. My mother had to do it.

108. George: You say your brother was held up by two men last night?

     Gracie: That's right. They held him up all the way home from the bar.

3.3 Avoiding Ambiguity: Definition

Because language is so important to logic, it is essential that we know what our words mean. An argument is made up of statements, and statements are made up of words; therefore, an argument can stand or fall on the basis of the meanings of the words involved. So we must look closely at the subject of *definition* and how it works.

Controversies often, surprisingly often, turn upon a crucial definition of a word or phrase. Consider the important role of the terms *abortion, sexual harassment, reasonable doubt, cutting Medicare, flat tax, obstruction of justice, hero,* and *child pornography* in such issues as abortion, feminism, the Simpson trial, the federal budget debate, the presidential election, Washington politics, and so on. Language *is* the context of all these controversies, and so the definitions of the words of our language—and the process of definition—must be taken into account by critical thinking about the controversies of our time.

There is an old question about which came first, the chicken or the egg. Here is the correct answer: If by *egg* you mean "chicken egg," then that's an egg that's laid by a chicken, and so the chicken came first. On the other hand, if by *egg* you mean "egg in general," then the egg came first, since dinosaurs laid eggs long before there were any chickens! We solved the problem by defining our terms.

Here's another example: If a tree falls in the forest when no one is around to hear it, does it make a sound? We define our terms: If by *sound* you mean "waves produced in air," then a tape recorder will show that there was a sound. But if by *sound* you mean "what someone hears," then there is no sound.

The American philosopher William James told a story about coming upon a group of men arguing near a large tree in the forest. There was a squirrel on the trunk of the tree, and as one of the men circled the tree, the squirrel always stayed on the side of the tree opposite him. The argument was about whether the man went around the squirrel as he went around the tree. Some of the people said the man in question certainly went around the squirrel; but the others said that since the squirrel's belly was always facing the man, then the man didn't go around the squirrel at all.

James, a good philosopher, solved the dispute by defining terms: If by *going around* you mean going north, east, south, and west of the squirrel, then north again, and so on, then the man goes around the squirrel. But if by *going around* you mean going from belly to side to back to side to belly again, then the man does not go around the squirrel. You just have to decide what you're going to mean by *going around*.

Logicians call this a **stipulative,** or **precising, definition.** It means assigning a meaning to a word for the purpose of keeping matters straight and unconfused. Verbal disputes (as opposed to real ones), such as those above, can often be cleared up by stipulating a meaning for a crucial word.

The precising definition reduces the vagueness of a term. For example, in this text we do not wish to consider every kind of argument—spats, disputes, quarrels, and so on—so we overcome the vagueness of the ordinary word by precising it (if we had just "invented" a word and stipulated its meaning, that would be a stipulative definition):

By *bug* we mean "insect" and "spider."

By *civil liberties* we mean the "right to free speech, thought, and religion."

By *thinking* we mean "reasoned thinking, which takes place as we work out problems, tell stories, plan strategies, and the like."

There are other types of definition, too. The **lexical, or reportive, definition** simply reports the way the word is actually used by people who speak the language. Here are some examples:

empty: containing nothing

top: the highest point of something

Technical or **theoretical definitions** are used to make technical language clear or to make a theory more acceptable and coherent. Examples include:

work: force × distance

decillion: the cardinal number represented by 1 followed by 33 zeroes

Persuasive ("loaded") **definitions** are used to influence attitudes by sneaking emotional content into the meaning of the word defined. These will come up again later, when we discuss the fallacies. Examples are

abortion: the murder of innocent babies

Democrat: a person who favors high taxes and low morals

Finally, the simplest form of definition, the **ostensive, or pointing, definition** is used when defining a word by pointing to or listing examples:

spoon: "one of these," you say   [*holding up a spoon*]

vegetation: trees, flowers, shrubs, and grass

Rules for Definition A safe method of defining a word is the method of **genus and specific difference.** A *genus* is a big set, and *species* are the little sets that make it up. An example of definition by genus and specific difference is

triangle: a plane figure (that's the genus) with three sides (that's the way it is specifically different from all other plane figures).

Two more examples are

exit: way (genus) out (specific difference from a way in)

doe: female (specific difference) deer (genus)

It is usually possible to come up with definitions, but certain rules should be observed:

1. **Avoid circular definitions.** These are definitions in which the word to be defined is part of the definition. For example:

   container: a utensil used to contain something

   square: a square-shaped figure

2. **Avoid definitions that are too broad.** These definitions include too much. For example:

   cat: a feline animal

   which includes lions and tigers; and

   television: visual entertainment

   which includes movies, live drama, and rock concerts.

3. **Avoid definitions that are too narrow.** These definitions include too little and narrow down the meaning of the word too much. For example:

   egg: reproductive cell of a chicken

   This is too narrow, for there are ostrich eggs, salmon eggs, snake eggs, and on and on. And so is

   exercise: a physical activity to develop skill

   because there are also mental exercises and spiritual exercises.

4. **Avoid negative definitions.** Most terms, have too many things to list that they do not mean. For example:

   cat: not a dog, not a horse, and on and on

   You would never complete such a definition. The same is true for

   jam: not jelly

   There are too many things that jam is not to list—it is not butter, not soup, and so on.

5. **Avoid definitions that are verbose.** Such definitions go on and on, in flowery and poetic language, but never tell the essentials. For example:

   honesty: a habitual inclination toward honorable and trustworthy behavior

   This is verbose. So is

   horse: the proud and noble steed of the knight, the cowboy, and the conquistador

   And, worst of all,

   net: fabric with large interstitial vacuities

Summary: Kinds of Definition

- The **stipulative, or precising, definition** assigns a meaning to a word for the purpose of keeping matters clear and unconfused. *Example:* By *short story* we mean any work of less than 15,000 words.

- The **lexical definition** is the standard, common meaning of a word in actual use. *Example:* bicycle: a two-wheeled vehicle powered by pedaling.

- The **technical definition** makes technical matters clear and definite. *Example:* Force = mass × acceleration.

- The **persuasive definition** tries to influence attitudes by sneaking biased content into the meaning of the word defined. Some logicians consider this a fallacy rather than a genuine kind of definition. *Example:* Abortion is the senseless slaughter of millions of innocent little babies.

- The **ostensive definition** gives the meaning of a word by pointing to or listing examples. *Example:* spoon: "one of these" you say [*holding up a spoon*]

Exercise 3.3   A. Find the type of definition in each of the following.

1. chair: piece of furniture used for seating one person

2. red: "the color of this" [pointing to a tomato]

3. dog: a useless pest

4. centimeter: a hundredth of a meter

5. circle: the set of all points equidistant from a given point

6. convene: to meet

7. donation: money contributed to further the Lord's work

8. Contras: freedom fighters

9. deficit: the Democrats' creation and the Republicans' problem

10. Let's agree that we mean by *tall* anyone over six feet.

11. volume: space occupied by an object

12. animal: such things as dogs, horses, fish, insects

13. war: the senseless destruction of human life

14. By *prayer partner* we mean anyone who sends $700 or more.

15. ohm: voltage per ampere

16. logic: the study of the principles of reasoning

17. By *argument* we mean a set of statements, one of which (the conclusion) is supported by the others (the premise).

18. By *person* we mean anyone who can make moral decisions.

19. fetus: an unborn child

20. mother: any woman who gives birth to a child

21. criminal: dangerous lawbreaker

22. cellar: an underground storage room

23. politics: the means by which the rich oppress the poor

24. selfish: concerned only with oneself

25. patriot: a person who loves his own country

26. euthanasia: killing someone for reasons of mercy

27. abortion: the termination of a fetus

28. abortion: the slaughter of innocent human beings

29. minister: to serve

30. surrogate: a person serving in place of another

31. triangle: a three-sided plane figure

32. figure: such things as triangles, squares, and circles

33. communism: such economic systems as those of China, Cuba, and Vietnam

34. bigot: a prejudiced, narrow-minded person

35. wrench: a tool used for twisting

36. fetus: an embryo

37. human: the highest animal

38. father: male parent

39. argument: dispute

40. rape: to have sexual relations by means of force

41. liberal: someone like Ted Kennedy or Jesse Jackson

42. conservative: someone who wishes to preserve old-fashioned values

43. death: the cessation of life

44. happiness: joy

45. attic: the topmost room of a house, often used for storage

46. flower: to blossom

47. education: the drawing forth of a person from the darkness of ignorance

48. justice: fairness

49. definition: the meaning of a word

50. love: to care

51. blue: "the color of this" [pointing to a blueberry]

52. inch: one-twelfth of a foot

53. convention: a coming together

54. Let's agree that by *short* we mean anyone under six feet tall.

55. politics: lies and nonsense

56. boat: vehicle for traveling over water

57. hen: female chicken

58. momentum: mass × velocity

59. love: the sweet mystery of life

60. politician: person such as Bush, Kennedy, Clinton, or Gore

61. sexist: one who discriminates against women

62. actor: someone who acts

63. By *fetus* we mean an unborn child.

64. actress: someone like Julia Roberts or Cybill Shepherd

65. fault: a serve that strikes the net

66. force: mass × acceleration

67. glamour: enticing charm

68. freedom: the ability to do as one wishes

69. art: madness given rational form

70. By *short story* we mean a written work of no more than 100 pages.

71. number: quantity

72. cat: *Felis domesticus*

73. Democrat: bleeding–heart liberal

B. Define the following words by genus and specific difference.

1. boy	2. boat
3. tax	4. fish
5. chair	6. girl
7. car	8. exhaustion
9. truck	10. bus
11. cartoon	12. gingivitis
13. kitchen	14. battleship
15. lamp	16. spoon
17. wheel	18. river
19. rabbit	20. animal
21. portrait	22. photograph
23. clock	24. book
25. knife	26. motion picture
27. jet	28. literature
29. cup	30. child
31. mask	32. winter
33. music	34. cowboy
35. movie star	36. soldier
37. chemistry	38. shoe
39. baby	40. chess
41. creek	42. pistol
43. ocean	44. rain

C. What is wrong with the following definitions?

1. boy: not a girl

2. dog: a canine animal

3. rabbit: mammal with long ears

4. cowboy: person who rides a horse

5. joy: not sadness

6. child: small person

7. soup: edible liquid made of meat broth

8. truck: sixteen wheeler

9. shoe: foot covering made of leather

10. ashtray: receptacle for holding cigarette ashes

11. square: figure with four sides

12. poetry: noblest and truest use of language

13. shape: shape of an object

14. desk: any object used as a desk

15. balloon: round rubber bladder filled with air

16. coffee: liquid containing caffeine

17. language: means of spoken or written communication

18. table: article of furniture

19. chair: article of furniture made of wood and fabric, used for seating one person

20. cold: absence of heat

21. mother: a woman who has borne offspring

22. vegetation: trees

23. contribution: money sent to Oral Roberts

24. yogurt: low-calorie dairy product

25. light: brilliant illumination of heaven's great orb

26. abortion: murder of innocent human beings

27. abortion: termination of a fetus

28. murder: killing of a human being

29. murder: intentional killing of a human being

30. time: a dome of many-colored glass

31. girl: not a boy

32. haiku: Japanese poem of seventeen syllables

33. engineer: man who drives a train

34. sadness: not joy

35. omelet: dish made with eggs

36. dwarf: small person

37. square: four-sided figure

38. mule: long-eared animal

39. history: record of the joys and sorrows, triumphs and failures, of humans

40. language: spoken communication

41. child: small person

42. car: four-wheeled vehicle

43. star: one of the billion points of light in the night sky

44. book: printed matter

45. computer: one who computes

46. stranger: a friend you haven't met yet

47. watch: timepiece

48. horse: four-legged animal

49. human: featherless biped

50. traitor: one who betrays his own people

D. Certain words and their definitions clearly play a crucial role in each of the following passages about abortion. Can you identify them? Can you formulate definitions for those words that would settle the dispute?

1. Good evening, ladies and gentlemen. The question before us is the crime of abortion. You are all aware that murder is a crime. Murder is the premeditated taking of a human life. An unborn child is a human life—a helpless and innocent human life. Therefore, abortion is murder and, therefore, a crime. Indeed, it is a crime unparalleled since the Nazi death camps, the wholesale slaughter of millions of innocent babies. Are you willing to allow such a mass murder to continue? Don't the pro-choice advocates realize that they are accomplices to murder?

2. Please don't let yourselves be swayed by the histrionics of the pro-lifers. A fetus is no more than a fertilized egg that cannot live outside the mother's body until the sixth month of pregnancy. An abortion is only a surgical procedure that terminates such a fetus. Whatever goes on in a woman's body is clearly her own private business and that of her physician. Criminalizing abortion would be a completely inappropriate invasion of a woman's privacy. Abortion should not be illegal, then, but should be up to the woman involved. America is a free country, so let's keep it free—for women, too.

3.4 Fallacies of Presumption

The **fallacies of presumption** all involve sneaking doubtful or false premises into the argument, presuming something is true when it's not.

Hasty Generalization   The fallacy of **hasty generalization** presumes that what is true of a few things is true of everything of that kind. Also called **converse accident,** it generalizes too quickly, with insufficient evidence. For example:

> *Chows have black tongues, so all dogs have black tongues.*

This is wrong because chows are only one breed of dog, and there are hundreds of breeds, most of which do not have black tongues. Here's another example:

> *One person died after taking Gudinol, so anyone who takes Gudinol will die.*

This is also a hasty generalization. Just because one bottle of Gudinol has been poisoned does not mean that they all have been. (On the other hand, it would not be irrational to stop taking Gudinol until more information is available.)

This fallacy moves, in an unwarranted manner, from the particular to the general and presumes that what is true in one or a few particular cases is true generally. For example:

> *My ex-husband was unfaithful. Therefore, no man should be trusted.*

In a later chapter, we will see that such an argument may be classified as a very weak inductive argument.

Not all such arguments are fallacious. Some statistical arguments, which go from a few samples to a conclusion about a whole population, are reliable. In the absence of scientific method, however, jumping from only a few instances to a general conclusion is risky. In fact, we ordinarily call this fallacy "jumping to conclusions."

Sweeping Generalization   The fallacy of **sweeping generalization** is the reverse of the hasty generalization. Also called **accident,** it goes from some statement that is often true to a statement about some particular thing to which, because of its special circumstances, the statement does not apply. For example:

> *I should never tell a lie, so I told the mad gunman where you were hiding.*

It is true that in general one shouldn't lie, but in some cases a lie is preferable to the truth.

Consider this example:

> *Haste makes waste, so there is no hurry with this heart attack victim.*

This kind of argument goes fallaciously from the general to the particular. It presumes that what is true usually must be true in every particular case, even when special circumstances render that inference false.

False Cause The fallacy of **false cause** presumes that if event A happened before event B, event A must have "caused" event B. This is of course not true. Just because event B follows event A, that doesn't prove that A caused B; something else might have caused B. Here are a few examples:

> *Let's not take Hilda on the picnic. Every time she comes along, it rains.*

Hilda might be a wet blanket, but she doesn't cause it to rain.

> *The witch doctor does a little dance, and then there's an eclipse. The tribe is impressed with the witch doctor's power.*

But we know that the dance didn't cause the eclipse.

> *A person has a cold and drinks lots of orange juice, and in a couple of days she is well. She concludes that the orange juice cured her.*

But we know that she might have gotten well in a couple of days anyway.

The late author Alexander King told of a man who every morning went to his door and knelt and said, "May this house be safe from tigers." A neighbor asked him why he did that. "To keep tigers away," the man replied.

"But there are no tigers around here," the neighbor said.

"See?" said the man. "It works!"

False Analogy In the fallacy of **false analogy,** two things are presumed to be more similar than they really are. For example:

> *If a dog has rabies, you put it out of its misery. So capital punishment is very appropriate because it's like putting a mad dog out of its misery.*

However, the mad dog is sick and doomed, and the criminal is not. And people aren't animals. So this is a **weak analogy.**

> *Why say cocaine is bad for you? If you take too many aspirin, that's bad for you, too. So cocaine is not a bad thing, it's just bad if you overdo it.*

This argument presumes that cocaine is inherently no more dangerous than aspirin, which is a mild patent medicine that doctors often recommend. Cocaine is *nothing* like aspirin. This is a bad analogy.

> *Why have gun control when practically everyone drives a car? Cars are as dangerous as guns.*

Guns are weapons only, whereas cars are practically a necessity. This is a bad analogy and makes a very weak argument.

Begging the Question The fallacy of **begging the question** is simply assuming the truth of what you're supposed to be trying to prove. It often involves saying the same thing in two different ways. For example:

> *Hugh is a nice young man. I am sure of this because I know Hugh would never do anything that wasn't nice.*

If you don't believe the conclusion (the first statement), you would not believe the premise (the second statement).

> *Koresh says he is the Son of the Most High, and I believe him because the Son of the Most High would never lie.*

This example is also called a **circular argument** because the conclusion ("Koresh says . . .") is supported by a premise ("the Son . . .") that assumes the truth of the conclusion, that is supported by. . . . You see the point.

> *We know carbon burns because we have found that it is combustible.*

This just says "Carbon burns because it burns." That's no argument because it begs (assumes) the very thing it's trying to prove.

> *Nobody is really honest because everybody is dishonest in some way.*

This says "Nobody's honest because nobody's honest." The appropriate response is yes, but why? What are your *reasons?*

Question-Begging Epithet A **question-begging epithet** is a name, label, or tag that tries to slip into an argument what should be argued for. It is a sly trick. For example:

> *Murdering babies should be outlawed, so vote against legalized abortion.*

We of course agree that murdering babies should be forbidden. But there must be reasons given for thinking that abortion is really murdering babies.

> *We can't trust the lies of the secular humanists. We must speak up against the teaching of evolution in our schools.*

Labeling the opposition and calling them liars all in one breath is an effective rhetorical trick. The point is presumably to show that evolution is a mistaken theory. "Secular humanists" is a term of abuse used by a certain kind of Christian

Fundamentalist, just as, say, "Bible-thumpers" is used by secular humanists to label their opponents. It's all a matter of irrational name calling and is a covert attempt to beg the question at hand—to cloud the issue and prejudice the audience.

Perhaps the best answer to such tactics is to say, "You need to *prove* that abortion is murder [or that evolution *is* mistaken, or whatever], and calling us names doesn't help. Play fair!"

Complex Question This is a simple trick. The fallacy of the **complex question** involves phrasing the question in such a way that answering it commits the other person to a certain hidden presumption. Here are four examples:

> *Have you stopped cheating your customers?*

If the answer is yes, that means he used to cheat them but he has now stopped. If the answer is no, that means he still cheats them; that he has cheated them in the past is presumed.

> *What makes you so stupid?*

This one, often used with children, is mean. And then there's the phone pitch:

> *When can we schedule an appointment for you to pick up your special prize and visit Condo Village?*

This presumes you "want" to see Condo Village, and the question is just "when." If you don't want to visit Condo Village, your response is "I don't want an appointment, thank you," but sometimes that doesn't do any good.

> *Are you as big a jerk as you were in high school?*

You must somehow speak to the hidden assumption: "I wasn't a jerk in high school."

Special Pleading The fallacy of **special pleading** happens when you apply the rules to everyone else but make an exception of yourself. We all tend to presume that we're special and should be catered to. Consider these examples:

> *I'm a bit overweight—not what you'd call "fat." Other people are "fat," but I'm just "a bit overweight."*

> *What I said about my military record wasn't exactly true, but I wasn't lying. And my wife was pregnant when I married her. And I'm not exactly on the board of directors of the parent company, but one of its subsidiaries. But all this was long ago, and it all just makes me more human, and my voters will stand by me because they know I stand for strict moral standards.*

The special pleader wants everybody else to play fair and go by the rules and love others and so on, but when it comes to applying the rules to himself, he eases up and cuts himself plenty of slack.

> *He was lying. You were exaggerating. I was protecting my family.*
>
> *I am firm. You are stubborn. He is pig-headed.*

That last example is thanks to the British philosopher Bertrand Russell, who realized that we always seem to see ourselves in the best light and others in the worst. It's human nature.

Fallacy of Black or White   The fallacy of **black or white,** also called the **false dilemma,** presumes that on a given question there are only two opposite positions, with no middle ground. A very common trick, it seems to clarify and simplify but in fact tends to warp and confuse everything. Here are three examples:

> *He who is not with me is against me.*

This presumes that there is no position that mediates the two options. One could, for example, be indifferent and prefer to stay out of the issue entirely.

During the Vietnam War, this slogan was popular:

> *America, love it or leave it.*

At that time there were strong feelings for, and against, the war. But the slogan falsely implied that, if you didn't agree with everything the government said and did, you weren't patriotic, which was false.

> *Either you're rich or you're poor.*

Clearly, this falsely omits the whole middle class of people who are neither rich nor poor. Marxists tend to commit this fallacy.

Gambler's Fallacy   The **gambler's fallacy** presumes that the longer it has been since a certain thing happened, the more likely it becomes that it will soon occur. This is wrong. If a (fair) coin is flipped once, the probability of getting heads is 1 out of 2, or ½. But even if heads has come up twenty times in a row, the probability of tails on the next throw is still just ½.

Consider the next examples:

> *It hasn't rained for a week, so we're surely due for a rain today.*

This is faulty logic. On any day during a dry spell, the probability of rain is low.

All my past five marriages have gone bad, so this time I'm due for a success.

Not likely.

Slippery Slope   The fallacy of the **slippery slope** is the presumption that once we give up a certain point, we will slide irrevocably to some awful disaster. The most notorious example of this fallacy was the argument that the loss of South Vietnam to the communists in the 1960s and 1970s would result in the loss of every other democratic country in Southeast Asia to communism. Some people still believe this, but a collapse has not yet happened.

Another notorious example is the argument that the existence of welfare for the needy is the first step to a socialist state. Still another is the argument that smoking marijuana leads inevitably to such drugs as cocaine and heroin.

Just because a certain step is taken does not "necessarily" mean that one cannot resist other, worse steps. One goodnight kiss might be as far as a given relationship will get; one step toward war need not become an ironclad commitment to actual war.

Exercise 3.4   A. What fallacy of presumption can you identify in the following?

1. A *Writer's Digest* ad: Before he became a bestselling author, John Grisham woke each day at 5:00 A.M., scribbled notes on a legal pad between sessions in court, mailed 26 submissions . . . and subscribed to WRITER'S DIGEST.

2. A *UFO UNIVERSE* magazine cover: "Who Pilots the Saucers?"

B. Identify each fallacy of presumption.

1. This egg is rotten, so the rest must be rotten, too.

2. He who hesitates is lost, so I'd better buy this car today.

3. He went to a psychiatrist, and now he's fine. So psychiatrists can really help.

4. Smoking is just a harmless habit, no worse than chewing gum.

5. We oppose pornography because we're against degrading smut.

6. The atheists who oppose school prayer must not be allowed to prevail.

7. Have you beaten that drinking problem?

8. Do you love me? Just answer yes or no.

9. I'm a moderate. He has no conviction.

10. I've lost three jobs, so I'm due for some good luck.

11. Either you agree on this point or we have nothing else to talk about.

12. Are you still cheating on your taxes?

13. I don't cheat, really. I exaggerate a little.

14. Cocaine is bad for you, so all drugs are bad for you.

15. We've had three dogs hit by cars, so this time we should have better luck.

16. Being a teacher is like being a prison warden; discipline is the most important thing.

17. *NYPD Blue* is a good TV show, so all TV shows are good.

18. We must not allow the pointy-headed intellectuals and eggheads to rule our lives.

19. I favor good citizenship because I value the person who takes her civic duty seriously.

20. The Red Rocket is cheap wine, so the Chateau Rothschild will be cheap, too.

21. Honesty is the best policy, so you won't mind if I tell you how ugly that wart on your forehead is.

22. Jim Bakker was corrupt so that just shows that all preachers are corrupt.

23. Thou shalt not kill. So capital punishment is wrong.

24. They weren't guilty of fornication. The baby was just a little premature.

25. Do you still believe that nonsense about reincarnation?

26. Do you want to pay cash for your subscription?

27. Either it's a Laborador Retriever or it's not.

28. Are you saved or damned?

29. These sluts on the covers of *Playboy* and *Penthouse* should be put in jail.

30. Life is like chess. You have to make your moves carefully and thoughtfully if you want to win.

31. Either you're a winner or you're a loser.

32. We must not give in to the effete intellectual snobs who want us to give up our right to hear arms.

33. Whom do you suppose you were in your previous existence?

34. You're either with us or against us.

35. Any of you too chicken to go can back out now.

36. I'm not fat; I'm just pleasingly plump.

37. I'm not bald; my hairline is just receding.

38. Jessica didn't pose nude for the money. She was just showing us what God had made.

39. Do you want hot dogs or spaghetti tonight?

40. I am thinking it over. He is paralyzed by indecision.

41. Would you rather watch Rosie O'Donnell or Oprah Winfrey?

42. I was shading the truth. She was lying through her teeth.

43. All or nothing.

44. I've been losing all night, so I'm sure to hit a winning streak soon.

45. Pat prayed and the hurricane turned away from the coast. So Pat's prayers are really effective.

46. He laid his hands upon her, and she was made whole.

47. Life is like football. You have to be rough and tough to come out on top.

48. The stock market has been going up for years, so it's sure to go down soon.

49. We can't listen to the lunatic fringe who says that a depression is coming.

50. I wasn't really cheating; I just wondered if she had the same answers.

51. Business is like basketball. You have to move when you get the ball.

52. Too many chefs spoil the broth. So I'm going to do this my way and forget the rest of the team.

53. IBM is a responsible company, so all American businesses are responsible.

54. The time I *do* spend with my family is *quality* time. Other businessmen forget their families entirely.

55. I once read a novel, and it wasn't any good, so I haven't read any more.

56. A penny saved is a penny earned. So I won't get this prescription filled.

57. Patriotism is a great thing because love of country is very important.

58. I know everything in the Reverend Schuller's book is true because Schuller says so in the Introduction.

59. The Ayatollah speaks truly because he is not a man who would ever lie.

60. The *New Yorker* is the best magazine there is because the editor says so.

61. The only way we can defeat the godless child killers is to start blowing up the abortion clinics.

62. How long will we allow the smut peddlers to continue to corrupt our children? We need strict censorship laws.

63. The bleeding-heart liberals want to keep us out of war even at the expense of our nation's dignity.

64. We worry about the rights of jailbirds and let the innocent suffer.

65. If you do not vote for this law, then you are against everything America stands for.

66. All the men are either too old or too young.

67. I'm slow to anger. He's a coward.

68. I enjoy a drink now and then. She's an alcoholic.

69. She's the type of person that you either love or hate.

70. Some Christians are hypocrites, so that tells me they all are.

71. I am flexible. He is spineless.

72. All that glitters is not gold, so I'm tossing this watch in the trash.

73. Silence is golden, so I'm not telling anyone about the fire.

74. Pass the Brady Bill today, and tomorrow the government will take all our firearms!

75. Either you agree with me or you're not a good American.

76. I am enthused. You are a fanatic.

77. He who hesitates is lost, so I'm launching the missiles now.

78. Richard Nixon was dishonest, so I'll never vote for another Republican.

79. Dan Quayle spoke in St. Louis, and three people were healed. So I'm voting for him.

80. Many Austrians were Nazis. Kurt Waldheim was Austrian, so he must have been a Nazi, too.

81. President George Bush insisted that the Soviets withdraw from Afghanistan, and they did. So I admire President Bush.

82. President George Bush said he would not raise taxes ("Read my lips") and he promised not to lie to us, so I believed him.

83. Two hundred and fifty-nine people died in the air crash in Lockerbie, So I'm never flying again.

84. *Roxanne* was a good movie, so all Steve Martin movies must be good.

85. Some Libyans are terrorists, so all Libyans are terrorists.

86. America is a capitalist country, so all Americans are capitalists.

87. Either George W. Bush is competent or he's not.

88. If Bill Gates could get rich and famous, everybody can.

89. What makes Donald Trump so greedy?

90. Some women want to be abused because they like rough treatment.

91. All communists are atheists because none of them believe in God.

92. Rush is not perfect because he has flaws like everyone else.

93. No philandering alcoholic should be made the secretary of defense.

94. If you are physically ill, you go to a medical doctor. So if you have spiritual problems, you should go to Madame Sosostris.

95. Women are like buses. If you miss one, another one will be along in a few minutes.

96. U.S.–Chinese relations are like a chess game.

97. The day after George Bush was elected, the stock market dropped 10 points, so the future looks bleak.

98. Never put off till tomorrow what you can do today, so I'm going to go ahead and steal that Porsche.

99. *The Perfect Storm* and *Mississippi Burning* were based on true stories, so all movies must have some basis in fact.

100. What makes Southerners such bigots?

101. No Democrat had been elected for sixteen years, so a Democrat was sure to be elected in 1992.

102. This apple is rotten, so the rest must be rotten, too.

103. He went to Madame Sosostris, and now he's fine. So she can really help.

104. Are you still the wimp you were in high school?

105. I have strong convictions. He's an extremist.

106. I've lost four jobs, so I'm due for some good luck.

107. Teaching is like business; you have to sell the students your subject.

108. Black widow spiders are poisonous, so all spiders are poisonous.

109. We can't allow the pansies to get control of the country.

110. Are we friends? Answer yes or no!

111. Are you saved or damned?

112. I was shading the truth a little, but she was lying through her teeth.

113. Curiosity killed the cat, so I'm not going to the doctor about this lump.

114. *Firestarter* wasn't any good, so I haven't read any more Stephen King novels.

115. All the boys in my class are either too short or too tall.

116. Either you're a capitalist or a communist.

117. Nicaragua has gone communist, so all other Central American countries will, too.

118. We shot down the Iranian airbus, and then Iran and Iraq started to negotiate. So maybe we should shoot down more civilian planes.

119. We will never submit to the coercion of Satan America.

120. We try to spread the truth; the Democrats are stooping to the lowest propaganda tactics.

121. Billy prayed with George, and we won the war.

122. I drank four quarts of grapefruit juice, and my cold cleared up in a few days.

123. I am trusting. Peggy is gullible.

124. Bill Cosby is rich and famous, so all black people are rich and famous.

125. The surgical termination of a fetus is hardly worth all this attention.

126. Are you still as frivolous as you were in college?

127. I'm concerned. You're panic stricken.

128. Well, it's either CNN or CBS.

129. Mercy killing is clearly murder.

130. Exxon is guilty of the Alaska oil spill because it was Exxon that did it.

131. I'm neat. You're fastidious.

132. I'm flirtatious. She's promiscuous.

133. What he said is true because it's a fact.

134. He massaged my back, and now the pain is all gone.

135. Jordan has joined Iraq, so all the other Arab countries will join Iraq, too.

136. I'm for capital punishment because I favor the death penalty.

137. After he married Sylvia, his writing improved immensely.

138. I'm against lazy welfare cheats.

139. Are you always as beautiful as you are now?

140. Are you going to tell me what you know about the robbery?

141. Why are you forcing me to do this?

142. Philosophy is a profound subject because it's about really deep stuff.

143. I'm tired of these un-American peace demonstrators.

144. Why are you always busy when I want to talk to you?

145. Atoms are mostly empty space; they're not solid. So this brick, which is made of atoms, is not solid, either.

146. I trust Arsenio because he said he would always tell me the truth.

147. I shaded the truth. You lied.

148. Ad: Which Bose product is best for you?

149. American business is in a slump, so the American company that makes the Bart Simpson dolls is in a slump.

150. Are these senators as stupid as they look?

151. If he has smoked marijuana it won't be long until he tries *hard* drugs.

152. Cover of *U.S. News and World Report* (7 November 1994): "Why Are You So Angry?"

153. Ad for Lipton Herbal Tea that shows a pretty girl getting a massage: We do for the inside of your body what this does for the outside.

C. Find the fallacies of presumption in the following letter to the editor.

Put Back Prayer in Schools[1]

Editor: Since the removal of prayer from our public schools, the crime rate within public schools has skyrocketed. And, alas the situation is worsening: police inspecting kids' lockers and searching the kids for drugs, knives and guns!

While I am a believer in the fact that a child's upbringing surely must begin in the home, is it not fair to assume that the return of prayer to the public schools just might be a most advantageous move in helping to restore our children's thinking regarding right from wrong?

Strange, is it not, that with so much of this drug and knife and gun business in our public schools making the newspapers these days, that nowhere have I read of these goings on in parochial schools. But then, parochial schools find the students beginning each and every day with prayer. Aloud.

Just a thought.

Jack Dillon
Wilmington

---

1. *Source:* Letter to the Editor, *Wilmington (N.C.) Star,* 17 February 1994. Reprinted with permission from Jack Dillon.

3.5 Fallacies of Irrelevance

Fallacies of irrelevance are tricks calculated to cloud the issue by introducing irrelevant considerations into the argument. They persuade by appealing not to reason but to feelings, prejudices, beliefs, and points and statements that have nothing to do with the real issue.

Abusive *ad Hominem* Ad hominem is Latin for "against the person." The **fallacy of abusive *ad hominem*** is an attack on a person rather than her argument. If you can cast doubt on a person's character or background, her argument will also seem doubtful. A person's character, however, has nothing to do with the soundness of her arguments, which should be evaluated on their own—on rational grounds. For example:

> *Do you realize that Mr. Smith is an ex-convict? So we can't trust his views on birth control, can we?*

> *Mrs. Chernev is a fascist, and so her arguments for abortion are hardly reliable.*

Such arguments commit the abusive *ad hominem* fallacy. They insult the person rather than confront his or her actual arguments.

Circumstantial *ad Hominem* The fallacy of **circumstantial *ad hominem*** attacks the person's circumstances rather than the person himself. It suggests that he is only being self-serving in arguing as he does. For example:

> *Bill is of course against higher property taxes. He has a lot of land.*

Having a lot of land might not be the reason why Bill is against property taxes. We should listen to his argument, whatever it is.

> *Of course, she's for Medicare. She's over sixty-five years old.*

She might have good reasons for favoring Medicare that have nothing to do with her own age. Indeed, she might be independently wealthy but socially concerned. There *are* times, however, when attacking a person's character may be appropriate. For example, if you know that the person whom your friend has chosen is a baby-sitter is untrustworthy, you should inform your friend.

Poisoning the Well More subtle than the simple insults of the abusive *ad hominem*, **poisoning the well** discredits the person in such a way that everything she says seems doubtful. For example:

> *Anyone who disagrees with me about this issue must be blind to the facts.*

As if the only reason anyone could disagree with me would be through ignorance or stupidity.

> *I'm just anxious to hear what lies and misinformation my opponent will to accept.*

Such an attack "poisons the well" of one's opponent's arguments by casting doubt on anything she might say.

Tu Quoque *Tu quoque* in Latin means "you're one, too." The fallacy of *tu quoque*, like the abusive *ad hominem*, argues that someone is wrong in his argument because of his imperfections. For example:

> A: *You shouldn't cheat in school.*
>
> B: *Didn't you ever cheat in school?*

Perhaps so, but that's irrelevant to whether B should cheat.

> *I can't say I've been absolutely faithful to my wife. But neither were Kennedy, Johnson, or Roosevelt. And what about you? Are you perfect?*

And so on.

Genetic Fallacy The **genetic fallacy** attacks the source of an argument or statement. Where an idea comes from has no bearing on its truth. For example:

> *You're against abortion? You must have been listening to Jerry Falwell.*
>
> *I've heard that slogan, "You only go around once in life" on television. It's a beer commercial, so the slogan must be shallow and phony.*

It well may be shallow and phony, but not just because you heard it in a beer commercial on television.

Appeal to Pity The fallacy of **appeal to pity** plays directly on our sympathy and thereby diverts attention to our emotions and away from the real issue.

> *Officer, I just couldn't have been speeding. My mother is so sick, and I guess I was thinking about her, and I haven't had any sleep . . .*

Your mother's illness might make the officer sympathetic, but it has nothing to do with whether you were speeding or not.

> *Members of the jury, the defendant grew up in poverty. Can you blind yourselves to that? You must follow your conscience and find her not guilty.*

The defendant's poverty is no argument for her innocence. (Of course, she should be presumed innocent until she is proven guilty. But in this situation, it appears that the prosecution has made its case.) On the other hand, an appeal to the judge's pity might work.

Appeal to Force   Also called the **appeal to fear,** the fallacy of **appeal to force** is a very bad argument but is often used and usually effective. It is simply a threat of unpleasant consequences if you do not agree (or at least say you agree). For example:

> *Well, if that's your opinion, you have a perfect right to it. But you'd better start looking for another job.*

This threat has no bearing on the truth of your opinion or the validity of your arguments. It only means you'd better change your mind. A more subtle example is

> *If you find this man innocent and let him go free, will you feel safe on the streets?*

This is just a subtle threat and has no bearing on the guilt or innocence of the defendant. It would be unlikely that he would come after the jurors anyway. But even if he did, that would not mean he is guilty in this case. The prosecutor wants to "scare" you into finding him guilty.

Appeal to Authority   The fallacy of **appeal to authority** is a fallacious reference to some person who is wrongly considered an authority on the subject at hand. Advertisements often use this tactic:

> *I'm not a doctor, but I play a doctor on TV, and . . . .*
>
> *We make money the old-fashioned way. We earn it.*

A TV doctor is of course no authority on patent medicine, and John Houseman was no expert on financial investment (as far as I know). He just looked authoritative. These are clearly fallacious appeals to authority. Then there is

> *Aristotle said a man's wife is his possession, like his children or his horse.*

As great as he was, just the fact that Aristotle said something doesn't make it true.

Appeal to Ignorance   The fallacy of **appeal to ignorance** turns our ignorance of a "disproof" into a proof. The basis of this argument is "You can't prove so-and-so is false, so it must be true." For example:

> *You say there are no witches. But how do you know, if you don't know what one looks like?*

Obviously, the fact that I don't know what witches look like is no argument that they exist!

> *You say there are no flying saucers. But there are plenty of UFOs, and you can't prove that some of them aren't flying saucers. So I'll continue to believe in them.*

The fact that I can't prove that there are no flying saucers is no proof that they exist. The *burden of proof* is on those who would try to show that they are real. Common sense presumes that they are not real, so some "evidence" must be given to those who say they are real.

Mob Appeal   The fallacy of **mob appeal** is widely used and can be very dangerous. It works on our desire to be one of the guys, a regular Joe, one of the crowd. Mob appeal proceeds by stirring up that feeling of wanting to fit in. For example:

> *Every good American will have to agree: Abortion is a crime.*

Even if every American *did* agree, that wouldn't make it true, no matter what's being discussed.

> *I know I can count on the real Christians out there to send their contributions, which are so badly needed.*

This implies that you will want to be one of the many people who will send money so that you can consider yourself a "good Christian." Many people do send money, but that doesn't mean it's the right thing to do.

> *Everybody else is doing it.*

This is no doubt the oldest and most popular form of this fallacy, for there is a Bible verse that states "Thou shalt not follow a multitude to do evil." On the other hand, if the issue *is* the popularity of something, then it is appropriate to ask whether most people like it. For example, an ice cream manufacturer needs to know what flavors most of its customers prefer.

Snob Appeal   Instead of appealing to your desire to fit in, the fallacy of **snob appeal** appeals to your desire to stand out—just the reverse of mob appeal. It tries to persuade us that a better class of people think a certain way and that therefore we should, too. It works on a natural desire to rise above the "common herd." For example:

> *Someone like you deserves the best.*

Whatever is being sold here is probably overpriced.

Owning this car means you've made it.

All status symbols work this way. People of course want them, whether they've really "made it" or not. They get things turned around—get the symbols first, make it big later. This little fallacy has put the population of America heavily in debt.

Do you think a Mastercard really enhances Angela Lansbury's possibilities? Or Robert Duvall's? Don't you suppose they have about all the possibilities they can handle as it is? They've made it and now they want to persuade the rest of us that a Mastercard is a superstatus symbol that will open grand possibilities for us. That's how the fallacy of snob appeal really works. You can probably think of a dozen commercials and advertisements that exploit this fallacy.

Irrelevant Thesis The fallacy of **irrelevant thesis** (also called **missing the point**) is a shrewd attempt to persuade us of one thing while really proving something else. The most dramatic examples of this occur in courts of law:

Ladies and gentlemen of the jury, look at the bloody clothes, the murder weapon. Imagine the helpless screams of the victim. Such a crime deserves no verdict except guilty, guilty!

This ploy is subtle, tricky, and dangerous. The fact that the crime was horrible, awful, and terrible is established, but that doesn't mean the defendant is guilty! That the crime was heinous is the irrelevant thesis.

Here's another example:

Millions of sick, old people live in this country, and therefore our conscience must insist that we vote for national health insurance.

The fact that there are many sick, old people certainly implies that "something" should be done, but it doesn't prove that national health insurance is the answer.

Exercise 3.5 A. Find the fallacy of irrelevance committed in the following passages. (You might have to imagine an appropriate argumentative context.)

1. We have ways of making you change your mind.

2. But, Mom, *everybody's* wearing them.

3. There are 7 million poor in this nation. The only answer is a welfare state.

4. My opponent has admitted to being an adulterer. So how can we take her seriously on any important issue?

5. The senator is a plagiarist. So how can he judge Mr. Bork?

6. Wilfred Brimly says oatmeal is the right thing to do.

7. Economic equality would be a good idea, except that it comes straight out of the pages of Karl Marx.

8. Can you prove there isn't a soul?

9. Yes, I did it, but my children were hungry.

10. Yes, I cheated on the test. Didn't you ever cheat when you were in school?

11. Seven astronauts were killed. This convinces me that the space program should be halted.

12. Naturally, Senator Kennedy thinks congressmen should be paid more.

13. Can you prove she didn't steal it?

14. Old Groundchuck aged whiskey—when you've really made it.

15. You've come a long way, baby.

16. My opponents are morally corrupt, so there's no need to listen to anything they say.

17. Of course, you say children should be seen and not heard. You don't have children.

18. Can Goetz prove they were trying to rob him?

19. I'm John Wayne for Valinil, the toughest painkiller you can get without a prescription.

20. The Bible says, "Thou shalt not kill."

21. The Bible says, "An eye for an eye."

22. But, gee, Sally, everybody else is doing it . . . .

23. You think it's okay? You must have been listening to Pat Robertson.

24. Pat Robertson says it's okay, so I'm going to do it, too.

25. Pat Robertson says fornication is a sin.

26. But didn't he do it?

27. You can't believe what she says about anything. She's corrupt and she's a liar.

28. Gorbachev was once a communist, therefore he can't be trusted.

29. No good American will support this treaty with the Syrians.

30. I believe what Billy Graham says about politics. He's a good person and a man of God.

31. Jessica's life was ruined by what happened, and she felt that appearing in *Playboy* was a way of getting over that and putting it behind her.

32. Naturally, you think criminals should be prosecuted. You've never broken the law.

33. I believe what Elizabeth Hurley says about cosmetics. She's so beautiful herself.

34. If everyone else is selling their stocks, so will I.

35. I'm going to watch *Friends*. Everyone says it's the best thing on TV.

36. All the other girls I graduated with are married now.

37. Biden is a politician, so you can't believe anything he says about Judge Thomas.

38. My opponent is well known for his poor judgment and loose morals, so we can't believe anything he says.

39. Most talk about depression is coming from the political left—the bleeding hearts.

40. General Haig favors more military spending, but of course he's a military man.

41. Jessica has nothing to be ashamed of. This poor girl was treated shamelessly by two moral bankrupts parading as men of God.

42. If you don't change your mind, you had better kiss your children good-bye.

43. Those of us who believe in democracy will never permit auto-import curbs.

44. If Oprah says Frank Sinatra was a great man, who am I to disagree?

45. No good Christian could vote for anyone but Pat Robertson.

46. Stealing from old people who can't defend themselves deserves punishment. I ask for a verdict of *guilty*.

47. No good Muslim could allow the menace of the Great Satan America to go unchallenged.

48. You may think you are right about this issue, senator, but the voters will tell you that you are wrong.

49. All women must stand together on this issue.

50. Can you prove the Iranians *didn't* do it?

51. There are thousands of abused wives in America. We must therefore stiffen the punishment for wife beating.

52. That might sound like a good idea, except that it comes directly from *The Sayings of Chairman Mao*.

53. My heart is breaking. I need to see the children. Please change your mind about the alimony.

54. The Beatles took drugs, and so did Elvis Presley and John Belushi. So why shouldn't I?

55. Please don't take away my pit bull. He's just a puppy. He didn't mean to chew up that girl's face.

56. Naturally, you'd say women are weaker. You're a man.

57. The deficit is an awful problem, so we must raise taxes.

58. You have the right to express yourself, of course. But you might have to do it in a work camp in Siberia.

59. No good American can condemn Colonel North's efforts on behalf of this country.

60. Shirley MacLaine believes in reincarnation, so it can't be a sensible idea.

61. Houdini, the great magician, believed in an afterlife, and so I do, too.

62. How can you stand there and accuse my poor old mother of causing trouble between us? You know that she's old and has been sick.

63. Karl Malden was a policeman on *Streets of San Francisco,* and he says it's risky to leave home without an American Express card. So I intend to get one right away.

64. Everybody's dieting and exercising, so I guess I will, too.

65. But exercise is good for you. Jane Fonda says so, as do Cheryl Ladd, Sheena Easton, and that bald-headed woman, too.

66. I don't believe anything she says. She supported the North Vietnamese during the Vietnam War.

67. Napoleon said that an army travels on its stomach.

68. Congratulations! You are one of the lucky people who qualify for our super investment deal.

69. St. Thomas Aquinas said that God created the world from nothing. That's good enough for me.

70. If you don't get saved, and right away, you might go to hell.

71. If you don't believe what I believe, you'll go to hell, where the fire is not quenched and the worm dieth not

72. Thinking that way will get you into plenty of trouble.

73. Child abuse is so widespread, and it's such an awful crime. So we ought to forget about due process for people accused of it.

74. AIDS is an awful, terrible, fatal disease. So people who have it should be locked up away from the rest of us.

75. Say, these arguments sound pretty good to me. But if Stanley says they're fallacies, they must be.

76. Lloyd Bentsen said Dan Quayle was no Jack Kennedy, so I'm voting Democratic.

77. Freud said that all boys love their mothers and are jealous of their fathers.

78. Cindy Crawford says Cover Girl is the best brand of cosmetics.

79. Can you prove you have never taken drugs?

80. You can vote for a Democrat if you want higher taxes.

81. Senator Barfe is a philanderer and an alcoholic, so how can we trust what he says about defense?

82. Lynn Redgrave recommends Weight Watchers meals.

83. Two hundred and fifty-nine innocent people were killed in the air crash over Lockerbie, so we should declare war on Libya.

84. Naturally, you'd say young people are lazy; you're an old man.

85. Joe Blather said Geoff Mush was a liar, and Blather is a top network newsman.

86. Every argument my opponent has offered comes straight from the warped mind of Jerry Falwell.

87. All the neighbors have children. I want some children, too.

88. Nobody believes in God anymore. None of my friends do. So I'm giving up believing in God, too.

89. If you stand up for Manson, you'll be laughed out of town.

90. Everybody knows that Manson killed all those people.

91. Look at the pictures of his victims—sweet, pretty, innocent young girls. You must find this monster *guilty!*

92. John Ritter says this videotape will help me get As.

93. Naturally, Richard Simmons says his videotape will help you lose weight. He's the one selling it.

94. B. F. Skinner, the great Harvard psychologist, said there is no such thing as "freedom."

95. Karl Marx predicted the end of bourgeoise capitalism and the rise of the classless society, so I'm giving away all my possessions.

96. Jimmy Swaggart visited a prostitute, so I don't trust anything he says about God.

97. Naturally, the surgeon general is against smoking; he's a nonsmoker himself.

98. Gee, Mom, everybody *else* is smoking crack.

99. Communism is a serious threat to democracy, so we should attack them with nuclear weapons right away.

100. My opponent is obviously such a complete jerk that nobody could possibly take him seriously.

101. But, Mom, everybody's got one.

102. But can O. J. prove he *didn't* do it?

103. Yes, I sold illegal drugs, but I had to make the payment on my new minivan.

104. Bill Vogel sportswear: You deserve to wear the very best.

105. My opponent is an adulterer, so we shouldn't even listen to her.

106. Naturally, I stole it. Haven't you ever stolen anything?

107. Naturally, a wimp like you would say fighting is wrong.

108. But what you're saying comes straight out of the pages of Marx's *Das Kapital*.

109. Elizabeth Hurley says Estee Lauder is great perfume; she should know because she's so beautiful.

110. The Bible says, "All is vanity."

111. If you don't change your mind, I'll have to change it for you.

112. No good Christian could vote for Trent Lott.

113. If you don't go to the prom with me, I guess nobody will.

114. Naturally, you'd say women are equal. You're a woman.

115. If you continue to think that way, you'll go to hell.

116. The communists are on the move everywhere. Therefore, we must vote this $200 billion budget for the Pentagon.

117. My opponent is not famous for his veracity, so we should be skeptical about what he's saying.

118. Look at the bruises on this man's face. Look at the wheelchair he's confined to. Can you possibly find this poor man guilty?

119. Socrates said that nobody does wrong except through ignorance.

120. Don't leave home without it!

121. Jerry Falwell says abortion is wrong.

122. That idea comes from Jerry Falwell, so it can't make any sense.

123. You have a right to your opinion, comrade. But that won't comfort you much in Siberia.

124. Lee Iacocca says that making money is the most important thing in life.

125. Ad for Folger's coffee: Is your coffee as *dark* as ours?

126. You have a right to your opinion, but you'd better not let the boss hear you saying that.

127. You can criticize our beloved Saddam, if you are ready to die for your beliefs.

128. President Reagan believed in astrology, and that's good enough for me.

129. No good American would undermine our troops by protesting against the war.

130. Yes, Dad, I beat my wife. You did too, didn't you?

131. I don't know why I embezzled. I had a lot of pressure on me at that point in time, and . . . well, it just happened.

132. Anyone who would say that is just plain dishonest.

133. You say teachers should be paid more, but of course you're a teacher yourself.

134. Would you still reject capital punishment if your daughter were raped and murdered?

135. The Catholic Church rejects abortion, and so do I.

136. That's a very unpopular view among educated people.

137. Be there or be square.

138. Deepak Chopra has said: To see love in the moment, you must clean the windows of perception (*The Path to Love*).

139. Carl Sagan believed in extraterrestrial life.

140. Can you prove that there is no extraterrestrial life?

141. The Breakfast of Champions.

142. Come on, don't be a nerd.

143. One person broke the chain, and the next day he was struck by lightning.

144. There are thousands of homeless people in America. The time for this tax hike in now.

145. Billy Graham, Pat Robertson, and Jimmy Swaggart all say that this is a holy war.

146. Saddam has said that it is a holy war.

147. King Hussein condemned the slaughter of civilians, but he was an Arab, after all.

148. Cybill Shepherd never wears anything but Shalimar.

149. Jury members, have you never done anything wrong?

150. Try a little of this. You can afford it now, can't you?

151. Pardon . . . would you have any Grey Poupon?

152. It costs a little more, but I'm worth it.

153. FDS—feel clean, feel confident.

154. Ad for Preferred Stock: The extrasmooth cologne for an extraspecial man.

156. A Maybelline ad: It's makeup made easy.   [This statement is under a photograph of Sarah Michelle Gellar.]

B. What fallacy of irrelevance can you find in the following editorial?

Thanks a Lot, Senator Lott[2]

If a hurricane were to hit the Gulf Coast of Mississippi, does anyone think a senator from that state would be posturing to deny federal disaster aid because of his political principles?

Of course not.

But Republican Sen. Trent Lott of Mississippi, who's also the Senate Majority Leader, continues to block $307 million to help North Carolinians who were victims of Hurricane Floyd last September.

In the latest effort to break the blockade of money, eight Congressmen from North Carolina—Democrats and Republicans—sent Sen. Lott a letter asking him to push for Senate approval of the relief money already approved by the House of Representatives.

Maybe this will be enough to get the naysayer from Mississippi to be sensible.

Sen. Lott says he's against the hurricane aid because it is part of a larger $13.1 billion emergency spending bill that he thinks includes some pet projects that shouldn't be funded.

This great stand on political principles, mind you, comes from a senator who's been trying to get Congress to approve $1.5 billion for a Mississippi shipyard to build a ship that the Navy says it doesn't need and doesn't want.

In the meantime, people in eastern North Carolina living in temporary trailers are awaiting money to help find permanent housing. Tobacco, cotton and peanut farmers are still waiting for help. Loans from the Small Business Administration aren't available to people who could use them.

A new Gallup Poll published the other day said people have declining trust in politicians, ranking Congress the worst.

With people like Sen. Lott holding back help from people who need it, is it any wonder?

---

2. *Source:* Editorial, *Morning-Star* (Wilmington, N.C.), 13 June 2000. Reprinted with permission.

3.6 Sophistries and Diversions

Sophistries are named after the ancient Greek Sophists, who taught the art of persuasion for money. In the Athenian democracy of the fifth century B.C., this art was very useful and, presumably, expensive. Socrates confessed at one point that he hadn't been able to afford the Sophists' course—which was ironic because Socrates was put to death for, among other things, "making the worse appear to be the better cause." That is sophistry.

Philosophically, the Sophists did not believe in much of anything—justice, beauty, goodness, or the like—so they taught the wealthy young Athenians to argue either side of any issue. They were much like our modern professors of law and debate coaches. **Sophistry** has come to mean the use of clever tricks and subterfuge—misleading, specious arguments and counterarguments intended to confuse the issue, foul up the discussion and get it off the track, and then appear to triumph in the end.

The Pooh-Pooh   The **pooh-pooh** (the **sneer**) dismisses a whole argument with a wave of the hand. Suppose the first speaker has argued at length for gun control. Then the second speaker says

> *Gun-control laws merely keep law-abiding citizens from owning guns and do nothing about real crime. There must be a better approach.*

Notice that whatever arguments the first speaker has offered have been pooh-poohed away with the word *merely*.

Here's another example:

> *National health insurance is merely another government boondoggle. We need to examine other, more sensible alternatives.*

No attempt is made to meet any specific argument or to present those other alternatives. It's a cheap trick, a sophistry.

The Straw Man   The **straw man** is a flimsy, silly version of the real argument. You set him up, kick him over, and pretend to have won a great victory. It's a shrewd misrepresentation of your opponent's argument. For example:

> *You say teachers should get higher salaries because they will be happier on the job? So why should they be any happier than the rest of us?*

The original argument was no doubt much more developed. There are other reasons for paying teachers well that go beyond "happiness on the job." Here's another example:

You say that outlawing drugs will mean our children will have to go to criminals to get them? That's ridiculous! We need a policy that will keep drugs away from our children!

And so on.

Refuting Examples   Refuting an example cited by your opponent might be appropriate sometimes. The fallacy of **refuting examples** pretends that one bad example spoils the whole argument. For example, suppose Tom is arguing that Medicare is necessary for the well-being of old people, and he mentions two local couples on Medicare as examples. Then Joe points out that one of those couples is actually very well off and doesn't really need Medicare:

The Parkers are well off, so that defeats Tom's whole argument!

That's going too far. One of Tom's examples is inappropriate; that doesn't mean his whole argument is wrong. Here's another example:

Tom: *Smoking is bad for your health. Consider Humphrey Bogart, Bob Fosse, and Hank Williams.*

Joe: *Hank Williams died of heart failure, so your whole argument goes up in smoke.*

Trivial Objections   These are what we could call "pot shots." No argument is totally immune to objections, but some objections are worthwhile and some are not. **Trivial objections** may be relevant, but they just aren't worth bringing up. Consider these two examples:

Mary: *Pornography should be outlawed because of the influence it can have on the minds of our children and because it dehumanizes women and turns them into things rather than people.*

Lee: *But can you imagine how much tax revenue would be lost to the government in that case—money that could support education, health, our military forces? Mary just hasn't thought this through.*

Tom: *More people should try the stock market. Last week I made seventy-three thousand dollars in two days.*

Mary: *But you have to consider the broker's fees. Those brokers make a lot of money. I'd say the stock market's a ripoff.*

The Red Herring   Fox hunters used to have a trick for training their dogs to stay on the fox's scent. They would drag a dead fish across the dogs' path; when the dogs went after the fish, the hunters would whip them back onto the right trail. The **red herring** is a diversion designed to pull the argument off track, away from the real subject. A new topic is sneaked into the discussion—one related to the real subject, of course—and the participants all chase it. For example:

> *What you say about Medicare has some merit, of course. But don't you get tired of all these minority groups sticking together the way they do? As if all women think the same way, for example. You can't find two women who agree on anything.*

The subject has been changed, hasn't it? The business about women disagreeing is a red herring, designed to pull the argument off the real subject, which is Medicare.

The Definitional Sulk

> A: *No Scotsman drinks gin.*
>
> B: *McBain drinks gin.*
>
> A: *Well, then, he's no true Scotsman, for no true Scotsman drinks gin.*

This trick is also called the "No-True-Scotsman" move. In the **definitional sulk,** A makes a claim that seems to be meant in the obvious way, B challenges it, and A goes into a definitional sulk by redefining a word and retreating to a narrower claim.

> A: *We were not at war in Vietnam.*
>
> B: *But fifty-eight thousand Americans were killed!*
>
> A: *By war I mean "declared by Congress." Congress never declared war on North Vietnam.*

Shifting Ground

> A: *Mr. President, you said in June that you did not know about the sale of guns to the Contras. Now you seem to be saying you did.*
>
> B: *I said I didn't "remember" okaying any such deal. I didn't say I absolutely didn't know about it.*

Here the president is **shifting ground**—from saying he "didn't know" to saying he "doesn't remember." A slick way to dodge trouble, this one is often used by politicians, as in

> A: *Do you still hold that the Bruiser is lying, now that he's here to defend himself?*
>
> B: *I never said he was lying. I said I believed he was mistaken.*

Hedging Hedging in an argument is avoiding any clear commitment and hiding behind a hedge of vague, or ambiguous, words. If the argument is disputed from one angle, it's easy to jump the other way by saying, "That's not what I meant."

> A: I think something must be done about this problem of vandalism in our schools.
>
> B: Are you saying we should expel the offenders? Even the superintendent's boy?
>
> A: Oh, no, no, I didn't mean anything so drastic. I meant we should try to come up with an acceptable policy of some kind.
>
> B: Acceptable to the school board, the parents, the students, or whom?
>
> A: Well, we'd want this policy to be acceptable to everyone concerned, hopefully.

And so on. This person, A, is saying nothing at all. That's the price you have to pay for playing it safe.

Shifting the Burden of Proof This sophistry is very similar to the fallacy of the appeal to ignorance. If you put forward a view and objections are made, you simply **shift the burden of proof** to your opponent. For example:

> A: You say you favor capital punishment? What if an innocent person is executed?
>
> B: No solution will satisfy everyone. How would you deal with the crime problem?

Or, more simply,

> A: You say national health insurance is necessary, but I don't hear you saying why.
>
> B: Well, why are you so convinced it wouldn't *work*? Tell us that.

Exceptions That Prove the Rule The word *prove* is from the Latin *probare*, "to prove or test." So **exceptions that prove the rule** don't prove the rule, if they are real exceptions, in the sense of proving it to be true. They test the rule, try it out. In fact, they disprove it, unless they are not really exceptions. For example:

> A: No president has been a very old person.
>
> B: There's Ronald Reagan.
>
> A: Just one case. He's the exception that proves the rule.
>
> A: No woman has ever been elevated to high office.
>
> B: There's Golda Meir, Margaret Thatcher, and Indira Ghandi.
>
> A: Well, they're just exceptions that prove the rule.

Exercise 3.6   A. Name the sophistry committed in each passage. The contexts of sophistries are back-and-forth arguments, speeches, and the like. Try to visualize the larger context for yourself.

1. All your talk about gun control is just silly. Guns don't kill people; people kill people.

2. You say gun control is unconstitutional. But tell me, what does a person need with a gun, anyway?

3. You say gun control is unconstitutional. But guns are very expensive, anyway. Have you priced any lately?

4. Gun control will just add to expensive red tape.

5. I didn't say I was totally against gun control. I just believe we should think about it, that's all.

6. All your argument is saying is that women are treated unfairly. But that's life.

7. Well, why are you *against* the ERA?

8. A: No beautiful women are smart.

   B: What about Cleopatra?

   A: She's just the exception that proves the rule.

9. A: So Chrysler *didn't* sell used cars as new?

   B: I didn't say that. I said such charges need to be examined carefully.

10. A: You say movie stars are greedy and self-centered. But what about Jerry Lewis?

    B: He's just the exception that proves the rule.

11. Well, why are you so against my proposal? Do you have a better idea?

12. A: Are you saying we should go to war?

    B: No, no. I only said that would be one option.

13. A: Smoking is bad for your health and that of those around you.

    B: Well, a person has to do something with her hands.

14. A: What are your reasons for saying there is life in space?

    B: I'm saying there *could* be.

15. What you say about the necessity for toxic-waste dumps is all very well, but the smell can be awful, like rotten eggs. I once tasted a rotten egg, and . . . .

16. A: Are you saying people with AIDS should be quarantined?

    B: I said that was one possibility.

17. What you say about medical costs is all very well, but everything else is going up, too. Just today I bought a lawn mower, and . . . .

18. Running may be good exercise, as you say, but I hate lacing up those sneakers. There's just so much time in you life. And don't you find that the older you get, the faster time seems to pass?

19. Well, if you don't like my gun-control bill, can you tell us why you're so against gun control?

20. What you said about the problem of illegal aliens puts me in mind of what a great movie *Casablanca* was.

21. All the ERA would do would be to force men and women to use the same restrooms, and that's silly.

22. If we did wipe out crime, what would TV shows like *NYPD Blue* be about?

23. A: No Americans are socialist.

    B: Michael Harrington is a socialist, and he's an American.

    A: Well, no *true* American could be a socialist.

24. A: Are you saying we should overthrow the government?

    B: No, no. I'm only saying we should vote against the present administration.

25. A: You say that all singers are egotistical? What about Britney Spears and Ricky Martin?

    B: They're just exceptions that prove the rule.

26. There have been a few changes in Russia. But Putin is still a communist, and you can't trust a communist.

27. You say that the passengers on Flight 103 (which was sabotaged and crashed in Lockerbie, Scotland) could have lived if they'd been warned? That's just silly. To tell every passenger of every terrorist warning would make air travel impossible.

28. All this talk about socioeconomic conditions is pointless. All we need to do is teach our children to "Just Say No."

29. All this talk about "a mother's love" is nonsense. Baby M's mother signed a *contract* and should abide by it.

30. Tom: No important network job has ever been held by a woman.

    Dave: There's Barbara Walters.

    Tom: She's just an exception that proves the rule.

31. All this talk about how serious the drug problem is is just silly. Television robs children of any meaningful childhood. I think we should outlaw TV.

32. What you say about the responsibilities of the state department in the case of Flight 103 is interesting. But people don't *have* to fly if they don't want to.

33. A: Are you saying that you did *not* use the special knowledge you had gained in government service to your profit after you had left government service?

    B: I am saying that I can recall no time at which I used such knowledge.

34. I can't understand why people are so concerned about apartheid in South Africa. Besides, *apartheid* isn't even an English word, is it?

35. A: You should quit smoking. Smoking causes cancer, emphysema, and heart disease and may complicate pregnancy.

    B: Well, but then I'd find something else that was stupid and dangerous to do.

36. Well, those are good reasons to quit smoking, I know, but I eat too much, too, and I'd hate to have to start dieting.

37. You say Coach Farber pressured professors to pass his players. But don't you admit that athletics is important to a college? Doesn't it build character?

38. A: No good coach would pressure professors to pass his players.

    B: Coach Farber did and he's a good coach.

    A: Well, he's not a really *good* coach.

39. A: Mr. Secretary, are you saying that state department employees were warned about the terrorist threat?

    B: I am saying that the information might have been available to some employees.

40. A: Are you saying that you're for communism?

    B: I'm only saying that the wealth of this country should be divided more equitably.

41. Well, how would *you* distribute the wealth?

42. A: Are you saying, that Mike Tyson is a wimp?

    B: No! No, I'm only saying he should perhaps have been a bit more forceful, you know, asserted himself more, you know what I mean.

43. A: I think all of us here want to do the right thing.

    B: You mean we should tell all the passengers about the terrorist threat?

    A: No, no, I haven't said that. But I don't think we should leave ourselves open to the charge that we didn't make an effort, uh. . . .

    B: So we shouldn't tell the passengers?

    A: Well, I think we should make at least an, uh, effort in that direction.

    B: So we should tell the passengers?

    A: Well, I don't think we should be alarmists. . . .

    B: Suppose we post a notice about the safety evaluation of this aircraft on the bulletin board in the lobby downstairs?

A: In that way our tails will be covered, I believe. And our people would have the information. Sounds good to me!

44. Well, what would *you* do about terrorist threats?

45. Mr. Tower, can you dissolve these suspicions?

46. I haven't said that we will cut social programs. All I'm saying is that we will have to tighten our belts.

47. A: No conservative is pro-choice on abortion.

    B: The secretary of education is a conservative, and he's pro-choice.

    A: Well, he's no *real* conservative.

48. All you're saying is that some women are oppressed. But look, life is hard for everybody.

49. A: Are you saying that we should break the treaty and start building nuclear weapons again?

    B: I'm just saying it's a mistake to trust the Russians completely.

50. Certainly, that move could lead to nuclear war, but then we could determine the effectiveness of our nuclear delivery system. And nobody could say that we backed down to the communists.

51. A: We must do what is necessary to protect our interests.

    B: Are you saying that we will go to war?

    A: No, no, I didn't say that.

52. Well, if you think my proposal is so inadequate, do you have a better idea?

53. Just think of the expensive red tape a gun-control law would cause.

54. You say that drunk driving kills all those people—but people need to have some fun, blow off steam, you know?

55. A: We should get tough on drug pushers.

    B: Do you favor giving them the death penalty?

    A: Well, I'm not saying that, but I'm in favor of taking strong measures.

56. A: It is highly probable that on one of the billions and billions of planets out there, there must be life.

    B: Are you saying that there is life in space?

    A: I'm saying that there certainly could be.

57. A: No Harvard man would drink Wild Irish Rose.

   B: Dr. Feebe is a Harvard man, and he drinks Wild Irish Rose.

   A: Well, he's no *true* Harvard man. No *true* Harvard man would ever drink Wild Irish Rose.

58. You say that smoking causes all these diseases. But people are mortal. Wars kill lots of people. We should be trying to stop wars.

59. All your arguments against smoking just boil down to this: Some people like to smoke, and some don't. So it's just a matter of taste.

60. A: I think that all these UFO sightings add up to something.

   B: Are you saying that there are flying saucers?

   A: I'm saying that there *could* be.

61. A: All rock stars take drugs—Boy George, the Beatles, the Who, John Belushi. . . .

   B: Ha! John Belushi wasn't a rock star! That proves you're totally misguided.

62. Capital punishment takes a lot of electricity. Somebody has to pay for that.

63. A: We should separate AIDS victims from the rest of society.

   B: You're saying that they should be quarantined?

   A: I'm saying that we should *think* about it.

64. A: I deeply believe that we should reassess our priorities with respect to nuclear power.

   B: You think that we should shut down nuclear plants?

   A: No, no, I didn't say that. I do believe that the subject calls for some rethinking, though.

65. A: I propose to take the lead on the drug issue. We'll declare war on drugs!

   B: You mean that you'll use the army?

   A: I fully intend to use every reasonable means to fight this scourge.

66. But in our attack on Granada, a number of weapons were lost. You can't dismiss that.

67. All your arguments for national health insurance just add up to one thing: higher taxes.

68. I'm frankly suspicious of my opponent's stand on these issues. It seems that she has something against the Pledge of Allegiance. Let's all say it: "I pledge. . . ."

B. Find the fallacies and sophistries in the following essay.

Creationism (Con)

The Bible-thumpers want to teach their backward, ignorant viewpoint to our innocent children. The issue is simple: Do you believe in fairy tales or in the simple facts? A pretty story or the truth?

Millions of years ago, as Carl Sagan tells us, there was a "big bang." Primordial matter flew out, and some of it congealed into galaxies of stars; some of those stars became suns, and those suns had planets. On one such planet, Earth, life evolved. It was a cosmic accident; there was no "Creation." The story of the Creation is just a wish fulfillment. We all want to have a heavenly father, so we made one up.

It is hard to understand how there could be people so backward, in this age of scientific progress, that they believe the old legend of God. Naturally, preachers will claim to believe it, for they make their living spouting this nonsense. But the rest of us have no excuse.

The real miracles of our times are cars and refrigerators and medicine. But they're all explicable in scientific terms.

We should respect the truth because facts are worthy of high regard. The universe is not a creation but an accident. It was not built but just happened.

Well-educated people have put religious nonsense behind them. I have spoken to five PhDs and none of them professed belief in God. The people who want creationism to be taught in the schools are always the poor and the ignorant. How long will they bury their heads in the sand? The choice is clear: ignorance or truth!

C. Find the fallacies and sophistries in the following essay.

AIDS Quarantine (Pro)

The people who have AIDS have contracted it by engaging in immoral, illicit, illegal, and unnatural acts. They have offended God and nature, and God and nature have sent a fitting punishment to them.

The only sensible course the rest of us can take is to quarantine the spreaders of this plague. We don't know enough about the disease to take chances with it. Can you get it from kissing? Nobody knows. Has medical science proved that you can't get it from using infected restroom facilities? If we want to be safe, quarantining is the only answer.

We quarantine people with small pox, even influenza. So why shouldn't we do the same with AIDS? Opponents want to say that it isn't necessary. But do they know? Can they prove it? Why should we expose our children to certain death, just to protect the feelings and sensibilities of homosexuals and drug addicts? It doesn't make sense.

AIDS is deadly. It has a 100 percent death rate. Something has to be done. Therefore, we should quarantine those people whom we know have it. Homosexuals and drug addicts won't like it, of course, but that's too bad.

Better safe than sorry. So we should start quarantining the homosexuals and addicts right away. If you don't have it yet, you've been lucky. But you shouldn't press your luck.

And I should just say that I'm not the only concerned American in favor of the AIDS quarantine. A number of senators feel the same way.

D. Find the fallacies and sophistries in the following article.

DNA Helps Uncover Truth[3]

Our View: Testing has proved to be a vital tool both to convict the guilty and to free the innocent

"There are some things you can't run from anymore," serial killer Danny Rolling said last year when he pleaded guilty to murdering five Gainesville, Fla., students.

What Rolling couldn't run from was the genetic evidence linking him to his crimes. His DNA profile matched that of semen found at the crime scenes.

Yet, despite that case and scores of other convictions and acquittals, use of such evidence is now in jeopardy—unnecessarily.

O. J. Simpson's lawyers, for example, steadily attack its use, as is their job. And a small group of critics in the scientific community last week seized on a California Supreme Court ruling to make their case.

The court ruled that for DNA tests to be admissible, they must follow scientifically accepted procedures. Since there is no agreement on every last procedure, they argue, no DNA evidence should be admitted.

Their concern for the innocent is admirable. But their standards are just too tight.

The fact is that DNA use in court is endorsed by most scientists and has shown to be more reliable than many eyewitnesses.

No one has proven anyone was wrongfully convicted as a result of errors or misrepresentation of DNA evidence. Meanwhile DNA testing has overturned the convictions of dozens of innocent people.

A third of DNA testing in Virginia's labs, for example, is used to exonerate suspects.

What's more, science has agreed upon acceptable standards for DNA testing.

The National Research Council set up a method for measuring the

---

3. *Source:* "DNA Helps Uncover Truth," *USA TODAY*, 31 October 1994. Copyright © 1994, USA TODAY. Reprinted with permission.

odds of one person's DNA profile matching another person's that most genetic scientists view as fair, if overly conservative. In some cases, the committee lowered odds of a mismatch to 1,000 to one that could have been as high as 10 million to one—a sensible precaution to protect defendants.

Critics complain about lack of quality control, but lab technicians now undergo proficiency tests by the American Society of Crime Laboratory Directors to ensure they follow proper procedures. And the society has accredited 16 of the nation's 50 federal, state and local DNA labs.

Such steps are why two longtime scientific rivals over DNA's use, MIT's Eric S. Lander and the FBI's Bruce Budowie, last week proclaimed DNA fingerprinting wars were over. "There is no scientific reason to doubt the accuracy of forensic DNA typing results," they wrote in *Nature* magazine.

Can DNA be made even more reliable? No question. And judges, defense attorneys and scientists must keep pressuring forensic labs to improve.

But DNA evidence has a place in court today—to protect the innocent and to put killers such as Danny Rolling away.

3.7 Summary

Informal fallacies are bad arguments that can *appear* to be good. They are so common that logicians have named and classified them. The fallacies of ambiguity occur when a word or phrase, or whole sentence, can be taken in more than one way in the same argument. Fallacies of presumption occur when we presume or assume the truth of some statement we have no justification for assuming. Fallacies of irrelevance occur when we bring considerations into the argument that has nothing or very little to do with the issue at hand. Sophistries are sly tricks we use to make it appear that we have a much stronger case than we do.

Because it does not fit easily into one of our four groups of informal fallacies and because it is such a devastating blunder when it occurs in an argument, we discussed inconsistency separately from the other informal fallacies. It occurs when two premises, or a premise and the conclusion, contradict each other.

Intellectual responsibility requires that we be cautious in ascribing fallacies to others and that we avoid the fallacies ourselves, however tempting they might be!

Other fallacies, unlike the ones in this chapter, are formal. We will discuss them in Chapter 4.

Summary: The Informal Fallacies

Fallacies of Ambiguity

- **Amphiboly** occurs when a whole sentence can be understood in two or more ways. *Example:* We stand behind every car we sell.

- **Equivocation** occurs when a word or phrase is used two different ways in the same argument. *Example:* Joe despises Mary, so Mary must be despicable.

- **Accent** occurs when improper emphasis on a word or phrase leads to an unintended conclusion. *Example:* Why shop somewhere else and be cheated?

- **Hypostatization** occurs when an abstraction is turned into a person or thing. *Example:* Old Man Winter buries the coast in snow.

- **Composition** occurs when what is true of a part is falsely applied to the whole. *Example:* Each sentence makes sense, so the whole essay makes sense. Composition also occurs when what's true distributively is falsely applied collectively. *Example:* A dog eats more than an insect eats, so all dogs eat more than all insects do.

- **Division** occurs when what is true of the whole is falsely applied to the parts. *Example:* Texas is a big state, so all Texans are big people. Division also occurs when what's true collectively is falsely applied distributively. *Example:* China's population is larger than Japan's, so each Chinese person is larger than each Japanese person.

Fallacies of Presumption

- A **hasty generalization (converse accident)** occurs when we jump to a conclusion from too few observations. *Example:* My first dog was bad tempered, so all dogs are bad tempered.

- A **sweeping generalization (accident)** occurs when we presume that what is true of many but not all cases applies to every particular case. *Example:* Haste makes waste, so don't rush me to the hospital with these chest pains.

- A **false cause** occurs when we presume that since A precedes B, A must *cause* B. *Example:* The Blessed Reverend laid her hands upon him, and his pain stopped, so . . . .

- A **false analogy (weak analogy)** occurs when we

presume two things are similar when they're not. *Example:* Life is like a box of chocolates . . . .

- **Begging the question** occurs when we assume the very statement we are trying to prove. *Example:* I know I can trust him because I'm confident that he's trustworthy.

- A **question-begging epithet** occurs when we use slanted words, tags, or labels that assume what we are trying to prove. *Example:* They should convict that murdering monster.

- A **complex question** occurs when we put a question in such a way that it falsely presupposes that the answer to another, hidden question has already been established. *Example:* Why are you so contrary?

- **Special pleading** occurs when we apply a rule or harsh judgment to everyone but ourselves. *Example:* I'm embellishing; she's lying.

- A **black or white fallacy (false dilemma)** occurs when we presume that there can be no middle ground. *Example:* You're either a success or a failure.

- A **gambler's fallacy** occurs when we presume that every loss brings us closer to a win. *Example:* I've lost money in the stock market every year. So I'm due for a break.

- A **slippery slope** occurs when we presume that one innocent first step must lead to a disaster. *Example:* Take one aspirin and soon you'll become a drug addict.

Fallacies of Irrelevance

- *Ad hominem* fallacies consist of two types: (1) The **abusive *ad hominem*** occurs when we attack the person rather than the argument. *Example:* My opponent, a congenital liar, is trying to mislead you. (2) The **circumstantial *ad hominem*** occurs when we unfairly imply that our opponent is self-serving because of his or her circumstances. *Example:* Naturally,

you'd oppose pay cuts for teachers; you're a teacher yourself.

- **Poisoning the well** occurs when we discredit the opposition's view in advance. *Example:* What foolish nonsense will the Congress trot out next?

- ***Tu quoque*** occurs when we pretend that two wrongs make a right: Since you did X, it's okay for *me* to do X. *Example:* You say I shouldn't cheat, but didn't *you* cheat when you were in school?

- A **genetic fallacy** occurs when we attack the *source* of the argument rather than the argument itself. *Example:* That point is one you must have found in Howard Stern's *Miss America.*

- An **appeal to pity** occurs when we play on the sympathies of the audience rather than argue for our own views. *Example:* If we find him guilty, his poor little children will have no father.

- An **appeal to force (appeal to fear)** occurs when we try to persuade by means of a threat. *Example:* Oh, yeah? Well, you'll think differently when I slap your face!

- An **appeal to authority** occurs when we cite someone who, though well known, is no expert on the subject being discussed. *Example:* These are the same kind of contact lenses that Linda Carter uses.

- An **appeal to ignorance** occurs when we turn our opponent's ignorance of contrary evidence into evidence of the truth of our statement. It is similar to *shifting the burden of proof* except that it "completes the proof." *Example:* Have you ever seen a ghost? No! So that proves there are none!

- **Mob appeal** occurs when we appeal to the desire to fit in, to go along with the crowd. *Example:* But, Mom, *everyone's* wearing them!

- **Snob appeal** occurs when we appeal to the desire to stand out. *Example:* "Old Groundhog Whiskey—when you've made it."

- An **irrelevant thesis (missing the point, *ignoratio elenchi*)** occurs when we purport to prove one point while actually proving another. Also called a *non sequitur. Example:* See the terrible knife wounds, the blood . . . . You must avenge this crime with a verdict of *guilty!*

Sophistries

- A **pooh-pooh** (the **sneer**) occurs when we dismiss a point with derision or with a cavalier wave of the hand, as not worth serious attention. *Example:* The poor have no bread? Then let them eat cake!

- A **straw man fallacy** occurs when we set up a weak version of an argument and refute it easily. Avoid committing this one when *finding* fallacies! *Example:* The only reason she favors the death penalty is that she wants *vengeance,* and that's a primitive view.

- **Refuting examples** occurs when we seize upon one bad example out of many good ones. *Example:* "Fruits are good for you—apples, grapes, turnips, pears."—"Ha! *Turnips* aren't fruits!"

- **Trivial objections** occur when we offer "pot shots." *Example:* But if there's no war, what will we do with all these new uniforms?

- A **red herring** occurs when we divert the discussion from the real subject to a related but different one. *Example:* I'm against assisted suicide. People can't do anything for themselves any more. That's why taxes are so high.

- A **definitional sulk** occurs when we try to win the argument by defining a crucial term in a biased way. *Example:* "No Democrat could ever vote for a Republican." "I'm a Democrat and I voted for Nixon." "Well, you're no *true* Democrat!"

- **Shifting ground** occurs when, upon being challenged, we change our position from a strong one to a weaker one. *Example:* "I did not give the order." "These three witnesses say you did." "Well, I don't *remember* giving the order."

- **Hedging** occurs when we avoid any clear statement in the first place so that we can easily avoid being pinned down. *Example:* "We should take *serious steps* to reduce crime." "So you favor the death penalty?" "Well, serious steps of *some* kind. We should get tough!"

- **Shifting the burden of proof** occurs when, instead of proving our claim, we challenge our opponent to disprove it (similar to *appeal to ignorance* but leaves conclusion "open"). *Example:* We can't prove he killed them, but just where *was* he when they were killed?

- **Exceptions that prove the rule** suggests that an exception shows that the rule *is* almost always true, but a *real* exception to a rule *disproves* the rule. *Example:* "No actors can direct." "What about Robert Redford?" "He's just the exception that proves the rule."

3.8 Applications

Violent Protest We will look for fallacies in the following essay, "Violent Protest Is Justified," by Frank Morriss. The critical analysis of the arguments that comprise the essay will be postponed until we have presented the techniques of modern symbolic logic in Chapter 5.

Before we begin, let's repeat our Golden Rule of critical analysis: Treat others' arguments as you would want others to treat yours. In finding fallacies, this means (1) don't find fallacies that aren't there; and (2) be objective and fair, as far as you are able, whether or not you agree with the material you are analyzing.

To get a sense of context, we should note that the *main conclusion* of Morriss's essay is

Killing abortion doctors is morally justified

which he supports by arguing that the Pensacola, Florida, killing of an abortion doctor was an attempt to save the innocent lives of the unborn babies that the doctor was about to murder. Since taking a "guilty" life is much more defensible than taking an "innocent" life, killing that doctor was justified. In a later analysis, we will consider other details in the essay. Given this perspective, we simply look for fallacies. For clarity's sake, we identify a few key words of each suspected fallacious passage; then we name the fallacy and briefly explain why this passage constitutes a fallacy or why it does not.

Bracketed numbers indicate where I believe that fallacies occur. In the numbered list that follows the essay, I identify each fallacy and briefly comment.

Violent Protest Is Justified[4]
by Frank Morriss

Any moral, or even humanly decent [1], society would consider the illustration in *Newsweek* (Feb. 11, 1993) obscene. It showed an unborn baby [2] and pointed out its various parts that might be harvested (or to be more honest, cannibalized) [3] for treatment of various diseases. Brain cells can help experimental surgery to treat Parkinson's disease, neurons "might treat" [4] spinal-cord injuries and multiple sclerosis, pancreatic cells "reduced patients' need for insulin," liver cells "helped one boy" with Hunter's syndrome, stem cells "might treat" sickle-cell anemia and other disorders.

---

4. *Source:* Frank Morriss, "How to Protect the Unborn When Law Permits Their Execution," *The Wanderer,* 25 March 1993. Reprinted with permission of *The Wanderer* and the author.

It might have been a chart such as once hung in old-fashioned butcher shops [5] showing areas of animals from which choice and less-choice cuts came for the kitchen. The caption to the *Newsweek* illustration betrays just what the attitude of the secularized, pagan society [6] of today is toward unborn life—"The Sum of Its Parts." If there is any doubt about what the article's intention might be, words of its headline should make it clear—" . . . saving a life is a moral imperative, yet we restrict the use of aborted fetuses." The headline goes on to call "the ethical landscape" of this issue a "minefield."

In Perspective

I cite this [7] as important in thinking about the tragedy in Pensacola, Florida, in which an abortionist "doctor" [8] was slain. The slaying may have deepened or widened the tragedy, but it did not of course create it. The tragedy was there, created by the mentality of the *Newsweek* illustration and by the pragmatic, sociological jurisprudence that has taken over control of our judiciary since the natural law legal philosophy was scuttled by [liberal Supreme Court justice] Oliver Wendell Holmes, Jr., and his ilk. [Natural, or true, law [9] was an 18th- and 19th-century legal philosophy that held certain human rights to be God-given and hence unassailable by the state.]

If the tragedy might be measured by blood [10], then that of the slain abortionist contributed a drop in what are streams of innocent blood flowing into America's sewers from its abortion abattoirs. For the first time, the blood of the guilty joined the rivers of it from the victims [11].

This makes some of the words coming from some on both sides rather meaningless, or at least not to the true issue. Much of the disavowal from the pro-life side and the indignation from the pro-death side implies that innocent and guilty life [12] are equal. They are, of course, ontologically and in the possession of human rights. But if that ends the matter, then deadly war may not be fought, the state may not execute, and no one can mount deadly defense in behalf of innocent life, either one's own or that of one's neighbor—and I take to be our neighbor any and all who face aggressive and malevolent evil [13] that we might stop.

This, incidentally, shows how pacifist or even the "seamless garment" ideas can muddy the ethical and logical waters concerning a vital issue. It also dignifies the "legalization" of what is morally and ethically perverse in essence. . . .

True Law and Morality

The force of the state should defend all innocent life. The right of true law exists only on one side—that which labels all slaying of the innocent murder to one degree or another, and the overt intention to slay such life never defensible. That this intention to slay the innocent is present in the case of abortion is undeniable. (The claim that some do not recognize abortion as the deliberate killing of an innocent human is inadmissible, for subjective opinion does not determine the moral or natural law reality.)

What, then, is the moral situation when the state refuses to protect some innocent life, and in fact gives mandate for its murder? Is all protection removed from that life? If, by some miracle, the unborn targets of abortionists were able to mount some defense by force against their attackers, some way to slay the "doctor" before he slayed them, could they be condemned for doing so? Alas, that cannot be expected to happen. The next question is, can someone who might act with such force on their behalf be accused of murder, as the abortionists certainly can be on the level of true law and morality? The same civil law that "legalizes" abortion cannot be cited when it judges deadly defense murder. It has lost its authority in this question. What that means in regard to actual cases of force on behalf of the unborn on the part of individuals or combinations of them, I leave to others. But I have no doubt that this is the real heart of the question about events in Pensacola.

It becomes, perhaps, clearer when we consider what actually happened. An abortionist left his car and was headed to the "clinic." There weapons of death aimed at the unborn, and them alone, awaited him. Within minutes— or certainly within an hour or two—he would have been using them to kill innocent life. No police were on hand to stop him. Indeed, were they there, representing the state or federal government, they would have instead facilitated his progress. All of this is certain fact.

What then is the moral, natural law quality of what was done by one who acted, almost certainly, with the intention of preventing what that abortionist clearly intended to do, as he had been doing in the past and would have continued to do had he been able? That is the question to be considered, and not whether the end justifies the means (it does not), or whether one must adopt a "seamless garment" attitude about all taking of life.

Nor does it deal with the real issue by saying or believing that what happened in Florida was a tactical blow to pro-life efforts, or thinking it might discredit those efforts. All such questions are important, but they must not determine our thought toward the central issue—what authority exists in defending innocent life for which no police (I mean state or judicial) defense is afforded? Does all authority in their defense vanish? If it does not, where does it exist?

If we are going to concede that all deadly force against aggressive evil is itself evil, then we must pretend we are helpless against any aggressive evil. That, of course, is the pacifist position. But, then, such pacifism is error, not truth. Some pro-lifers hastening to present "clean hands" in regard to what happened in Florida have, unfortunately, taken a pacifist stance. And of course the enemies bent on the "right" to take innocent life would be glad to have pacifism prevail on one side—the pro-life side—but not on theirs. Indeed, that is the hypocritical stand of all aggressors.

Let it be said honestly and openly, the moral aggressors at Pensacola were the abortionists and their agents, encouraged by pseudo-law that in the case of the unborn countenances and authorizes deadly aggression, identical to that for which we executed Nazis after the Nuremberg trials.

Historical Precedents

Most historians would give their sympathy, if not their outright approval, to Charlotte Corday, who slew "the Toad." Marat [a leader of the French Revolution], in his bathtub. She felt, with reason, that he had betrayed the true Revolution and led it into a swamp of blood. She added his blood to that swamp. I know of no one who mourned the passing of the agitator Marat.

The fictional "Scarlet Pimpernel" [from the similarly entitled 1934 novel about the French Revolution by Baroness Emmuska Orczy] did not, at least ordinarily, resort to killing to rescue royalists from the guillotine. But I doubt if any reader or viewer of the exploits of this English "rescuer" would have complained had he killed a few Jacobins and their agents in order to save some helpless persons being hauled to the place of execution, where the ground was so blood-soaked that, it is said, horses reared back in terror at the smell.

I suggest that what happened in Florida had, at the very least, the coloration of Corday's assassination and the Pimpernel's refusal to accept French revolutionary "law" as the final determination—certainly not a moral determination.

Indeed, the traditional ethical teachings based on the natural law can be cited more precisely to the case in Florida than to the two events in Revolutionary France, one historical, the other fictional.

It should be realized that it is certain that good morality cannot allow the killing of the unborn to continue, and that there will be those of good and informed conscience who will act in one way or another to bring it to an end, whether that can be accomplished by ordinary "legal" means or not. The question then becomes what actions can a true and valid conscience indicate.

Frank Morriss, a teacher at the Colorado Catholic Academy, is the author of The Conservative Imperative *and* The Divine Epic *and has, since 1950, been a columnist for several Roman Catholic journals.*

1. "any . . . humanly decent" (poisoning the well): As if whoever disagrees with him is *not* humanly decent.

2. "unborn baby" (question-begging epithet):—Is a fetus a *baby?*

3. "cannibalized" (question-begging epithet, false analogy):—*But* so is "harvested"; is fetal tissue a *crop?*

4. Morriss is *hedging* with such phrases as "might treat."

5. "butcher shops" (false analogy) [But there *is* a disquieting similarity of the two kinds of charts.]

6. "secularized pagan society" (poisoning the well with tiresome, insulting rhetoric)

7. "this" (amphiboly): Not clear what "this" refers to.

8. "doctor" (accent): As if abortionists are not real doctors. The following are left to you to name and explain or to explain why it is *not* a fallacy:

9. "or true, law"

10. "tragedy . . . measured by blood"

11. "victims"

12. "innocent . . . guilty"

13. "malevolent evil"

The *issue* is whether violence against abortion doctors is morally justifiable. The *main argument,* put informally for the present, is that (in reference to the Pensacola case) killing the abortion doctor is an attempt to save innocent lives (the fetuses), by taking a guilty life (the abortion doctor). Taking a guilty life to save innocent life is—like self-defense or defense of an innocent neighbor—justifiable.

Our approach is to look for fallacious passages; when we think that we have found one, we identify it by quoting a few key words; then we name the fallacy and briefly explain why or why not the passage is an instance of that fallacy. Make positive comments when they are warranted.

Can you find more fallacies in the essay?

Ross Perot Speech Here we apply our list of fallacies to a political speech. Bracketed numbers indicate where I believe that fallacies occur. In the numbered list that follows the speech, I identify each fallacy and briefly comment.

Excerpts of a Speech for the 1996 Reform Party National Convention
by Ross Perot

What about Franklin Delano Roosevelt, got us through World War II, a depression, sorry, man in a wheelchair will be in an uphill climb. It's all visually, all acting, no substance. Guess what, if you get elected acting, what do you think you do after you get elected? Keep on acting. Right. Got it. Now, in business the customer is king [1]. In politics today the special interests who pay for the campaigns are king and the voter is just out there on the fringe somewhere.

You are the customer, but you have no effective voice and it's something we're stuck with. We've got to change that.

If you question that, just look at the amount of money the special interest [2] get. For example, there's one [2] that gives several million dollars a year to both parties, doesn't care who wins. Gets 500 million dollars subsidy from the U.S. government. Strike the word "U.S. government" and put in the words "out of your pocket."

Okay. We're going to change that for sure. Campaigns last too long, cost too much, we can do them in a much shorter period of time. Get the price down, and that's what we have to do.

The thing I want to talk about in the time I have left here, is you need to understand that Washington incorrectly assumes we will always have an endless supply of tax money.

The facts are, tax money does not fall out of the sky. It comes off the sweat of the brow of millions of hard working Americans [3]. That's where tax money comes from. There is no tax money until farmers, truck drivers, plumbers, electricians, the people who make the world go around, pay it. And it should be handled like water in the desert, very, very carefully, not thrown away and given to the special interests.

Now, you don't have tax money if people don't have jobs. Now, Washington always assumes an endless supply of tax money, but only if people have jobs, and if you don't have a job [4], you don't pay taxes, you do get Medicaid and you do get on welfare, and that's a triple hit in the economy. The greatest thing we can do is put our people to work [4]. And, believe me, they would like to go to work.

Okay. To get part of the overall plan to solve this problem is a growing, expanding tax base which can only come if you have a growing, expanding job base, and to put it in perspective in the 1950s [5], 90 percent of the goods we bought in this country were made in the good old U.S.A. That number has dropped to only 50 percent of the goods we buy in the U.S.A. are made in the U.S.A., and it will continue to drop as long as we have these stupid, one-sided trade deals [6].

Very quickly I will show you the graphs that show you how the dollar has deteriorated against the deutsche mark and against the yen since 1950 and you will realize who is winning and who is losing [7], and you will also realize—I have to tell you this, that at the end of 1950 our workers made four times as much as the German workers and fifteen times as much as the Japanese workers, and today both the German and Japanese workers make more [8] than our workers.

Now, I got a lot of other subjects I would like to talk to you about, particularly the schools and what have you. We're out of time and I don't want to keep you here longer than you can stand it. So let me just bring this thing down to a conclusion here about how we solve these problems [9]. And this is what it's going to take.

The reason we can't [10] solve these problems now is because Congress doesn't understand the process to go through. But solving these problems is far more complex than putting a man on the moon [11] and yet in Washington they do not follow a rational, logical design and engineering process to improve these programs.

Under our current legislative system [12] in Washington, they start with a noble cause and just an artist's sketch, not a detailed blueprint, massive legislation and nationwide implementation, and nothing works. That's like building a skyscraper from the artist's sketch, and then bringing in people to build it that haven't built a building before, and then later on bringing in the electricians and the plumbers and what have you. That's not the way you build a building, right? It's not the way you design these systems.

Here's what we have to do. We must first create a detailed plan, a blueprint, using the leading experts [13], not lobbyist or special interests. Right now they wouldn't let doctors around the Medicaid plan the last time around. Just think it through now. They've got brilliant poets, bee keepers, what have you, nobody understood medicine. Tomorrow you're going to fly home, let's get some pilots that never flew [13] before and have the experience of our life. I don't think so. I made the point. Next step is to develop preliminary cost estimates [14], which we know won't be very good. Then explain all of this in great detail [15] to the American people, get their okay that this makes sense.

Then we know that one shoe won't fit every foot, but they never figured that out on our social programs because they assume that everything is the same. Can we agree that the perfect health care system for Los Angeles would be quite different from the perfect health care system for a small rural town [16] in Wyoming?

You will find all this out as you go into the next step, pilot testing, optimize and debug [17] these programs, then for the first time you know how well they work. You know what your real costs are and you have made them work through the pilot testing phase, then when you mass produce [17] them across the country, you can do it with certainty that they will work and produce results for you.

Then the last step is recognize and reward people who come up with better ideas. Don't freeze them by law and make them better every day. At that point we can make them work and there's no question [18] about it.

If you elected me president I would put together task forces [19] immediately to go to work on all of this. FDR [20] brought dollar a year men to Washington. We would bring those same fine people but not pay them a dollar this time because they will come as great citizens and work night and day to solve these problems for all of you. You will know every step of the way [20].

Now, we may have a program you love and in pilot testing it turns into a mess and we stop it right there and that won't break us, right? We won't go broke on pilot testing [21].

Now, I would like to learn a little bit from history before we leave today and have you listen to the words of professor Alexander Tyler, Scottish historian who in 1787 said, "A democracy can only exist until the voters discover they can vote themselves money from the public treasury. From that moment on, the majority always votes for the candidates promising people benefits from the treasury" [22]. With the results that a democracy always

collapses [23] under loose fiscal policy. The average age of the world's greatest democracies has been 200 years [24]. George Washington was sworn in 207 years ago. The clock is ticking [24].

I will summarize everything I have said with these words. The budget should be balanced. The treasury should be refilled. The public debt should be reduced and the arrogance of public officials should be controlled.

Do you agree with that? Thank you. As you know, those are not my words. Cicero [25] spoke those words 2000 years ago. Human nature never changes. We always wait, keep the status quo until after a disaster occurs. We can't do that. We've got to have the will to move now, and I know you do, and we've got to get this message across the nation.

I want to thank all of you so much for coming. I want you to know that I'm absolutely committed to this. And I know you are, too. Together, we will get it done. We will be in Valley Forge. We'll all be in Valley Forge next weekend. If you can't be there, watch it on CNN and C-SPAN and we will pick it up where we left off tonight.

But we will, we will leave our children a country where they can climb every mountain [26], forge every stream and follow every rainbow until they find their dream.

Thank you very much. Privilege to be with you. Thank you very much. Thank you very much.

1. "customer is king" (false analogy): The customer is often conned, not treated like a king. Customers' "wants" are manipulated by hot-shot psychologists and marketing experts.

2. "the special interest" and "there's one" (innuendo): Worthless without a name. Is Perot scared to tell us? What good would he be to us if he won't tell us what he knows?

3. "sweat . . . hard working Americans" (mob appeal): And from stockbrokers, realtors, rock musicians, Rosanne, and executives of RJR Nabisco, to name only a few. Some of these people do sweat.

4. "if you don't have a job" and "greatest thing . . . is . . . work" (sweeping generalization): This makes sense. Most work is good, but it must be worthy of a human being.

5. "in the 1950s" (red herring): Doesn't help put problem in perspective, just changes the subject.

6. "stupid . . . trade deals" (hasty generalization): They might be stupid, but deals can't just be forced on our trade partners. Perot oversimplifies ruthlessly.

7. "winning . . . losing" (black or white fallacy): What game is being played? Who's getting the biggest salary? Maybe we enjoy life more?

8. "German and Japanese make more" (false cause): Why not? Do we work as hard?

9. "how we solve these problems": Get ready.

10. "the reason we can't" (false cause): Congress doesn't understand engineering and logic.

11. "more complex than . . . moon": But Perot is going to show us the way! Pooh-pooh?

12. "current legislative system": Does he mean democracy?

13. "first . . . a plan . . . leading experts" and "pilots that never flew" (red herring): Still talking about why current system fails. Another insult to our intelligence.

14. "cost estimates": This process goes on now. No help, no breakthrough here.

15. "explain in . . . detail": The American people are busy trying to make a living, pay taxes. Remember Hillary Clinton's health plan? Nobody understood it, though it might have been good. The mechanic goes over with the customer the costs of fixing his or her car, but it often comes down to trust. The U.S. public doesn't understand military purchasing, a disappointment. We have experts aplenty in Washington already.

16. "small rural town": Point not obvious. What does it mean?

17. "optimize and debug" and "mass produce" (hedging, false analogy): Why didn't we think of this (empty jargon) before?

18. "no question" (begging the question): Why will they work? Because they will!

19. "task forces": We have plenty already.

20. "FDR . . . every step of the way" (appeal to authority, hasty generalization): Will these experts get it right this time?

21. "pilot testing" (false analogy): For example, try nationalizing the airlines or the computer industry as a "pilot test."

22. " 'benefits from the treasury' " (appeal to authority): Assumes people have no conscience.

23. "a democracy always collapses" (ambiguity): So we must turn to fascism?

24. "200 years . . . ticking" (appeal to fear). We'd better hurry!

25. "Cicero" (appeal to authority): Ancient Rome had budget problems? Rome was not a democracy. Balance the budget? That's it?

26. "climb every mountain" (cliché): A fresh, original song when Rodgers and Hammerstein wrote it. A cliché at this point. Clichés indicate a lazy mind.

Much, or even most, of what Perot says rings true. He has a sense of humor and effectively stings the two major parties, but his discourse is centered upon a very weak analogy between business and politics. Though he seems to have a grasp of the economic situation, he is only able, it seems, to tell us what's wrong with "our present legislative system," but not what he will do about it. He intends to use experts and task forces, which are already commonplace in Washington. He has no answers, only slogans and clichés. He gets applause from his abuse of the present system.

But there is something sinister about Perot's attack on the legislative system when it is tied to his almost complete avoidance of solutions. It's as if he wants us to trust him to come up with the right answers and fix all the problems. This is worrisome, for obvious reasons. Blind faith in a leader has a fascist aura.

Government is not a business, but Perot can't get away from the belief that it should respond to a business approach. The army might not be cost effective, for example, but it can be necessary in many situations. The same goes for many government projects.

Perot seems to be a decent man who understandably has let his self-made wealth go to his head. Wealth does not qualify a person to be president. If it did, we could elect Madonna, or John Dupont, or Bill Gates.

Exercise 3.8   What fallacies can you find in the following editorial?

Court Says No to Sly Tactics[5]

Our View: But "partial-birth" debate is revived, benefiting no one

Abortion is a sensitive and painful subject in any context. But particularly so in the case of what critics have labeled partial-birth abortions. These are gruesome procedures, usually performed late in pregnancy, that involve partially extracting a fetus, legs first, cutting the skull and draining its contents.

For more than five years, groups opposing abortion rights have used that gruesome picture as a wedge to limit abortion more generally. They've prodded 30 states into passing vaguely written laws that undermine the right of women and their doctors to choose abortion when necessary. Not accidentally, those laws criminalize less-vivid procedures commonly used for midterm abortions. It's an attempt to ban abortion by stealth.

All of which is reason to celebrate Wednesday's Supreme Court decision striking down those laws. But the court's equivocal 5–4 ruling also ensures that the lies and distortions that have characterized the debate on both sides will be revived—not least in the presidential campaign, where George W. Bush favors partial-birth-abortion bans and Al Gore opposes them.

This is no way to settle abortion law. A broad consensus on abortion already exists. The public strongly supports access to abortion in the first three months of pregnancy, when more than 88% of abortions occur. That hasn't changed much in 30 years. And while the public strongly opposes abortion in the last months of pregnancy 81% in the latest Gallup Poll say it's acceptable when a woman's health is endangered.

Advocates of partial-birth-abortion bans say they want to stop late-term abortion of well-formed fetuses. But there's little to keep them from doing so. They need only heed the polls and previous high court's rulings saying there must be exceptions permitted for the health and the life of the mother.

This they won't do. With the public opposing the partial-birth procedure 66%–29%, they hope the issue can be used to restrict abortion rights more broadly, starting with deceitful laws such as those rejected by the court Wednesday.

---

5. *Source:* Editorial, *USA TODAY,* 29 June 2000. Copyright 2000, USA TODAY. Reprinted with permission.

CHAPTER THREE: INFORMAL FALLACIES

The justices struck down Nebraska's ban on partial-birth procedures, which threatened doctors with 20 years in prison for any act fitting the law's imprecise terms. It provided no exception to protect women's health. And it would prohibit some abortions performed before fetal viability—an area in which states are forbidden to legislate.

But even if states could structure a constitutional ban, as one of the justices in the majority suggested, telling doctors how to treat their patients is a poor way to legislate. The choice of a safe and effective abortion method should be a matter only for the professional judgment of the physician and the preferences of the woman.

In the end, abortion law cannot and should not be changed based on emotional reactions to a rare procedure. But thanks to those who feel they can't win the argument on the merits, hyperbole and hysteria will be with us for some time.

CHAPTER FOUR

The Syllogism

Aristotelian logic, also called *traditional logic* or *syllogistic logic,* was invented in the fourth century B.C. and is still being taught today, despite the development of a more inclusive and powerful symbolic logic in the late nineteenth and early twentieth centuries. Aristotle (ca. 384–322 B.C.) invented the practice of using letters to stand for classes of things, thereby inventing *formal* logic. **Syllogisms,** very natural and very close to the arguments in ordinary language that they formalize, can be extended to deal with a surprising number of forms of arguments, as you will see in the examples and exercises that follow.

The main theoretical drawbacks of syllogistic logic are (1) it can only analyze arguments that have or can be paraphrased into the three-statement syllogism and (2) the problem of **existential import,** which is the assumption that the classes to which the subjects of statements refer must have some members. We do not have to assume this, however, to employ the most useful features of this kind of logic.

4.1 Categorical Statements

In actual controversies, arguments may take many forms. The logician's task is to provide a general method for telling good, valid arguments from bad, invalid ones. As we learned in Chapter 1, arguments are valid or invalid in virtue of their *form* alone, not their subject matter. Now if we just knew which argument forms were valid and which were not *and* if we could recognize the form of an argument just by looking at it, we could always tell if a given argument was valid or not! This would make the analysis and evaluation of argumentative material much easier and more methodical.

As mentioned earlier, Aristotle developed the first such logical system. He was the first person, as far as we know, to use letters to stand for words. He believed that any argument could be expressed in a few categorical statements. A **categorical statement** is about relations of classes or sets of things. There are four kinds of categorical statements, illustrated by the following examples:

A: *All sailors are poets.*

E: *No sailors are poets.*

I: *Some sailors are poets.*

O: *Some sailors are not poets.*

In each statement the subject term is "sailors" and the predicate term is "poets." Taking each kind of statement in turn, we can describe them in this way:

A: "All sailors are poets" is called a **universal affirmative statement:** universal because it's about *all* sailors and affirmative because it affirms that they are poets. It has the form "All *S* are *P*," where *S* stands for the *subject term* (and, incidentally, "sailors"), and *P* stands for the *predicate term* (and, again incidentally, "poets").

E: "No sailors are poets" is called a **universal negative statement.** It is about all sailors and denies that any of them are poets. It has the form "No *S* are *P*."

I: "Some sailors are poets" is called a **particular affirmative statement** because it affirms that some (at least one) sailor is a poet. Its form is "Some *S* are *P*."

O: "Some sailors are not poets" is called a **particular negative statement.** It denies that some particular sailors are poets. It is symbolized "Some *S* are not *P*."

Each statement kind can be pictured by means of Venn diagrams. **Venn diagrams,** invented by John Venn (1834–1923), are a very useful method of representing categorical statements and syllogism. For example, an A-statement ("All *S* are *P*") looks like this:

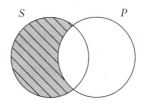

We shade out the space in the S-circle that is *empty*—that is, where the sets involved have no members—leaving all S in the P-circle.

An E-statement, "No S are P," looks like this:

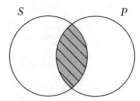

We again shade out the space that is empty, leaving no S in P; that is, all the S is *outside* the P-circle.

An I-statement, "Some S are P," looks like this:

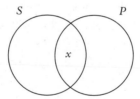

There is at least one member of S in P, represented by x.

An O-statement, "Some S are not P," looks like this:

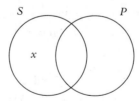

There is at least one S, represented by x, which is *not* in P.

(*Note:* The regions that are shaded out are empty; the regions with an x have at least one member; and the blank regions might have members or not—we don't know.)

The point to these diagrams is that they will help us formally evaluate the validity of a large class of arguments called categorical syllogisms, as we will see later. But first we examine the logical relationships of the four kinds of categorical statements with one another.

Exercise 4.1   Classify the following statements as A, E, I, or O. Identify each sentence as universal or particular, affirmative or negative, and draw its Venn diagram.

1. All cats are felines.

2. No dogs are feline.

3. Some dogs are mutts.

4. Some cats are not pets.

5. Some dogs are not mutts.

6. All dogs are canine.

7. No Methodists are Baptists.

8. Some Democrats are Christians.

9. No Christians are Buddhists.

10. No Democrats are Republicans.

11. All socialists are communists.

12. No Christians are socialists.

13. No married men are philanderers.

14. Some senators are not philanderers.

15. Some heads of state are not women.

16. All battleships are expensive things.

17. Some televangelists are visitors in motels in New Orleans.

18. Some prostitutes are not televangelists.

19. No priests are dishonest people.

20. Some adolescents are immature people.

21. No cats are canines.

22. All Methodists are Christians.

23. Some dogs are not cats.

24. All television commercials are ridiculous things.

25. No signers of the Declaration of Independence were Germans.

26. Some Democratic congressmen are believers in frugality.

27. Some former members of the National Guard are senators from Indiana.

28. No conservatives are liberals.

4.2 Translations

Although many statements are not standard-form categorical statements, they can often be translated into standard form. Consider:

1. Singular statements such as "Socrates is a wise man": We just call "Socrates" "the set of all persons identical to Socrates" and symbolize the whole thing as "All *S* are *W*."

2. Statements that have adjectives, rather than class nouns, as predicates—as in "Socrates is old": We translate this into "Socrates is an old person" and symbolize it as "All *S* are *O*." The set of persons is what we call the *universe of discourse,* the set of all things that we are discussing.

3. Statements without a form of the verb *to be* as in "All birds can fly": We translate this into "All birds are flyers" and symbolize it as "All *B* are *F*."

4. Statements in nonstandard order, as in "Rodents are all nasty": We translate this as "All rodents are nasty things" and symbolize it as "All *R* are *N*."

5. Statements using words other than *all, no, some,* and the like, as in "Every student must turn in his or her paper": This becomes "All students are students who must turn in their papers" and is symbolized as "All *S* are *P*." "I'll argue with anyone" becomes "All people are people I'll argue with" and is symbolized as "All *P* are *A*" (the *A* is for those people I'll argue with—not *P*, which would come out "All *P* are *P*," which obviously would be confusing).

6. Statements with no quantity words such as *all, every,* and *any,* as in "Dogs hate cats": This is translated as "All dogs are haters of cats" and symbolized as "All *D* are *H*."

7. Statements with *only,* as in "Only members may enter": This is translated "All people who may enter are members" and symbolized as "All *E* are *M*." (*Note:* "All *M* are *E*" means "All members are people who may enter," which is *not* equivalent to the original statement.) Another example is "Only elephants have trunks" and is rendered as "All animals with trunks are elephants" and symbolized as "All *T* are *E*."

8. Statements that look nothing at all like standard-form statements: A little ingenuity may be necessary. Consider "Not all dogs are vicious." This just means "Some dogs are not vicious animals," symbolized as "Some *D* are not *V*." Or "Nobody but a veteran could understand" becomes "All people who understand are veterans," which is symbolized as "All *P* are *V*."

9. Parameters: Some statements may be translated readily by means of a well-chosen term. For "The artistic are eccentric," we would use "people" as the parameter: "All artistic people are eccentric people." For "She follows me

everywhere," we would use "places": "All places where I go are places where she follows me." For "I get weak whenever you're near," we use "times": "All times you're near are times when I get weak."

Exercise 4.2   A. Translate the following statements into standard form and then symbolize.

1. Socrates is a philosopher.

2. Aristotle is wise.

3. Democrats are all liberals.

4. Everybody loves a lover.

5. All that glitters is not gold.

6. There's no time like the present.

7. No news is good news.

8. What's past is prologue.

9. Dogs are man's best friend.

10. He who hesitates is lost.

11. Cowboys love their horses.

12. Women are fickle.

13. Clint Eastwood is a star.

14. Users are losers.

15. The winner is Miss Utah.

16. None but the brave deserves the fair.

17. Only a fool never changes her mind.

18. Only nonsmokers may sit in this section.

19. These are the times that try one's soul.

20. Not all dogs are vicious.

21. Not everyone is honest.

22. We'll meet tomorrow.

23. Cybill Shepherd is glamorous.

24. Candy is fattening.

25. Whenever you're ready, I am, too.

26. Trespassers will be shot.

27. Shoplifters will be prosecuted.

28. There's no place like home.

29. Only the perpetrator could know where the victim was buried.

30. Not all businessmen are greedy.

31. Nobody knows the trouble I've seen.

32. Nobody knows you when you're down and out.

33. When you're smiling, the whole world smiles with you.

34. Cry and you cry alone.

35. Tomorrow is another day.

36. Nobody likes a sore loser.

37. Oatmeal. It's the right thing to do.

38. I'm not Herb.

39. Nothing ventured, nothing gained.

40. Of making many books there is no end.

41. The poor man's wisdom is despised.

42. When the swallows come back to Capistrano, I'll be coming back to you.

43. The course of true love never did run smooth.

44. Where there's smoke, there's fire.

45. We make money the old-fashioned way.

46. There's no business like show business.

47. Aristotle invented formal logic.

48. Beauty is as beauty does.

49. To the victor belong the spoils.

50. My house is your house.

51. Every dog has his day.

52. Life's but a passing shadow.

53. Nobody cares.

54. All men are created equal.

55. Mike has a red Mustang.

56. The poor are with you always.

57. Blessed are the meek.

58. Only the pure in heart may enter here.

59. Those under 21 years of age may not buy alcoholic beverages.

60. Nobody but a child could understand.

61. Some companies don't care how they poison the environment.

62. Some big American companies have operations in South Africa.

63. No American company should support apartheid.

64. John Wayne was patriotic.

65. Bob Geldof initiated LiveAid.

66. Bob Geldof was never one of the Rolling Stones.

67. Some farmers have lost their farms.

68. Not all stock traders are honest.

69. Inside traders are all dishonest.

70. Former Attorney General John Mitchell went to jail.

71. Friends of William Bennett wished him luck with the drug problem.

72. Every time I get a raise, my insurance goes up.

73. Congresswomen deserve a raise.

74. Not only congresswomen deserve a raise.

75. Not every multinational corporation is based in the United States.

76. Plato is a philosopher.

77. Socrates is immortal.

78. Nobody is cuter than Britney Spears.

79. Women are indecisive.

80. Women are not indecisive.

81. Not everyone is dishonest.

82. I really enjoy old Bob Hope movies.

83. Boozers are losers.

84. Nobody skates as well as Katarina Witt.

85. Whenever you're ready, so am I.

86. All's well that ends well.

87. There's no place like home.

88. Only veterans are eligible.

89. None but the lonely heart can know my sorrow.

90. Nobody likes pizza as much as I do.

91. I love Whitney Houston.

92. Nobody likes a smart aleck.

93. Ross Perot has big ears.

94. Only those who forsake all hope may enter here.

95. I'll match wits with anyone here.

96. Not all southerners are bigoted.

97. Only the lonely can know how I feel tonight.

98. Whither thou goest, I will go.

99. Someday you'll fall in love.

100. Nobody but Ted Koppel could interview the Ayatollah.

B. Find some categorical statements in the following editorial. Translate them into standard form as A-, E-, I-, or O-statements.

Editorial from the *Telegram & Gazette*[1]

The acquittal of Dr. Jack Kevorkian in a test case of Michigan's hastily enacted law prohibiting assisted suicide will serve to widen the public debate on this difficult and troubling subject.

So will a recent ruling by a federal judge in Washington state that assisted suicide—along with abortion—is included within the constitutional right to privacy.

Jurors in the Kevorkian case cited uncertainties over the doctor's motives, the wisdom of the two-year-old law under which he had been prosecuted and the precise location of where he had helped a 30-year-old man end his suffering from a degenerative nerve disease.

Kevorkian's opponents say the jury took advantage of loopholes in the law, and that a wave of assisted suicides will follow.

Kevorkian himself underscored the dilemma: "Obviously, what are needed are guidelines on this, and that is the first priority to me."

Establishing those guidelines will be a long, grueling and divisive process.

For some physicians, abetting death for any reason goes against the grain in a profession dedicated to sustaining life. Yet compassion

---

1. *Source:* Editorial, *Telegram & Gazette* (Worcester, Mass.) 6 May 1994. Editorial reproduced with permission of the *Telegram & Gazette,* Worcester, Mass.

and the urge to ease hopeless suffering are also age-old facets of the healer's art.

With more patients and their relatives opting to decline extraordinary life-support procedures in terminal situations, there is a gradual shift in public opinion on how we face death. One poll found that 57 percent of Americans consider it proper for physicians to provide lethal pills or, in extreme cases, to administer a lethal injection.

It will be the task of medical ethicists, physicians, lawmakers and legal experts to consider the many issues surrounding this life-and-death matter.

But the fact that the Michigan jury refused to see criminality in Kevorkian's action, coupled with the Washington court ruling, underscores growing public approval of physician-assisted suicide in certain types of cases.

While realizing the immense complexity of this issue, we agree with those who prefer death with dignity to suffering without hope.

4.3 Squares of Opposition

The four kinds of categorical statements have certain logical relationships to one another, regardless of their subject matter. These formal relationships can be illustrated by means of the traditional square of opposition (Figure 4.1).

It should be obvious that if A is true, O cannot be true. For example, if "All sailors are poets," it cannot be true that "Some sailors are not poets," and vice versa. A and O are **contradictories** of each other.

Likewise, for E and I, if "No sailors are poets," it cannot be true that "Some sailors are poets." So E and I are also contradictories. If E is true, O must be true (if *S* and *P* have members).

If "All sailors are poets," then "Some sailors are poets" (given that there *are* some sailors). But if "Some sailors are not poets," it does *not* follow that "All sailors are poets." This relation between A and I is called **subalternation** (A is superaltern and I is subaltern). The same relation holds between E and O: If "No sailors are poets," then "Some sailors are not poets" (if, again, we assume there are sailors); but from "Some sailors are not poets," it does not follow that "No sailors are poets."

A and E are **contraries.** If "All sailors are poets," it cannot also be true that "No sailors are poets" (if we assume there are sailors). *But* A and E may both be false: It can happen that "All sailors are poets" is false (because "Some sailors are not poets") and also false that "No sailors are poets" (because "Some sailors *are* poets"). Contraries can both be false but cannot both be true.

I and O are **subcontraries.** They cannot both be false, but both may be true. If it is false that "Some sailors are poets," it must be true that "Some sailors are not

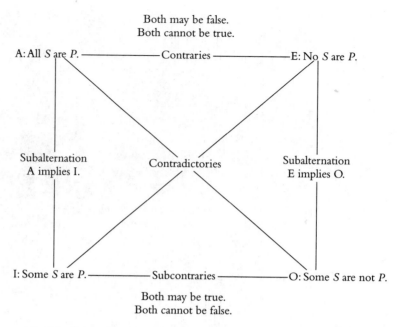

Both may be false.
Both cannot be true.

A: All *S* are *P.* —————— Contraries —————— E: No *S* are *P.*

Subalternation
A implies I.

Contradictories

Subalternation
E implies O.

I: Some *S* are *P.* ————— Subcontraries ————— O: Some *S* are not *P.*

Both may be true.
Both cannot be false.

Figure 4.1   Traditional Square of Opposition

poets" and vice versa. But it can happen that "Some sailors are poets," and "Some sailors are not poets."

These relationships provide us with several means of what logicians call **immediate inference.** If we know a certain A-form categorical statement is true, we can infer quite a few other statements by means of the square of opposition.

The **traditional square of opposition,** as we have seen, assumes that there exist things in the sets referred to in categorical statements. This is what logicians call the **existential viewpoint.** Modern symbolic logic does not make this assumption, however, and so we have a very streamlined modern square of opposition (Figure 4.2).

According to the modern square of opposition, A and O are still contradictories, as are E and I. For example:

All vampires are monsters

still contradicts

Some vampires are not monsters

whether there are any vampires or not.

No vampires are monsters

still contradicts

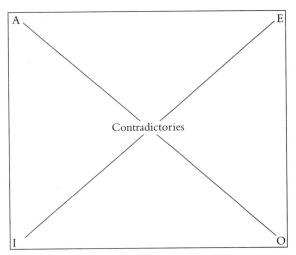

Figure 4.2   Modern Square of Opposition

Some vampires are monsters.

If one is true—whether there are any vampires or not—the other is false, but A and I are no longer contraries.

All vampires are monsters

does not imply that

Some vampires are monsters

because A does not, under the hypothetical viewpoint, have existential import.

To understand this intuitively, realize that one might say, "Yes, yes, all vampires are monsters, if there were any, but there aren't, and it is *not* true to say that *some* are." The same is true with E and O.

Nor does contrariety survive under the hypothetical viewpoint. Both A and E might be false, but both also might be true:

All vampires are monsters

might be true, and

No vampires are monsters

might be true as well. If nothing is a vampire, nothing is a vampire that is not a monster!

So it makes a difference whether we make the *existential presupposition* that all sets have members, as Aristotle did. In actual contexts we have to choose between the traditional square and the modern one on the basis of which seems to fit the kinds of things we are talking about.

Execise 4.3   A. This exercise involves using squares of opposition.

1. Using the traditional square of opposition, assume that the statements in the first column are *false*. What can you infer about the truth of the statements in the remaining column?

   (1) E   I O A
   (2) A   E O I
   (3) I   E O A
   (4) O   E I A

2. Using the modern square of opposition, assume that the statements in the first column are *true*. What can you infer about the truth of the statements in the remaining column?

   (1) E   I O A
   (2) I   E O A
   (3) O   I E A
   (4) A   E I O

B. Assume that the classes in the following statements have members. If the first statement is true, what can be inferred about the other statements (T or F)?

1. All cats are feline. No cats are feline. Some cats are feline.

2. No dogs are feline. Some dogs are not feline. Some dogs are feline.

3. Some ministers are television personalities. No ministers are television personalities. All ministers are television personalities.

4. Some fruits are not apples. All fruits are apples. Some fruits are apples.

5. All sports are games. No sports are games. Some sports are not games.

6. No candidates are acceptable ones. Some candidates are acceptable ones. All candidates are acceptable ones.

7. Some fires are accidents. Some fires are not accidents. No fires are accidents.

8. Some men are jerks. No men are jerks. All men are jerks.

9. Some actors are not vain people. All actors are vain people. No actors are vain people.

10. No musicians are religious people. Some musicians are not religious people. All musicians are religious people.

11. All senators are honest people. Some senators are not honest people. No senators are honest people.

12. Some murderers are people who should be executed. No murderers are people who should be executed. Some murderers are not people who should be executed.

13. All fetuses are babies. Some fetuses are babies. No fetuses are babies.

14. No fetuses are persons. Some fetuses are persons. All fetuses are persons.

15. All Down syndrome babies are babies who should be allowed to die. Some Down syndrome babies are babies who should be allowed to die. No Down syndrome babies are babies who should be allowed to die.

16. Some very sick people are people who should be euthanized. No very sick people are people who should be euthanized. All very sick people are people who should be euthanized.

17. All AIDS victims are people who die. Some AIDS victims are not people who die. No AIDS victims are people who die.

18. Some young people are alcoholics. Some young people are not alcoholics. All young people are alcoholics.

19. All smokers are people who will die. Some smokers are people who will not die. No smokers are people who will die.

20. Some Mississippians are farmers. No Mississippians are farmers. All Mississippians are farmers.

C. Assume that none of the classes in Exercise B have members. Then, if the first statement is true, what can be inferred about the others (T or F)?

D. Restate some of the statements in the following editorial as standard-form categorical statements. For each one, tell whether it is assumed that the classes involved have members.

Editorial from the *Boston Herald*[2]

Common decency should have prevented NBC Nightly News from broadcasting the autopsy photo of President John F. Kennedy earlier this week.

Clearly, a picture can sometimes tell a story more dramatically than prose.

But not this time. John Kennedy has been dead nearly 30 years. The picture showed nothing new, nothing that the public doesn't already know, nothing that words cannot illustrate better, and nothing to sustain or refute continuing rumor.

---

2. *Source:* Editorial, *Boston Herald,* 23 May 1992. Reproduced with permission.

> The full, close-up photograph of the late president's face, neck and head, a photograph taken illicitly by a Secret Service technician, served only to shock. Rep. Joseph P. Kennedy, nephew of the late president, railed against NBC on the House floor for broadcasting the graphic photo.
>
> "I want the people of this chamber to know how outrageous an act I feel that was, how harmful to my family I feel that was, how harmful I hope that the American people feel that was."
>
> NBC wasn't covering the news when it aired this photo. It was capitalizing on it. News coverage should be legitimate, fair, and relevant. Last Monday, NBC Nightly News was none of these.

4.4 Immediate Inference

We can infer certain things from just one statement:

1. **Conversion:** *We construct the converse of a categorical statement by simply switching subject and predicate.* The converse of "All S are P" is "All P are S," which does *not* follow. "Some P are S" follows by limitation. The converse of "No S are P" is "No P are S," which follows. The converse of "Some S are P" is "Some P are S," which follows. The converse of "Some S are not P" is "Some P are not S," which does *not* follow.

2. **Obversion:** *We construct the obverse of a statement by changing it from affirmative to negative, or from negative to affirmative, and negating the predicate term.* The obverse of "All S are P" is "No S are non-P," which follows. The obverse of "No S are P" is "All S are non-P," which follows. The obverse of "Some S are P" is "Some S are not non-P," which follows. The obverse of "Some S are not P" is "Some S are non-P," which follows. So the obverse *always* follows and is equivalent to the original statement.

3. **Contraposition:** *We form the contrapositive of a statement by switching subject and predicate and negating both.* The contrapositive of "All S are P" is "All non-P are non-S," which follows. The contrapositive of "No S are P" is "No non-P are non-S," which does *not* follow. The contrapositive of "No S are P" is "No non-P are non-S," which does *not* follow. The contrapositive of "Some S are P" is "Some non-P are non-S," which does *not* follow.

Table 4.1 provides a summary.

Some of the inferences in Table 4.1 are obvious, and some are not. Some such sentences can be found only in government documents, especially income-tax instructions. Here are some examples:

Table 4.1 Summary: Immediate Inference

	Converse	*Obverse*	*Contrapositive*
All *S* are *P*.	Some *P* are *S*. (by limitation)	No *S* are non-*P*.	All non-*P* are non-*S*.
No *S* are *P*.	No *P* are *S*.	All *S* are non-*P*.	
Some *S* are *P*.	Some *P* are *S*.	Some *S* are not non-*P*.	
Some *S* are not *P*.		Some *S* are non-*P*.	Some non-*P* are not non-*S*.

All Scots are Britons.

It follows, by limitation, that "Some Britons are Scots" (converse), that "No Scot is a non-Briton" (obverse), that "All non-Britons are non-Scots" (contrapositive), and that "Some Britons are Scots," by limitation.

No Scots are Protestants. No Protestants are Scots (converse), and all Scots are non-Protestants (obverse).

Some Scots are Protestants. So some Protestants are Scots (converse), and some Scots are not non-Protestants (obverse).

Some Scots are not Protestants. So some Scots are non-Protestants (obverse), and some non-Protestants are not non-Scots (contrapositive).

Exercise 4.4   A. Assume that the sets in the following exercises have members. If the first statement is true, what can be inferred about the others?

1. All frogs are amphibians. No frog is a nonamphibian. All nonamphibians are nonfrogs. Some frogs are not amphibians.

2. No frogs are reptiles. No reptiles are frogs. All frogs are nonreptiles. Some frogs are not reptiles.

3. Some southerners are Georgians. Some Georgians are southerners. Some southerners are not non-Georgians. All southerners are Georgians.

4. Some southerners are not Georgians. Some southerners are non-Georgians. Some non-Georgians are not nonsoutherners. All southerners are Georgians.

5. All cats are furry animals. Some cats are not furry animals. All nonfurry animals are noncats. No cat is a nonfurry animal.

6. No cats are reptiles. Some cats are reptiles. No reptiles are cats. All cats are nonreptiles.

7. Some teachers are women. No women are teachers. Some teachers are not nonwomen. Some women are teachers.

8. Some teachers are not men. No teachers are men. Some teachers are non-men. Some nonmen are not nonteachers.

9. Some heads of households are not men. All heads of households are men. Some heads of households are nonmen. Some nonmen are not nonheads of households.

10. All logic courses are worthwhile things. Some logic courses are not worthwhile things. No logic course is a nonworthwhile thing. No logic course is a worthwhile thing.

11. Some AIDS victims are addicts. Some addicts are AIDS victims. All addicts are AIDS victims. Some AIDS victims are not nonaddicts.

12. All alcoholics are drivers. Some alcoholics are not drivers. All nondrivers are nonalcoholics. No alcoholic is a nondriver.

13. Some businessmen are ethical people. No ethical people are businessmen. Some businessmen are not nonethical people. Some ethical people are businessmen.

14. No birth control devices are infallible devices. Some birth control devices are infallible devices. No infallible devices are birth control devices. All birth control devices are noninfallible devices.

15. Some prisoners are innocent people. Some innocent people are prisoners. Some prisoners are not noninnocent people. All prisoners are innocent people.

16. All dogs are mammals. No dog is a mammal. Some dogs are not mammals. All nonmammals are nondogs.

17. Some teachers are men. No men are teachers. Some teachers are not nonmen. Some nonmen are teachers.

18. Some heads of households are not men. All heads of households are men. Some nonmen are not nonheads of households. No heads of households are men.

19. No cats are dogs. No dogs are cats. All cats are nondogs. Some cats are dogs.

20. All Democrats are non-Republicans. Some Democrats are Republicans. No Democrats are Republicans. No Republicans are Democrats.

B. In any of Exercise A, does it matter whether you assume that the classes in question have members? Where?

C. Assume the information on the following Fulbright scholarship form is true. Translate the eligibility requirements into categorical statements. What can be inferred about the eligibility of the applicants described after the following sample exercise?

Suppose applicant 1 is a permanent resident at the time of application but is not yet a U.S. citizen.

Answer: Since U.S. citizenship is required and permanent resident status is not sufficient, applicant 1 is not eligible for an award.

1. Applicant 1 received a Fulbright award only two years before the starting date of the new award.

2. Applicant 2 lived abroad for the ten years immediately preceding this application.

3. Applicant 3 wants support for her dissertation research abroad.

4. Applicant 4 is a permanent U.S. resident with U.S. citizenship.

5. Applicant 5 wants a grant to attend a professional congress.

Fulbright Scholar Awards Abroad[3]

Introduction

The Fulbright Scholar Program is a collection of country and regional programs, an array of opportunities for lecturing and researching abroad. About 1,000 awards in over 100 countries are available. The grants are distributed by country and region, vary in financial support and length of stay, and sometimes tied to very specific appointments, and at other times are unrestricted. The general announcement of award opportunities is issued in the spring. Occasionally, supplemental announcements are released later in the year.

Fulbright awards are normally granted for periods ranging from two to twelve months. Lecturing awards are usually not available for the summer months only, nor are grants available for attendance at professional congresses and meetings. . . .

Basic Eligibility Requirements

- U.S. citizenship at the time of application; status as a permanent resident is not sufficient.

- For lecturing—in most instances, a doctoral degree at the time of application and postdoctoral college or university teaching experience at the level and in the field in which the lectureship is sought.

- For research—a doctoral degree at the time of application or, in some fields, recognized professional standing as demonstrated by experience, publications, compositions, exhibitions, etc.

- In some cases, foreign language proficiency as specified in the awards announcement.

---

3. *Source:* Council for International Exchange of Scholars, Washington, D. C.

- Medical clearance is required for the issuance of a grant and a medical report will be requested of successful candidates at a later date. . . .

Other Factors Affecting Eligibility

Applicants in the performing and creative arts are usually expected to have the terminal degree in their fields. This also may be the case for certain professional fields, such as library science. For junior lecturing awards in Teaching English as a Foreign Language, a master's degree in TEFL or TESOL may be sufficient.

- Applicants who have held previous Fulbright scholar awards are eligible to apply if three years will have elapsed between the a date of one award and the starting date of the new award. Preference, however, is given to applicants who have not already had lecturing or research grants.

- Scholars who have already held two (or more) Fulbright scholar awards are not prohibited from making application for an additional grant. Applicants should keep in mind, however,

that preference will be given to those who have not participated in the program and who do not have substantial recent experience abroad.

- Persons who have lived abroad for the full ten–year period immediately preceding application are not eligible to apply.

- Predoctoral students interested in financial support for dissertation research abroad are not eligible to apply under this program. Research grants announced through CIES cannot be used for dissertation purposes. See awards announcement for suggestions of funding agencies for doctoral dissertations or graduate study abroad.

The Fulbright Program is funded and administered by the United States Information Agency. Funding is also provided by participating governments and cost sharing by host institutions in the U.S. and many countries. The presidentially-appointed J. William Fulbright Foreign Scholarship Board is responsible providing policy guidance for the program and making the final selection of all grantees.

4.5 Categorical Syllogism

A **categorical syllogism** has three categorical statements. First is the **major premise,** which contains the **major term,** which is the **predicate** of the conclusion. Next is the **minor premise,** which contains the **minor term,** which is the **subject** of the conclusion. Last comes the **conclusion.** For example:

(A) *All poets are mariners. [major premise]*

(A) <u>*All mariners are sailors. [minor premise]*</u>

(A) *(Therefore) All sailors are poets. [conclusion]*

This syllogism is in standard form: major premise, minor premise, conclusion. "Poets" is the major term, the predicate of the conclusion. "Sailors" is the minor term, the subject of the conclusion. "Mariners" is the middle term, which connects the major and minor terms.

The **mood** of a syllogism is a list of the statement forms involved. The syllogism above has a mood of AAA because all its statements are type A. The **figure** of a syllogism depends upon the arrangement of the middle term. There are four possible figures:

	1			2			3			4	
M	*P*		*P*	*M*		*M*	*P*		*P*	*M*
<u>*S*</u>	<u>*M*</u>		<u>*S*</u>	<u>*M*</u>		<u>*M*</u>	<u>*S*</u>		<u>*M*</u>	<u>*S*</u>
S	*P*		*S*	*P*		*S*	*P*		*S*	*P*

Figure 4.3 illustrates it more simply. The figure of the preceding example is

P   *M*

<u>*M*   *S*</u>

S   *P*

which is the fourth figure in Figure 4.3.

Our example, then, is a AAA-4 syllogism. Finding the mood and figure of a syllogism specifies it completely. A syllogism has three statements, each of which can be one of four possible statement-forms (A, E, I, or O), which means that there are $4 \times 4 \times 4 = 64$ possible moods. There are four possible figures (1, 2, 3, or 4), so there are $64 \times 4 = 256$ possible syllogisms.

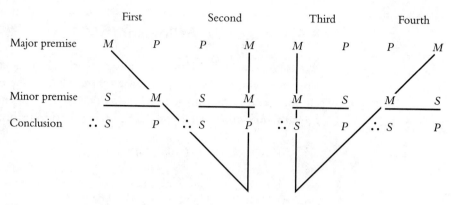

Figure 4.3   The Four Figures of the Syllogism

Logicians have made a list of syllogisms that are valid. One way to determine whether a given argument is valid is to determine its mood and figure and then check the following list:

VALID SYLLOGISMS

AAA–1	EAE–2	IAI–3	AEE–4
EAE–1	AEE–2	AII–3	IAI–4
AII–1	EIO–2	OAO–3	EIO–4
EIO–1	AOO–2	EIO–3	

(This list presupposes that the sets involved have members—more on this later.) Is the following syllogism valid?

All mammals are warm-blooded creatures.

Some vertebrates are mammals.

Therefore, some vertebrates are warm-blooded creatures.

This has the form

All M are W

Some V are M

∴ *Some V are W*

which has the mood AII and the figure 1. So this is an AII-1 syllogism, which according to our list is valid.

Here's another example:

All senators are congressmen.

No senators are representatives.

Therefore, no congressmen are representatives.

This has the form

All S are C.

No S are R.

∴ *No C are R.*

This is not in standard form, however. The minor premise (which contains the minor term *C*) and the major premise (which contains *R*) must be reversed, to give

No S are R

All S are C

∴ *No C are R*

which has the mood EAE and the figure 3. EAE-3 is *not* on the list, so the syllogism is invalid.

The whole point to formal syllogistic logic is simply this: Given any argument in ordinary language, if it can be expressed as a syllogism, we can tell whether it is valid by looking at its form alone—no matter what its content! Whether the premises are true or not is of course another very important matter; not all valid arguments are sound. (*Remember:* A **sound argument** must be valid and have true premises.)

Furthermore, not every argument can be expressed as a categorical syllogism. To deal with those that cannot, we need a more powerful logical system. But first we discuss an alternative method of testing the validity of categorical syllogisms: the Venn diagram.

Exercise 4.5   Symbolize each argument in standard form and tell the mood and figure. Then check the list of valid syllogisms to see whether it is valid.

1. All cats are feline; no felines are dogs; therefore, all cats are dogs.

2. No cats are vegetables; all turnips are vegetables; so no cats are turnips.

3. Some vegetables are carrots; no carrots are animals; so some vegetables are not animals.

4. Some cats are not poets; all poets are humans; so no cats are humans.

5. All poets are musicians; no musicians are vegetables; so no poets are vegetables.

6. No actors are gentlemen; some gentlemen are not vegetables; so some actors are not vegetables.

7. All sailors are musicians; some musicians are poets; so some sailors are poets.

8. No coaches are dishonest people; some dishonest people are women; so some women are not coaches.

9. All terriers are dogs; no cats are dogs; so no cats are terriers.

10. All parrots are birds; no birds are mammals; so no parrots are mammals.

11. All politicians are dishonest; no dishonest people are reliable; therefore, no politician is reliable.

12. No Democrats are Republicans; all Republicans are conservatives; so no Democrats are conservatives.

13. Some addicts are AIDS victims; no AIDS victims are priests; so some addicts are not priests.

14. No passengers were informed. Some state department employees were informed. So no passengers were state department employees.

15. All fetuses are babies. All babies are persons. So all fetuses are persons.

16. No congresswoman was one who voted for the pay increase; all those who voted for the pay increase are greedy people; so no congresswoman is a greedy person.

17. No syllogism on the list is an invalid syllogism. Some of these syllogisms are on the list. So some of these syllogisms are not invalid.

18. Some multinational corporations are based in Japan. All those corporations based in Japan are not regulated by U.S. laws. So some multinational corporations are not regulated by U.S. laws.

19. Some American-controlled multinationals are companies operating in South Africa. Companies operating in South Africa are companies that took advantage of the blacks (because apartheid made it possible to pay blacks very low wages). So some American-controlled multinationals are companies that took advantage of blacks in South Africa.

20. American companies that supported apartheid for high profits are immoral companies. Some American companies are companies that supported apartheid for high profits (IBM, Ford, Exxon, and over 300 others). So some American companies are immoral companies.

21. All dogs are canines. No canines are cats. So no cats are dogs.

22. Some Republicans are poets; no poets are boxers. So no Republicans are boxers.

23. All national guardsmen are patriotic people. Some senators are national guardsmen. So some senators are patriotic people.

24. All musicians are poets. So no musicians are actors, because no actors are poets.

25. Some sailors are not athletes. All sailors are Republicans. So some athletes are not Republicans.

4.6 Venn Diagrams

Another way to test the validity of syllogisms is the Venn diagram. In Section 4.1 we symbolized each type of categorical statement by means of two circles. To symbolize a whole argument, which necessarily includes three terms, we use three circles.

Consider the following argument:

All mariners are poets

All sailors are mariners

∴ *All sailors are poets*

that has the form

All M are P.

All S are M.

∴ *All S are P.*

This is an AAA-1 syllogism—which, from the list in Section 4.5, we know is valid.

We can also use the following method: First draw three circles and label them *S, P,* and *M:*

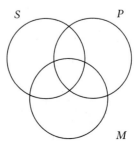

Then diagram the first statement (the major premise), "All *M* are *P*":

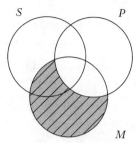

shading out all *M*'s not in *P.* Next diagram the second statement (the minor premise), "All *S* are *M*":

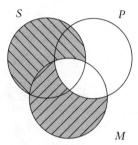

We do not diagram the conclusion. Instead, we look to see if the conclusion, "All *S* are *P*," has appeared already; it has. All the *S* that's left is in *P,* so our argument is valid.

To make this clear, let's number each section of the final diagram:

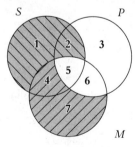

Section 1 is empty; 2 is empty; 3 contains all the *P*'s that are not *S*'s or *M*'s; 4 is empty; 5 contains all *S*'s that are also both *P*'s and *M*'s; 6 contains all *M*'s that are *P*'s; and 7 is empty. Clearly, all the *S*'s there are, are in section 5, and all these *S*'s are also *P*'s. So "All *S* are *P*," which is the conclusion we were seeking.

Now let's consider this syllogism:

Some preachers are Methodists.	*which has*	*Some P are M.*
No Methodists are spies.	*the form*	*No M are S.*
∴ *Some spies are not preachers.*		*Some S are not P.*

This is an IEO-4 syllogism, which is invalid according to our list. But let's test it with a Venn diagram. (When you have a universal premise and a particular one, always diagram the universal statement first. You'll see why.) The universal premise here is "No *M* are *S*":

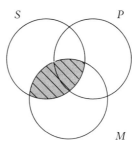

Then diagram "Some *P* are *M*":

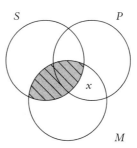

(If we had tried to diagram "Some *P* are *M*" first, we wouldn't have known where to put the *x*.) And now we ask: Is there some *S* that is not *P*? No. So the argument is invalid.

Now let's try this syllogism:

All monkeys are primates.	*All M are P.*
Some simians are monkeys.	*Some S are M.*
∴ *Some simians are primates.*	*Some S are P.*

This is an AII-1 syllogism, which is valid, but let's test it with a Venn diagram. Diagram "All *M* are *P*" (the universal premise is always first):

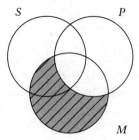

Then diagram "Some *S* are *M*":

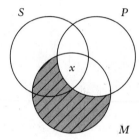

Now we ask: Is there some *S* that are *P*? Yes; it is represented by *x*. So the conclusion follows and the syllogism is valid.

Here's one more example:

All actors are thespians.	*All A are T.*
Some thespians are diabetics.	*Some T are D.*
∴ *Some actors are diabetics.*	*Some A are D.*

This is an AII-4 syllogism, which is invalid, but let's test it with a Venn diagram. First diagram "All *A* are *T*":

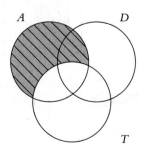

then diagram "Some *T* are *D*":

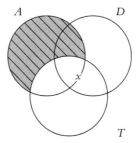

(*Note:* The *x* goes on the *A*-line because, although we know it goes in both *T* and *D*, we don't know whether it goes in *A*.) The *x* is not clearly in *A*, so the argument is invalid.

Exercise 4.6   A. Test each syllogism in Exercise 4.5 with a Venn diagram.
B. Put each syllogism into standard form, name its mood and figure, and test its validity with a Venn diagram.

1. All martyrs are Christians. All Christians are religious people. So all martyrs are religious people.

2. Some judges are conservatives. All conservatives are honest people. So some judges are honest people.

3. Some senators are plagiarists. No plagiarists are honest people. So some senators are not honest.

4. Some dogs are males. All dogs are vertebrates. So some males are vertebrates.

5. Some cats are not Persians. No Persians are Siamese. So some cats are not Siamese.

6. Some Democrats are conservatives. Some Republicans are conservatives. So some Democrats are Republicans.

7. Some cowboys are Texans. All cowboys are equestrians. So some Texans are tough people.

8. Some cowboys are not Texans. All cowboys are equestrians. So some Texans are not equestrians.

9. No Democrats are Republicans. All Republicans are conservatives. So no Democrats are conservatives.

10. No Democrats are Republicans. All conservatives are Republicans. So no Democrats are conservatives.

11. No poets are nonmusicians. Some musicians are nonvegetables. So all poets are nonvegetables.

12. No parrots are nonbirds. All nonmammals are nonbirds. So all nonmammals are nonparrots.

13. Some sailors are nonpirates. No sailor is a nonmariner. So some mariners are not nonpirates.

14. No cats are nonfelines. All dogs are nonfeline. So all dogs are noncats.

15. Some actors are not nongentlemen. All nongentlemen are nonmen. So some actors are not men.

16. All coaches are honest. Some dishonest people are women. So some coaches are not women.

17. All nonbirds are nonparrots. All birds are nonmammals. So all parrots are nonmammals.

18. No nonsailors are nonmusicians. Some poets are musicians. So some sailors are not nonpoets.

19. All police are marksmen. Some marksmen are sharpshooters. So some police are not nonsharpshooters.

20. Some cowboys are non-Texans. No Texan is a nonequestrian. So some cowboys are not equestrians.

21. Some congressmen are not wealthy. No senator is a noncongressman. So some senators are not wealthy.

22. Some AIDS victims are addicts. Some addicts are not rational. So some AIDS victims are irrational.

23. All NRA members are gun owners. Some gun owners are madmen. So some NRA members are madmen.

24. No New Yorkers are rude. Some rude people are bigots. So no New Yorkers are bigots.

25. Some coaches pressure professors to give their players passing grades. Anyone who'd do that is not ethical. So some coaches are unethical.

4.7 Rules and Formal Fallacies of the Syllogism

We have still another method of determining the validity of a categorical syllogism, called the rules of the syllogism.

As we pointed out earlier, A-statements and I-statements are *affirmative,* and E-statements and O-statements are *negative.* Another idea that is necessary for the "rules" method is that of **distribution.** A statement distributes a term if and only if it refers to *all* members of the class which that term designates. For example, the A-statement

All mariners are sailors

distributes the term "mariners," saying something about *all* of them, and the E-statement

No mariners are sailors

also distributes the term "mariners" because it says about *all* mariners that every one is *not* a sailor. Furthermore, it also distributes "sailors" because it says that *no* sailor can be a mariner.

An I-statement such as

Some mariners are sailors

is *undistributed* in both terms. It says nothing about *all* mariners nor about all sailors.

Finally, an O-statement such as

Some mariners are not sailors

says nothing about all mariners, but it does (oddly enough) refer to all sailors, saying that *none* of them is any one of the mariners referred to by the subject term.

The subject term is distributed in A- and E-statements, and E-statements distribute both subject and predicate terms. I-statements distribute neither subject nor predicate term, and O-statements distribute the predicate term. The following sums this all up:

A: All S are P.
  Distributes S.

E: No S are P.
  Distributes both S and P.

I: Some S are P.
  Distributes neither.

O: Some S are not P.
  Distributes P.

A valid categorical syllogism follows the next six rules.

1. *There must be exactly three terms, each of which has the same meaning throughout the syllogism.* Breaking this rule commits the **fallacy of four terms.** (Some logicians would insist that the argument in question cannot in this case be a syllogism at all.) For example:

> All politicians are people who want fame.
>
> All famous people are well-known people.
>
> ∴ All politicians are well-known people.

"People who want fame" does not mean the same as "famous people."

2. *The middle term must be distributed in at least one premise.* Breaking this rule commits the **fallacy of the undistributed middle.** For example:

> Some Democrats are honest people.
>
> Some Republicans are honest people.
>
> ∴ Some Democrats are Republicans.

The middle term "honest people" is not distributed in the premises and could therefore refer to entirely distinct parts (subclasses) of the other two terms.

3. *A term distributed in the conclusion must also be distributed in the premises.* Breaking this rule is either the **fallacy of the illicit minor** or the **fallacy of the illicit major.** For example:

> No cats are realtors.
>
> All cats are vertebrates.
>
> ∴ No vertebrates are realtors.

Here the minor term "vertebrates" is distributed in the conclusion (an E-statement) but not in the premises, where it is the predicate of an A-claim. Since the class of vertebrates is not referred to as a whole in the premises, it cannot be referred to in the conclusion. This is an example of the illicit minor fallacy.

4. *There cannot be two negative premises.* Breaking this rule commits the **fallacy of exclusive premises.** For example:

> No smokers are healthy people.
>
> No Olympic contenders are smokers.
>
> ∴ No Olympic contenders are healthy people.

Here the premises exclude too much, and no conclusion can be derived from them.

5. *If either premise is negative, the conclusion must be negative as well.* Breaking this rule is the **fallacy of drawing an affirmative conclusion from a negative premise.**

For example:

> *No sailors are fliers.*
>
> *Some fighters are sailors.*
>
> ∴ *Some fighters are fliers.*

The *exclusion* of sailors from the class of fliers does not justify the *inclusion* of fighters in that class.

6. *A particular conclusion (I or O) cannot follow from two universal premises.* The violation of this rule is called the **existential fallacy.** For example:

> *All people without sin are people who may cast stones.*
>
> *No dentists are people who may cast stones.*
>
> ∴ *Some dentists are people who are not without sin.*

This is invalid because its conclusion asserts that there are people without sin, while its premises do *not* assert that. For example:

> *All judges are lawyers.*
>
> *No people without sin are lawyers.*
>
> ∴ *Some people without sin are not judges.*

These rules apply only to standard-form categorical syllogisms. Some logicians combine rules 4 and 5 into a single rule to the effect that the number of negative statements in the premises must be the same as the number of negative claims in the conclusion; some logicians exclude rule 1 entirely, since a "syllogism" with four terms is by definition not a categorical syllogism at all.

Exercise 4.7   State the following arguments as standard-form categorical syllogisms and use the rules and fallacies of the syllogism to test their validity:

1. No cats are dogs. Some dogs are not spaniels. So no cats are spaniels.

2. No ladies are rock stars. All ladies are church-goers. So no rock stars are church-goers.

3. All carrots are vegetables. No cats are vegetables. So some cats are carrots.

4. Some birds are parrots. Some parrots are edible things. So some birds are edible things.

5. No coaches are dishonest people, so some women are coaches, because women are not dishonest people.

6. Some Palestinians are Arabs. No Arabs are Jews. So some Palestinians are not Jews.

7. Some nuclear plants are not safe plants. Unsafe plants are plants that should be shut down. So some nuclear plants are plants that should be shut down.

8. Some drug addicts are thieves. Some thieves are murderers. So some drug addicts are murderers.

9. Some cats are males. All cats are vertebrates. So some males are vertebrates.

10. Some dogs are not chows. No chows are poodles. So some dogs are not poodles.

11. Some cowboys are wranglers. All wranglers are tough hombres. So some cowboys are tough hombres.

12. No Republicans are Democrats. All Democrats are liberals. So no Republicans are liberals.

13. No poets are nonmusicians. Some musicians are not tough hombres. So all poets are tough hombres.

14. No plagiarists are honest people. Some senators are plagiarists. So some senators are not honest people.

15. No parrots are nonvertebrates. All nonvertebrates are nonmammals. So all parrots are nonmammals.

16. No coaches are dishonest, so some women are not dishonest, because some coaches are women.

17. No cats are nonfeline, so all dogs are noncats, since no dogs are feline.

18. Some birds are parrots, so some birds are singers, because some parrots are singers.

19. Some Democrats are conservatives. No conservatives voted for Clinton. So some Democrats did not vote for Clinton.

20. Some chemicals are toxic substances. All toxic substances are dangerous substances. So some chemicals are dangerous substances.

21. Some wealthy people are successful politicians. Some successful politicians are dishonest people. So some wealthy people are dishonest people.

22. Some alcoholics are child abusers. All child abusers are emotionally disturbed people. So some alcoholics are emotionally disturbed people.

23. No secular humanists are Fundamentalists. All Fundamentalists are creationists. So no secular humanists are creationists.

4.8 Enthymemes and Sorites

Enthymemes   **Enthymemes** are categorical syllogisms that have a premise or a conclusion left out. We have discussed such arguments already, in a general way, in Chapter 1 when we examined suppressed premises. As we saw there, the way we discover suppressed elements of deductive arguments is simply to *ask what is needed to make the argument valid* (or strong, if the argument is inductive). For example, this argument

> *Killing a person is murder*
>
> ∴ *Abortion is murder*

is not valid as it stands. But it is obvious what premise is suppressed:

> *Abortion is killing a person.*

When we supply this premise, we get a valid argument (and while we're at it, let's put the whole argument in standard form):

> *All cases of killing a person are cases of murder.*
>
> supp → *All cases of abortion are cases of killing a person.*
>
> ∴ *All cases of abortion are cases of murder.*

We can of course challenge that premise, as pro-choice people probably would. However, the argument is valid, which we could easily establish with a Venn diagram.

Actual arguments require more thought. Consider this passage from "Encourage Student Prayer":

> The action taken Monday by the Supreme Court in favor of student-initiated graduation prayer was a step in the right direction. It moves the courts closer to the public's view. Polls consistently show that 95% of this country's population believes in God.   (Tom Minnery, *USA TODAY,* 27 June 1995.)

We paraphrase the argument and put it into standard form:

All actions identical to Monday's in favor of school prayer are actions that move closer to the public view.

∴ *All actions identical to Monday's . . . are steps in the right direction.*

This is invalid as it stands, but perhaps we can find a suppressed premise. The thought process works this way:

All M are P: (All Monday-actions are ones that move closer to public view.)

∴ *All M are S: (All Monday-actions are steps in the right direction.)*

The formal validity of the argument requires a statement that binds the minor term *M* with the major term *S,* by means of the middle term *P.* That must be

All P are S

which we fill out with the appropriate subject matter:

All actions that move closer to the public view are steps in the right direction.

Now we have the complete argument:

All actions identical to Monday's . . . are actions that move closer to the public's view.

supp → *All actions that move closer to the public's view are steps in the right direction.*

∴ *All Monday-actions are steps in the right direction.*

This is a valid argument, but the suppressed premise is not plausible, for we can imagine the public being in the wrong. (*Important:* Not everyone will agree with this analysis. But in critical thinking there is room for disagreement, as long as we are able to give *reasons* for our judgments.)

Sorites   Sometimes several syllogisms are strung together in a chain. Such an argument, called a **sorites,** is valid only if all its constituent arguments are valid. Usually, only the premises of each syllogism and the final conclusion are stated. For example:

All politicians are dishonest. Dishonest people are untrustworthy. Some untrustworthy people are criminals. So some politicians are criminals.

To test this, we break it down into its constituent arguments, put them in standard form (major premise first, and so on), supply the missing conclusions, and test each argument with a Venn diagram:

(1) All dishonest people are untrustworthy

All politicians are dishonest

∴ All politicians are untrustworthy

which is symbolized and tested:

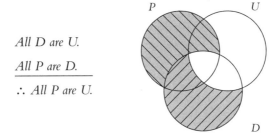

All D are U.

All P are D.

∴ All P are U.

Argument (1) is valid, so we go on to the next argument.

(2) Some untrustworthy people are criminals

All politicians are untrustworthy [the conclusion of (1)]

∴ Some politicians are criminals

which is symbolized and tested:

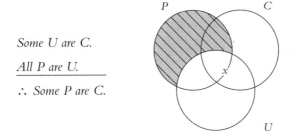

Some U are C.

All P are U.

∴ Some P are C.

Argument (2) is not valid, so the whole sorites is invalid.

Exercise 4.8   A. In each enthymeme, supply the suppressed premise or suppressed conclusion and then test for validity with a Venn diagram.

1. All dogs are vertebrates, so all dogs are mammals.

2. All dogs are mammals, so all dogs are vertebrates.

3. Socrates was wise and the wise are precious.

4. Abortion is taking an innocent life, so abortion is murder.

5. It is wrong to kill, and capital punishment is killing.

6. People with AIDS are immoral, so they don't deserve medical care.

7. Men of God should be trusted, and Jim Bakker is a man of God.

8. Judge Molehill smoked marijuana, so he can't be a Supreme Court justice.

9. Judge Bork can't be a Supreme Court justice. He has a beard.

10. Judge Kennedy has no beard, so he can be a Supreme Court judge.

11. Tom was a user and users are losers.

12. Some fleas are vicious. So some fleas should be exterminated.

13. No Democrat is conservative. So all conservatives are Republicans.

14. No liberals are conservatives. All Democrats are liberals.

15. All young people like rock music, and people who like rock music are liberals.

16. Ducks are birds and all birds can fly.

17. Herman is an insider trader, so he'll soon be indicted.

18. Some books are pornographic. Pornographic books should be suppressed.

19. No nice doggy likes beer; Spuds is a nice doggy.

20. All government programs are being examined, and Social Security is a government program.

21. No Marxist is a Republican, but some Republicans are liberals.

22. The best whiskey is the most expensive. Chivas is expensive.

23. We build cars that make sense. You want a car that makes sense.

24. Pickles that snap are good pickles. Our pickles snap.

25. Some Americans can't read. People who can't read are disadvantaged.

26. Any company that operated in South Africa in the 1970s implicitly supported apartheid. Conrok, Inc., operated in South Africa.

27. Anyone who believes in evolution is being misled by Satan. The school superintendent believes in evolution.

28. Any movie that portrays premarital sex favorably is immoral. *Splendor in the Grass* portrays premarital sex favorably.

29. Some recent movies are pornographic. All pornography should be illegal.

30. Any economic plan that ignores the homeless is unrealistic. The president's plan ignores the homeless.

31. We need a source of energy that we can really count on. We can really count on nuclear energy.

32. GM has agreed to pay $3 million in damages to black workers who sued them for racial discrimination. Any company that does that must have been guilty.

33. Over 30 million people buy U.S. Savings Bonds, so savings bonds must be safe.

34. Any public official who makes $89,500 a year is overpaid. Congressmen make $89,500 a year.

35. Pete Tweety makes ten times the average annual American income. The average American makes $20,000 a year.

36. Nobody wants an alcoholic and a womanizer as secretary of defense. So nobody wants Fred Flintstone as secretary of defense.

37. Anyone who understands Latin American politics is a political heavyweight. So Dan Quayle is a political heavyweight.

38. When you have an LQ-13, you have a lot of computer. So you have a lot of computer.

39. You want to buy an AK-47. No sensible person wants to buy an AK-47.

40. After John Tower retired from the Senate in 1985, he received over $750,000 in consulting fees from six Pentagon contractors. No such person could possibly be ethical.

41. All dogs are mammals, so all dogs are vertebrates.

42. It is wrong to kill, and abortion is killing.

43. Jerry Falwell can be trusted because he's a man of God.

44. John Belushi was a loser because he was a user.

45. People with AIDS don't deserve medical help because they are immoral.

46. Jill is precious because she's intelligent.

47. Freddy must be destroyed because he's a madman.

48. Freddy is not real because he's a dream creature.

49. The best whiskey is expensive. Old Groundhog is expensive.

50. No nice camel smokes, and Joe smokes.

B. Break down each sorites into its constituent arguments and test with Venn diagrams.

1. No politicians are honest. Dishonest people are not trustworthy. Nobody likes an untrustworthy person. So nobody likes a politician.

2. Some dogs are mongrels. No mongrel is registered. Unregistered animals are not expensive. So some dogs are not expensive.

3. No movie is realistic. Unrealistic movies are misleading to young people. Anything that misleads the young is immoral. So all movies are immoral.

4. Some books are classics. Some classics are erotic. Some erotic books are in our local bookstore. So some classics are in our local bookstore.

5. None but the brave deserve the fair. Those who deserve the fair are great heroes. Lancelot is a great hero. So Lancelot deserves the fair.

6. Gwenivere is a fair damsel. Gwenivere is married to King Arthur. Any damsel married to King Arthur should not be courted by Lancelot. So some fair damsels should not be courted by Lancelot.

7. Only the lonely know how I feel. People who know how I feel are sensitive souls. Sensitive souls are unlucky in love. So the unlucky in love know how I feel.

8. I'm bad. The bad are rich and famous. Some people who are rich and famous are superstars. So I'm a superstar.

9. Whom the gods would destroy, they first drive mad. The gods drove Marilyn mad. Marilyn was a superstar. So the gods would destroy some superstars.

10. People who hate Americans just don't understand them. Some Iranians hate Americans. People who don't understand Americans think they are infidels. So some Iranians think Americans are infidels.

11. Some dogs are mutts. No mutt is a purebred. Nonpurebreds are not expensive. So some dogs are not expensive.

12. No lawyers are honest. Dishonest people are untrustworthy. Nobody likes an untrustworthy person. So nobody likes a lawyer.

13. No books are realistic. Unrealistic books are a waste of time. Any waste of time is immoral. So all books are immoral.

14. Only the wicked contemplate murder. People who contemplate murder are dangerous. Dangerous people make poor friends. So the wicked make poor friends.

15. Nobody but rock stars are really free. Anyone who is really free is happy. Britney is happy. So Britney is really free.

16. I'm really bad. The really bad are superstars. All superstars are rich and famous. So I'm rich and famous.

17. Whoever loves Belinda Carlisle loves pop-rock. People who love pop-rock have good taste. Some people with good taste like Megadeth. So some people who love Belinda Carlisle also like Megadeth.

18. Some teachers can't teach. Some people who can't teach are grouchy. All grouchy people are unpleasant. So some teachers are unpleasant.

19. Whom the gods would destroy, they first drive mad. Whom the gods drive mad, they give great riches. Whom the gods give great riches, they love. So whom the gods would destroy, they love.

4.9 Summary

The logic of the categorical syllogism is very useful in analyzing and evaluating arguments that can be expressed in categorical statements. The four categorical statements can be represented by a Venn diagram:

A: All *S* are *P:*

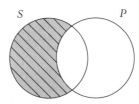

E: No *S* are *P:*

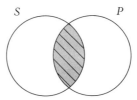

I: Some *S* are *P:*

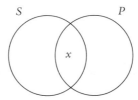

O: Some *S* are not *P:*

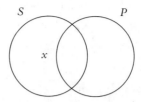

These statements are related in several ways that can be exhibited by the traditional square of opposition (if we assume *S* and *P* must have members) or the modern square of opposition (if we do not assume *S* and *P* have members). Furthermore, the operations of conversion, obversion, and contraposition allow us to make valid, immediate inferences from each categorical statement.

By translating an argument into standard form and specifying its mood and figure, we can test its validity in any of three ways: by the list of valid syllogisms, the use of Venn diagrams, or the rules of the syllogism. For example, the argument

Some mariners are punks	is symbolized	*Some M are P*
All sailors are mariners		*All S are M*
∴ *Some sailors are punks*		∴ *Some S are P*

and diagrammed:

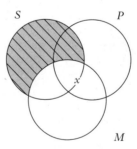

This is an IAI-1 syllogism, which is not in the list of valid syllogisms. The Venn diagram shows that it is invalid, and it breaks rule 2, committing the fallacy of the undistributed middle.

An enthymeme is a syllogism with an unstated premise or conclusion. In analyzing such an argument, we supply the premise that will make the syllogism valid, trying always to be objective and fair.

A sorites is a string of syllogisms with suppressed conclusions. To analyze a sorites we take two of its premises, combine them, and derive their conclusion, which we combine with another premise to get another conclusion, and so on, until we get the final conclusion. Each syllogism can then be tested for validity.

The point of all these techniques is to be able critically to analyze all arguments that can be somehow expressed, translated, or paraphrased as standard-form categorical syllogisms. But, as we will see in Chapter 6, not all arguments can be treated as categorical syllogism.

4.10 Applications

The Death Penalty   Here we apply what we know about the syllogism to the issue of the death penalty. The following editorial is about Supreme Court Justice Harry Blackmun's announced decision to oppose all executions. Blackmun's reason for that decision? The death penalty cannot be applied fairly. The editorial argues that Blackmun has abandoned his oath to judge every case by the facts and the Constitution.

Our procedure is to find the syllogisms, as well as enthymemes and sorites, translate them into standard form, symbolize them, and supply suppressed premises and conclusions. Then we test them for validity.

At this point we need to introduce the idea of the **subargument,** which is an argument that supports the premises of the main argument.

On Death Sentences[4]

If a Supreme Court nominee had told the Senate Judiciary Committee what Justice Harry Blackmun said in an opinion on Tuesday, that nominee's chances of confirmation would be zero. And rightly so. For in saying that he'll never vote to uphold a death sentence, Mr. Blackmun did more than deliver his moral judgment on the fairness of capital punishment. He abrogated his sworn duty to judge each case as its facts fit the U.S. Constitution.

In effect, Mr. Blackmun, 85, says that he already has *prejudged all* future death penalty cases. His fine, learned mind has served American justice well in his 20-plus years on the court. But as his career closes, so has his mind closed—at least on this most divisive of issues. No appellant expecting—as every appellant has a *right* to expect—an open judicial mind need knock.

Forget about whatever facts a future death penalty appeal may

---

4. *Source:* Editorial, *Miami Herald,* 24 February 1994. Reprinted with permission of *Miami Herald,* via CCC.

bring. Forget that a future appellant may well be Danny Rolling, confessed white butcher of five white college students. Do the death penalty's biases, which Justice Blackmun has adjudged to be incurably skewed against blacks and poor people, apply to white killers too?

No other issue is as visceral, as intractable to normal reasoning processes, as capital punishment. Abortion comes close, but only close. Some people can rationalize a woman's right to an abortion but cannot rationalize the *state's* right, for any reason, to take a life.

Yet Justice Blackmun's error need not involve capital punishment, or abortion. The issue really lies in another plane. In that plane, wherein rests a judge's duty, there is room for only one overriding principle, one enduring passion, one inviolable standard: fealty to the law.

It is not a jurist's prerogative to rule this way or that because a law is "good" or "bad." On the contrary. A judge takes an oath *not* to apply personal beliefs to the law.

It's the duty of legislators to do that. A society's laws reflect its beliefs and mores and values as legislators construe and codify those standards. Legislators may, and do, pack laws with absurdities or contradictions.

Judges are free to remark upon those absurdities and contradictions— but they can't revoke or change those that are lawful. If a statute comports with the applicable constitution, either state or U.S., a judge must apply the law, absurdity and contradiction and all.

Otherwise, unimaginable chaos and injustice would ensue. Suppose a Catholic judge interpreted the Bill of Rights according to papal encyclicals, not the Constitution. Suppose another religion teaches another judge that physical infirmity is God's punishment, and that those so "punished" don't deserve equal opportunity. Suppose a third judge's God teaches that women are inferior to men (or vice versa), or that racial or ethnic minorities are born inferior.

A judge may in fact hold odd personal beliefs—and still be a good judge. The litmus test requires covering personal beliefs, neck to ankles, with the jurist's black robe. It requires applying the law even when—especially when—the application of it runs counter to the judge's personal convictions.

This is the battle in which, on capital punishment, Mr. Blackmun has surrendered. It grieves his admirers to see the lion so felled by the thorn, with Androcles nowhere to be found.[5]

---

5. In a legend Androcles, an early Christian, pulls a thorn from a lion's paw. When the Romans throw Androcles to the lions, the lion that he helped spares his life.

The main conclusion is

> *Blackmun has abandoned his oath.*

The subarguments (whose conclusions are the main premises) are

> *(1) All judges identical to <u>B</u>lackmun are <u>p</u>rejudging judges.*
>
> *All <u>p</u>rejudging judges are judges who will <u>n</u>ot judge by facts and the Constitution.*
>
> *All judges who will not judge by facts . . . are judges who have abandoned their oath.*
> _____
>
> ∴ *All judges identical to Blackmun are judges who have abandoned their oath.*

This is not a syllogism but a sorites. So we symbolize and break it into its constituent arguments:

> *All P are N.*
>
> *All B are P.*
> _____
>
> ∴ *All B are N.*

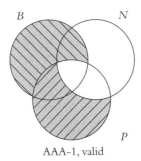

AAA-1, valid

> *All N are A.*
>
> *All B are N.*
> _____
>
> ∴ *All B are A.*

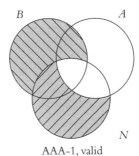

AAA-1, valid

Translated back into ordinary language, "All *B* are *A*" says

> *Blackmun abandoned his oath.*

The next subargument

> *(2) No law that applies to <u>w</u>hites, too, is biased (<u>u</u>nfair).*
>
> <u>*The <u>d</u>eath penalty applies to <u>w</u>hites (like Danny Rolling), too.*</u>
>
> ∴ *The <u>d</u>eath penalty is not biased (<u>u</u>nfair).*

is translated into standard form

No law that applies to whites, too, is a biased law

All laws identical to the death penalty are laws that apply to whites, too

∴ *No laws identical to the death penalty are biased laws*

and is symbolized and tested:

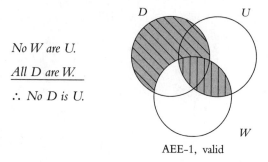

No W are U.

All D are W.

∴ *No D is U.*

AEE-1, valid

The next subargument

(3) All ċhaotic situations are ṣituations that we should avoid

All situations where judges use p̱ersonal beliefs are situations that would be ċhaotic

∴ *All situations where judges use p̱ersonal beliefs are ṣituations that we should avoid*

is symbolized and tested:

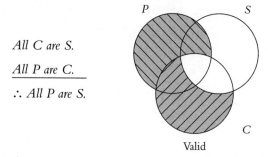

All C are S.

All P are C.

∴ *All P are S.*

Valid

"All *P* are *S*" means "All situations where judges apply personal beliefs are situations that we should avoid."

Argument (1) gives us the main conclusion directly, but argument (2) gives us

The death penalty is not biased

which would indicate that Blackmun was wrong about the death penalty but would be irrelevant to whether Blackmun has abandoned his oath. But (3) gives us

Judges should not apply their own personal beliefs.

If we supply the premise that

Judges that apply their personal beliefs are abandoning their oaths

we get the desired conclusion. This supplied premise, however, is more or less dubious depending upon one's view of what Supreme Court justices are supposed to do.

With this comment we have stepped out of the area of pure logic and entered the realm of critical thinking. So let's compose our critical observations in a brief summary (but the *fallacies* in the editorial are left to you!).

CRITICAL SUMMARY: "ON DEATH SENTENCES"

The editor thinks that judges who apply their personal values rather than the facts and the Constitution have abandoned their oaths as judges. This is surely mistaken. We don't want judges' decisions to be mechanical.

Would we have chaos if judges applied their personal values? No, because all judges have personal values upon which they act, and always have had such values, and yet the legal system has not fallen into chaos.

What's more, the claim that laws applying to both whites and minorities are therefore "fair" overlooks the manifest injustices of our society. Robbing a store is illegal for both rich and poor, but rich people hardly ever rob stores. To ignore the realities of racism and socioeconomic conditions is wrong.

Again, the preceeding analysis is not the *only* way of thinking through the editorial, but it is more than a mere statement of opinion. It is a reasoned critical evaluation with which you might reasonably disagree. You might find more arguments, for example, or you might disagree with the way I gathered the statements into arguments.

Logic, not to mention critical thinking, is not cut and dried.

Helms on AIDS   Our next application is an editorial about North Carolina Senator Jesse Helms's opposition to federal spending on AIDS.

Editorial from the *Record*[6]

Sen. Jesse Helms, R–N.C., wants to reduce—or even block—federal spending for those with AIDS. He says AIDS sufferers bring on the disease with their "deliberate, disgusting, revolting conduct." He also says more federal money is spent on AIDS, the ninth leading killer in America, than on diseases that kill more people.

---

6. *Source:* Editorial, *Record* (Hackensack, N.J.), 6 August 1995. Reproduced with permission of the *Record* (Bergen County, N.J.).

Unfortunately, Mr. Helms' argument is filled with half-truths and innuendo.

It's true that many people with AIDS are responsible for their plight. The disease is spread by dirty needles used for taking drugs and by unprotected sex among homosexuals—and to a lesser extent heterosexuals. Mr. Helms is entitled to his opinion on homosexual sex. Fortunately, it's not universally shared.

But many AIDS sufferers have no responsibility for getting the disease. Ryan White, the teenage boy who is a symbol for the fight against AIDS, got the virus through his treatment for hemophilia. Many men and women get AIDS from sexual partners who neglect to tell them they are HIV-infected. Some babies are born with AIDS because of their infected mothers.

And many people who got AIDS through sexual activity knew nothing at the time about how the disease is spread.

Mr. Helms also misleads us when he suggests that Washington spends more on AIDS than on heart disease and cancer, the nation's two biggest killers. Federal spending is greater for AIDS if you consider only the amount spent on research, prevention, and housing. But if you consider the amount spent for Medicare and Medicaid, in addition to these other expenditures, the federal outlay for heart disease ($36.3 billion) and cancer ($16.9 billion) is far more than for AIDS ($6 billion).

Let's also keep in mind that cancer and heart disease are partially brought on by personal conduct. Like smoking, for starters.

The main conclusion is

We should reject Helms's contention that AIDS spending should be cut.

The main arguments are

Helms argues that AIDS sufferers bring the disease on themselves and therefore AIDS funding should be cut.

This essay contradicts this. Many AIDS sufferers do not bring it on themselves—for example, Ryan White, unknowing sex partners of infected people, and babies born to infected mothers.

Helms argues that AIDS gets more funds than diseases such as cancer and heart disease, which kill more people, and therefore AIDS funding should be cut.

This essay points out that if you include Medicare and Medicaid spending, cancer and heart disease each get more funds than AIDS.

So the *Record* editorial rests on the effective strategy of challenging Helms's premises. The argument in standard form is

> *All arguments identical to <u>H</u>elms's argument on AIDS are arguments with <u>f</u>alse premises*
>
> supp → *All arguments with <u>f</u>alse premises are arguments that should be <u>r</u>ejected*
>
> ∴ *All arguments identical to <u>H</u>elms's argument on AIDS are arguments that should be <u>r</u>ejected*

which, of course, means simply

Helms's argument on AIDS should be rejected.

The whole argument is symbolized and tested:

All H are F.
All F are R.
∴ All H are R.

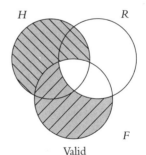

Valid

Look for fallacies and then write a brief critical summary. Again, you might not agree with my analysis. You need only state *your* arguments.

A Murdered Girl With the translation methods we have learned so far, we do not approach an actual argument in ordinary English. Consider this passage:

> My deputy, who performed the autopsy, called me to the table upon which the young actress lay. "It's strange," he said. "The police say she was shot, but there's no bullet in her brain—and no exit wound through which it escaped." [Thomas Noguchi, *Coroner* (New York: Simon & Schuster, 1983).]

The translation is

All gunshot wounds to the <u>b</u>rain are wounds that <u>r</u>esult in exit wounds or a bullet in the brain.

<u>T</u>his wound is not (No wound identical with this wound is) one that <u>r</u>esulted in exit wounds or a bullet in the brain.

∴ *[implicit, unstated conclusion] <u>T</u>his wound is not (No wound identical with this wound is) a gunshot wound to the <u>b</u>rain.*

It is symbolized as

All B are R.

No T are R.

∴ *No T are B.*

In standard form it is

All gunshot wounds to the <u>b</u>rain are wounds that <u>r</u>esult in either a bullet in the brain or an exit wound.

No wound identical with <u>t</u>his wound is one that <u>r</u>esulted in exit wounds or a bullet in the brain.

∴ *No wound identical with <u>t</u>his wound is a gunshot wound to the <u>b</u>rain*

We then symbolize and test it:

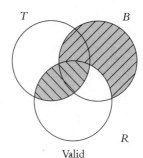

All B are R.

No T are R.

∴ *No T are B.*

Valid

(The wound turned out to have been made by the spike of a woman's high-heeled shoe.)

Exercise 4.10   A. In the following essay, find the sorites, supply suppressed premises, put the constituent syllogisms in standard form, and test for validity.

Don't Fear Gun Laws[7]

Our View: Some say gun laws prompt violence by extreme right; but such violence is the reason laws are needed

Right-wing paramilitary groups have been quick to disavow Timothy McVeigh, the prime suspect in the Oklahoma City bombing. Leaders of the Michigan Militia, one of the larger such associations, say McVeigh and two others were "silenced" and "told to leave" because of their "anarchist rhetoric."

If true, that's to their credit. The trouble is that such "militias" have used expanded federal gun controls as a rallying point for arming themselves for resistance—an anarchist notion itself. According to those who track the groups, two recent gun laws—one requiring a background check for handgun purchases and the other banning the sale of scores of firearms—are seen as particularly ominous steps toward the disarming of citizens.

That's way off base. The aim is not to seize guns, just control them better. Banning assault-style semiautomatics is the act of a nation fearful for its own safety, not an act of tyranny.

And the background check isn't Big Brother. It's a small inconvenience that has prevented thousands of felons from acquiring guns on the open market.

We ought to go further. Registration and licensing, as we do with cars and drivers, would make us all safer without violating anyone's legitimate gun privileges. But until last Wednesday, Congress was moving fast in the other direction. At least four bills had been introduced to repeal the assault-weapons ban or undermine the handgun-purchase background check.

What will happen to those bills now that McVeigh—who reportedly "never went anywhere unarmed," who embraced the anarchy of unfettered gun rights, and who was carrying a semiautomatic pistol loaded with "cop-killer" bullets at the time of his arrest—is in custody? A quick legislative burial wouldn't be inappropriate.

Even comprehensive gun laws wouldn't have prevented the Oklahoma bombing. But they could well help deter other acts of violence by giving law enforcement the means of tracking gun ownership and controlling the most dangerous weapons.

The fight against terrorism will always cause some inconvenience to law-abiding citizens—airport metal detectors are one example. But against the daily terror that guns bring to our streets, comprehensive gun laws need be no more of a sacrifice. They should be no less, either.

---

7. *Source:* "Don't Fear Gun Laws," *USA TODAY,* 24 April 1995. Copyright 1995, USA TODAY. Reprinted with permission.

B. In the following letter to the editor, find a sorites, put it into standard form, and test its constituent syllogisms for validity.

Home's in Cuba[8]

Editor: I just wanted to comment about the Cuban boy, Elian Gonzalez. A lot of people feel this little boy should remain in the United States with his family here. I feel he should be reunited with his father and family in Cuba.

All children should be with their parents whenever possible. We should ask ourselves this question. "How would we feel if our little boy or girl was taken into another country and the family and government there did not let him come back to us?"

We would call that kidnapping. This is a serious crime and no one I know wants to lose a child this way. It would be a shame for our wonderful country to be labeled as a country that helps in this type of crime. I hope the best interest of the child is put forth.

Wendy Carter
Wilmington

---

8. *Source:* Letter to the Editor, *Star-News* (Wilmington, N.C.), 23 January 2000. Reprinted by permission of the author.

CHAPTER FIVE

Truth-Functional Logic

Despite the usefulness of syllogistic logic, the vast majority of arguments in ordinary language are not neat syllogisms with two premises, three terms, and a conclusion—which necessitated the addition of some special rules and methods, as we saw in Chapter 4. So when modern symbolic logic was invented and developed by Gottlob Frege (1848–1925) in the nineteenth century and developed by Bertrand Russell (1872–1970) and others in the twentieth century, the subject was finally liberated from the strictures of Aristotle's syllogism.

Also called the **sentential calculus** and the **propositional calculus, truth-functional logic** concerned itself not so much with the "carriers of truth-value" statements but with the important little words that bind sentences or statements together: *and, or, not, if,* and *then,* to name a few.

A whole metaphysical view of the world evolved on the basis of this new logic, and a new kind of philosophy called *analytic philosophy* was gradually developed by Russell and by Ludwig Wittgenstein (1889–1951). The world, according to this view of reality, is the class of all facts. Facts could be simple (atomic) facts such as "It's raining" and "Today is Tuesday" or compound facts—for example, "It's Tuesday and it's raining" and "It's raining or it's snowing." These simple atomic facts could be represented by p's and q's. Now there was a clear way to determine the truth-values of complex statements, even long series of statements. Moreover, a long argument composed of many statements could be tested mechanically for validity by means of truth tables.

Best of all, certain argument forms could be shown to be formally valid by means of truth tables, and then these valid argument forms could be used as rules in writing lengthy proofs. Most of these innovations, and more that are presented in Chapter 6, were due to Frege.

A theoretical (or philosophical) problem concerns whether the world indeed conforms to a truth-table delineation of reality rather than to the subject–predicate structure of the syllogism. Are the statements represented by the *p*'s and *q*'s those things that really exist? What is the nature of *truth?* Many philosophers insist that a statement is true if it corresponds with the facts; for example, "It's raining" is true if it is indeed raining.

Other philosophers and logicians see truth differently, arguing that truths come not individually but in whole fabrics of belief. W. V. O. Quine (1908–2000) espoused such a view. Such grand philosophical questions need not dissuade us from applying logic whenever we can, however. Whatever kind of thing our T's and F's and our *p*'s and *q*'s and so on stand for, we can still do our analyses.

5.1 Basic Symbols

Despite its limitations, the worst of which is the difficulty of capturing actual argumentation in categorical statements, the logic of the syllogism has been used and elaborated upon from the time of Aristotle, throughout the Middle Ages, on up to this century. And, as we saw in Chapter 4, it is still useful.

Since the nineteenth century a different kind of logic has been developed that is more powerful because it can accommodate many more arguments of greater length and complexity. Modern symbolic logic has proved useful in the areas of the foundations of mathematics and the development of the theoretical basis for the electronic circuitry of digital computers; more recently, it has played a role in efforts to develop artificial intelligence. This role is due to the age-old desire of the logician to develop an entirely symbolic language.

An important difference between syllogistic logic and truth-functional logic is this: Syllogism uses letters to stand for *classes,* but truth-functional logic uses letters to stand for *statements.* For example, the statement "The Braves will win" is symbolized in categorical logic by "All *B* are *W,*" but in truth-functional logic by "*W.*"

As we did in categorical logic, we try to use a letter that helps us remember what it stands for—for example:

The sun is <u>u</u>p: *U*

Today is <u>W</u>ednesday: *W*

The secretary is <u>e</u>n route to Sarajevo: *E*

Tom has been <u>j</u>ailed for illegal drug possession: *J*

I <u>l</u>ike to get my hamburgers at MacDonald's: *L*

These simple statements are called **atomic statements.** To form **compound statements,** we use certain symbols that stand for important words called **logical connectives** (Table 5.1). The following shows how these connectives are used:

Table 5.1 Logical Connectives

Connective	Name	Meaning	Sample Translation
·	Conjunction	And	$A \cdot B$ means "A and B"
v	Disjunction	Or	A v B means "A or B"
~	Negation	Not	$\sim A$ means "not A."
⊃	Implication or conditional	Implies or if . . . then	$A \supset B$ means "A implies B," or "If A, then B."
≡	Equivalence or biconditional	Is equivalent to or if and only if	$A \equiv B$ means "A is equivalent to B," or "A if and only if B."

I'm h̲ungry and I'm t̲hirsty.	$H \cdot T$
J̲eff will join and so will T̲ammy.	$J \cdot T$
Today is either M̲onday or T̲uesday.	M v T
Today is not S̲unday.	$\sim S$
If A̲l walks out, then B̲etty will, too.	$A \supset B$
G̲inger will dance if and only if F̲red dances.	$G \equiv F$

We use **punctuation** in truth-functional logic, to avoid ambiguity. When more than two letters appear in a translated statement, we use parentheses, brackets, or braces to show the range of the connectives. Here are some examples:

A̲nn and B̲ill went home, or C̲indy lied.	$(A \cdot B)$ v C
A̲nn went home or B̲ill and C̲indy lied.	A v $(B \cdot C)$
A̲nn or B̲ill went home, and C̲indy lied.	$(A$ v $B) \cdot C$
If A̲nn goes home, so will B̲ill and C̲indy.	$A \supset (B \cdot C)$
If A̲nn's going home means B̲ill will go, too, then C̲indy lied.	$(A \supset B) \supset C$
If either A̲nn and B̲ill went home or C̲indy lied, then D̲ave will sing.	$[(A \cdot B)$ v $C] \supset D$
If E̲sther insists, then if either A̲nn and B̲ill went home or C̲indy lied, then D̲ave will sing.	$E \supset \{[(A \cdot B)$ v $C] \supset D\}$

When the negation sign appears, it affects only the expression that immediately follows. So in $\sim A \cdot B$, the negation sign affects only A; but in $\sim(A \cdot B)$, it affects both A and B. For example:

It is not the case that A̲nn went home, but B̲ill did.	$\sim A \cdot B$
Neither A̲nn nor B̲ob lied, but C̲indy did.	$\sim(A$ v $B) \cdot C$

We examine more such translations later in the chapter. Logicians call symbolic expressions that are unambiguous and meaningful **well-formed formulas** (WFFs).

These symbols do not work exactly like their English counterparts, however, so, to define them more exactly, we use **truth tables.**

Conjunction The **conjunction** symbol · is used to mean "and," as in "Tom and Jerry are present," which is symbolized $T \cdot J$; "Tom is present but Jerry is not" is symbolized $T \cdot \sim J$. The conjunction sign can mean *and, but, also, still, although, furthermore, nevertheless, moreover,* and *yet.*

The truth table for · (and) works like this: p and q are **statement variables** that stand for any statements whatever, and T and F stand for true and false. We write *guide columns* for p and q so that we account for every possible combination of truth-values, and we write the corresponding *resultant column* under the controlling connective, · (and). The controlling connective determines the truth-value of the whole expression.

Guide Columns   Whole Expression

p	q		p	·	q
T	T		T	T	T
T	F		T	F	F
F	T		F	F	T
F	F		F	F	F

↑ resultant column

This truth table means that $p \cdot q$ is true *when and only when* p is true *and* q is true. It represents all the possible situations, all the possible combinations of truth values of p and q: when p is true and q is true, when p is true and q is false, when p is false and q is true, and when both p and q are false. It shows that the one and only case in which $p \cdot q$ is true is when both p and q are true.

How do we know that we have listed "every possible case"? Because each row represents one possible combination of truth-values: When p is true, q can be true or false; when p is false, q can be true and false. That accounts for every possibility, each represented by a row of the truth table. Notice that if we have n statement-letters, the truth table will have 2^n rows. If we have two statements, as we do in our example, we need $2^2 = 4$ rows. If we need to do a truth table involving three statements, our truth table requires $2^3 = 8$ rows, and so on. The number of rows doubles with each additional statement.

In the preceding truth table, as we said, the resultant column is the column whose truth-values are those of the whole expression above it, and the truth-values are written under the main connective of the symbolic statement.

Suppose p stands for "Rosanne dances" and q stands for "Tom sings." Then $p \cdot q$ will stand for "Rosanne dances and Tom sings." The truth table looks like this:

Guide Columns   **Whole Expression**

p	q
T	T
T	F
F	T
F	F

	$p \cdot q$	
T	T	T
T	F	F
F	F	T
F	F	F

↑ resultant column

(The resultant column is filled in by looking at the first two columns—"Guide Columns"—and the definition of the · symbol.) This tells us that "Rosanne dances and Tom sings" is true if and only if "Rosanne dances" is true *and* "Tom sings" is true.

Disjunction The **disjunction** symbol in logic means "one or the other or possibly both." For example, "Either Tom or Jerry will be there" is symbolized $T \vee J$. If they cannot both be there, we add "but not both," or $\sim(T \cdot J)$.

The truth table for v (or) works this way:

Guide Columns   **Whole Expression**

p	q
T	T
T	F
F	T
F	F

	$p \vee q$	
T	T	T
T	T	F
F	T	T
F	F	F

↑ resultant column

This shows that $p \vee q$ is true in every case *except* when *both* p and q are false.

Negation The statement "Machines cannot think" is symbolized $\sim M$, as is "It is not the case that machines can think" and "It is false (not true) that machines can think."

The **negation** symbol ~ (not) has a simple truth-table definition:

p	$\sim p$	
T	F	T
F	T	F

↑ resultant column

which obviously means that $\sim p$ is false when p is true, and vice versa. For example, if p stands for "I like *MTV*," then $\sim p$ is "I do not like *MTV*," which is true when p is false, and vice versa.

Parentheses Parentheses are handled like this: Suppose p stands for "Jay is funny" and q stands for "Dave is funny." Then $\sim(p \cdot q)$ means that not both are funny. The truth table for this statement is the following (the controlling connective is $\sim$):

p	q		$\sim$	$(p$	$\cdot$	$q)$
T	T		F	T	T	T
T	F		T	T	F	F
F	T		T	F	F	T
F	F		T	F	F	F

↑ resultant column

This truth table shows us that both Jay and Dave are not funny, except in the case when both Jay is funny and Dave is funny. [Notice that the resultant column is lined up under the $\sim$ sign because it governs the whole expression $\sim(p \cdot q)$. It is the result of negating the next-to-resultant column found under the $\cdot$.] In general $\sim(p \cdot q)$ is true except when p and q are both true.

The truth table for $\sim(p \vee q)$—for example, for "Neither Jay nor Dave is funny"—is the following:

p	q		$\sim$	$(p$	$\vee$	$q)$
T	T		F	T	T	T
T	F		F	T	T	F
F	T		F	F	T	T
F	F		T	F	F	F

↑ resultant column

which means that neither is funny only if Jay is not funny *and* Dave is not funny.

Material Implication The truth table for $\supset$ (if . . . then) is the following:

p	q		$p \supset q$
T	T		T
T	F		F
F	T		T
F	F		T

If p and q are both true, then the conditional $p \supset q$ is true. If p is false, then $p \supset q$ is true—whether q is true or false. If q is true, then $p \supset q$ is true—whether p is true or false. Put more succinctly, $p \supset q$ is true when either p is false or q is true. This relation is called **material implication** and does not refer to the *meaning* of the statements connected.

Note: In $p \supset q$, p is called the *antecedent*, and q is called the *consequent* of the conditional. The statement $p \supset q$ does not assert that q is true, but only that it is true *if* the antecedent *p* is true. So *p* ⊃ *q* does not quite match the ordinary if . . . then because that can have several meanings, as in

If Clinton is firm, Gingrich will weaken.

If it's square, it has corners.

If all cats are mammals and all mammals are animals, then all cats are animals.

If you don't leave, I'll call the police.

Logicians use ⊃ to mean just this: *p* ⊃ *q* is true if and only if ~(*p* · ~*q*) is true; that is, *p* implies *q* if and only if it is *not* the case that *p* is true when *q* is false.

All the following statements mean the same thing, and all can be symbolized *C* ⊃ *T*:

If machines can play chess, then they are able to think.

Machines can play chess only if they are able to think.

Machines are able to think, if they can play chess.

Machines are able to think, given that they can play chess.

Machines are able to think, provided that they can play chess.

Machines are able to think, on the condition that they can play chess.

Machines can play chess implies (entails) that they are able to think.

Machines playing chess is a sufficient condition for their being able to think.

Unless machines can think, they cannot play chess.

Machines can't play chess unless they can think.

Notice that "Machines can think only if they can play chess" is *not* equivalent to the above statements.

For example, "If we take Bob, it will rain" is true in *every* case, except where we take Bob and it doesn't rain. If we don't take Bob, then it may still be true that *if* we took him it would rain. And if we take him and it rains, then it is clearly true that if we take him it rains (not that he caused it!). But if we take him and it doesn't rain, then our statement "If we take Bob, it will rain" is clearly false.

Another example: "If I lie down, I'll fall asleep." This is false *only* if I lie down and do not fall asleep. It is true if I don't lie down, whether I fall asleep or not, and it is true if I do lie down and do fall asleep. The truth table says just this, no more and no less: *p* ⊃ *q* is false only if *p* is true and *q* is false.

It is worth noting here that *p* ⊃ *q* is equivalent to ~(*p* · ~*q*), which you can verify by comparing their truth tables. In ordinary language this means that "If *p*, then q" is true *if and only if* "It is not true that q is false when p is true." For example, the following two statements mean the same thing:

> *If you keep that up, I'll call the police.*
>
> *Either you stop that or I'll call the police.*

This equivalence rule, which allows us to replace such statements with each other, is called material implication. We write this

$$p \supset q \equiv \sim(p \cdot \sim q)$$

where $\equiv$ means "is equivalent to," which means that (1) the two expressions have the same truth-value or (2) one is true if and only if the other is true *and* one is false if and only if the other is false. This is a stronger relationship than implication. If the "if" occurs somewhere other than the front of a sentence, we rearrange it so that the statement following the "if" comes first. That statement is called the *antecedent,* and the one following is the *consequent.* So it is important to note that $A \supset B$ is *not* equivalent to $B \supset A$. "Tom speaks unless Jerry speaks" is symbolized $T \supset \sim J$.

Necessary and Sufficient "Tom's speaking is a *necessary* condition for Jerry's speaking" is symbolized $J \supset T$. "Tom's speaking is a *sufficient* condition for Jerry's speaking" is symbolized $T \supset J$. The biconditional if and only if, $\equiv$, stands for truth-functional equivalence or material equivalence. It means that two statements have the same truth value, *not* that they mean the same thing.

Exercise 5.1   A. Symbolize the following:

1. Tom is pleased.

2. Tom is pleased and so is Julie.

3. Neither Chuck nor Bob will join.

4. Either Chuck or Bob will join.

5. Either Gore will win or Bush will win.

6. Both Jack and Bobby were involved with Marilyn.

7. I'll have eggs and bacon.

8. I won't take algebra.

9. Jackson won't become vice-president.

10. I like Cybill and Bruce.

11. It's not morning yet.

12. Neither Reagan nor Gorbachev understood the INF Treaty.

13. Alf is not human.

14. New York is bigger than Chicago.

15. Neither you nor I can go.

16. Either you're joking or I'm not staying.

17. My favorite comic books are *Thor* and *Donald Duck*.

18. Dolphins are not really fish but marlin are.

19. He's both an addict and an alcoholic and either asleep or unconscious.

20. I'll have two pancakes, bacon, two eggs, orange juice, coffee, and either toast and jelly or biscuits and honey.

B. If *A*, *B*, and *C* are true and *X*, *Y*, and *Z* are false, which of the following statements are true? Brackets [ ] and braces { } work as they do in algebra.

1. A

2. $A \cdot B$

3. $A \cdot X$

4. $(A \cdot B)$ v X

5. $(A \cdot X)$ v Y

6. $\sim(A$ v $B)$

7. $[A$ v $(B \cdot C)] \cdot \sim[(A \cdot C)$ v $(A \cdot B)]$

8. $\sim[(A \cdot X)$ v $\sim(A \cdot B)]$

9. $\sim B$ v $\sim X$

10. $\sim\{\sim B$ v $\sim C)$ v $(Y \cdot \sim Z)] \cdot [(\sim A$ v $X)$ v $B]\}$

C. Based on these statements,

Let *A* stand for "George W. Bush won the 2000 presidential race"

Let *B* stand for "Santa Claus lives at the North Pole"

Let *C* stand for "Bismark is the capital of Idaho"

which of the following statements are true?

1. $A \cdot B$

2. $A \cdot \sim C$

3. $\sim\{\sim[(B \cdot C)$ v $(B \cdot C)]\}$

4. $\sim[(A$ v $\sim B)$ v $(A \cdot \sim C)$ v $(\sim B)]$

5. $\sim\{\sim[\sim B \cdot \sim C)] \cdot A\}$

D. If *A*, *B*, and *C* are true and *D*, *E*, and *F* are false, which of the following statements are true?

1. $A \supset B$

2. $A \supset D$

3. $D \supset A$

4. $(A \vee B) \supset F$

5. $(A \supset B) \supset (D \supset B)$

6. $(D \supset E) \vee (A \supset F)$

7. $[(A \vee B) \supset (B \supset C)] \supset (D \vee B)$

8. $[(A \vee B \supset (B \supset E) \vee C] \supset (D \vee E \vee F)$

9. $\{[(A \vee B) \supset (C \vee D) \supset F] \supset [(A \supset B) \vee F]] \supset (B \vee E)\}$

10. $[(D \supset B) \cdot (B \supset C) \cdot (A \supset D)] \vee \{[(C \supset E) \vee (B \vee C)] \supset B\}$

E.   Assuming these statements are true,

A: Erik and Lyle killed their parents

B: Elena maimed her husband

C: Family values have broken down

which of the following are true?

1. $(A \cdot B) \supset \sim C$

2. $(A \cdot B) \supset C$

3. $(A \vee B) \supset C$

4. $C \supset (A \vee B)$

5. $\sim C \supset \sim (A \cdot B)$

5.2 Some More Argument Forms

Consider this argument:

> *If I fell asleep, I missed the news.*
>
> *I fell asleep.*
>
> ∴ *I missed the news.*

We can show this argument to be valid by means of a Venn diagram, but first we must translate it into categorical statements:

All my falling-asleep-today times are my missed-the-news today times.

All news times today are my falling-asleep times.

∴ All news times today are my missed-the-news-today times.

Then we symbolize and diagram it:

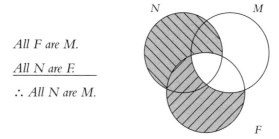

All F are M.

All N are F.

∴ All N are M.

It is valid, but the translation is very tortured. There is an easier way to do it. We can symbolize it

$F \supset M$

F

$\therefore M$

And so its general form is what logicians call **modus ponens** (MP):

$p \supset q$

p

$\therefore q$

We can prove that any argument with this general form is valid, by means of a truth table:

Sentences		Premises		Conclusion
p	q	$p \supset q$	p	$/ \therefore q$
T	T	T	T	T
T	F	F	T	F
F	T	T	F	T
F	F	T	F	F

(every possible case)

The guide columns ("Sentences") ensure that we have examined every possible case: where p and q are both true, where p is true and q is false, where p is false and q is true, and where both p and q are false. The next two columns ("Premises") list the truth-values (T or F) of the premises in every case, and the last column ("Conclusion") lists every possible truth-value of the conclusion.

The first row states that when p and q are true, the premises $p \supset q$ and p are also true, and the conclusion q is also true. And so on for the other rows. (*Note:* An argument in which the premises are all true and the conclusion false is always invalid!)

So now we ask: Is it possible for the premises to be true and the conclusion false? Can we find a row in which $p \supset q$ and p are true and q is false? That is, is there a row that states the following?

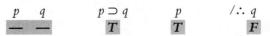

p	q		$p \supset q$		p		$/\therefore q$
—	—		*T*		*T*		*F*

No, so the argument form MP is valid. It will never take true premises and produce a false conclusion, so the argument we began with is valid.

But consider this:

> *If I fell asleep, I missed the news*
>
> *I did not fall asleep*
>
> ∴ *I did not miss the news*

which has the form

> $p \supset q$
>
> ~p
>
> ~q

This is invalid. In the truth table for this argument form, there is a row in which the premises are true and the conclusion is false:

p	q		$p \supset q$		~p		$/\therefore$ ~q
F	*T*		*T*		*T*		*F*

This means the argument *cannot* be valid!

I might have stayed awake but missed the news anyway because, for example, the house caught fire. The above invalid argument form is called the **fallacy of denying the antecedent.**

Now look at the following argument:

> *If I fell asleep, I missed the news.*
>
> *I missed the news.*
>
> ∴ *I fell asleep.*

We symbolize it as

$F \supset M$

M

$\therefore F$

And so its general form is

$p \supset q$

q

$\therefore p$

which we test with a truth table:

p	q	$p \supset q$	q	$/\therefore p$
T	T	T	T	T
T	F	F	F	T
F	T	T	T	F
F	F	T	F	F

Is there a row that ends in T T F? Yes, the third row, so this argument form (the **fallacy of affirming the consequent**) is invalid. In other words, this argument form gives a false conclusion with true premise in case p is false and q is true. In our original example, this would be the case where I did not fall asleep but I missed the news anyway (perhaps I was watching a "Tom and Jerry" cartoon on another channel).

Then there is the **hypothetical syllogism** (HS). An example is

If Jim resigns, Jerry will take over

If Jerry takes over, Satan will be the victor

∴ If Jim resigns, Satan will be the victor

which we symbolize as

$R \supset T$

$T \supset S$

$\therefore R \supset S$

which has the general form

$p \supset q$

$q \supset r$

$\therefore p \supset r$

and which we prove by means of a truth table (three statements means we need
$2^3 = 2 \times 2 \times 2 = 8$ rows):

Guide Columns			*Premises*		*Conclusion*
p	*q*	*r*	*p* ⊃ *q*	*q* ⊃ *r*	/∴ *p* ⊃ *r*
T	*T*	*T*	*T*	*T*	*T*
T	*T*	*F*	*T*	*F*	*F*
T	*F*	*T*	*F*	*T*	*T*
T	*F*	*F*	*F*	*F*	*F*
F	*T*	*T*	*T*	*T*	*T*
F	*T*	*F*	*T*	*T*	*T*
F	*F*	*T*	*T*	*T*	*T*
F	*F*	*F*	*T*	*T*	*T*

This time we have *eight* rows to account for all the possible cases. (In general, if
we have *n* sentence-letters, we will have 2^n rows. If we have four statements to
deal with, we have $2^4 = 2 \times 2 \times 2 \times 2 = 16$ rows. If we have five statements, we
will have $2^5 = 2 \times 2 \times 2 \times 2 \times 2 = 32$ rows.)

Now we ask: Is there any row that looks like this?

p	*q*	*r*	*p* ⊃ *q*	*q* ⊃ *r*	/∴ *p* ⊃ *r*
—	—	—	*T*	*T*	*F* . . .

That is, is there any row in which all the premises are true and the conclusion
false? No. That means that when the premises are true, the conclusion is true; that
proves the argument form HS is valid. Since our original argument has this form,
it's valid, too. (*Remember:* No argument with true premises and a false conclusion
can be valid.)

Testing an argument a bit more directly is permissible. We use capital letters
that indicate which statements we mean rather than *p*'s and *q*'s. Suppose we are
confronted with this argument:

If Hillary talks, Bill will listen.

Bill won't listen.

∴ *Hillary won't talk.*

We can symbolize this as

$H \supset B$

~*B*

∴ ~*H*

and test it:

H	B		H ⊃ B		~B		/∴ ~H
T	T		T		F		F
T	F		F		T		F
F	T		T		F		T
F	F		T		T		T

There is no row that ends in T T F, and so the argument, which incidentally has the form

$$p \supset q$$

$$\underline{\sim q\qquad}$$

$$\therefore \sim p$$

and which is called **modus tollens** (MT), is valid. (*Note:* With two premises, we look for a T T F; with three premises, T T T F; with four premises, T T T T F; and so on.) Here's one more example:

> *Either Hillary will talk or Bill will.*
>
> *Hillary will not talk.*
>
> ∴ *Bill will talk.*

We symbolize this as

H	B		H v B		~H		/∴ B
T	T		T		F		T
T	F		T		F		F
F	T		T		T		T
F	F		F		T		F

↑ resultant column

No row ends in T T F. So this argument, the form of which is called **disjunctive syllogism** (DS), is valid.

Dilemmas The **dilemma** is a combination of hypothetical and disjunctive statements. For example:

> *Either Jack will fly the plane or Katy will.*
>
> *If Jack flies the plane, Lucy will go along.*
>
> *If Katy goes along, so will Max.*
>
> ∴ *Either Lucy will go along or Max will.*

Its most general logical form is

> *Either J or K*
>
> *If J, then L*
>
> *If K, then M*
> _____
>
> ∴ *Either L or M*

which is symbolized

> *p v q*
>
> *p ⊃ r*
>
> *q ⊃ s*
> _____
>
> ∴ *r v s*

This can easily be shown to be valid with a truth table.

The dilemma is among the most powerful forms of argument. Like the horns of a charging bull, its alternatives seem to leave you with no escape. For example:

> *Either you'll get old or you'll die young.*
>
> *If you get old, that's sad.*
>
> *If you die young, that's sad, too.*
> _____
>
> ∴ *Either way, it's sad.*

There are three standard ways of responding to the dilemma:

1. "*Going between the horns.*" This means you reject the either–or statement. Perhaps you won't die young or get old, either, but perhaps you will get middle-aged and die then. But that's sad, too.

2. "*Grasping it by the horns.*" This means you deny one of the alternative conclusions. It's not sad to get old; many old people are happy.

3. *The counterdilemma.* You offer another dilemma, made of the same elements, whose conclusion negates the original conclusion: Either you'll get old or you'll die. If you get old, that's good, because you'll live a long time. If you die young, that's good, because you won't have to suffer through old age. So either way, it's good!

Here's another example: Either the first lady knew or she didn't. If she knew, she lied to the committee. If she didn't know, she's incompetent.

1. Going between the horns: She forgot.

2. Grasping it by the horns: She knew but was making a secret effort to spare the innocent.

3. The counterdilemma: Either she knew or she didn't. If she knew, she was making a secret effort to spare the innocent. If she didn't know, it was because her subordinates were willing to risk their careers to protect her while they did as they believed she would have approved. Therefore, either the first lady was making a secret effort or her subordinates were willing and so on.

Exercise 5.2   A. Symbolize the following arguments and test their validity by means of truth tables.

1. If Meg says yes, Dennis will divorce her. She does say yes. So Dennis will divorce her.

2. Either Meg or Cameron will be upset. Meg will not be upset. So Cameron will be upset.

3. You can get Madonna's photo if you clear it with Sara. You cannot clear it with Sara. So you cannot get Madonna's photo.

4. Either Ollie is guilty or Ronnie is. Ollie is guilty. So Ronnie is not.

5. If Pete agrees, so will Tilly. If Tilly agrees, so will George. So if Pete agrees, so will George.

6. If Heidi is guilty, she should be prosecuted. If she is prosecuted, she should tell all. She should not tell all. So she is not guilty.

7. If she sees him standing there, she'll never dance with another. She does not see him standing there. So she will dance with another.

8. If Michael appears, Lisa Marie is waiting. Michael does not appear. So Lisa Marie is not waiting.

9. Either Michael or Britney will appear. If Michael appears, we'll hear "Bad." If Britney appears, we'll hear "Oops! I Did It Again." So we'll hear either "Bad" or "Oops! I Did It Again."

10. If the king is abducted, Elton will be happy. If Elton is happy, Tony will be delighted. The king is abducted. Therefore, Tony will be delighted.

11. If Bush loses, Gore would become president. Bush did not lose. So Gore did not become president.

12. If Congress does not raise taxes, social problems will increase. If social problems increase, crime will increase. If crime increases, it will not be a more compassionate world. So if Congress will not raise taxes, it will not be a more compassionate world.

13. If taxes increase, the poor and the middle class will suffer most. Taxes will not increase. So the poor and the middle class will not suffer.

14. Either the Supreme Court will overturn *Roe v. Wade* (in the case of *Webster v. Reproductive Health Sciences*) or publicly funded abortions will continue. Publicly funded abortions will not continue. Therefore, the Supreme Court will overturn *Roe v. Wade*.

15. If Justice Stephens votes to overturn *Roe v. Wade,* so will Justice Kennedy. Stephens will vote to overturn *Roe v. Wade*. Therefore, so will Kennedy.

B. Test the following argument forms for validity by means of truth tables.

1. $p \supset q$

   p

   $\therefore q$

2. $p \supset q$

   $\sim q$

   $\therefore \sim p$

3. p

   $\therefore p \lor q$

4. $p \lor q$

   $\sim q$

   $\therefore p$

5. $p \supset q$

   $q \supset r$

   $r \supset s$

   $\therefore \sim s \supset \sim p$

6. $p \lor \sim p$ (show that this is *always* true)

7. $p \supset q$

   $q \supset r$

   $\therefore p \supset r$

8. p

   q

   $\therefore p \cdot q$

9. $(p \supset q) \cdot (r \supset s)$

   $p \lor r$

   $\therefore q \lor s$

10. $p \supset q$

    $\sim p$

    $\therefore \sim q$

11. $p \lor q$

    $q \lor r$

    $\therefore p \lor r$

12. $p \lor q$

    $\sim p$

    $\therefore q$

13. $p \cdot q$

$\therefore p$

14. $p \supset q$

$\therefore p \supset (p \cdot q)$

15. $(p \supset q) \lor (r \supset s)$

$p \cdot r$

$\therefore q \cdot s$

16. $p \supset q$

$q \supset r$

$r \supset s$

$s \supset t$

$\sim t$

$\therefore \sim p$

C. Respond to the following dilemmas.

1. Either Tom knew about the wiring or he didn't. If he did, he was dishonest. If he didn't, he was incompetent. So either he was dishonest or incompetent.

2. Either she will leave him or she won't. If she does, she'll feel like a failure. If she doesn't, she will continue to be abused. So either she'll feel like a failure or be abused.

3. Either he will live or he will die. If he lives, he will continue to suffer; if he dies, his life will be over. So either he will suffer or his life will be over.

4. Either she's a spy or she's a criminal. If she's a spy, she's dangerous. If she's a criminal, she's dangerous. So either way, she's dangerous.

5. You can open it now or wait until Christmas. If you open it now, it'll spoil your Christmas. If you wait, you'll be driven mad by curiosity. So either your Christmas will be spoiled or you'll be driven mad by curiosity.

6. Either Ratscough will take responsibility or he won't. If he does, he faces criminal prosecution. If he doesn't, he'll have to betray the president. So either he'll face prosecution or betray the president.

7. If I watch *Survivor*, I'll miss *20/20*. If I watch *20/20*, I'll miss *Survivor*. So either way I'll miss a good show.

8. Either Ben or Alex must win. If Ben wins, then Alex must die. If Alex wins, Ben's family will be destroyed. So either Alex must die or Ben's family will be destroyed.

9. Either I'll lose my job or I won't. If I do, I'll be out of work. If I don't, I'll have to continue to put up with the Big Boss. So either I have to put up with the Big Boss or I'll be out of work.

10. Either I'll feed the stray dog or I won't. If I do, it will hang around. If I don't, it might starve. So either it will hang around or it will starve.

11. If Juice Plus cured his rheumatoid arthritis, O. J. was lying about being unable to use the knife. If it did not cure his arthritis, he was lying in the commercial he made. So either way O. J. is a liar.

12. If he doesn't resign, he'll be crucified by the press. If he does resign, he'll be presumed guilty. Either he will resign or he won't. So either he'll be crucified by the press or presumed guilty.

13. Either we celebrate now or later. If we celebrate now, we might jinx the race. If we don't, then we might never get to celebrate at all. So either we jinx the race or never get to celebrate.

14. You can drink the rest of the water now or wait until you need it more. If you drink it now, you can't drink when you need it more. If you wait, you will become dehydrated and die. So either you can't drink it when you need it or you will become dehydrated.

15. Either you trust the president or you don't. If you do, you'll be damaged when the scandal comes out. If you don't, you'll be called treacherous. So either you'll be damaged or you'll be called treacherous.

16. Either evolution should be dropped or creationism should be taught. If evolution is dropped, students will not get a one-sided view. If creationism is added, students will get both sides of the issue. So either way, students will not get a one-sided view.

17. Either the Supreme Court will reverse *Roe v. Wade* or it won't. If it does, women will go to backstreet butchers. If it doesn't, millions of fetuses will be aborted. So either women will go to backstreet butchers or millions of fetuses will be aborted.

18. Either we will go to nuclear power or we will use fossil fuels. If we go to nuclear power, we will have nuclear accidents. If we use fossil fuels, we will destroy the ozone layer. So either we will have nuclear accidents or we will destroy the ozone layer.

19. Either I will have the baby or have an abortion. If I have the baby, I'll have to drop out of school and get a job to take care of it. If I have an abortion, I'll feel guilty. So either I'll have to drop out of school or I'll feel guilty.

20. If we divorce, the children will suffer. If we don't, we'll suffer. Either we'll get a divorce or not. So either we or the children will suffer.

D. In the following editorial, pick out all arguments that exemplify truth-functional argument forms found in this chapter (MP, HS, and so on) and also the formal fallacies (fallacy of denying the antecedent and so on), if any.

Control, Yes; but Don't Ban Human Cloning[1]

Our View: Stopping human cloning research is simply unrealistic; whatever happens, science marches on

Scientists around the world are racing toward the moment when human cloning is not just thinkable, but totally doable. Despite new calls from alarmed federal lawmakers, there is no way to stop the science. And despite the concerns of everyone else, there's not yet any need to.

To be sure, the current alarms over human cloning—conditioned as much by fiction as by fact—resonate deeply. Members of Congress now want to ban federal funding of human cloning research. And some, following the lead of several European nations, want to outlaw such research entirely.

But there's a better way to handle the matter, and it's already been tested. In the early 1970s, breakthroughs in genetic engineering sparked similar uneasiness among lawmakers, consumers and scientists. They worried that the newly developed ability to move genetic material between species might produce mutant lifeforms and deadly new pathogens.

None of those fears came true, and today we enjoy the benefits of genetic engineering in everything from tomatoes to insulin. That's because instead of overreacting, lawmakers and the scientific establishment created a federal advisory panel to establish biosafety standards and review applications for new experiments. The public was reassured and the science marched on.

That model can work today, with similar benefits. A federal panel would allow regulators to help modulate the pace and direction of cloning research. And it would provide the context for continuing public debate. For example, some scientists oppose cloning research on human embryos, but not on clusters of human cells *before* they form an embryo. That's a super-fine line, and it needs to be thoroughly discussed before the nation takes sides.

Also, such engagement gives American consumers a first-look at any new medical benefits that the research produces. Among the hoped-for outcomes—new organs for needy transplant patients.

Finally, the regulatory process can be left flexible. If new hazards—biological or ethical—are discovered, then the regulations can be tightened. But if our fears are unwarranted, they can be eased.

---

1. *Source:* Editorial, *USA TODAY,* 18 March 1997. Copyright 1997, USA TODAY. Reprinted with permission.

On the other hand, if human cloning research is outlawed, it will merely be driven offshore. And if it is denied funds, it will be driven entirely into the hands of commercial laboratories. Either way, the science marches on—to the beat of someone else's drum.

So far, federal lawmakers have had a busy year legislating medical options. They have debated hospital stays, diagnostic techniques and procedures. Now, some want to outlaw an entire field of medical opportunity. They warn about scientists who play God. The real threat, though, is posed by lawmakers who play doctor.

5.3 Deductive Proofs

Rules of Inference   Since we know that the argument form modus ponens (MP) is valid, whenever we see an instance of that form, we know that the inference is valid, so we can skip the use of truth tables. We can use MP as a rule of inference. This method is the basis of deductive proofs.

Consider the following argument:

If Ann joins, so will Bob. If Bob joins, Charles will resign. If Charles resigns, Dave will pitch a fit. Ann will join. So Dave will pitch a fit.

Proving this argument with a truth table would require sixteen rows and twelve columns. Instead, we symbolize it, using the underlined letters above—for example, A for "Ann joins"—and write it this way:

$A \supset B$

$B \supset C$

$C \supset D$

$A \quad /\therefore D$

Next we number each premise:

(1) $A \supset B$

(2) $B \supset C$

(3) $C \supset D$

(4) $A \quad /\therefore D$

Then we use the rule we have learned already, MP, and write the next step:

    (5) B   1, 4 MP

which means we get *B* from lines (1) and (4) and the rule MP. This is because

    (1) A ⊃ B

    (4) A   _____

    ∴ *B*

is clearly an instance of

    p ⊃ q

    p   _____

    ∴*q*   *(MP)*

Next we write

    (6) C   2, 5 MP

which means we get *C* from lines (2) and (5) and MP (again). Finally,

    (7) D   3, 6 MP

which is the conclusion we wanted to prove.

In Section 5.2, we also proved the validity of the argument forms hypothetical syllogism (HS), disjunctive syllogism (DS), and modus tollens (MT). This means we can use these argument forms as rules in deductive proofs. Let's try proving the following:

    If <u>A</u>rgentina responds, <u>B</u>razil will declare war.

    If <u>B</u>razil declares war, so will <u>C</u>hile.

    Either <u>P</u>araguay will respond or <u>A</u>rgentina will.

    <u>P</u>araguay will not respond.

    Therefore, <u>C</u>hile will declare war.

We first symbolize the argument and number the premises:

    (1) A ⊃ B

    (2) B ⊃ C

    (3) P v A

    (4) ~P   */ ∴ C*

We want to get *C* from the premises and the rules. *C* is found in line (2), implied by *B*. *B* is in line (1), implied by *A*. *A* is in line (3), which states *P* v *A*. Line (4) states ~*P*. By the rule DS, we can get *A* from lines (3) and (4), so let that be our first step:

(5) A   3, 4   DS

Then we get *B* from (1) and (5) and the rule MP:

(6) B   1, 5   MP

We get *C* from (2) and (6) and MP:

(7) C   2, 6   MP

which is what we wanted to prove. The smart approach is obviously to work backward from the conclusion.

Here's another example:

If Einstein is right, time travel is impossible.

If time travel is impossible, Star Trek is nonsense.

If Star Trek is nonsense, so is Star Wars.

If Star Wars is nonsense, Katharine Hepburn was Princess Leia.

Katharine Hepburn was not Princess Leia.

Therefore, Einstein is wrong (not right).

We symbolize it and number the premises:

(1) R ⊃ I

(2) I ⊃ T

(3) T ⊃ W

(4) W ⊃ L

(5) ~L   /∴ ~R

We want to prove ~*R*, which we get from line (1) and ~*I* and MT. We get ~*I* from line (2) and ~*T* and MT, ~*T* from line (3) and ~*W* and MT, and ~*W* from line (4) and ~*L* and MT. Line 5 states ~*L*, so our first step is

(6) ~W   4, 5   MT

and then

(7) ~T   3, 6   MT

(8) ~I   2, 7   MT

(9) ~R   1, 8   MT

which is what we wanted to prove.

We could have proved it another way:

(1) $R \supset I$

(2) $I \supset T$

(3) $T \supset W$

(4) $W \supset L$

(5) ~L   /∴ ~R

(6) $R \supset T$ 1, 2   HS

(7) $R \supset W$ 6, 3   HS

(8) $R \supset L$ 7, 4   HS

(9) ~R   8, 5   MT

So far we have introduced the following rules of inference:

1. modus ponens (MP):

$p \supset q$

$\underline{p}$

∴ q

2. Modus tollens (MT):

$p \supset q$

$\underline{\sim q}$

∴ ~p

3. Hypothetical syllogism (HS):

$p \supset q$

$\underline{q \supset r}$

∴ $p \supset r$

4. Disjunctive syllogism (DS):

$p \lor q$

$\underline{\sim p}$

$\therefore q$

We have also proved them all valid by means of truth tables. Let's add the following:

5. Conjunction (Conj):

p

$\underline{q}$

$\therefore p \cdot q$

6. Simplification (Simp):

$\underline{p \cdot q}$

$\therefore p$

7. Addition (Add):

$\underline{p}$

$\therefore p \lor q$

8. Constructive dilemma (CD):

$(p \supset q) \cdot (r \supset s)$

$\underline{p \lor r}$

$\therefore q \lor r$

9. Absorption (Abs):

$\underline{p \supset q}$

$\therefore p \supset (p \cdot q)$

10. Excluded middle (EM) (*not* a rule of inference):

$p \lor \sim p$

(Logicians disagree about the status of this principle, or "law of thought." We include it here because, although we might not often need it, it is both true and useful.)

All these rules can be proved by means of truth tables (and in fact you have already proved them all in Exercise 5.2B). These argument forms can now be used as rules in deductive proofs.

Here's another example:

If Bush chooses Jackson as his running mate, he will lose the South. If he does not choose Jackson, he will lose the black vote. If Bush loses the South or loses the black vote, then Pennsylvania will secede, and Bush will lose the election. So Pennsylvania will secede or I'll be surprised.

The proof is

(1) J ⊃ S

(2) ~J ⊃ B

(3) (S v B) ⊃ (P · L)   /∴ P v I

(4) J v ~J   EM

(5) (J ⊃ S) · (~J ⊃ B)   1, 2   Conj

(6) S v B   5, 4   CD

(7) P · L   3, 6   MP

(8) P   7   Simp

(9) P v I   8   Add

For our final example in this chapter, we return to Justice Blackmun's stand on the death penalty. This time we state the arguments somewhat differently, for we can now deal with much larger pieces of argumentation.

> **On Death Sentences[2]**
>
> If a Supreme Court nominee had told the Senate Judiciary Committee what Justice Harry Blackmun said in an opinion on Tuesday, that nominee's chances of confirmation would be zero. And rightly so. For in saying that he'll never vote to uphold a death sentence, Mr. Blackmun did more than deliver his moral judgment on the fairness of capital punishment. He abrogated his sworn duty to judge each case as its facts fit the U.S. Constitution.
>
> In effect, Mr. Blackmun, 85, says that he already has *prejudged all* future death penalty cases. His fine, learned mind has served American justice well in his 20-plus years on the court. But as his career closes, so has his mind closed—at least on this

2. *Source:* Editorial, *Miami Herald,* 24 February 1994. Reprinted with permission of *Miami Herald,* via CCC.

most divisive of issues. No appellant expecting—as every appellant has a *right* to expect—an open judicial mind need knock.

Forget about whatever facts a future death penalty appeal may bring. Forget that a future appellant may well be Danny Rolling, confessed white butcher of five white college students. Do the death penalty's biases, which Justice Blackmun has adjudged to be incurably skewed against blacks and poor people, apply to white killers too?

No other issue is as visceral, as intractable to normal reasoning processes, as capital punishment. Abortion comes close, but only close. Some people can rationalize a woman's right to an abortion but cannot rationalize the *state's* right, for any reason, to take a life.

Yet Justice Blackmun's error need not involve capital punishment, or abortion. The issue really lies in another plane. In that plane, wherein rests a judge's duty there is room for only one overriding principle, one enduring passion, one inviolable standard: fealty to the law.

It is not a jurist's prerogative to rule this way or that because a law is "good" or "bad." On the contrary. A judge takes an oath *not* to apply personal beliefs to the law.

It's the duty of legislators to do that. A society's laws reflect its beliefs and mores and values as legislators construe and codify those standards. Legislators may, and do, pack laws with absurdities or contradictions.

Judges are free to remark upon those absurdities and contradictions—but they can't revoke or change those that are lawful. If a statute comports with the applicable constitution, either state or U.S., a judge must apply the law, absurdity and contradiction and all.

Otherwise, unimaginable chaos and injustice would ensue. Suppose a Catholic judge interpreted the Bill of Rights according to papal encyclicals, not the Constitution. Suppose another religion teaches another judge that physical infirmity is God's punishment, and that those so "punished" don't deserve equal opportunity. Suppose a third judge's God teaches that women are inferior to men (or vice versa), or that racial or ethnic minorities are born inferior.

A judge may in fact hold odd personal beliefs—and still be a good judge. The litmus test requires covering personal beliefs, neck to ankles, with the jurist's black robe. It requires applying the law even when—especially when—the application of it runs counter to the judge's personal convictions.

This is the battle in which, on capital punishment, Mr. Blackmun has surrendered. It grieves his admirers to see the lion so felled by the thorn, with Androcles nowhere to be found.[3]

---

3. In a legend Androcles, an early Christian, pulls a thorn from a lion's paw. When the Romans throw Androcles to the lions, the lion that he helped spares his life.

The main conclusion is

Blackmun has abandoned his oath

and the main argument is

If Blackmun intends never to vote to uphold a death sentence, he is prejudging all such cases.

If he prejudges them, he must not be judging each case by the facts and the Constitution.

If he is not judging each case in that way, he must be applying his personal beliefs.

Any judge who applies his personal beliefs is abandoning his oath.

Blackmun intends never to vote to uphold another death sentence.

∴ *Blackmun has abandoned his oath.*

Now we write this as a deductive proof:

(1) ~I ⊃ P

(2) P ⊃ ~J

(3) ~J ⊃ B

(4) B ⊃ A

(5) ~I   /∴ A

(6) P   1, 5   MP

(7) ~J   2, 6   MP

(8) B   3, 7   MP

(9) A   4, 8   MP

The "Danny Rolling" argument might be treated as follows:

If Blackmun is right, the death penalty is not fair to blacks and the poor.

If it were unfair in that way, it would not apply to white murderer Danny Rolling.

But it does apply to him.

∴ *Blackmun is wrong.*

The deductive proof is

(1) B ⊃ ~F

(2) ~F ⊃ ~D

(3) D   /∴ ~B

(4) ?

Here we have a problem! We know that D is equivalent to $\sim(\sim D)$, which we need in order to proceed. So far we have no such rule, which we might naturally call the rule of double negatives. In the next section, is a list of such rules, called rules of replacement.

Other arguments, good and bad, are in this essay, which I encourage you to analyze. Certain other tactics are also employed, such as the "Androcles and the Lion" comment and the outrageous (to some) analogy that this writer draws between abortion and murder: If a woman has a right to an abortion, then surely the *state* has the right to execute people.

Rules of Replacement If we try to prove the following argument,

> *Either she committed suicide or she was murdered*
>
> *She was not murdered*
>
> *If she committed suicide, she was depressed about something*
>
> ∴ *She was depressed about something*

which we symbolize as

$S \vee M$

$\sim M$

$S \supset D$ / ∴ D

we find that we need a rule that says that $S \vee M$ is equivalent to $M \vee S$. We can use the rule DS to get S from $S \vee M$ and M and then get D from $S \supset D$ and S by the rule MP. The rule looks like this:

$p \vee q \equiv q \vee p$

To skip such a step would defeat the whole purpose of deductive proofs, which are meant to guarantee rigor. So let's demonstrate that $p \vee q = q \vee p$, with a truth table:

p	q		p	$\vee$	q	$\equiv$	q	$\vee$	p
T	T		T	T	T				
T	F		T	T	T				
F	T		T	T	T				
F	F		F	T	F				

↑ resultant column

Two statements are shown to be logically equivalent if each is true when the other is true and each is false when the other is false. In the preceding truth table, this is the case. The columns under *p* v *q* and *q* v *p* are exactly alike, so the two expressions are logically equivalent. The same is true of (*p . q*) = (*q . p*), which you can prove for yourself.

The rule we have proved, called **commutation** (Com), can be applied to expressions *within* a line of a proof—unlike the rules of inference that apply only to whole lines. Our proof looks like this:

(1) S v M

(2) ~M

(3) S ⊃ D   / ∴ D

(4) M v S   1   Com

(5) S   4, 2   DS

(6) D   3, 5   MP

A number of rules of replacement, including commutation, which we need, can be proved by means of truth tables:

1. De Morgan's laws (DM):

    $\sim(p \cdot q) \equiv (\sim p \text{ v} \sim q)$

    $\sim(p \text{ v } q) \equiv (\sim p \cdot \sim q)$

2. Commutation (Com):

    $(p \cdot q) \equiv (q \cdot p)$

    $(p \text{ v } q) \equiv (q \text{ v } p)$

3. Association (Assoc):

    $p \text{ v } (q \text{ v } r) \equiv (p \text{ v } q) \text{ v } r$

4. Distribution (Dist):

    $p \cdot (q \text{ v } r) \equiv (p \cdot q) \text{ v } (p \cdot r)$

5. Double negative (DN):

    $p \equiv \sim\sim p$

6. Transposition (Trans):

    $(p \supset q) \equiv (\sim q \supset \sim p)$

7. Implication (Imp):

    $(p \supset q) \equiv (\sim p \text{ v } q)$

8. Equivalence (Equiv):

$$(p \equiv q) \equiv (p \supset q) \cdot (q \supset p)$$

$$(p \equiv q) \equiv (p \cdot q) \lor (\sim p \cdot \sim q)$$

9. Exportation (Exp):

$$(p \cdot q) \supset r \equiv p \supset (q \supset r)$$

10. Tautology:

$$p \equiv (p \lor p)$$

$$p \equiv (p \cdot p)$$

We now have ten rules of inference (if we include excluded middle) and ten rules of replacement—twenty rules of deduction in all. Let's look at an argument in ordinary language to which we can apply a variety of these rules:

> *If either the suspect or her husband was at home at the time of the murder, then her alibi is true, and she is innocent. If she is innocent, she will consent to a polygraph test. But she will not consent to a polygraph test. Therefore, the suspect was not at home at the time of the murder.*

First, we symbolize and number the premises:

(1) $(S \lor H) \supset (A \cdot I)$

(2) $I \supset C$

(3) $\sim C$ /∴ $\sim S$

Now we try to prove *S*:

(4) $\sim I$	2, 3	*MT*
(5) $\sim I \lor \sim A$	4	*Add—rule of inference*
(6) $\sim A \lor \sim I$	5	*Com—rule of replacement*
(7) $\sim(A \cdot I)$	6	*DM—rule of replacement*
(8) $\sim(S \lor H)$	1, 7	*MT—rule of inference*
(9) $\sim S \cdot \sim H$	8	*DM—rule of replacement*
(10) $\sim S$	9	*Simp—rule of inference*

Doing a deductive proof involves spelling out every simple mental step from the premises to the conclusion. Although this method of proving the validity of an argument might seem tedious, many actual arguments will yield only to the powerful machinery of modern symbolic logic. Such arguments may be found in newspapers, magazines, professional books, and journals; in medicine, law, science, and technology; and on and on. (And, of course, there are always federal income-tax instructions.)

What if we suspect that one of these lengthy arguments is invalid? Not being able to devise a proof is not in itself a proof of invalidity. The failure might be due only to a lack of ingenuity in constructing the proof. We need a method of proving the invalidity of such arguments, and we will turn to that in Section 5.4.

Exercise 5.3   A. Give the justification for each step of the following proofs, using the rules of inference. Here's a sample:

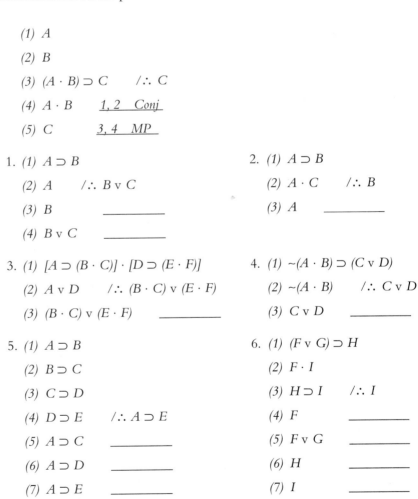

(1) A

(2) B

(3) (A · B) ⊃ C   /∴ C

(4) A · B   <u>1, 2   Conj</u>

(5) C   <u>3, 4   MP</u>

1. (1) A ⊃ B

  (2) A   /∴ B v C

  (3) B   _____

  (4) B v C   _____

2. (1) A ⊃ B

  (2) A · C   /∴ B

  (3) A   _____

3. (1) [A ⊃ (B · C)] · [D ⊃ (E · F)]

  (2) A v D   /∴ (B · C) v (E · F)

  (3) (B · C) v (E · F)   _____

4. (1) ~(A · B) ⊃ (C v D)

  (2) ~(A · B)   /∴ C v D

  (3) C v D   _____

5. (1) A ⊃ B

  (2) B ⊃ C

  (3) C ⊃ D

  (4) D ⊃ E   /∴ A ⊃ E

  (5) A ⊃ C   _____

  (6) A ⊃ D   _____

  (7) A ⊃ E   _____

6. (1) (F v G) ⊃ H

  (2) F · I

  (3) H ⊃ I   /∴ I

  (4) F   _____

  (5) F v G   _____

  (6) H   _____

  (7) I   _____

7. (1) $A \supset B$

(2) $C \supset \sim D$

(3) $A \vee (\sim\sim D \cdot \sim\sim B)$

(4) $\sim(A \cdot B)$ /∴ $\sim A \vee \sim B$

(5) $A \supset (A \cdot B)$ _____

(6) $\sim A$ _____

(7) $\sim\sim J \cdot \sim\sim B$ _____

(8) $\sim\sim D$ _____

(9) $\sim A$ _____

(10) $\sim A \vee \sim B$ _____

8. (1) A

(2) $A \supset B$ /∴ $B \vee C$

(3) B _____

(4) $B \vee C$ _____

9. (1) $S \supset T$

(2) $U \vee \sim T$

(3) $\sim U \cdot \sim V$ /∴ $\sim S$

(4) $\sim U$ _____

(5) $\sim T$ _____

(6) $\sim S$ _____

10. (1) $(A \supset B) \cdot (C \supset D)$

(2) $(B \supset T) \cdot (D \supset U)$

(3) A /∴ $T \vee U$

(4) $A \supset B$ _____

(5) $B \supset T$ _____

(6) $A \supset T$ _____

(7) T _____

(8) $T \vee U$ _____

B. Prove the following arguments valid by means of the rules of inference.

1. $A \supset B$

$A \cdot C$ /∴ $B \vee C$

2. $A \supset B$

$A \vee (P \cdot Q)$

$\sim B \cdot \sim E$ /∴ P

3. $Q \supset R$

$(Q \cdot R) \supset S$

$(Q \cdot T) \supset U$ /∴ $Q \supset U$

4. $(A \vee B) \supset C$

$(C \vee D) \supset E$

$D \vee A$

$\sim D$ /∴ E

5. $A \supset B$

$B \supset C$

$D \supset E$

$A \vee D$ /∴ $C \vee E$

6. $A \supset B$

$(B \cdot C) \supset D$

$\sim(B \cdot D)$ /∴ $\sim A$

7. $A \supset B$
   $B \supset C$
   $\sim C$
   A v E $/ \therefore E$

8. $A \supset B$
   $C \supset D$
   A v C $/ \therefore (A \cdot B)$ v $(C \cdot D)$

9. $A \supset B$
   $B \supset C$
   $\sim C$
   A v E $/ \therefore E$

10. $A \cdot B$
   $A \supset C$ $/ \therefore C$

C. Using the rules of inference, symbolize and construct a deductive proof for each of the following arguments.

1. If there was no capsule residue, she did not commit suicide. She either committed suicide or she was murdered. There was no capsule residue. So she was murdered.

2. If you buy stocks now you'll lose money. Either you buy stocks now or later. You won't buy stocks later. So you'll lose money.

3. Dolly and Linda will record new songs this year. If Dolly records a new song, it will be a hit. So Dolly's song will be a hit.

4. If Bruce meets Tiffany, he'll fall in love with her. He will not both fall in love with Tiffany and also marry her. So if he meets Tiffany, he won't marry her.

5. If Phil or Bill wins, then Jesse and Al lose. Phil wins. So Jesse loses.

6. If Ross picks Larry, he'll lose the South. If he loses the South, he won't win the election. Either he will pick Larry or he is not wise. If he is not wise, he'll lose the election. So either he'll lose the South or he'll win the election.

7. If Democrats win, we'll have higher taxes. If Republicans win, social programs will be cut. Either Democrats or Republicans will win. If we have higher taxes, inflation will rise. If social programs are cut, crime will rise. So either inflation or crime will rise.

8. If it rains, the drought will be over. If it rains and the drought is over, the crops will be saved. If the crops are saved, the farmers will not be bankrupted. Either the farmers will be bankrupted or the meteorologist is mistaken. It will rain. So the meteorologist is mistaken.

9. If I have no brothers or sisters, then my father's son must be me. If I am my father's son and my father's son is this man's father, then I am this man's father. I have no brothers or sisters. My father's son is this man's father. So I am this man's father or something is wrong somewhere.

10. I'll buy either a Subaru or a Toyota. If I buy a Subaru, I'll get good mileage. If I get a Toyota, I'll get a rebate. I won't get a Subaru. So I'll buy a Toyota and get a rebate.

11. Either the mayor or the police chief is corrupt. If the mayor is corrupt, so is the governor. If the police chief is corrupt, so are all the police officers. But the police officers are not all corrupt. So the mayor and the governor are corrupt.

12. If Noriega smuggles drugs, he is a criminal. If he is a criminal, he should be arrested. He smuggles drugs. So he is a criminal and should be arrested.

13. If Dukakis is of Greek descent, he loves philosophy. He is of Greek descent. So he loves philosophy.

14. If you're successful, you can afford cocaine. If you can afford it, you'll become addicted. If you become addicted, you'll play better basketball. So if you're successful, you'll become addicted and play better basketball or die of an overdose.

15. If you smoke, you'll get lung cancer. If you get lung cancer, you'll die young. If you die young, your family will be left destitute, and your wife and daughter will turn to prostitution. You smoke. So your daughter will turn to prostitution.

16. Either Marilyn committed suicide or she was murdered. If Dr. Noguchi is a licensed coroner, his word can be trusted. If he can be trusted, Marilyn did not commit suicide. But if she was murdered, there was a coverup, and people in high places are implicated. Dr. Noguchi is a licensed coroner. Therefore, people in high places are implicated.

17. If the heat wave continues, there will be no rain. If there is no rain, the drought will worsen, and crops will be destroyed. If crops are destroyed, there will be shortages of produce, and food prices will go up. The heat wave will continue, if the meteorologists know what they're talking about. They do know what they're talking about. So food prices will go up.

18. If Donald is there, Mickey will also be there. If both Donald and Mickey are there, the kids won't be disappointed. If either the kids are not disappointed or Henry doesn't get sick, the trip will be a success. Donald is there. So the trip will be a success.

19. If he is guilty, he should resign. If he is not guilty, he should explain his actions. Either he is guilty or the prosecutor is incompetent and the Justice Department is corrupt. He should not resign, and everybody knows it. So the prosecutor is incompetent.

20. If *The Satanic Verses* is blasphemous, it will offend millions of fundamentalist Muslims. If it offends fundamentalist Muslims, the Ayatollah will put a price on Salman Rushdie's head. If the Ayatollah puts a price on Rushdie's head, his life will be in danger. If Rushdie's life will be in danger, the book must be suppressed. So if *The Satanic Verses* is blasphemous, then Rushdie's life will be in danger, and the book must be suppressed.

D. Find, symbolize, and construct a deductive proof for an argument in the following editorial.

Protect Access to Clinics[4]

Our View: If local law enforcement officials cannot protect women, then Congress must step in

By a resounding majority, U.S. senators did a resoundingly right thing this week. They voted 69–30 to make it a federal crime to block access to abortion services and clinics, destroy clinic property or intimidate patients.

Not a moment too soon. In many states, for many years, anti-abortion agitators have conducted an unbridled reign of terror against clinics, abortion providers and abortion seekers. The National Abortion Federation has counted 329 violent incidents this year alone, including:

- One murder
- One attempted murder
- One bombing
- Eight arsons
- 15 bomb threats
- 66 death threats

The bombing and arsons alone have cost nearly $4 million, but the true losses are far more grave. Hundreds and thousands of women have been denied their constitutional rights through intimidation, confrontation—even murder.

Defenders of this pogrom say that clinic blockades are no different from the civil disobedience practiced by Martin Luther King Jr.

That grotesque rhetorical gargle is outrageous. Abortion opponents absolutely have a right to speak out and make protest. But bullying, fire-bombing, hate mail and murder are the tools of social fascism, not civil disobedience. If state and local law enforcement is unable to protect citizens from that—and in many places, it either cannot or will not—Congress has no choice but to order the federal government to do the job.

The new laws can't by themselves quell the campaigns of fear and intimidation. But violent, interstate efforts to deprive women of reproductive rights must not be tolerated. That's why even many senators who oppose abortion voted for the legislation.

Here's hoping that by the end of today, a House majority displays similar integrity and resolve. This is legislation that, individually and collectively, all Americans need to see enacted.

---

4. *Source:* Editorial, *USA TODAY,* 18 November 1993. Copyright 1993, USA TODAY. Reprinted with permission.

E. Give the justification for each step in the following proofs. Use the rules of inference and the rules of replacement.

1. *(1) R ⊃ S*

    (2) ~S v T   /∴ R ⊃ T

    (3) S ⊃ T _____

    (4) R ⊃ T _____

2. *(1) A v ~B*

    (2) B v (A v C)

    (3) ~A   /∴ C

    (4) ~B _____

    (5) A v C _____

    (6) C _____

3. *(1) A ⊃ B*

    (2) B ⊃ C

    (3) ~C   /∴ ~ (A v B)

    (4) ~B _____

    (5) ~A _____

    (6) ~A · ~B _____

    (7) ~(A v B) _____

4. *(1) (A ⊃ B) · (B ⊃ C)*

    (2) D ⊃ E

    (3) A v D   /∴ B v E

    (4) A ⊃ B _____

    (5) (A ⊃ B) · (D ⊃ E) _____

    (6) B v E _____

5. *(1) A v (B v C)*

    (2) ~A · ~B   /∴ C

    (3) ~A _____

    (4) B v C _____

    (5) ~B · ~A _____

    (6) ~B _____

    (7) C _____

6. *(1) A ⊃ B*

    (2) ~B v D   /∴ A ⊃ D

    (3) B ⊃ D _____

    (4) A ⊃ D _____

7. *(1) (A ⊃ B) v (C · D)*

    (2) ~C · ~B /∴ ~A

    (3) ~C _____

    (4) ~B _____

    (5) ~A _____

8. *(1) T ⊃ V*

    (2) ~(V · W)   /∴ T ⊃ ~W

    (3) ~V v ~W _____

    (4) V ⊃ ~W _____

    (5) T ⊃ ~W _____

9. *(1) ~A ⊃ ~B*

    (2) ~A ⊃ ~C

    (3) A ⊃ B

    (4) A ⊃ C   /∴ B ≡ C

    (5) B ⊃ A   ＿＿＿＿＿

    (6) C ⊃ A   ＿＿＿＿＿

    (7) B ⊃ C   ＿＿＿＿＿

    (8) C ⊃ B   ＿＿＿＿＿

    (9) (B ⊃ C) · (C ⊃ B)   ＿＿＿＿＿

    (10) B ≡ C   ＿＿＿＿＿

10. *(1) A ⊃ B*

    (2) C ⊃ D

    (3) ~B v C

    (4) A   /∴ D

    (5) B   ＿＿＿＿＿

    (6) B ⊃ C   ＿＿＿＿＿

    (7) A ⊃ C   ＿＿＿＿＿

    (8) A ⊃ D   ＿＿＿＿＿

    (9) D   ＿＿＿＿＿

F. Prove the following arguments, using the rules of replacement.

1. *~A v B*

   A   /∴ B

2. *A ⊃ B*

   ~B v C

   C ⊃ D

   A   /∴ D

3. *A v B*

   A v C

   [A v (B · C)] ⊃ D

   D ⊃ E   /∴ E

4. *(A v B) ⊃ C*

   C ⊃ D

   ~D   /∴ ~B

5. *~A v B*

   B ⊃ C

   D ≡ E

   ~C

   ~C v D   /∴ A ⊃ E

6. *(A · B) ⊃ C*

   (B ⊃ C) ⊃ D   /∴ A ⊃ D

7. *A ⊃ B*

   ~A ⊃ C

   ~B   /∴ C

8. *(A · B) ⊃ C*

   ~ C

   ~B   /∴ ~ A

9. *A* v (*B* · *C*)   10. ~*A* v *B*

   (*A* v *B*) ⊃ ~*D*   ~*B* v *C*

   D   /∴ *C*   ~*C*   /∴ ~(*B* v *C*)

G. Symbolize and construct proofs for the following arguments, using the rules of replacement.

1. He has either had too much wine or he has cholera. If the nausea stopped, then he can't have cholera. His nausea has stopped. So he must have had too much wine.

2. Not both Tyson and Spinks will win. Tyson will win. So Spinks will not win.

3. Miss Jones will accept the job if it is offered, as long as there are no strings attached. She will not accept the job, even though there were no strings attached. So she wasn't offered the job or there were strings attached.

4. It is not the case that Tom either disagrees or refuses to speak up. But he either agrees or he refuses to speak up. So he agrees.

5. If Ollie North is guilty, he will be punished. If he is punished, he will be repentant. He will not be repentant. So he is not guilty.

6. If the child's mother or father had examined him, the bruises would have been discovered, and the child would have been taken to a doctor. If he had been taken to a doctor, he would have lived. The child did not live. So neither his mother nor his father examined him.

7. If Dolly Parton had married Buddy Holly, her name would have been Dolly Holly. But if her name was Dolly Holly, she would have failed in show business. Either she did not fail or she married Buddy Holly.

8. If Einstein is right, time travel is impossible. Either time travel is possible or *Star Trek* is nonsense. *Star Trek* is not nonsense. So Einstein is wrong.

9. If Ames is found guilty, he will be pardoned by either Tom or Bob. He will not be pardoned by Tom. So he will be pardoned by Bob or he will not be found guilty.

10. If you break the law and are caught, you'll have to pay a fine. Paying a fine will mean you'll think twice next time, and if you think twice next time, then you'll profit from the experience. If you don't register for draft, you'll break the law, and you'll be caught. You won't register for the draft. So you'll be caught, and you'll profit from the experience.

11. If there are witches, there are hexes. If there are hexes, some illnesses are caused by magic. But if some illnesses are caused by magic, then either medical science is in the dark or it is dishonest. But medical science is not dishonest, and it is not in the dark. So there are no witches.

12. If I get drunk again, my wife will walk out. I can't go to the office party unless she goes with me. If she walks out, she won't go with me to the party. Either I go the party or my boss will be angry and I'll be fired. So if I get drunk again, I'll be fired.

13. If Pete Rose is innocent, the press was wrong to impugn his integrity. Either he is innocent or the investigators were stupid and inadequate. The investigators were neither stupid nor inadequate. So Pete Rose is innocent and the press was wrong to impugn his integrity.

14. If the captain of the *Vincennes* knew the plane was a civilian plane, he was a vicious murderer. If he didn't know, he was incompetent. He was not a vicious murderer. So he was incompetent or something was wrong with the most technologically sophisticated ship in history.

15. If Al or Betty shows up, then Charles and Dorothy will leave. Charles will not leave. So Al won't show up.

16. If Clinton was a good president and the country recognizes that fact, Gore will be elected. If Clinton was not a good president, Gore will not be elected. If Gore is elected, then we'll go to war in the Middle East. If he is not elected, taxes will go up. Taxes will not go up. So Clinton was a good president.

17. Either Alice will not drive or Betty will stay home. Either Betty will not stay home or Cindy will bring the ammunition. Cindy will not bring the ammunition. Therefore, it will not be the case that Betty will stay home or Cindy will bring the ammunition.

18. If Willie or Waylon appears, so will Hank, Jr. If Hank, Jr., appears, the audience will go wild. The audience will not go wild. So Waylon will not appear.

19. Either there is no Santa Claus or Betty lied to me. If Betty lied, so did Charles. If there is a tooth fairy, then Rudolph exists, and if Rudolph exists, there is a tooth fairy. Either there is a tooth fairy or Charles did not lie. So if there is a Santa Claus, then Rudolph exists.

20. Either Waldheim is innocent or the pope was wrong to grant him an audience. Either Waldheim is innocent or he was a Nazi. If Waldheim is innocent or the pope was wrong to grant him an audience and he was a Nazi, then we should let bygones be bygones. If we should let bygones be bygones, then none of us really knows right from wrong. So none of us really knows right from wrong.

21. Either Smith is guilty or Congress will be embarrassed. If Smith is guilty, he should be punished. Smith should not be punished. So Congress will be embarrassed.

22. If Williams is not guilty, he should be exonerated. If he is guilty, he should not be exonerated, and he should be punished. Therefore, either he should be exonerated or he should be punished.

23. If Senator Jones prevails, the poor will suffer. If he does not prevail, Republicans will suffer. So either the poor or the Republicans will suffer.

24. If the B-1 bomber does not work, the Pentagon has wasted $28 billion. Either the B-1 does not work or the Stealth bomber does not work. If the Stealth bomber does not work, the Pentagon will waste $70 billion. Neither the B-1 nor the Stealth works. So the Pentagon has wasted $28 billion and will waste $70 billion.

25. Unless Arafat is a changed man, he cannot be trusted. If the PLO has sworn to destroy Israel, then Arafat is not a changed man. The PLO has sworn to destroy Israel and fully intends to do it. So Arafat fully intends to destroy Israel and cannot be trusted.

H. Symbolize and construct a proof for an argument in the following editorial, using the rules of replacement.

Protect Everyone's Rights in Surrogate Motherhood[5]

Our View: Laws banning the practice send it underground; we need laws to protect the rights of all the parties

A billboard that appeared in Texas recently read "Womb for Rent." A Houston woman willing to bear a child for an infertile couple was looking to top the going surrogate rate of $10,000–$20,000, and newspapers refused her ads.

Thursday, news emerged that might interest folks thinking about taking up her offer. Among other legal woes, Whitney Neuhaus, 43, faces federal mail-fraud and money-laundering charges that could send her away for 20 years.

Five years after New Jersey's ghastly Baby M case focused attention on the risks of surrogate motherhood, little has been done to protect the innocent.

Only 19 states have any laws on the subject, mostly limitations. A few unwisely make surrogacy for profit a crime.

The Baby M case, in which a surrogate mother reneged on a contract with a childless couple, showed what's needed.

New Jersey's Supreme Court ruled such contracts illegal, and a vicious custody battle followed. By the time the couple won, the girl had been shuffled between homes for two years. The issue landed in court because New Jersey law did not cover surrogacy. It still doesn't.

The simplistic response—banning surrogacy—is no answer at all. Such laws only send the practice

---

5. *Source:* Editorial, *USA TODAY,* 19 November 1993. Copyright 1993, USA TODAY. Reprinted with permission.

underground, leaving parents, surrogates and children with nowhere to turn if they are abused, exploited, cheated or deceived.

The right course: Write law—particularly contract law—that sets clear rules and protects all parties.

California lawmakers offered a model for that kind of reform last year. Their bill—vetoed by a governor who preferred to leave the issue to the courts—would have assured that all involved clearly understood their rights, responsibilities and options and that both parents and surrogate would be counseled and examined thoroughly.

Most important, it guaranteed the child's rights.

That costs next to nothing and protects everyone.

No one knows how many babies have been born to surrogates. Most go home to happy endings. But when troubles arise, sound law is their best defense.

5.4 Proving Invalidity

An inability to give a proof of an argument does *not* mean that the argument is invalid. The trouble might simply be due to a lack of ingenuity. However, there is a neat method of proving invalidity, called the **short truth-table method.** An argument is shown to be invalid by this method if a row can be found in its truth table in which the premises are all true and the conclusion false. For example:

If Mary attends, we'll sing "Dixie."

Mary won't attend.

Therefore, we won't sing "Dixie."

We symbolize this as

(1) $M \supset S$

(2) $\sim M$ $/ \therefore \sim S$

Now we ask: Is there an assignment of truth values to the constituent sentences that will make the conclusion false and the premises true? The conclusion, $\sim S$, will be false only if S is true. So we write

__Premises__

M	S		$M \supset S$		$\sim M$	$/ \therefore \sim S$
			F	**T**		**FT**
T			**T**		**T**	↑ resultant column

Next we must make the premises true. The premise ~M will be true only if M is false, so we write

M	S		$M \supset S$			~M		/∴ ~S
F	**T**		**F**	**T**		**F**		**T**
—	—			**T**		**T**		**F**

which makes $M \supset S$ true as well. So we have found a row of the truth table that gives us T T F—a row, that is, in which the premises are true and the conclusion is false, which means the argument is invalid.

Here's another example;

If Smith shows up, Wilson will resign.

Either Smith shows up or Rogers will be embarrassed.

Rogers will be embarrassed.

So Wilson will resign.

Symbolized, this is

$S \supset W$

$S \vee R$

R /∴ W

We first make the conclusion false:

S	W	R		$S \supset W$		$S \vee R$		R		/∴ W
	F			**F**						**F**

Then we make the premises true:

S	W	R		$S \supset W$		$S \vee R$		R		/∴ W
F	**F**	**T**		**F**	**F**		**F**	**T**		**T**		
—	—	—			**T**			**T**		**T**		**F**

S has to be false so that $S \supset W$ is true (since W is false), and so R has to be true so that $S \vee R$ is true and R is true. Therefore, we have a row in which the premises are true and the conclusion false—T T T F. This proves that the argument is invalid.

If a conclusion can be wrong in several ways, we must be sure to check all those ways if earlier ways of falsifying the conclusion do not allow making all the premises true. For example:

If Sam agrees, so will Jed.

Jed will agree.

So Sam and Jed will agree.

Symbolized, this is

$S \supset J$

J $/\therefore S \cdot J$

We make the conclusion false (by letting J be false):

S	J		$S \supset J$		J		$/\therefore S \cdot J$
F	**T**		**T**		**F**		**F**

It appears that we can't get T T F. But if we instead let S be false, we get

S	J		$S \supset J$		J		$/\therefore S \cdot J$
F	**T**		**T**		**T**		**F**

which shows the argument is invalid.

Exercise 5.4   A. Show the following arguments to be invalid by the short truth-table method.

1. If the Vietnam War was pointless, 58,000 young Americans died for nothing. If we lost the war, it was pointless. So the Vietnam War was pointless.

2. Either you stop cursing or I won't listen. If you stop cursing, I'll buy you a teddy bear. If you don't, I won't. So either I won't buy you a teddy bear or I won't listen.

3. If Aristotle was Plato's student and Plato was Socrates' student, then Socrates was not Aristotle's student. Plato was Socrates' student and Alexander the Great was Aristotle's student. So Socrates was not Aristotle's student.

4. If all that glitters is not gold, then your bracelet is only gold plated. If your bracelet is only gold plated, then either Johnny is trying to trick you or he was cheated himself. Johnny was not cheated. So he is trying to trick you.

5. If death is the end, then the soul is not immortal. Either the soul is immortal or Jimmy Swaggart is mistaken. So Jimmy Swaggart is mistaken.

6. If Jimmy Swaggart is morally corrupt, he will not continue preaching. Either he will continue preaching or give up his faith. If he gives up his faith, his followers will be disillusioned and will no longer believe in God. So he is not morally corrupt.

7. If there is no God, there is no standard of right and wrong. If there is no standard of right and wrong, everything is permissible. But everything is not permissible. So there is no God.

8. If Keats wrote "Ode on a Grecian Urn" he was a great poet. If Coleridge wrote "Xanadu" he was a great poet. Both men were great poets. So Keats wrote "Ode on a Grecian Urn."

9. If people descended from apes, we are no more than animals, if Lorenz is right. But Lorenz is not right. So it is not true that we are no more than animals.

10. If Lisa Bonet appears nude again, Bill Cosby will explode and have her fired. If Cosby has her fired, she will have a successful movie career, and it will be the best thing that ever happened to her. So even if Bill Cosby explodes, he will not have her fired.

B. For each of the following arguments, first test for invalidity by the short truth-table method and then, if the argument cannot be shown to be invalid, prove its validity by a deductive proof.

1. If I go north, I'll find Simmons. But if it gets dark before I see Simmons, I'll never take him alive. I'll go north. So either I'll take Simmons alive or I'll never find him.

2. I'll either watch *Friends* or *20/20*. If I watch *20/20,* I'll miss seeing Jennifer Aniston. My whole week will be spoiled if I miss seeing Jennifer Aniston. My whole week will not be spoiled. So I'll watch *Friends.*

3. If the dog sees the cat, the dog will chase the cat. If the dog chases the cat, either he'll catch it and kill it or it will fight him and scratch his eyes out. The dog sees the cat, so it will scratch his eyes out.

4. If Elvis is still imitated, then he still lives. If he still lives, then he will never die. If he will never die, he is immortal. If he is immortal, he is as great as Socrates. He is not as great as Socrates. So he is not still imitated.

5. If Ted Koppel questions Rush Limbaugh, he will show Rush up as a wimp. But if Rush is not a wimp, he cannot be shown up as one, and so either Rush is not a wimp or Ted Koppel will not question him.

6. If William F. Buckley's IQ is over 150, then he is very intelligent. But if he were very intelligent, he wouldn't be a conservative. He is a conservative. So his IQ cannot be over 150.

7. The dead man must be the other man's son or his brother, because the other man says that the dead man's father is his own father's son. If the dead man's father is the other man's father's son and the other man has no brothers or sisters, then the dead man cannot be his brother. Therefore, the dead man is the other man's son.

8. If the hurricane turned away, then either it was Pat Robertson's prayers or it was an act of God. If it was Pat Robertson's payers, then Pat Robertson has the power to turn hurricanes away. If he can do that, then he could have saved all the 58,000 soldiers who were killed in Vietnam. If he could have done that and didn't, he must have been uncaring. If he didn't have such power as he claimed, he is a phony.

9. If Israel gives up the West Bank or the Gaza Strip, its territorial integrity will be compromised. Israel has a right to be suspicious of Arafat if Arafat has sworn to destroy Israel. So Israel will not give up the West Bank.

10. Either *Nightline* or *Crossfire* is the best show on TV. If *Nightline* is the best, we have Ted Koppel to thank. If *Crossfire* is best, we have to thank either Pat Buchanan or Ted Turner. But the people on *Crossfire* often talk at once, which is not true about *Nightline*. So *Nightline* is the best show on TV.

11. If it rains, I'll be disappointed. If it doesn't rain, the farmers will be disappointed. So either the farmers or I will be disappointed.

12. If the next president does not raise taxes, the deficit will grow and Social Security will dry up. Either the deficit will not grow or Social Security will not dry up. So the president will raise taxes.

13. If I don't get any sleep, I'll won't be able to pass the test. If I don't stay up and study, I won't pass the test. But if I stay up and study, I won't get any sleep. So I won't pass the test.

14. Every event has a cause, and human actions are events. Anything that has a cause is not free. If human actions are not free, then I have no moral responsibility. If I have no moral responsibility, then I can't be blamed for anything I do. So I can't be blamed for anything I do, if every event has a cause.

15. If *Maury* is as bad as *Montel,* I will stop watching TV and take up reading. If *Another World* is as bad as *All My Children,* then Erica should be proud. Either *Maury* is as bad as *Montel* or Erica should not be proud. Therefore, *Another World* is as bad as *All My Children.*

16. Either David left his slingshot at home or Goliath is in trouble. If Goliath is in trouble, then God must be on David's side. If God is on David's side, then David's mother packed his slingshot and a chicken salad sandwich in his backpack. So Goliath is in trouble.

17. If Arafat is sincere, Sharon should negotiate. Arafat is not sincere. So Sharon should not negotiate.

18. Fred will dance with either Ginger or Rita. If he dances with Rita again, Ginger will fly into a rage. If she flies into a rage, she will harm Fred or Rita, and Fred will hire Charles Bronson to shoot her. Fred will not dance with Ginger, and he will hire Charles Bronson to shoot her.

19. If Hugh Grant is guilty, he should not be acquitted. If he should not be acquitted, then someone else should be punished. So someone else should be punished.

20. If Richard resigns, Al will be pleased. If Richard is vindicated, George will be pleased. So either George or Al will be pleased.

5.5 Summary

Truth-functional logic uses letters to stand for whole statements. Compound statements are constructed from atomic statements by means of connective symbols:

· for *and*

v for *or*

~ for *not*

⊃ for *if . . . then*

≡ for *if and only if* (or *equivalence*)

These connectives are defined by means of truth tables, and then these distinctions are used to test arguments involving these symbols for validity. For example, the argument form

$p \supset q$

$\underline{\sim q}$

$\therefore \sim p$

can be tested this way:

Atomic Statements		**Premises**		**Conclusion**
p	q	$p \supset q$	$\sim q$	$/\therefore \sim p$
T	T	T	F	F
T	F	F	T	F
F	T	T	F	T
F	F	T	T	T

↑ resultant column
(governed by controlling connective ~)

No row shows that

$p \supset q$	$\sim q$	$/\therefore \sim p$
T	T	F

—which would represent the possibility of having all true premises and a false conclusion—so this argument form (called modus tollens) is valid.

We can also develop a list of argument forms and rule of replacement that can be used to write lengthy deductive proofs without doing large truth tables. For example:

(1) A ⊃ B

(2) $B \supset C$

(3) $C \supset D$

(4) $\sim D$ $/\therefore \sim A$

We want to prove $\sim A$ from the premises:

(5) $\sim C$ 3, 4   MT

(6) $\sim B$ 2, 5   MT

(7) $\sim A$ 1, 6   MT

Proving invalidity of a deductive argument uses the short truth-table method, in which we set the conclusion to be false and find a set of truth values for the atomic statements that makes all the premises true. If this can be done, the argument is invalid.

5.6 Applications

Spousal Abuse Evidence in Court Trials The prosecution in the O. J. Simpson trial believed that evidence of a history of spousal abuse was very relevant to the question of Simpson's guilt. Many people agreed; but the defense, and many supporters of the famous defendant, disagreed.

In the following editorial, we look for an argument that can be proved by a truth table, an argument that can be shown invalid by the short truth-table method, and an argument that can be expressed and demonstrated as a deductive proof.

Old Charges Can Thwart Justice for O. J.—or You[6]

Our View: Events Thursday show why past events shouldn't automatically be admissible in court

You've heard a lot of terrible tales this week about O. J. Simpson.

How O. J. threatened to cut off the heads of Nicole's boyfriends if they ever drove her cars.

How he beat Nicole in the 1970s when they were just beginning their relationship.

---

6. *Source:* Editorial, *USA TODAY.* 13 January 1995. Copyright 1995, USA TODAY. Reprinted with permission.

How he threw her into a wine cellar.

Prosecutors hurled those and nearly 60 other allegations at the actor and former football star Wednesday.

But, oops, on Thursday, those three allegations and another dozen ugly ones were withdrawn.

Having imbedded them in the public mind one day, L.A. prosecutors decided the unproven slurs were no longer part of its case the next. At least for awhile.

This action demonstrates again why allegations don't constitute truth. And it shows why courts must beware of allowing prosecutors to present any evidence they choose to prove a person committed a crime.

Simpson, for example, isn't on trial for the awful things he may have done to Nicole in the 1970s, 1980s or 1990s. He's on trial for her gruesome murder and that of Ronald Goldman on the night of June 12, 1994.

Thus, Judge Lance Ito must decide which, if any, of the domestic violence evidence is relevant to showing Simpson committed that crime.

Some advocates for victims of domestic violence say that a history of abuse is always relevant. One act of violence usually leads to more heinous ones. And a woman's most likely murderer is her ex-spouse.

All that may be true. But it doesn't prove a thing. Because for every case where a batterer kills his ex-spouse, there are a thousand cases where he did nothing at all. The same is true with former robbers, burglars, drug dealers and, even, rapists.

Past misdeeds may show someone was or is a bad person. They don't prove that person committed a particular crime.

And that's where the attention of juries must be focused—on the crime for which a person is on trial, not on his character or past history.

How to draw the line? Cautiously, with the right to fair trial in mind.

Prior acts can provide a motive for a crime or show the intent to commit one. They may display a pattern of behavior leading to its commission.

Otherwise, though, they are irrelevant. Worse, when they involve numerous old and unproven accusations, they are distracting and dangerous. Each one can result in a mini trial of its own, diverting the attention of jurors from the crime at hand.

Trials should be about showing who committed a crime, why they did it and how it was done; not about past misdeeds or character assassination.

The following argument can be symbolized and proved by means of a truth table:

Not every spouse abuser is one who goes on to commit murder.

If not every spouse abuser goes on to commit murder, then prior misdeeds don't prove a thing.

∴ *Prior misdeeds don't mean a thing.*

We symbolize this as

N

$N \supset {\sim}P$

∴ ${\sim}P$

and test it with a truth table:

N	P	N	$N \supset {\sim}P$	$/ \therefore {\sim}P$
T	T	T	F	F
T	F	T	T	T
F	T	F	T	F
F	F	F	T	T

(The N column serves both as a guide column and a premise column.) Because no row shows that

N	$N \supset {\sim}P$	$/ \therefore {\sim}P$
T	T	F

this argument is valid. Next we express (paraphrase) the argument:

O. J.'s prior acts are unproven.

If prior acts do not show motive, intent, or pattern, they are not relevant.

If prior acts are not relevant and are unproven, they are distracting and dangerous.

If prior acts are distracting and dangerous, trials should not be about them.

∴ *Trials should not be about prior acts.*

We then symbolize it:

(1) U

(2) ${\sim}M \supset {\sim}R$

(3) $({\sim}R \cdot U) \supset D$

(4) $D \supset {\sim}T$ $/ \therefore {\sim}T$

But, after a few tries, it appears we cannot give a deductive proof of this argument. So we try a short truth-table proof of invalidity:

U	M	R	U	D	T	U	~M ⊃ ~R	(~R · U) ⊃ D	D ⊃ ~T	/∴ ~T
T	*T*	*T*	*T*	*F*	*T*	*T*	*T*	*T*	*T*	*F*

For this assignment of values to the sentence letters, there *is* a row in which the premises are true and the conclusion false, and so the argument is invalid.

With one adjustment to premise (3), however, we can have an argument that *is* valid. Perhaps our paraphrase of the third premise is not accurate. Does the author want to say that any prior acts that are not proven *and* not relevant are dangerous, or might he or she only want to say that any prior acts that are not proven *or* not relevant are dangerous?

With this amendment our argument can be symbolized

(1) U

(2) ~M ⊃ ~R

(3) (~R v U) ⊃ D

(4) D ⊃ ~T   /∴ ~T

and proved:

(5) U v ~R   1   Add

(6) ~R v U   5   Com

(7) D   3, 6   MP

(8) ~T   4, 7   MP

This interpretation seems more likely, and by the logician's Golden Rule, we are bound to give the arguer the benefit of the doubt. As always, there is more than one way to paraphrase the passage in this essay. The second premise seems unused and unnecessary because the arguer never states that the abuse evidence does not show motive, intent, or pattern of behavior—perhaps because such abuse *does* tend to establish a pattern. An important question, from a critical thinking point of view, is whether any of that abuse evidence was or could be proven to be relevant. The jury in this controversial case apparently did not think so.

Violent Protest

This essay was discussed before (see Section 3.8). There we looked for informal fallacies. This time we will try to find arguments, one that can be tested by a truth table, one that can be expressed and demonstrated as a deductive proof, and one that can be shown invalid by the short truth-table method.

Violent Protest Is Justified[7]
by Frank Morriss

Any moral, or even humanly decent, society would consider the illustration in *Newsweek* (Feb. 11, 1993) obscene. It showed an unborn baby and pointed out its various parts that might be harvested (or to be more honest, cannibalized) for treatment of various diseases. Brain cells can help experimental surgery to treat Parkinson's disease, neurons "might treat" spinal-cord injuries and multiple sclerosis, pancreatic cells "reduced patients' need for insulin," liver cells "helped one boy" with Hunter's syndrome, stem cells "might treat" sickle-cell anemia and other disorders.

It might have been a chart such as once hung in old-fashioned butcher shops showing areas of animals from which choice and less-choice cuts came for the kitchen. The caption to the *Newsweek* illustration betrays just what the attitude of the secularized, pagan society of today is toward unborn life— "The Sum of Its Parts." If there is any doubt about what the article's intention might be, words of its headline should make it clear—". . . saving a life is a moral imperative, yet we restrict the use of aborted fetuses." The headline goes on to call "the ethical landscape" of this issue a "minefield."

In Perspective

I cite this as important in thinking about the tragedy in Pensacola, Florida, in which an abortionist "doctor" was slain. The slaying may have deepened or widened the tragedy, but it did not of course create it. The tragedy was there, created by the mortality of the *Newsweek* illustration and by the pragmatic, sociological jurisprudence that has taken over control of our judiciary since the natural law legal philosophy was scuttled by [liberal Supreme Court justice] Oliver Wendell Holmes, Jr., and his ilk. [Natural, or true, law was an 18th- and 19th-century legal philosophy that held certain human rights to be God-given and hence unassailable by the state.]

If the tragedy might be measured by blood, then that of the slain abortionist contributed a drop in what are streams of innocent blood flowing into America's sewers from its abortion abattoirs. For the first time, the blood of the guilty joined the rivers of it from the victims.

This makes some of the words coming from some on both sides rather meaningless, or at least not to the true issue. Much of the disavowal from the pro-life side and the indignation from the pro-death side implies that innocent and guilty life are equal. They are, of course, ontologically and in

---

7. *Source:* Frank Morriss, "How to Protect the Unborn When the Law Permits Their Execution," *The Wanderer,* March 25, 1993. Reprinted with permission of *The Wanderer* and the author.

the possession of human rights. But if that ends the matter, then deadly war may not be fought, the state may not execute, and no one can mount deadly defense in behalf of innocent life, either one's own or that of one's neighbor—and I take to be our neighbor any and all who face aggressive and malevolent evil that we might stop.

This, incidentally, shows how pacifist or even the "seamless garment" ideas can muddy the ethical and logical waters concerning a vital issue. It also dignifies the "legalization" of what is morally and ethically perverse in essence. . . .

True Law and Morality

The force of the state should defend all innocent life. The right of true law exists only on one side—that which labels all slaying of the innocent murder to one degree or another, and the overt intention to slay such life never defensible. That this intention to slay the innocent is present in the case of abortion is undeniable. (The claim that some do not recognize abortion as the deliberate killing of an innocent human is inadmissible, for subjective opinion does not determine the moral or natural law reality.)

What, then, is the moral situation when the state refuses to protect some innocent life, and in fact gives mandate for its murder? Is all protection removed from that life? If, by some miracle, the unborn targets of abortionists were able to mount some defense by force against their attackers, some way to slay the "doctor" before he slayed them, could they be condemned for doing so? Alas, that cannot be expected to happen. The next question is, can someone who might act with such force on their behalf be accused of murder, as the abortionists certainly can be on the level of true law and morality? The same civil law that "legalizes" abortion cannot be cited when it judges deadly defense murder. It has lost its authority in this question. What that means in regard to actual cases of force on behalf of the unborn on the part of individuals or combinations of them, I leave to others. But I have no doubt that this is the real heart of the question about events in Pensacola.

It becomes, perhaps, clearer when we consider what actually happened. An abortionist left his car and was headed to the "clinic." There weapons of death aimed at the unborn, and them alone, awaited him. Within minutes— or certainly within an hour or two—he would have been using them to kill innocent life. No police were on hand to stop him. Indeed, were they there, representing the state or federal government, they would have instead facilitated his progress. All of this is certain fact.

What then is the moral, natural law quality of what was done by one who acted, almost certainly, with the intention of preventing what that abortionist clearly intended to do, as he had been doing in the past and would have continued to do had he been able? That is the question to be considered, and not whether the end justifies the means (it does not), or whether one must adopt a "seamless garment" attitude about all taking of life.

Nor does it deal with the real issue by saying or believing that what happened in Florida was a tactical blow to pro-life efforts, or thinking it might discredit those efforts. All such questions are important, but they must not determine our thought toward the central issue—what authority exists in defending innocent life for which no police (I mean state or judicial) defense is afforded? Does all authority in their defense vanish? If it does not, where does it exist?

If we are going to concede that all deadly force against aggressive evil is itself evil, then we must pretend we are helpless against any aggressive evil. That, of course, is the pacifist position. But, then, such pacifism is error, not truth. Some pro-lifers hastening to present "clean hands" in regard to what happened in Florida have, unfortunately, taken a pacifist stance. And of course the enemies bent on the "right" to take innocent life would be glad to have pacifism prevail on one side—the pro-life side—but not on theirs. Indeed, that is the hypocritical stand of all aggressors.

Let it be said honestly and openly, the moral aggressors at Pensacola were the abortionists and their agents, encouraged by pseudo-law that in the case of the unborn countenances and authorizes deadly aggression, identical to that for which we executed Nazis after the Nuremberg trials.

Historical Precedents

Most historians would give their sympathy, if not their outright approval, to Charlotte Corday, who slew "the Toad," Marat [a leader of the French Revolution], in his bathtub. She felt, with reason, that he had betrayed the true Revolution and led it into a swamp of blood. She added his blood to that swamp. I know of no one who mourned the passing of the agitator Marat.

The fictional "Scarlet Pimpernel" [from the similarly entitled 1934 novel about the French Revolution by Baroness Emmuska Orczy] did not, at least ordinarily, resort to killing to rescue royalists from the guillotine. But I doubt if any reader or viewer of the exploits of this English "rescuer" would have complained had he killed a few Jacobins and their agents in order to save some helpless persons being hauled to the place of execution, where the ground was so blood-soaked that, it is said, horses reared back in terror at the smell.

I suggest that what happened in Florida had, at the very least, the coloration of Corday's assassination and the Pimpernel's refusal to accept French revolutionary "law" as the final determination—certainly not a moral determination.

Indeed, the traditional ethical teachings based on the natural law can be cited more precisely to the case in Florida than to the two events in Revolutionary France, one historical, the other fictional.

It should be realized that it is certain that good morality cannot allow the killing of the unborn to continue, and that there will be those of good and informed conscience who will act in one way or another to bring it to an end, whether that can be accomplished by ordinary "legal" means or not. The question then becomes what actions can a true and valid conscience indicate.

Frank Morriss, a teacher at the Colorado Catholic Academy, is the author of The Conservative Imperative *and* The Divine Epic *and has, since 1950, been a columnist for several Roman Catholic journals.*

For a truth-table proof, we state the argument and symbolize it:

If innocent and guilty life are equal, then war, capital punishment, and defense of the innocent are all wrong.

War, capital punishment, and defense of the innocent are not all wrong.

∴ *Innocent and guilty life are not equal.*

$E \supset W$

$\sim W \qquad / \therefore \sim E$

Next we set up a truth table:

E	W	$E \supset W$	$\sim W$	$/\therefore \sim E$
T	T	T	F	F
T	F	F	T	F
F	T	T	F	T
F	F	T	T	T

There is no row with premises true and conclusion false, so this argument—which is modus tollens—is valid.

An argument that can be treated as a deductive proof is

If all deadly force is wrong, we are helpless against aggressive evil.

The pacifist position is that we are helpless against aggressive evil.

Pacifism is error, not truth.

∴ *Not all deadly force is wrong.*

Next we symbolize it:

(1) $D \supset H$

(2) $P \equiv H$

(3) $\sim P$ $/\therefore \sim D$

(4) $(P \supset H) \cdot (H \supset P)$ 2   Equiv

(5) $(H \supset P) \cdot (P \supset H)$ 4   Com

(6) $H \supset P$ 5   Simp

(7) $\sim H$ 6, 3   MT

(8) $\sim D$ 1, 7   MT

This is valid, but the premises leave a lot to be desired. "Pacifism is error, not truth" is not backed up, and to identify pacifism with "we are helpless against agressive evil" is surely mistaken—not every response to evil need include deadly force.

An argument that fails the short truth-table test is

The doctor was about to kill innocent life

If so, either the police or the pro-life gunman had to defend the innocent life

The police were not there (and wouldn't help anyway)

∴ *The pro-life gunman had to shoot the doctor*

and symbolized:

(1) K

(2) $K \supset (P \lor G)$

(3) $\sim P$ $/\therefore S$

We try to prove it,

(4) $P \lor G$ 2, 1   MP

(5) G 4   DS

and we get no further. So we try a short truth-table disproof:

K	P	G	S	K	K ⊃ (P ∨ G)	~P	G	/∴ S
T	**F**	**T**	**F**	**T**	**T**	**T**	**T**	**F**

which shows the argument's invalidity. In concrete terms, even if the gunman was morally required to take some action in defense of innocent life, it does not follow that he had to shoot anybody. The outcome of this case bears this point out.

There is more to say about this essay, but further observations are left to you. It must be pointed out that such an essay as this one is a hopeful event, whether we agree with Morriss or not, because he is willing to write an argumentative essay presenting his reasons for what he thinks. As Thomas Jefferson said: "Error may be tolerated as long as reason is left free to combat it." And we must never discount the possibility that we may be mistaken.

Exercise 5.6   Find an argument in the following editorial that can be expressed as a deductive proof or can be proved invalid by the short truth-table method.

Editorial from the *Washington Times*[8]

The controversy over the Supreme Court case of NOW vs. Scheidler, decided by the court on Monday, obviously centers on the meaning of the court's ruling for abortion protesters and the future of the organizations that mobilize them. Those organizations, like Operation Rescue, were as disappointed at the court's ruling as their adversaries, like the National Organization for Women, which brought the suit, were elated. But there is a larger issue at stake in this ruling, and whatever the results of the court's decision for abortion, the right to life or the right to protest abortion, it is likely that this larger issue will be the one that future legal experts will study as what is important in the case.

That issue is the meaning and application of the Racketeer Influenced and Corrupt Organizations (RICO) statute, under which NOW brought its lawsuit against Randall Terry of Operation Rescue and Joe Scheidler of the Pro-Life Action Network. The RICO law was passed by Congress in 1970, and the legislative history and language of the law make clear that the intent of the lawmakers was to facilitate federal law enforcement activities against organized crime, particularly the Cosa Nostra and similar outfits. One of the salient features of RICO is its concept of an "enterprise," which means more than simply a discrete organization. Under the law's "enterprise" language— which defines an "enterprise" as "any individual, partnership, corporation, association, or other legal entity and any union or group of individuals associated in fact though not a legal entity"—federal law enforcement can take measures, such as wiretaps, against a wide range of persons loosely associated with each other for shadowy or criminal purposes.

But RICO also was explicitly written so that its scope was confined to activities affecting "interstate or foreign commerce." That language reflected the federal authority under the Constitution's commerce clause

---

8. *Source:* Editorial, *Washington Times,* 26 January 1994. Copyright © 1994 News World Communications, Inc. Reprinted with permission of the *Washington Times.*

to make such a law, and by limiting the law's scope to interstate and foreign commerce, the Congress also limited the application of the sometimes awesome power it granted law enforcement.

It was with those limitations in mind that two lower courts had dismissed the NOW suit on the grounds that the defendants, the abortion protesters, did not harbor the "economic motive" the commerce language of the law apparently required. The importance of the Supreme Court's ruling is that, as Chief Justice Rehnquist stated in his opinion for the court, "We hold only that RICO contains no economic motive requirement."

Moreover, he and the court also rejected the lower court's opinion that the abortion protesters' actions, if they lacked an "economic motive," did not affect interstate commerce. ". . . predicate acts," Mr. Rehnquist held, "such as the alleged extortion (by the abortion protesters), may not benefit the protesters financially but still may drain money from the economy by harming businesses such as the clinics. . . ."

Thus, the Court succeeded in travelling far beyond what both the language of RICO and the will of the lawmakers seemed to intend, and in doing so, it may have crafted a federal weapon that can be used for purposes that have nothing to do with either organized crime or violent and illegal abortion protests. Virtually any activity, legal or not, may have the effect of "draining

money from the economy by harming businesses," but that is clearly not what RICO was intended to cover and prohibit.

Clark Forsythe, a spokesman for the anti-abortion group Americans United For Life, pointed directly to this danger in a statement just after the ruling. "The Court's ruling," he noted, "may bankrupt not only pro-life organizations, but other political activists throughout the nation. Other targets of the RICO sledgehammer may include animal-rights activists, environmentalists and anti-nuclear war protesters." Any or all of those kinds of activism, which often are no less unruly and violent than anything opponents of abortion have mounted, could reasonably be interpreted as "draining money from the economy" and thus be subject to lawsuits brought by their adversaries under the new-made RICO law.

The court's expansion of RICO authority is part of a consistent pattern it has shown in other cases, and as in those other cases, it noted that limitations in the law must be placed there by Congress, not judges. That is a fair comment, and a clear invitation to lawmakers to draft their laws more carefully. No doubt lawmakers should do so. No doubt they did not do so with RICO. But no doubt either that the court's ruling nevertheless does move well beyond the law that lawmakers at the time thought they were making, and it does so in a way that could backfire on any group, left or right, that treasures the right of protest.

 CHAPTER SIX

Quantifiers

Gottlob Frege, whom we discussed in Chapter 5, invented not only truth-functional logic but also introduced quantifiers. This made it possible to include syllogistic logic, or *predicate logic,* within the structure of truth-functional logic. This means, as we see in this chapter, that a statement Aristotle would have symbolized as "All *S* is *P*," Frege symbolized as "(*x*) (S*x* ⊃ P*x*)"—which reads as "For all *x*, if *x* is *S*, then *x* is *P*."

Bertrand Russell saw early in the twentieth century that the quantifiers made it possible to "dissolve" certain age-old philosophical problems. Consider the statement "The present king of France is bald." Traditional logic would symbolize this as "All *K* is *B*," and the problem would naturally arise—there is no present king of France! But it seems that if I must *refer* to the present king of France, then the present king of France must *exist* somehow. Many philosophers thought at that time that indeed the present king of France, and Pegasus, and all fictional beings besides, must possess *some* kind of existence.

Quantifiers and variables solve this problem neatly. We simply paraphrase "The present king of France is bald": "For every *x*, if *x* is the present king of France, then *x* is bald," which does not commit us to the existence of the present king of France. Indeed, even "There is no present king of France" can be paraphrased "It is not the case that there is an *x* such that *x* is the present king of France" and symbolized in the notation we introduce in this chapter.

Furthermore, quantifiers make it possible to subsume traditional logic (the syllogism) under quantified truth-functional logic.

Not that all philosophical problems were thereby solved, but at this point the advocates of the "ideal language" movement were encouraged to think that logic could be a logically perfect language that would show us the true picture of reality. These hopes were later dashed by Wittgenstein himself, but many philosophers and logicians still harbor these hopes.

6.1 Quantifiers

The method of deductive proof we presented in Chapter 5 will not work on the following simple argument:

All sailors are poets.

Jeff is a sailor.

∴ *Jeff is a poet.*

It is clearly valid, but when we symbolize it we get

S

J

∴ P

which does not conform to any of our rules. The method of the syllogism could be employed, of course, but only very awkwardly. We would have to translate "Jeff" as "the set with only one member identical to Jeff," which seems very artificial. Now consider this:

All sailors are poets.

Jeff is a sailor or Steve is a sailor.

Steve is not a sailor.

∴ *Jeff is a poet.*

Again, the argument is obviously valid, and yet it cannot be proven by either a Venn diagram or a deductive proof. So what do we do? We need to greatly extend the range of deductive proofs.

So first let's use lowercase letters—*a, b, c,* and so on—to stand for individual things and people and capital letters—*A, B, C,* and so on—to stand for **predicates.** For example, to symbolize the sentence "Al is bald," we write *Ba. B* stands for "is bald" and *a* stands for "Al." To symbolize "Bob is curious," we write *Cb.* To symbolize "Socrates is mortal," we write *Ms.*

We continue to use the symbolism of truth-table logic so that "Al is bald and Bob is curious" is written *Ba · Cb,* "Al is bald or Bob is curious" becomes *Ba* v *Cb,* and "Al is not bald" is *~Ba.*

Next we introduce the **variable** *x,* which will stand for any of the individuals *a, b, c,* and so on. So if we wish to write "Everything is wet," we write

(x) Wx

The symbol (x) is called a **universal quantifier** and reads as "Every x is such that" or "For every x." So we read the symbol (x) Wx as "Every x is such that x is wet" or "For every x, x is wet."

Suppose we wish to symbolize "Something is on fire." We write

$(\exists x)\ Fx$

which reads as "There is an x such that x is on fire" or "For some x, x is on fire." The symbol $(\exists x)$ is called the **existential quantifier.**

These simple but profound symbolic innovations allow us to test syllogisms (and many more arguments) by means of the rules of deduction. However, we need a few more rules about how to use quantifiers, which we will formulate in Section 6.2.

But first we must look at a few examples of how to translate ordinary statements into the symbolism of quantifiers. The standard-form categorical statements, for instance, are translated and symbolized as follows:

A-FORM

A: *All sailors are poets.*

We translate this into

For every x, if x is a sailor, then x is a poet
and then symbolize it:

$(x)\ (Sx \supset Px)$

E-FORM

E: *No sailors are poets.*

We translate this into

For every x, if x is a sailor, then x is not a poet
and then symbolize it:

$(x)\ (Sx \supset Px)$

I-FORM

I: *Some sailors are not poets.*

We translate this into

For some x, x is a sailor, and x is a poet
and then symbolize it:

$(\exists x)\ (Sx \cdot Px)$

O-FORM

O: *Some sailors are not poets.*

We translate this into

   For some x, x is a sailor, and x is not a poet
and then symbolize it:

   (∃x) (Sx · ~Px)

Here are some more complex examples—statement, translation, and symbolization (in that order):

   All the people at the party were drunk.

   For every x, if x was at the party, x was drunk.

   (x) (Px ⊃ Dx)

(Here we have limited the *range* of things that *x* can be to *people.*)

   All nonmembers who attended the party were over fifty years old.

   For every x, if x was a nonmember and x attended the party, then x was over fifty years old.

   (x) [(~Mx · Ax) ⊃ Fx]

(The brackets show the *scope* of the quantifier extends over the whole expression.)

   Some rich people think that they own the country.

   For some x, x is rich and x thinks that he/she owns the country.

   (∃x) (Rx · Tx)

   Some people are liars, and some are not.

   For some x, x is a liar, and for some x, x is not a liar.

   [(∃x) Lx] · [(∃x) ~Lx]

   Something is rotten in the state of Denmark.

   For some x, x is rotten and x is in Denmark.

   (∃x) (Rx · Dx)

   Not all birds can fly.

   For some x, x is a bird, and x cannot fly.

   (∃x) (Bx · ~Fx)

All logicians love puzzles, and so do all mathematicians.

For every x, if x is a logician, x is a lover of puzzles, and if x is a mathematician, x is a lover of puzzles.

(x) [(Lx ⊃ Px) · (Mx ⊃ Px)]

Other letters besides *x* can be used in quantifiers. For example:

Sometimes I think of Glana and recall the sweet, hot summers that we spent together.

For some (time) t, t is a time that I think of Glana, and t is a time that I recall the sweet, hot summers that we spent together.

(∃t) (Tt · Rt)

Someday my prince will come.

For some t, t is a time when my prince will come.

(∃t) Pt

Every girl and every boy deserve happiness.

For every girl x, x deserves happiness, and for every boy y, y deserves happiness.

(x) Dx · (y) Dy

(The range of *x* is girls; the range of *y* is boys.)

Capitalists and socialists are materialistic and narrow minded.

For every x, if x is a capitalist, x is materialistic and narrow minded, and if x is a socialist, x is materialistic and narrow minded.

(x) {[Cx ⊃ (Mx · Nx)] · [Sx ⊃ (Mx · Nx)]}

Sometimes much ingenuity is needed to symbolize such sentences. Here are some mistakes to avoid:

No elves are dwarfs

should *not* be symbolized

~(x) (Ex · Dx)

for that means

Not every x is such that x is an elf and x is a dwarf; that is, not every elf is a dwarf

and it should *not* be symbolized as

(x) Ex · ~Dx

for that expression, with parentheses missing, is meaningless. The right way to symbolize it is

$\sim(\exists x)\ (Ex \cdot Dx)$

which means

There is no x such that x is both an elf and a dwarf.

Here's another example:

Some elves are not dwarfs

should *not* be symbolized

$\sim(\exists x)\ (Ex \cdot Dx)$

for that means

There is no x such that x is both an elf and a dwarf

which means

No elves are dwarfs.

The proper way to symbolize it is

$(\exists x)\ (Ex \cdot \sim Dx)$

which reads

There is an x such that x is an elf and not a dwarf.

This is an appropriate point at which to present the **logical relations** (LR) between (x) and $(\exists x)$: Where P is any predicate,

LR1: $(x)\ Px \equiv \sim(\exists x)\ \sim Px$

which means that "If every x is P, there is no x that is not P," and vice versa.

LR2: $(\exists x)\ Px \equiv \sim(x)\ \sim Px$

which means that "If some x is P, then not every x is not P," and vice versa.

LR3: $(x)\ \sim Px \equiv \sim(\exists x)\ Px$

which means that "If every x is not P, then it is not the case that some x is P," and vice versa.

LR4: $(\exists x) \sim Px \equiv \sim (x)\ Px$

which means that "If some x is not P, then not every x is P," and vice versa.
Here are some examples:

(1) Everything is beautiful

can be written either

(x) Bx   (For every x, x is beautiful.)

or

$\sim (\exists x) \sim Bx$ *(There is no x that is not beautiful.)*

(2) Something is amiss

can be written

(∃x) Ax   (For some x, x is amiss.)

or

~(x) ~Ax   (It is not the case that every x is such that x is not amiss.)

(3) Not everyone who goes to college learns much

is written

~(x) (Cx ⊃ Lx)   or   *(∃x) (Cx · ~Lx)*

which also means

Some people who go to college don't learn a lot.

In Section 6.2 we see how to incorporate such quantified statements into deductive proofs. Even though this is a book on practical logic, knowing something about the powerful analytic capabilities of modern symbolic logic is not impractical. The exercises show that actual occasions in which we need those capabilities do arise.

Exercise 6.1   Translate the following sentences into quantificational symbolism.

1. Some scientists are poets.

2. All actors are wealthy.

3. Some actors are not wealthy.

4. No honest people are actors.

5. The wise will understand why we do not seek revenge.

6. Not all technology is good.

7. Some Arabs are not Palestinians.

8. None but the brave deserve the fair.

9. He who hesitates is lost.

10. There's no time like the present.

11. There's no fool like an old fool.

12. All men and women are mortal.

13. Honesty is always the best policy.

14. There's no place like home.

15. Where there's life, there's hope.

16. Every dog has his day.

17. You can always tell a Harvard man.

18. Trespassers will be shot.

19. Violators will be shot.

20. Violators will be prosecuted.

21. Some people who drink are able to avoid getting drunk.

22. Not every businessperson is dishonest.

23. No Greeks are immortal.

24. All that glitters is not gold.

25. What's past is prologue.

26. If you ever need me, I'll be there.

27. Some multinational corporations operate in South Africa.

28. All who doubt me should read my lips.

29. You're no Jack Kennedy.

30. Sometimes terrorism is understandable.

31. All existentialists are atheists.

32. Some existentialists are not atheists.

33. Only a Democrat could vote for Dukakis.

34. No black people voted for Bush.

35. Some heterosexuals get AIDS.

36. No prophylactic device is foolproof.

37. Not all smokers get cancer.

38. All neo-Nazis are Germans.

39. The race is not to the swift, nor the battle to the strong.

40. Drug addicts are miserable.

41. A word to the wise is sufficient.

42. Some AIDS victims are homosexuals, and some are not.

43. The early bird catches the worm.

44. He that troubleth his own house shall inherit the wind.

45. Not all cabinet members are womanizers.

46. Those who can't, teach.

47. Rapists are cowardly and cruel.

48. Christina Onassis died either from natural causes or from an overdose.

49. Everybody wants Nintendo.

50. Leveraged buyouts always result in layoffs.

51. Every time we take Dan, it rains.

6.2 Quantifier Rules

To include quantified statements in deductive proofs, we need four more rules. These rules assume that the *universe* of *x*—its range of possible values—includes at least one individual.

1. **Universal instantiation** (UI):

   If (x) Px, then Pa.

That is, where *P* is any predicate and *a* is some individual, "If everything is *P,* then *a* is *P.*" This rule works as follows:

> *All poets are sailors.*
>
> *Al is a poet.*
>
> ∴ *Al is a sailor.*

We symbolize it

> *(1) (x) (Px ⊃ Sx)*
>
> *(2) Pa*   */∴ Sa*

and prove it this way:

> *(3) Pa ⊃ Sa*   *1*   *UI*
>
> *(4) Sa*   *3, 2*   *MP*

(If the poet had been Tom or Bill, we could have used *t* or *b* in the proof. If "everything" is *P,* then *t* is *P,* too, and *b,* and so on.)

  2. **Universal generalization** (UG): If *Pa* then, if *a* is any arbitrarily selected individual, *(x) Px;* that is, if any *a* you select is *P,* then everything is *P.* For example:

> *All poets are sailors.*
>
> *All sailors are mariners.*
>
> ∴ *All poets are mariners.*

We symbolize it

> *(1) (x) (Px ⊃ Sx)*
>
> *(2) (x) (Sx ⊃ Mx)*   */∴ (x) (Px ⊃ Mx)*

and prove it:

> *(3) Pa ⊃ Sa*   *1*   *UI*
>
> *(4) Sa ⊃ Ma*   *2*   *UI*
>
> *(5) Pa ⊃ Ma*   *3, 4*   *HS*
>
> *(6) (x) (Px ⊃ Mx)*   *5*   *UG*

This rule works because if any arbitrary individual we pick is such that $Pa \supset Ma$, then every x is such that $Px \supset Mx$—that is, $\sim(x)$ $(Px \supset Mx)$.

3. **Existential instantiation** (EI):

If (∃x) Px, then Pa.

That is, if there is something that is P, we can *call* it a, as long as a hasn't been used in the proof already. For example:

All poets are sailors.

Some criminals are poets.

∴ Some criminals are sailors.

We symbolize it

(1) (x) (Px ⊃ Sx)

(2) (∃x) (Cx · Px)   /∴ (∃x) (Cx · Sx)

and prove it

(3) Ca · Pa	*2*	*EI (Always use EI before UI.)*
(4) Pa ⊃Sa	*1*	*UI*
(5) Pa · Ca	*3*	*Com*
(6) Pa	*5*	*Simp*
(7) Sa	*4, 6*	*MP*
(8) Ca	*3*	*Simp*
(9) Ca · Sa	*8, 7*	*Conj*

(We save the last step until we have introduced rule 4.)

4. **Existential generalization** (EG):

If Pa, then (∃x) Px.

That is, if something in particular is P, then there is some x that is P. For example, we can complete the proof in rule 3 by writing

(10) (∃x) (Cx · Sx)   9   EG

Those are all the rules we need to deal with quantified statements, but let's do one more example:

All Iranians are Arabs. Some Iranians are Muslims. So some Arabs are Muslims.

(1)	$(x) (Ix \supset Ax)$			
(2)	$(\exists x) (Ix \cdot Mx)$		$/\therefore$	$(\exists x) (Ax \cdot Mx)$
(3)	$Ia \cdot Ma$	2	EI	(Always use EI before UI.)
(4)	$Ia \supset Aa$	1	UI	
(5)	$Ma \cdot Ia$	3	Comp	
(6)	Ma	5	Simp	
(7)	Ia	3	Simp	
(8)	Aa	4, 7	MP	
(9)	$Aa \cdot Ma$	8, 6	Conj	
(10)	$(\exists x) (Ax \cdot Mx)$	9	EG	

These four rules apply only to the standard quantified statements $(x)\ Px$ and $(\exists x)\ Px$; that is, they do *not* apply to such statements as $\sim(x)\ Px$ and $\sim(\exists x)\ Px$. This means that such statements must always be transformed into the standard quantified statements by means of the list of logical relations between (x) and $(\exists x)$ presented in Section 6.1:

LR1: $(x)\ Px \equiv \sim(\exists x)\ \sim Px$

LR2: $(\exists x)\ Px \equiv \sim(x)\ \sim Px$

LR3: $(x)\ \sim Px \equiv \sim(\exists x)\ Px$

LR4: $(\exists x)\ \sim Px \equiv \sim(x)\ Px$

So with the following argument,

Not everyone is dishonest. Nobody is perfect. Therefore, some honest people are imperfect.

we symbolize it

(1)	$\sim(x)\ \sim Hx$		
(2)	$(x)\ \sim Px$	$/\therefore$	$(\exists x) (Hx \cdot \sim Px)$

and then we rewrite $\sim(x)\ \sim Hx$ as $(\exists x)\ Hx$:

(3)	$(\exists x)\ Hx$	1	LR2
(4)	Ha	3	EI
(5)	$\sim Pa$	2	UI

(6) Ha · ~Pa   *4, 5*   *Conj*

(7) (∃x) (Hx · ~Px)   *6*   *EI*

Note: We must use EI before UI because we must never use *a* with EI if it has been used already. The reason? We wish to avoid the following kind of mistake:

There are cats and there are dogs, so there are cats that are also dogs.

We symbolize it

(1) (∃x) Cx

(2) (∃x) Dx   */∴ (∃x) (Cx · Dx)*

and "prove" it:

(3) Ca   *1*   *EI*

(4) Da   *2*   *EI*   *the mistake!*

(5) Ca · Da   *3, 4*   *Conj*

(6) (∃x) (Cx · Dx)   *5*   *EG*

Exercise 6.2   A. Prove the following quantified arguments.

1. No Democrats are Republicans. Jesse is a Democrat. So Jesse is not a Republican.

2. All actresses are vain. Some beautiful women are not vain. So some beautiful women are not actresses.

3. All wrestlers are strong. No florists are strong. So no florists are wrestlers.

4. Only Democrats are liberals. Some cowboys are liberals. So some cowboys are Democrats.

5. Some secretaries are musicians. No musicians are untalented. So some secretaries are talented.

6. Not all politicians are honest. All politicians are either Republicans or Democrats. So some people who are either Republicans or Democrats are dishonest.

7. All pit bulls are vicious. Some pets are pit bulls. So some pets are vicious.

8. Not everyone who is called is chosen. All florists are chosen. So some who are called are not florists.

9. Some televangelists have unusual hobbies. Nobody with an unusual hobby is perfectly virtuous. So some televangelists are not perfectly virtuous.

10. He who hesitates is lost. Not all Presbyterians do not hesitate. So some Presbyterians are lost.

6.3 Proving Invalidity of Quantified Arguments

To prove the invalidity of quantified arguments, there are two methods. The first is very simple. In response to the argument

All psychologists are intelligent

Some intelligent people are corrupt

Therefore, some psychologists are corrupt

we offer the following analogous (and obviously invalid) argument:

All kittens are animals.

Some animals are kangaroos.

Therefore, some kittens are kangaroos.

This shows the argument about psychologists, which has the same form, to be ridiculous and of course invalid.

Another, more complicated method of proving invalidity is a variation on the short truth-table method, which we used with deductive proofs. Consider again our argument about psychologists. We symbolize it

(1) (x) (Px ⊃ Ix)

(2) (∃x) (Ix · Cx)   /∴ (x) (Px · Cx)

and consider what it means. Suppose there is only one individual *a*. Then the whole quantified argument is equivalent to

Pa ⊃ Ia

Ia · Ca   /∴ Pa · Ca

which can easily be proved invalid by using the short truth-table method:

Pa	*Ia*	*Ca*	*Pa ⊃ Ia*	*Ia · Ca*	/∴ *Pa · Ca*
F	*T*	*T*	*F T*	*T T*	*F T*
			T	*T*	*F*

This proves the quantified argument invalid because it is invalid for the universe with just one individual *a*.

But consider this argument:

Some people are intelligent. Therefore, all people are intelligent.

We symbolize it as

(1) (∃x) Ix   /∴ (x) Ix

We first suppose there is only one individual *a,* in which case the whole quantified argument is equivalent to

Ia   /∴ Ia

which still looks valid. So we must look at a universe that contains two individuals, *a* and *b.* If there are two individuals, (∃x) Ia is equivalent to Ia v Ib, and (x) Ix is equivalent to Ia · Ib, and so our original quantified argument is equivalent to

Ia v Ib   /∴ Ia · Ib

and we can now use our short truth-table method:

Ia	Ib		Ia v Ib			/ ∴ Ia · Ib	
T	*F*		*T*	*F*		*T*	*F*
				T			*F*

Here we find that the premise is true and the conclusion false, and so the argument is invalid.

More complicated arguments might require that we try universes with three, four, or more individuals to prove invalidity.[1]

Exercise 6.3   Prove the invalidity of the following arguments by both the short truth-table method and the method of analogous argument. No exercise requires looking at a universe with more than two individuals.

1. Some actors are belligerent. Some engineers are belligerent. So some actors are engineers.

2. Some doctors are senators. All surgeons are doctors. So some surgeons are senators.

3. All communists are socialists. Some Americans are socialists. So some Americans are doctors.

4. All candidates are ambitious. All ambitious people are ruthless. So all ruthless people are candidates.

---

1. There is much more to know about quantifiers. The following books are recommended: Copi, Irving, *Introduction to Logic,* New York: Macmillan, 1982. Gustason, William, and Dolph E. Ulrich, *Elementary Symbolic Logic.* New York: Holt, Rinehart & Winston, 1973. Kneale, William, and Martha Kneale, *The Development of Logic,* Oxford: Clarendon Press, 1962.

5. Some animals are vicious. Some animals are cats. So some cats are vicious.

6. Some Teamsters are corrupt. Some corrupt people belong to the Mafia. So some Teamsters belong to the Mafia.

7. Some famous people have beards. Some people with beards are grandfathers. So some famous people are grandfathers.

8. No communists are senators. Not all senators are Democrats. So some communists are not Democrats.

9. Some astrologers are fakes. Some palm readers are fakes. So some astrologers are palm readers.

10. If anyone deserves an A, it's the person who has done all her homework. The girls have done all their homework. So they deserve A's.

6.4 Summary

Some arguments, including syllogistic arguments, cannot be expressed as deductive proofs without the use of symbols called quantifiers: (x), which means "For every x," and $(\exists x)$, which means "There is an x." The quantifier (x) is called the universal quantifier, and $(\exists x)$ is called the existential quantifier. Following are some examples of translations from ordinary language into the symbolic notation of quantifiers:

Some legislators are not honest: $(\exists x) (Lx \cdot Hx)$

Somewhere over the rainbow, blue birds fly: $(\exists x) (Ox \cdot Fx)$

To include quantifiers in deductive proofs, we need four more rules: universal instantiation (UI), universal generalization (UG), existential instantiation (EI), and existential generalization (EG). By means of these rules, we can reduce a quantified statement to one that refers to only one member. This reduced statement is then manipulated by the rules of deductive proofs, and the result is generalized again into a quantified statement.

To prove invalidity, we use a slightly more complicated version of the short truth-table method.

Syllogisms can be proved by these methods but can usually be handled more easily by Venn diagrams. Extended quantified arguments that involve several quantified statements, however, usually need to be treated as quantified deductive proofs.

6.5 Applications

The Death Penalty   We treat the main argument of this editorial, which we examined in Chapters 4 and 5, as a quantified deductive proof.

On Death Sentences[2]

If a Supreme Court nominee had told the Senate Judiciary Committee what Justice Harry Blackmun said in an opinion on Tuesday, that nominee's chances of confirmation would be zero. And rightly so. For in saying that he'll never vote to uphold a death sentence, Mr. Blackmun did more than deliver his moral judgment on the fairness of capital punishment. He abrogated his sworn duty to judge each case as its facts fit the U.S. Constitution.

In effect, Mr. Blackmun, 85, says that he already has *prejudged all* future death penalty cases. His fine, learned mind has served American justice well in his 20-plus years on the court. But as his career closes, so has his mind closed—at least on this most divisive of issues. No appellant expecting—as every appellant has a *right* to expect—an open judicial mind need knock.

Forget about whatever facts a future death penalty appeal may bring. Forget that a future appellant may well be Danny Rolling,

confessed white butcher of five white college students. Do the death penalty's biases, which Justice Blackmun has adjudged to be incurably skewed against blacks and poor people, apply to white killers too?

No other issue is as visceral, as intractable to normal reasoning processes, as capital punishment. Abortion comes close, but only close. Some people can rationalize a woman's right to an abortion but cannot rationalize the *state's* right, for any reason, to take a life.

Yet Justice Blackmun's error need not involve capital punishment, or abortion. The issue really lies in another plane. In that plane, wherein rests a judge's duty, there is room for only one overriding principle, one enduring passion, one inviolable standard: fealty to the law.

It is not a jurist's prerogative to rule this way or that because a law is "good" or "bad." On the contrary. A judge takes an oath *not* to apply personal beliefs to the law.

---

2. *Source:* Editorial, *Miami Herald,* 24 February 1994. Reprinted with permission of *Miami Herald,* via CCC.

It's the duty of legislators to do that. A society's laws reflect its beliefs and mores and values as legislators construe and codify those standards. Legislators may, and do, pack laws with absurdities or contradictions.

Judges are free to remark upon those absurdities and contradictions—but they can't revoke or change those that are lawful. If a statute comports with the applicable constitution, either state or U.S., a judge must apply the law, absurdity and contradiction and all.

Otherwise, unimaginable chaos and injustice would ensue. Suppose a Catholic judge interpreted the Bill of Rights according to papal encyclicals, not the Constitution. Suppose another religion teaches another judge that physical infirmity is God's punishment, and that those so "punished" don't deserve equal opportunity. Suppose a third judge's God teaches that women are inferior to men (or vice versa), or that racial or ethnic minorities are born inferior.

A judge may in fact hold odd personal beliefs—and still be a good judge. The litmus test requires covering personal beliefs, neck to ankles, with the jurist's black robe. It requires applying the law even when—especially when—the application of it runs counter to the judge's personal convictions.

This is the battle in which, on capital punishment. Mr. Blackmun has surrendered. It grieves his admirers to see the lion so felled by the thorn, with Androcles nowhere to be found.[3]

The premises are

All judges identical to <u>B</u>*lackmun are* <u>p</u>*rejudging judges.*

All <u>p</u>*rejudging judges are judges who will not judge by* <u>f</u>*acts and the* <u>C</u>*onstitution.*

All judges who will not judge by <u>f</u>*acts and the* <u>C</u>*onstitution are judges who have* <u>a</u>*bandoned their oath.*

No law that applies to <u>w</u>*hites, too, is biased (*<u>u</u>*nfair).*

The <u>d</u>*eath penalty applies to* <u>w</u>*hites (like Danny Rolling), too.*

All <u>c</u>*haotic situations are situations we should* <u>a</u>*void.*

All situations where judges use <u>p</u>*ersonal beliefs are situations that would be* <u>c</u>*haotic.*

---

3. In a legend Androcles, an early Christian, pulls a thorn from a lion's paw. When the Romans throw Androcles to the lions, the lion that he helped spares his life.

We symbolize the statements as

(1) $(x) (Bx \supset Px)$

(2) $(x) [Px \supset \sim(Fx \cdot Cx)]$

(3) $(x) [\sim(Fx \cdot Cx) \supset Ax]$ $/ \therefore (x) (Bx \supset Ax)$

(4) $(y) (Wy \supset \sim Uy)$

(5) $(y) (Dy \supset Wy)$ $/ \therefore (y) (Dy \supset \sim Uy)$

(6) $(z) (Cz \supset Az)$

(7) $(z) (Pz \supset Cz)$ $/ \therefore (z) (Pz \supset Az)$

(8) $Ba \supset Pa$	1	UI
(9) $Pa \supset \sim(Fa \cdot Ca)$	2	UI
(10) $\sim(Fa \cdot Ca) \supset Aa$	3	UI
(11) $Ba \supset \sim(Fa \cdot Ca)$	8, 9	HS
(12) $Ba \supset Aa$	11, 10	HS
(13) $Wb \supset \sim Ub$	4	UI
(14) $Db \supset Wb$	5	UI
(15) $Db \supset \sim Ub$	14, 13	HS
(16) $Cc \supset Ac$	6	UI
(17) $Pc \supset Cc$	7	UI
(18) $Pc \supset Ac$	17, 16	HS
(19) $(x) (Bx \supset Ax)$	12	UG *Blackmun has abandoned his oath.*
(20) $(y) (Dy \supset \sim Uy)$	12	UG *The death penalty is not unfair.*
(21) $(z) (Pz \supset Az)$	18	UG *We should avoid situations where judges apply their personal beliefs.*

We find three conclusions here, which depend on some very dubious premises. Surely, we expect Supreme Court justices to use their wisdom and experience and not behave mechanically. Just because the death penalty applies to whites as well as blacks does not mean that it applies equally to blacks and whites. Social problems and racism exist and no doubt affect justice for minorities.

Gun Laws We treat the main argument of this editorial, which we examined in Chapter 4, as a quantified deductive proof.

Don't Fear Gun Laws[4]

Our View: Some say gun laws prompt violence by extreme right; but such violence is the reason laws are needed

Right-wing paramilitary groups have been quick to disavow Timothy McVeigh, the prime suspect in the Oklahoma City bombing. Leaders of the Michigan Militia, one of the larger such associations, say McVeigh and two others were "silenced" and "told to leave" because of their "anarchist rhetoric."

If true, that's to their credit. The trouble is that such "militias" have used expanded federal gun controls as a rallying point for arming themselves for resistance—an anarchist notion itself. According to those who track the groups, two recent gun laws—one requiring a background check for handgun purchases and the other banning the sale of scores of firearms—are seen as particularly ominous steps toward the disarming of citizens.

That's way off base. The aim is not to seize guns, just control them better. Banning assault-style semiautomatics is the act of a nation fearful for its own safety, not an act of tyranny.

And the background check isn't Big Brother. It's a small inconvenience that has prevented thousands of felons from acquiring guns on the open market.

We ought to go further. Registration and licensing, as we do with cars and drivers, would make us all safer without violating anyone's legitimate gun privileges. But until last Wednesday, Congress was moving fast in the other direction. At least four bills had been introduced to repeal the assault-weapons ban or undermine the handgun-purchase background check.

What will happen to those bills now that McVeigh—who reportedly "never went anywhere unarmed," who embraced the anarchy of unfettered gun rights, and who was carrying a semiautomatic pistol loaded with "cop-killer" bullets at the time of his arrest—is in custody? A quick legislative burial wouldn't be inappropriate.

Even comprehensive gun laws wouldn't have prevented the Oklahoma bombing. But they could well help deter other acts of violence by giving law enforcement the means of tracking gun ownership and controlling the most dangerous weapons.

The fight against terrorism will always cause some inconvenience to law-abiding citizens—airport metal detectors are one example. But against the daily terror that guns bring to our streets, comprehensive gun laws need be no more of a sacrifice. They should be no less, either.

---

4. *Source:* "Don't Fear Gun Laws," *USA TODAY*, 24 April 1995. Copyright 1995, USA TODAY. Reprinted with permission.

The main conclusion is

All gun laws requiring background checks or banning assault weapons are at worst an inconvenience, like airport detectors.

The main premises are

Background check laws are for controlling guns, not for seizing citizens' guns.

Bans on assault weapons are laws that aim to make us safer and to calm our fears of the terror of street violence (if not of such acts as McVeigh's), not to impose tyranny on us.

All laws that control guns but do not seize them or that make us safer but do not impose tyranny are no worse than airport metal detectors.

We symbolize the statements and write them as a quantified deductive proof as

(1) $(x) [Bx \supset (Cx \cdot {\sim}Sx)]$		
(2) $(x) \{Ax \supset [(Mx \cdot Fx) \cdot {\sim}Tx]\}$		
(3) $(x) \{(Cx \cdot {\sim}Sx) \lor [(Mx \cdot Fx) \cdot {\sim}Tx] \supset {\sim}Wx\}$ $/\therefore (x) [(Bx \lor Ax) \supset {\sim}Wx]$		
(4) $Ba \supset (Ca \cdot {\sim}Sa)$	1	UI
(5) $Aa \supset [(Ma \cdot Fx) \cdot {\sim}Ta]$	2	UI
(6) $(Ba \lor Aa) \supset \{(Ca \cdot {\sim}Sa) \lor [(Ma \cdot Fa) \cdot {\sim}T]\}$	4, 5	CD
(7) $\{(Ca \cdot {\sim}Sa) \lor [(Ma \cdot Fa) \cdot {\sim}Ta]\} \supset {\sim}Wa$	3	UI
(8) $(Ba \lor Aa) \supset {\sim}Wa$	6, 7	HS
(9) $(x) [(Bx \lor Ax) \supset {\sim}Wx]$	8	UG

The comments about McVeigh, which I left out of the deductive proof, obviously do not help the author's argument.

Exercise 6.5   Treat the main argument of this editorial, which also appeared in Chapter 4, as a quantified deductive proof.

Editorial from the *Record*[5]

Sen. Jesse Helms, R-N.C., wants to reduce—or even block—federal spending for those with AIDS. He says AIDS sufferers bring on the disease with their "deliberate, disgusting, revolting conduct." He also says more federal money is spent on AIDS, the ninth leading killer in America, than on diseases that kill more people.

Unfortunately, Mr. Helms' argument is filled with half-truths and innuendo.

It's true that many people with AIDS are responsible for their plight. The disease is spread by dirty needles used for taking drugs and by unprotected sex among homosexuals—and to a lesser extent heterosexuals. Mr. Helms is entitled to his opinion on homosexual sex. Fortunately, it's not universally shared.

But many AIDS sufferers have no responsibility for getting the disease. Ryan White, the teenage boy who is a symbol for the fight against AIDS, got the virus through his treatment for hemophilia. Many men and women get AIDS from sexual partners who neglect to tell them they are HIV-infected. Some babies are born with AIDS because of their infected mothers.

And many people who got AIDS through sexual activity knew nothing at the time about how the disease is spread.

Mr. Helms also misleads us when he suggests that Washington spends more on AIDS than on heart disease and cancer, the nation's two biggest killers. Federal spending is greater for AIDS if you consider only the amount spent on research, prevention, and housing. But if you consider the amount spent for Medicare and Medicaid, in addition to these other expenditures, the federal outlay for heart disease ($36.3 billion) and cancer ($16.9 billion) is far more than for AIDS ($6 billion).

Let's also keep in mind that cancer and heart disease are partially brought on by personal conduct. Like smoking, for starters.

---

5. *Source:* Editorial, *Record* (Hackensack, N.J.), 6 August 1995. Reproduced with permission of the *Record* (Bergen County, N.J.).

CHAPTER SEVEN

Induction

The principle of induction states that we can trust the laws of nature to operate in the future as they have in the past. But how can we justify this principle, except inductively? We would be using induction to justify induction. Induction has always served us well in the past, so it should do so in the future. However, this clearly commits the fallacy of begging the question!

This problem was given its classic statement by David Hume (1711–1776) in his *Enquiry Concerning Human Understanding.* A more recent riddle of induction has been offered by Nelson Goodman (1906–): Suppose all the emeralds that we have so far observed are green. This no more justifies the claim that all emeralds are green than it does the claim that all emeralds are green before January 1, 2100, and blue otherwise. The same data confirm two different conclusions: (1) All emeralds are green, *and* (2) all are green up until January 1, 2100, and blue thereafter. Goodman called these latter emeralds "grue."

Despite these theoretical problems, scientists, and the rest of us, continue to use induction.

7.1 Analogical Reasoning

Not all arguments are deductive arguments, in which the conclusion is supposed to be guaranteed. Some arguments are merely intended to show the conclusion is *probable.* These arguments are called **inductive.**

The most common kind of inductive argument is the **argument from analogy.** To draw an analogy is to point out one or more respects in which two or more things are similar. For example, we say that the heart is like a pump, or even that it is a pump, for the obvious reason that the heart pumps blood in a way similar to, or analogous to, the way a pump pumps liquids. We often say that the brain is like a computer, or that the computer is like the brain, because they are similar, or analogous, in that both receive information and process it in various ways—both *calculate.*

These are true analogies in that they assert similarities but not identities. Recall our discussion in Chapter 3 about the fallacy of false analogy. Some analogies fail in being false or in being too far-fetched—that a soldier is similar to a paid killer or that being a rock star is analogous to being an Ancient Greek god. The similarities are too slight to support a genuine analogy, at least without further elaboration.

The argument from analogy uses such similarities to argue that, if two or more things have certain similarities, then they probably have further similarities. For example:

> *Nick liked* Apollo 13, Saving Private Ryan, *and* The Green Mile. *Each movie featured Tom Hanks. So, since* Cast Away *also featured Tom Hanks, Nick will probably like it as well.*

The *form* of this argument from analogy begins to emerge when we paraphrase it as follows:

> *A (Apollo 13), S (Saving Private Ryan), and G (The Green Mile) have qualities Q1 (featuring Tom Hanks) and Q2 (being liked by Nick).*
>
> *C (Cast Away) also has quality Q1 (featuring Tom Hanks).*
> _____
>
> ∴ *C (Cast Away) will probably have Q2 (being liked by Nick).*

This has the form

> *A, S, and G have Q1 and Q2.*
>
> *C has Q1.*
> _____
>
> ∴ *C probably has Q2.*

This is *not* a deductive inference, so the conclusion is not at all certain. Any number of factors might intervene to render it weak. On the other hand, it is not unreasonable. Someone who liked those other movies will probably like *Cast Away.*

The argument from analogy can take another, rather different form. Suppose Betty bought a holly bush, an azalea bush, and a boxwood at the Garden Center; all three plants have flourished; and she is pleased. She now wants to buy a juniper bush, and she thinks she will be pleased if she buys it at the Garden Center.

We first paraphrase it:

H (the holly bush), A (the azalea bush), and B (the boxwood) have all had the qualities Q1 (being bought at the Garden Center) and Q2 (has flourished).

J (the juniper bush) has quality Q1 (being bought at the Garden Center).

∴ J (the juniper) will also have the quality Q2 (has flourished).

Symbolized, this argument has the form

H, A, and B have the qualities Q1 and Q2.

J has quality Q1.

∴ J probably has Q2

The following analogical argument has a slightly different form:

Tour guides Anna and Bill both speak English, French, and German.

Anna also speaks Spanish.

∴ Bill probably speaks Spanish, too.

This argument (not a very strong one) has the following symbolized form:

A and B have Q1, Q2, and Q3.

A also has Q4.

∴ B probably has Q4 as well.

Using certain criteria, we can evaluate the strength (not the validity—only deductive arguments are valid or invalid) or weakness of such analogical arguments. One way to assess such an argument is to consider whether it would be strengthened or weakened by the addition of certain factors:

1. *The more observed cases with the quality in question, the stronger is the analogy.* For example, the more Tom Hanks movies that I've seen, the more likely is my conclusion that I will like the next one.

2. *The more similarities among the observed cases, the weaker is the argument.* If all the Tom Hanks movies that I've seen were directed by the same person (and this one is not), the analogy is weakened.

3. *The more similarities between the observed cases and the new case, the stronger is the argument.* If all the Tom Hanks movies that I have seen also costarred Meg Ryan and this one does, too, the analogy is strengthened.

4. *Consider the relevance of the analogy.* If all the Tom Hanks movies that I have seen have been romantic comedies but this one is not, the analogy is weakened.

5. *The broader the conclusion, the weaker is the analogy.* If I conclude that I would like *every* movie that Tom Hanks ever made, the analogy is weakened.

Here's another example:

You have always enjoyed a cup of coffee upon rising in the morning. So this morning you expect to enjoy your regular cup of coffee, too.

Now consider how the following added factors will affect your induction:

1. *You have enjoyed your coffee every morning for twenty years.* This fact would increase the number of observed cases and therefore strengthen your argument.

2. *You have always had Maxwell House, but this morning the only coffee you have in the house is economy instant.* That would seriously increase the dissimilarity between observed and unobserved cases and weaken your inductive argument.

3. *You like any kind of coffee, strong or weak, perked or dripped, hot or cold.* This heterogeneity among observed cases would greatly increase the likelihood of your enjoying your coffee this morning.

4. *You conclude that not only will you enjoy your coffee but also that your whole day will be wonderful and you'll get an A on every test or a promotion at work.* That greatly increases the sweep of your conclusion and diminishes the likelihood of its coming true.

5. *You believe that the reason you have always enjoyed your coffee is that you've drunk it out of your favorite cup that has a decal of Tweety Bird on the side, and so you've bought a pound of economy instant.* There is presumably a very low correlation between the cup and the enjoyableness of the coffee that's in it; on the other hand, it could be argued that there is indeed a positive correlation between one's favorite cup and the joy of drinking coffee from it.

6. *This morning you get up with a headache, and you haven't studied for your biology test today.* These dissimilarities, between observed cases and this new one, might very well spoil this morning's coffee and render your inductive argument weak and improbable.

Here's a final example:

You have made money in the stock market every month for the past several months, so you expect to make money this month, too.

Let's see how the following added factors will affect your inductive argument:

1. *You have made money in the market every month for five years.* This fact would increase the number of observed cases and therefore strengthen your analogy.

2. *You have always bought blue-chip stocks, but this month you bought an unknown.* This would decrease the similarities among the observed cases and therefore weaken your induction.

3. *You have always bought a wide variety of stocks in big companies, small companies, blue chips, and unknowns.* This would increase the dissimilarities among the observed cases and therefore strengthen your induction.

4. *You conclude that not only will your stocks increase in value but also that they will double.* This greatly increases the breadth of your conclusion and weakens the whole argument.

5. *You have always bought your stocks through a certain broker, and you've bought more stocks through that same broker again this month.* The broker's advice is relevant to how successful you are in the market, so this strengthens your argument.

Exercise 7.1   Decide whether the added facts would weaken or strengthen the inductive analogy.

A.   You have read three books by Nick D'Amour, and you have enjoyed them immensely, so you buy another and you expect it to be enjoyable, too.

1. You have read ten books by D'Amour and enjoyed them.

2. All books by this author that you've read have been romances set in Europe, but this one is a Gothic novel set in Australia.

3. The books by this author that you have read have included a romance novel, a suspense story, and a mystery, and you've liked them all.

4. You conclude that this novel will equal *Wuthering Heights* and will finally teach you all about life and love.

5. All the books by this author that you've read have featured a rock musician as the hero, and you are a rock musician—but this latest book is about a surly tax accountant.

6. You've just strained your eyes studying for a creative writing course exam.

B.   You have averaged 24 points in the six basketball games that you've played in this season. You expect to score that much in the next game.

1. You have played only two games so far this season.

2. All the games that you've played so far have been home games.

3. You've averaged 24 points in both home games and away games, when you were well and when you were ill and injured, when the regular coach was there and when he was not.

4. You conclude that you'll average 30 points in this game, that the other players will be in top form, and that you'll go all the way to the state finals.

5. Your confidence is based on the fact that you're wearing your lucky rabbit's foot (rather than on your scoring average).

6. The starting forward is sick, and his replacement hogs the ball.

7.2 Inductive Generalizations

Logicians distinguish several types of inductive generalization. In this section we discuss universal generalization and causal generalization (including Mill's methods).

In **universal generalization,** the conclusion is about *all* or *none* of the members of a population. For example:

All observed ravens are black.

∴ *All ravens are black.*

No observed pigs have wings.

∴ *No pigs have wings.*

In general, the form of a universal generalization is

All (or none) of the observed P's are Q's.

∴ *All (or none) of . P's are probably Q's.*

The questions that we must ask of a universal generalization are as follows:

1. Is the sample on which the generalizations based *big* enough?

2. Is the sample *representative* or *biased?*

3. Does the conclusion make *too* strong of a claim?

4. Have disconfirming instances been *ignored?*

Suppose a television station, during a program that features a fundamentalist evangelist, asks the audience to call in to say whether they favor prayer in school. Fifty people call in, and all favor school prayer. The station concludes that *all* its listeners favor school prayer.

We apply our critical questions:

1. Is the sample *big* enough? Yes. The station could discover a lot about its audience of, say, 20,000 people, from a sample of 50. But . . . .

2. Is the sample *representative?* No, it is *biased,* for two reasons. First, mostly religious people, of a fundamentalist bent, would be watching that program; second, polls are notoriously unrepresentative because only those who are enthused about school prayer will go to the trouble of phoning in.

3. Is the conclusion *too* strong to be supported adequately by the evidence? Yes. It would be stretching the evidence even to say that *most* of their listeners favor school prayer.

4. Have disconfirming instances been *ignored?* No, because all calls have been noted. But disconfirming instances have been made unlikely by the biased sampling.

Next we consider causal generalization. By *cause,* the logician means a necessary and sufficient condition: If *A* causes *B,* then *A* is necessary and sufficient for *B. A* is necessary of *B* if and only if, whenever *A* does not happen, *B* cannot happen. *A* is sufficient for *B* if and only if, whenever *A* happens, *B* must happen. So if *A* causes *B,* then whenever *A* happens, *B* happens, and whenever *A* does not happen, *B* does not happen.

So when we look for a cause, we are looking for an event or thing that whenever it happens the effect must follow, and when it does not happen, the effect does not follow.

A **causal generalization** is an inductive argument that concludes that one event or thing causes another, as in

Most lung cancers occur in smokers.

∴ *Smoking probably causes lung cancer.*

This kind of reasoning is very important to the doctor who is looking for the cause of a set of symptoms, a diagnosis; to the medical researcher who is searching for the cause and cure for cancer, polio, or AIDS; to the police pathologist who is looking for the cause of a certain homicide; to the police investigator who is looking for the perpetrator of a series of crimes; to the military scientist who wants to know why a certain weapon is ineffective; to the sociologist who is searching for the cause of the high poverty rate in a certain city; to the political manager who wants to know why his candidate lost so badly in a certain primary; to the saleswoman who wants to know why she sold so many more lawn mowers in one town than in another; to the astronomer who wonders why a certain pinpoint of light has appeared in his telescope; to a computer scientist who wants to know why her program works so well for companies A and B but not for company C; to the psychologist who wants to help his patient avoid the mistakes that she has made in her previous relationships that have left her lonely and miserable.

These people are looking for *causes*. It is not only the scientist who searches for causes, but all of us, so we can all profit from a bit of methodological thought about causes. The English philosopher John Stuart Mill (1806–1873) set forth a list of simple and sensible methods of making inductive inferences about causes.

1. The **method of agreement.** The reasoning here is that where the effect is present the cause must be present. So the one feature that is common to a number of cases where a certain effect occurs must be the cause. For example, Bill, Janie, and Richard all came down with hepatitis and we know that

> *Bill shared a syringe with Chuck, Eva, and Beatrice.*
>
> *Janie shared a syringe with Chuck, Eva, and Amy.*
>
> *Richard shared a syringe with Chuck, Amy, and Beatrice.*

Therefore, it is likely that Bill, Janie, and Richard caught hepatitis from Chuck. (At least if we assume that they got hepatitis from sharing a needle with someone.)

2. The **method of difference.** This method recognizes that any feature that is present when the effect is *not* present must *not* be the cause. For example, Al has bad breath, but Beatrice doesn't, and Cathy does, but Elmer doesn't. Now we find out that

> *Al had a hot dog with chili and onions.*
>
> *Beatrice had a hot dog with chili and mustard.*
>
> *Cathy had a hot dog with mustard and onions.*
>
> *Elmer had a hot dog and a salad.*

It makes sense to infer that the feature that caused the bad breath was onions, because hot dogs, chili, mustard, and salad were eaten by the two individuals without bad breath. (Again, we must assume that one of the items listed caused the bad breath.)

3. The **method of concomitant variation.** If a feature is present to a greater degree in cases where the effect is also present to a greater degree, this feature is likely the cause of the effect. For example:

> *Bill has two cavities, and the dentist discovers that Bill eats one chocolate bar a day. Betty has four cavities, and she eats two chocolate bars a day. Wallace has twelve cavities, and he eats three chocolate bars a day.*

It makes sense to infer that the chocolate bars are causing the cavities. (Again, we must assume that we have not overlooked some other feature.)

These methods can be combined. For example:

Joey had anchovies, hamburger, and mushrooms on his pizza and became ill.

Paula had anchovies, hamburger, and peppers on her pizza and became ill.

Dwanna had hamburger, peppers, and mushrooms on her pizza and did not become ill.

The features present in all cases in which illness was caused were anchovies and hamburger. But Dwanna had hamburger and did not become ill, so the cause of the illness must be the anchovies. Mill called this the **combined method of agreement and difference.** More generally, suppose *A, B,* and *C,* are possible causes of effects *x* and *y.* The agreement method can show that, for example, *A* and *B* are not present with *x,* and the difference method can then show that when *A* and *B* are present, *y* is absent. The combined method then shows that *C* is the probable cause, to a greater degree of likelihood than either method does by itself.

These methods are not infallible. We always have to assume that the cause lies among the features we have listed, and that might not be the case. Consider this famous old joke:

Friday I had straight scotch with a Polish sausage, and the next morning I had an awful hangover. Then Saturday I had straight bourbon with a Polish sausage, and next morning I had an awful hangover. Then Sunday I had straight gin with a Polish sausage, and the next morning I had an awful hangover. So I'm giving up that Polish sausage.

Exercise 7.2   Use Mill's methods to find the cause in the following examples. State which method you're using.

1. Of the following, what causes the headaches?

   Joan drinks coffee, smokes, is overweight, and has headaches.

   Paul drinks coffee, eats tuna-salad sandwiches, jogs, and has headaches.

   Milton drinks coffee, eats tuna-salad sandwiches, jogs, and has headaches.

2. Of the following, what poisoned Marge and Chris?

   Marge was poisoned. She had eaten caviar, ice cream, and a cheeseburger.

   Hal wasn't poisoned. He had eaten ice cream, a cheeseburger, and potato salad.

   Chris was poisoned. He had eaten caviar, french fries, and a corn dog.

3. Of the following, who is the likeliest suspect among the partygoers?

Joyce was murdered at a party that was attended by Slade, the baron, and Doris.

Charles was murdered at a party that was attended by Doris, the baron, and Millie the model.

Farnsworth was murdered at a party that was attended by Slade, the baron, and Millie the model.

4. Of the following, what is causing the better grades?

Jim did not do his homework after every class, but he studied all night before the exam and scored 71 points.

Betty did her homework after every class, but she did not cram for the exam the night before and scored 90 points.

Joe did his homework after every class, studied all night before the exam, and scored 82 points.

5. Of the following, what is causing the weight loss?

Dave walked one mile daily for a month, did not diet, and lost two pounds.

Jan walked two miles daily for a month, dieted, and lost five pounds.

Orson walked three miles daily for a month, did not diet, and lost three pounds.

6. Of the following, living in which town seems to cause cancer?

Dale lived in Los Alamos, Oak Ridge, and New York and developed cancer.

Patty lived in New York, Los Alamos, and Chicago and did not develop cancer.

LaBelle lived in Oak Ridge, New York, and Chicago and developed cancer.

7. Of the following, what causes the bad grades?

Jennifer parties once a week and is an A student.

Tommy parties twice a week and is a B student.

Johnny parties every night and is flunking out of college.

8. Of the following, which microbes are causing the disease?

Al's blood contains types A, B, and C microbes, and he has castorides simplex.

Bob's blood contains types A, D, and E microbes, and he has castorides simplex.

Chuck's blood contains types A, F, and G microbes, and he has castorides simplex.

9. Of the following, what makes these young men popular with the crowd?

Tony plays football, drives a sports car, and is popular with the crowd.

Bruce plays basketball, drives a van, and is popular with the crowd.

Rodney plays baseball, doesn't drive, and is popular with the crowd.

10. Of the following, what's the secret of being popular with the crowd?

Tony plays football, drives a sports car, writes poetry, and is popular with the crowd.

Herb plays no sport, drives a sports car, does not write poetry, and is not popular with the crowd.

Bruce plays basketball, drives a van, writes poetry, and is popular with the crowd.

Mel plays no sport, does not drive, writes poetry, and is popular with the crowd.

7.3 Hypothetical Reasoning

Scientific inquiry: How did human beings come to be here on Earth?

Explanation A: The most widely accepted scientific explanation for human life on Earth is the theory of evolution: the process of adaptation of species to their surrounding environment in a gradual development from simple to more complex organisms over some 3.5 billion years.

Explanation B: The Bible says clearly that God created the world and the various forms of life, around 6000 years ago. The biblical account was inspired by God and is therefore without error. If any so-called theory, fact, or evidence—scientific or historical—contradicts Scripture, then by definition it must be wrong.

To evaluate a scientific explanation, logicians have generally agreed on these criteria:

1. The facts to be explained must be *deducible* from the proposed explanation (or hypothesis).

2. The explanation must be *testable.* Our observations need to confirm or disconfirm the hypothesis.

3. The explanation should not conflict with other scientific explanations that are already well confirmed.

4. A range of observable facts must be deducible from the explanation (hypothesis). It should explain more than just the facts at hand.

5. The explanation should be simple. The simpler explanation is the better one.

So let's look at the two human-origin explanations with regard to our criteria:

1. Are the facts of human origins deducible from evolution? Yes. Human beings, the theory states, have been produced by a very long process of adaptation.

Are the facts of human existence deducible from divine creation? Yes. Indeed, everything in the universe is deducible from the creation account.

2. Is the divine-creation explanation *testable?* What would disconfirm it? Nothing. Whatever the facts are in the world or in the universe, creation caused them.

    What would *disconfirm* evolution as an explanation of the fact of humans? Any number of things: Earth is only a few thousand years old, or all putatively billion-year-old fossils are actually only 6000 or 10,000 years old or are fakes, or no stars are over 6000 light-years away.

3. Does the divine creation conflict with other, well-confirmed theories? Yes—for example, the existence of dinosaur fossils and the big bang.

    Does evolution square with the rest of science? Yes. It fits with astronomers' belief that the universe is very old—some 15 billion years old.

4. Are several observable facts deducible from the divine creation? If God did create humans, as Genesis says, then a whole range of predictions can be made. Indeed, the Bible makes predictions (prophecies)—for example, the final judgment. Creationists claim that many events—for example, Israel's becoming a nation—have come to pass in past years, but these events have not been interpreted the same way by everyone. Why are zebras striped, or why do giraffes have such long necks? The same answer for all such questions is that God created it that way. A hypothesis that explains everything explains nothing.

5. Is evolution simple? Yes. Natural selection is wonderfully simple. Living things that have certain traits survive and reproduce. Those that do not, die out. So traits that enable survival tend to persist.

    Is the divine creation simple? Not very. You must believe in a being who is good, powerful, and knowing—perfect. This becomes more and more complicated.

The Scientific Method Mill's methods, though useful in inductive reasoning, all assume that the cause of the fact(s) in question is to be found in the rather narrow sphere of our present knowledge. Not all acientists agree on the specifics of the scientific method, but perhaps most would acknowledge that it involves at least the following elements:

1. States the problem.

2. Formulates a hypothesis.

3. Deduces the implications.

4. Tests the implications.

5. Draws a conclusion.

No scientific statement can be certain because it is always possible that a counterexample will turn up. Even if you have observed a million white swans, the next one might be some other color.

The essence of the scientific method is observation. A statement that cannot be tested by observation is not a scientific statement. Some scientists and philosophers think that such a "statement" is not really a statement at all.

There is much more to say about the scientific method. A hypothesis must be relevant to the facts to be explained *and* internally coherent. Furthermore, it ought to jibe with the rest of scientific knowledge and be capable of generating some predictions that can be tested.

Let's construct an example of the scientific method: Most people before Galileo (and perhaps even today) believed that a heavy object drops faster than a lighter object. But it is easy (once Galileo did it!) to prove that the two objects will in fact drop at the same rate. For example, drop one quarter from one hand and a roll of quarters from the other; they will hit the ground at the same time. This shows that the force of gravity exerts the *same* force on everything, heavy or light, large or small.

The problem: Do heavier objects fall faster than light ones?

The hypotheses: (1) Heavier objects fall faster; (2) heavier objects do not fall faster.

The implication: If the heavier objects fall faster, a heavy object (a roll of quarters) will hit the ground before the lighter object (a quarter).

The test: We drop the two objects, and they hit the ground at the same time.

The conclusion: Hypothesis (1) is probably false, which means hypothesis (2) is probably true.

We have ignored air friction, which is practically the same for the quarter and the roll of quarters. (If we used a quarter and a feather, the result would have been different because the feather, which has much more surface area than the coin, encounters more wind drag, or friction resistance, which slows it considerably. The force of gravity is the same. In a vacuum, the coin and the feather would fall at the same rate.)

Heavier things do not fall faster than lighter ones. As simple a truth as this might seem to us, it provoked the interest of such great scientists as Galileo, Newton, and Einstein.

Exercise 7.3   Some people believe that science is all settled—cut and dried and reported in schoolbooks. But this fascinating question is still controversial among scientists: Are we alone? Is there life elsewhere in the universe?

Given what you now know about induction and the scientific method, what critical remarks can you make about the following two essays? How is it possible that these two scientific essays can come to two entirely opposite conclusions?

There Is Probably Intelligent Life Elsewhere in the Universe[1]

Many scientists believe that the physical laws and processes that resulted in the appearance of life on Earth have also been at work throughout the rest of the universe.

Organic matter has been found in meteorites (chrondites) and has been detected by radio telescopes in the vast gaseous clouds of interstellar space. These organic molecules formed naturally, out of inorganic matter, throughout the cosmos. This is compelling evidence that chemical evolution has produced them.

The outer planets of our solar system—Jupiter, Saturn, Uranus, and Neptune—have been discovered to have atmospheres very similar to the atmosphere of primitive Earth—an abiotic stew of hydrogen, methane, ammonia, and water vapor. On Earth this preorganic mix was acted upon by the natural energy sources of sunlight and lightning—a natural, physical process.

If that process occurred here on Earth, it most probably has begun to occur on the other planets. And if animal life, and even intelligent life, has appeared on Earth, it seems highly probable that it will appear—indeed, has already appeared—elsewhere in the cosmos.

---

1. *Source:* Thora W. Halstead, "Exobiology," in *McGraw-Hill Concise Encyclopedia of Science and Technology,* 3d ed., ed. Sybil Parker (New York: McGraw-Hill, 1994).

> ### There Is Probably No Intelligent Life Elsewhere in the Universe[2]
>
> Although life of a very simple kind, like bacteria, might exist in other areas of the universe, the complex lifeforms on Earth have been produced by a large number of very extraordinary sequences, chance events, and conditions unlikely to be reproduced anywhere else.
>
> In 1976 two *Viking* robot spacecrafts detected no life on Mars, no organic matter at all. If Mars has no life, it is unlikely that the more distant planets, which are even more dissimilar to Earth, could have any life.
>
> Moreover, the fossil record of Earth shows that the appearance of complex organisms was abrupt, not gradual. The "Cambrian explosion" of life occurred some 3 billion years after simple lifeforms originated. This makes any kind of gradual evolutionary process improbable. The flourishing and survival of life on Earth greatly depended on the lucky circumstance of Earth's nearness to the Sun.
>
> So the appearance of complex life on Earth was a matter of luck, and therefore the existence of similar life, not to mention intelligent life, in other places in the universe, is improbable in the extreme.

7.4 Probability and Statistical Reasoning

Information about contemporary issues such as abortion often comes to us in the form of **probabilities** and **statistics**. We are told, for example, that 77.9 percent of all legal abortions in 1981 were administered to unmarried women, 28 percent of all legal abortions in that year were given to women under twenty years of age, and so on. So it will be useful to look briefly at how we arrive at such data and interpret what they mean.

Probability   Let's use the symbols $P(A)$ to stand for "the probability of A." To calculate $P(A)$, we divide the number of positive possible outcomes in a given situation by the total possible outcomes:

$$P(A) = \frac{\text{Positive outcomes}}{\text{Total possible outcomes}}$$

---

2. *Source:* Peter Ward, "The Rare Earth Hypothesis," in *A Brief History of Science,* ed. John Gribbin (New York: Barnes & Noble, 1998).

For example, a coin has two faces: heads and tails. So the probability of getting heads on one toss is

$$P(A) = \frac{\text{Positive outcomes}}{\text{Total possible outcomes}} = \frac{1}{2}$$

A single die has six sides, numbered 1 through 6, so the probability of getting a 3 is

$$P(3) = \frac{\text{Positive outcomes}}{\text{Total possible outcomes}} = \frac{1}{6}$$

The probability of getting a head *or* a tail on one toss of a coin is

$$P(H \text{ v } T) = \frac{\text{Positive outcomes}}{\text{Total possible outcomes}} = \frac{2}{2} = 1$$

which is a certainty. The probability of getting either a 3 or a 5 on one toss of a die is

$$P(3 \text{ v } 5) = \frac{\text{Positive outcomes}}{\text{Total possible outcomes}} = \frac{2}{6} = \frac{1}{3}$$

These are simple situations, but we can assign numerical values to more complex cases. Suppose you know that 20 percent of the eggs in a store are spoiled. That means that the probability of getting a spoiled egg, by choosing it at random, is

$$P(S) = \frac{20}{100} = \frac{1}{5}$$

which is simple arithmetic.

Scientific and technical information is often expressed in terms of probabilities. For example, if out of 50,000 people who smoke, 200 get cancer, then what is your probability (other factors being equal) of getting cancer if you smoke? You can figure it out:

$$P(C) = \frac{200}{50,000} = \frac{2}{500} = \frac{1}{250}$$

Suppose you want to assign a probability to an event in a situation where counting all the outcomes would be impractical. For example, what is the probability of getting a fresh banana out of a whole crate? You take what statisticians call a **random sample:** Make sure that all bananas have an equal chance of being chosen and then pick out ten, say (without looking). Then if five of the ten you picked are fresh, the probability of getting a fresh banana is

$$P(F) = \frac{5}{10} = \frac{1}{2}$$

Here's another example: When a meteorologist calls for a 20 percent chance of rain in a certain area, she means that rainfall will be observed in two places out of ten.

Whatever the method used to assign probabilities to simple outcomes, we can calculate more complex probabilities by using a set of rules or laws called the *probability calculus:*

1. The **law of negation:** If the probability of getting a certain outcome is $P(A)$, then the probability of *not* getting that outcome is

$$P(\sim A) = 1 - P(A)$$

For example, if the probability of getting a rotten egg from a carton is ½ then the probability of getting a fresh egg is

$$1 - P(F) = 1 - P(R) = 1 - \frac{1}{12} = \frac{11}{12}$$

2. The **law of conjunction:** The probability of getting *both* of two different outcomes, A and B, is

$$P(A \cdot B) = P(A) \times P(B, \text{ given } A)$$

which means the probability of A and B is the product of the probability of A and the probability of B given A. For example, suppose you want to get two heads on two tosses of a coin. The probability of this is

$$P(H1 \cdot H2) = P(H1) \times P(H2, \text{ given } H1)$$
$$= \frac{1}{2} \times \frac{1}{2} = \frac{1}{4}$$

Here, H1 is getting heads on the first toss, and H2 is heads on the second toss. Notice that the probability of getting heads on the second toss, given that you got heads on the first toss, is *still* ½. Remember the Gambler's fallacy!)

Here's another example: What is the probability of getting an ace on one draw from a standard deck of cards and another ace on the next draw? Here, A1 is the number of chances of getting an ace from a standard (fifty-two-card) deck, and A2 is the number of chances of getting an ace from the fifty-one cards that are left. So

$$P(A1 \cdot A2) = P(A1) \times P(A2, \text{ given } A1)$$
$$= \frac{4}{25} \times \frac{3}{51}$$
$$= \frac{12}{2652} = \frac{1}{221}$$

3. The **law of disjunction:** The probability of getting *either* of two positive outcomes is

$$P(A \text{ v } B) = P(A) + P(B) - P(A \cdot B)$$

which says that the probability of getting *A* or *B* is equal to the probability of *A*, plus the probability of *B*, *minus* the probability of getting *both A and B.*

What is the probability of getting heads on *either* the first toss or the second toss of a coin? Look at the possible outcomes:

Heads on the first toss $\rightarrow$ H H $\leftarrow$ Heads on the second toss
$\rightarrow$ H T
T H $\leftarrow$
T T

$P(H1)$, the probability of getting heads on the first toss, is ¾; H H and H T are the two positive outcomes out of the four possible outcomes. $P(H2)$, the probability of getting heads on the second toss, is also ¾; H H and T H are the two positive outcomes. Because H H has been counted twice, we subtract its probability, $P(H1 \cdot H2)$, which is ¼. Therefore,

$$P(H1 \text{ v } H2) = P(H1) + P(H2) - P(H1 \cdot H2)$$
$$= \frac{2}{4} + \frac{2}{4} - \frac{1}{4}$$
$$= \frac{3}{4}$$

We could get the same result by looking at the table and counting positive outcomes, 3, and dividing by the total possible outcomes, 4. Drawing up such a table is not always easy, however, so it's wiser to rely on the equation.

Sometimes probabilities are expressed as **odds.** Odds *for* are equal to the ratio of positive outcomes to negative outcomes, and odds *against* are equal to the ratio of negative outcomes to positive outcomes. For example, the odds for getting a 3 on one roll of a die is

$$\frac{\text{Positive outcomes}}{\text{Total possible outcomes}} = \frac{1}{6}$$

whereas the odds against getting a 3 are

$$\frac{\text{Negative outcomes}}{\text{Positive outcomes}} = \frac{5}{1}$$

which is usually expressed as "5 to 1." A fair wager in this case would bet $5 against $1 that the 3 won't come up.

Exercise 7.4   What is the probability of the following?

1. Getting a 6 on one roll of a die

2. Getting 10 on one roll of a die

3. Getting "snake eyes" (1 and 1) or "boxcars" (6 and 6)

4. Drawing an ace or a king

5. Getting at least one head on two tosses of a coin

6. Getting at least one head on three tosses of a coin

For Exercises 7–10, a standard deck is fifty-two cards in four suits (spades, clubs, hearts, and diamonds, each with thirteen cards—A, K, Q, J, 10, 9, 8, 7, 6, 5, 4, 3, and 2).

7. What is the probability of drawing an ace from a standard deck of fifty-two cards?

8. What is the probability of drawing the ace of spades?

9. What is the probability of drawing an ace, replacing it, and then drawing a king?

10. What is the probability of drawing an ace, *not* replacing it, and then drawing another ace? What are the odds against this outcome?

11. If there is a 60 percent chance of rain, what is the probability that it will rain in any given place?

12. If there is a 60 percent chance of rain and a 50–50 chance (even odds) of your getting wet if it does rain, what is the probability of it raining and your getting wet?

13. A coin is tossed three times. What is the probability of getting heads every time? What are the odds against it?

14. The odds against Tom's quitting smoking are 5 to 1. The odds are 2 to 1 against his getting cancer if he doesn't stop. The odds against his survival if he gets cancer are 10 to 1. What are the odds against Tom's surviving?

15. Suppose I bet $5 against your $2 that you will not get heads at least once from three tosses of a coin. Would you take the bet?

16. The probability of Richard's passing logic is ¼. But the probability of his passing calculus "if" he passes logic is ½. The probability that he will graduate if he passes both logic and calculus is ⅔. What is the probability that Richard will graduate?

17. In Exercise 16, what are the odds against Richard's graduating?

18. If you are female, the odds against your making a salary of over $30,000 are (let's say) 18 to 1. If you are under thirty years old, the odds against your making over $30,000 are (let's say) 20 to 1. So if you are both female and under age thirty, what are the odds against your making over $30,000?

19. What are the odds against your rolling a 7 with a pair of dice?

20. What are the odds against your rolling an 8 and then another 8 with a pair of dice?

Statistics In **statistical reasoning** (another kind of inductive generalization), a few observations are taken to represent the whole population.

Statistics, a substantial field of mathematics, is very complex and powerful; statistical surveys and arguments based on them are commonplace today. Although we have room here for only a brief discussion of statistical arguments, we should ask certain questions when confronted with statistical arguments.

Statistical evidence is usually gathered by polling or looking at a **sample,** which is a small portion or percentage of a **population,** which is the whole set of items about which we want to learn more. If all things or persons in a sample are found to have a certain feature, it is argued that all members of the whole population have that feature.

Suppose a television station wants to know how many of its viewers think talk shows are not worth watching. They put an announcement on the screen at 3:00 P.M., right after *Chatting with Joe Blow,* with the question "Are talk shows worth watching?" and a 900 number to call (at a charge of 50 cents per call). Their results are 500 calls, of which 300 are positive and 200 are negative. They conclude that 60 percent of viewers think that talk shows are worth watching.

So now let's apply our questions:

1. Was the sample random? No, because talk-show fans were more likely than any other viewers to see the question and phone in.

2. Was it aimed at the appropriate audience? No, because it includes only those people who were watching a talk show, rather than *all* viewers, including those who prefer prime-time shows, soap operas, and so on.

3. Was the question phrased in a neutral way? No, because it is challenging and provocative, and therefore likely to elicit responses from those with strong feelings favoring talk shows.

4. Were the pollsters biased? No doubt the station's producers hope that people watch their programs and, perhaps unintentionally, bias their sample in favor of talk shows. This factor is often hard to assess objectively. Also, this poll was taken in such a way that the results are not very informative. A *self-selected survey*—one in which the samples select themselves (viewers decide to call or not)—is unreliable, for reasons we have already mentioned. The same would go for mail-in polls in publications and the like.

5. How large was the sample? Five hundred callers is a rather large sample, which is good, but the sampling methods are bad, so the poll is something of a waste.

6. Does the survey tell us the median, mean, mode, or midrange? When it concludes that 60 percent of viewers approve of talk shows, this is the *mean* of the data. They probably just count each yes vote as 1 and each no vote as 0, then sum all the individual 1s and divide that (300) by the total number of individuals in the sample (500) and get

$$\frac{300}{500} = \frac{3}{5} = .6 = 60 \text{ percent}$$

Consider the following information about household finances.

Information Please Almanac[3]

Household Income

Median household income declined by 3.5 percent in real terms between 1990 and 1991 from $31,203 to $30,126. This decline in income is the effect of the most recent recessionary period which began in July of 1990 and ended in March of 1991.

The real median income of White households declined by 3.0 percent to $31,569, and for Asian and Pacific Islander households by 9.0 percent to $36,449. The median income of Black households ($18,807) and of Hispanic origin households ($22,691) showed no significant change.

The real median earnings of male year-round, full-time workers with earnings increased between 1990 and 1991 by 2.0 percent to $29,421. This increase was accompanied by composition changes in the male work force and a decline of 1.3 million year-round, full-time workers. Real median earnings of women working year-round, full-time with earnings, on the other hand, remained unchanged at $20,553. As a result, the female-to-male earnings ratio decreased to .70. The ratio had increased from .60 in 1980 to a record high of .72 in 1990.

---

3. *Source: Information Please Almanac,* ed. Otto Johnson and Vera Dailey (Boston: Houghton Mifflin Co., 1994), 828. (Original source: U.S. Bureau of the Census.)

Poverty Increased

There were 35.7 million persons (14.2 percent) below the official government poverty level in 1991, up from 33.6 million (13.5 percent) in 1990. The 1991 poverty rate for Whites (11.3 percent) was higher than in 1990, whereas the 1991 rates for Blacks (32.7 percent) and Hispanics (28.7 percent) did not change significantly.

The poverty rate for children under 18 continued to be the highest of all age groups (since 1975) at 21.8 percent. The corresponding figure for persons 18 to 64 and for persons 65 years or older was 11.4 percent and 12.4 percent, respectively.

Between 1990 and 1991, the poverty rate for families increased from 10.7 percent to 11.5 percent, representing an increase of 613,000 poor families. About two-thirds of this increases was due to the rise in the number of female householder families with no husband present below the poverty level.

The poverty rates for Whites, related children under 18, and persons in households maintained by females with no husband present increased significantly from 1990 to 1991. However, significant increases did not occur for Blacks, Hispanics, elderly persons, or persons in married-couple families.

One-Person Households

In 1989, there were 22.4 million single-person households, representing almost a quarter of all occupied housing units. About 53 percent of householders living alone were renters (representing 35 percent of all renters) and 47 percent owned their own homes (representing 18 percent of all homeowners).

For homeowners living alone, the median age of their houses was 31 years, compared to the median age of 25 years for all owner-occupied homes. Women living alone tended to own older homes (median age of 33 years) than those owned by men living alone (median age of 28 years). The median value of homes owned by persons living alone was $59,800, 21 percent lower than the $75,400 median for all owner-occupied units.

Homeownership

In 1991, 64 percent of households were owner occupied. The homeownership rate ranged from a low of 15 percent for householders under 25, to a high of 81 percent for householders 65 to 69. The homeownership rate was 79 percent for persons 70 to 74 years or older.

The homeownership rate for married-couple families in 1991 was 79 percent. The corresponding rates for families maintained by a male with no wife present and female with no husband present were 54 percent and 44 percent, respectively. Among one-person households, the homeownership rate was 43 percent for males and 54 percent for females.

Among States, homeownership rates in 1991 rates ranged from 53 percent in New York to 74 percent in Pennsylvania. The homeownership rate in the District of Columbia was 35 percent.

There were 107.3 million housing units in the Nation in 1991: 61 million were owner occupied, 34.2 million were renter occupied, and 12 million were vacant.

Here are some relevant questions we might ask about these statistics:

1. Was the sample taken randomly? A random sample is one in which every person or thing in the population has an equal chance of being selected.

2. Did the poll target the right population? Was it done by phone? By mail? By e-mail?

3. Were survey questions phrased in a neutral way?

4. Were the pollsters themselves unbiased? Are they Democrats investigating economic conditions under a Republican administration, or vice versa?

5. How large was the sample size? The larger the better, up to a point, after which a much larger increment must be added to the sample to produce a very small gain in accuracy. Pollsters indicate the reliability of a survey by means of what statisticians call the **margin of error,** which is based on the degree of reliability of similar polls taken in the past. We do not pursue this rather complicated concept any further here, except to offer an illustration: Suppose the Census Bureau based its figures on household income on a poll of 1000 households and then reported that income declined by 3.5 percent, with a margin of error of ±.5 percent. This means that they think the actual outcome is between 3.0 percent and 4.0 percent. If they polled 10,000 households, they might be able to reduce the margin of error to ±2.0 percent, which would mean they could expect the actual results to be 3.3 percent and 3.7 percent. The *Almanac* gives no margin of error for these figures, but there is one. **Certainty** could be achieved only by polling every member of the population, which would be unrealistic and prohibitively expensive.

6. Does the survey tell us the median, the mean, the mode, or the midrange? All these terms have different meanings. The Census Bureau's statistics in our example are given in terms of the median. The **median** is the number that, when the data are put in ascending order, occurs in the middle of the list. For example, suppose they found the following incomes in the 1990 poll:

$42,127
39,541
31,203   (the median)
20,416
15,651

The mean, on the other hand, is not the same thing. The **mean** is the arithmetic average, found by dividing the sum of the individual values by the total number of individuals in the sample. For the imaginary data above, the mean would be

$ 42,127
39,541

$$31,203$$
$$20,416$$
$$\underline{15,651}$$

$148,938 divided by 5 = $29,787.60

which differs from the median by $1415.40—a significant difference.

The **mode** is the number in a set of data that occurs most frequently. In the Census Bureau data on household income, if the mode had been the object of the survey, rather than the median, more data would have been gathered. Suppose it had looked like this:

$20,000
30,000
40,000
15,000
14,000
12,000
30,000
30,000

The mode is $30,000.

The **midrange** is found by adding the highest number to the lowest number in the data and dividing by 2. For the imaginary data, the midrange is

$$\frac{\$40,000 + \$12,000}{2} = \frac{\$52,000}{2} = \$26,000$$

Notice that the impression we get from the median income is that American households are doing okay, because $31,203 per year is not poverty-level income. But the official poverty level in 1991 was between $6932 (for a person living alone) to $27,942 (for a family of nine or more members). So the relevance of median incomes to some serious concerns is not always very great.

7.5 Summary

There are several kinds of inductive argument. Analogical arguments have the form

a, b, and c have qualities A and B.

d has the quality A.

∴ *d probably has quality B.*

Analogical arguments may be evaluated by these criteria:

1. The more observed cases with the quality in question, the stronger is the argument.

2. The more similarities (and the fewer dissimilarities) among observed cases, the weaker is the argument.

3. The more similarities (and the fewer dissimilarities) between observed cases and new cases, the stronger is the argument.

4. The greater the relevance of the analogy, the stronger is the argument.

5. The broader the conclusion, the weaker is the argument.

Inductive generalization, unlike analogical arguments, have conclusions that are about whole classes of things rather than individuals. An inductive generalization states that if a portion of a class has a certain quality, then the whole class has that property.

A universal generalization has the following form, where S is a sample of a certain class or population P:

Every (or no) member of sample S of population P has the quality Q.

∴ *Every (or no) member of S has the quality Q.*

This kind of inductive argument is reliable only if the sample is representative and not biased. The sample should be a random sample in which every individual member of P has an equal chance of being chosen for observation.

A special type of inductive generalization is statistical generalization, in which the conclusion is stated in terms of a percentage of the target population. Two important statistical concepts are sample size and margin of error.

A causal generalization concludes that one event or thing causes another. It has the general form

x always is present if and only if y is present.

∴ *x causes y.*

The search for a cause may be guided in a general way by Mill's methods:

1. The method of agreement: The cause must be present where the effect is present.

2. The method of difference: The cause cannot be present where the effect is absent.

3. The method of concomitant variation: A variation in a cause should be closely followed by a variation in its effect.

[In Mill's joint method of agreement and difference, the agreement method (the cause is present when the effect is present) and the difference method (the cause is absent when the effect is absent) are used together.]

These methods can suggest causal hypotheses to be tested by the scientific method, in which the hypothesis is used to deduce testable predictions. [Scientific method: (1) State the problem, (2) formulate a hypothesis, (3) deduce the implications, (4) test the implications, and (5) draw a conclusion.]

7.6 Applications

The Death of Marilyn Monroe (Coroner's Case No. 81128) At 4:30 on Saturday afternoon, August 4, 1962, psychiatrist Ralph Greenson visited his most famous patient, Marilyn Monroe, at her home in Brentwood, California. She was drugged and despondent. She told him that she had been expecting to see "someone very important" that evening, but the meeting had been canceled. She was also very upset about not being able to sleep. Greenson talked to her for two hours and then left, feeling that she was okay.

At about 7:40 she called him again, and then called Joe DiMaggio, Jr., son of her ex-husband. Both men found her "cheerful." But at 8:00 she received a call from her close friend Peter Lawford, brother-in-law of President John Kennedy and Attorney General Robert Kennedy. Lawford recalled later that she asked him to "say good-bye to the president" and that her voice was slurred.

Much later, at 3:30 A.M., Eunice Murray, a psychiatric nurse–housekeeper chosen for Marilyn by Greenson, noticed a light under Marilyn's bedroom door. It was unusual for Marilyn to be up so late. Not wishing to waken Marilyn unnecessarily, Murray called Greenson, who came over. Marilyn's door was locked from the inside, so he broke a window and let himself in.

Marilyn was nude on the bed, dead, with the phone in her hand.

At 4:25 A.M. Greenson reported the death to the Los Angles police. At the scene the police found an empty bottle of Nembutal that had been prescribed the day before by another doctor, Hyman Engleberg, as well as an empty bottle of chloral hydrate. Both drugs were sleeping pills. No drinking glass was found. No needle was found.

The autopsy was performed by Thomas Noguchi. Drug concentration in Marilyn's blood was 8.0 mg% of chloral hydrate, and in her liver was 13.0 mg% of Nembutal. Either dose would have been fatal; both together certainly killed her.

Noguchi went over her body with a magnifying glass but found no needle marks. He found a fresh bruise on her lower left back. Her body was unkempt, her fingernails dirty, and her hair frizzy and burned by bleach.

He found no pill residue in her stomach. This fact has led some experts to conclude that she did not take an overdose of pills but was injected. Some people have even speculated that she was murdered. But Noguchi has argued that the stomach of a habitual drug user passes such substances on to the intestines quite readily, and so the lack of such residue does not prove that no pills were ingested orally.

"Probable Suicide," Noguchi wrote on his autopsy report.

On the other hand, a witness said she saw Robert Kennedy and a man with a doctor's bag enter Marilyn's home on the night of her death. Robert Kennedy had indeed flown to San Francisco from Washington on August 3, the day before Marilyn's death, to give a speech to the bar association the following Monday. (Why arrive three days early for one speech?) Rumors abounded that Marilyn was sexually involved with both President Kennedy and his brother, having been introduced to them by Peter Lawford, and that her depression at the time of her death was caused specifically by their attempts to cut their ties with her. She was both famous and emotionally unstable (she had attempted suicide at least twice before) and was therefore especially dangerous to them. She might even have threatened them with exposure.

The Kennedys might have had Marilyn murdered, then, so that she would not embarrass the president. Or perhaps the Mafia or Jimmy Hoffa, both serious enemies of Robert Kennedy, injected Marilyn that night and then forced her to call Robert Kennedy to her aid, thus setting him up for a seriously damaging situation or blackmail.

But if Marilyn was murdered, that fact would have had to be covered up by Greenson, Murray, Noguchi, the Los Angeles police, the Los Angeles district attorney, the FBI (whose files indicate that Robert Kennedy never went to Brentwood that weekend), the president, the attorney general, the Mafia, and on and on. Such a massive coverup would seem to be unthinkable. But then there was Watergate. . . .

These murder scenarios rest on the fact that Noguchi found no pill residue in Marilyn's stomach. Another hard-to-explain fact is that Greenson had injected Marilyn the day before she died. Why didn't Noguchi find a needle mark from that injection? If he missed that one, perhaps he missed the one that caused her death as well?

Another possibility is that Marilyn, already sedated heavily but unable to get to sleep, took another large dose of sleeping pills, not realizing that she was overdosing. Or perhaps someone else (one of her doctors?) gave her another dose by injection on top of the drugs she had ingested gradually during the day, thereby killing her. This is suggested by the statements of the people to whom she talked on Saturday, to the effect that she was "drugged and despondent" and frantic about not being able to sleep.

Did Marilyn Monroe, the world's most famous actress, commit suicide? Was her death an accident? Or was she murdered?

Donald Spoto's more recent account in his *Marilyn Monroe: The Biography* (New York: HarperCollins, 1993) asserts that Marilyn *never* locked her door and that Murray later said so. Furthermore, Murray first told police that she called Greenson at about midnight, but later changed her story to match Greenson's, who lied in order to avoid the obvious question of why he would wait until 4:30 A.M. to notify the police.

No evidence exists to support any conspiracy involving the Kennedys, the mob, the FBI, or the CIA. Greenson himself later stated that Marilyn was making future plans, which dilutes the suicide angle.

How must she have ingested a fatal dose of drugs? Orally? No, for there was no pill-dye residue in her stomach. By injection? A lethal injection would have killed her much sooner and be present at a much higher level in the blood and would have left a bruise, but there was no needle mark of any kind.

Her colon was discovered to be discolored in a way consistent with a rectal administration of drugs—that is, an enema. No suicide would go to all the trouble of giving herself an enema when she could simply wash down a lot of pills with water. So Spoto concludes that she was given an enema of chloral hydrate, which interfered with the body's production of the enzymes that metabolize Nembutal. Greenson was tired, having spent the day dealing with Marilyn, so he gave Murray instructions to give Marilyn an enema of chloral hydrate so that she could sleep. As a male psychiatrist, he could hardly do it himself. Furthermore, when the police arrived, Murray was doing laundry—a very odd thing to be doing with Marilyn lying dead in the bedroom. Dirty sheets are consistent with the involuntary expulsion of the enema upon Marilyn's death—and Murray's desire to destroy evidence.

For these reasons Spoto concludes that Marilyn Monroe's death was an accidental overdose of Nembutal mixed with chloral hydrate—the Nembutal ingested gradually by mouth and the chloral hydrate *per anus.*

Hardly glamourous. Forensic science is a mix of induction and deduction, involving such subjective elements as human motivations, habits, and emotions; but like all scientific endeavors, it searches for the truth that lies hidden among the facts, suspicions, and misinformation. Spoto's conclusion seems reasonable, plausible. Murray lied and she was doing the laundry at a very unusual time and under very unusual circumstances. But there could have been some other cause for her strange behavior—perhaps compulsive cleanliness or a very poor memory. Furthermore, although to some people Marilyn seemed to be making plans for the future, she seemed to others—especially Greenson—depressed and unable to sleep without medication.

Since we are looking for the cause, let's try to apply Mill's methods to the evidence:

1. *The method of agreement.* What is common to a number of cases of which Marilyn's is one? She was famous but emotionally disturbed and dependent on psychiatrists and drugs. This was also true of Kurt Cobain, Janis Joplin, Elvis Presley, James Dean, and many others. Some of their deaths were by suicide; others were the result of wild, careless, childish behavior. Few were by murder, and assassins of the famous often want to be famous themselves and do not effectively hide their crimes. So this method, applied to Marilyn's case, suggests not murder but recklessness.

2. *The method of difference.* Fame is not the cause. Many famous people are not self-destructive. Emotional problems alone cannot be the cause, for millions of emotionally disturbed people do not commit suicide. Money, sex appeal, divorce, a family history of madness—many people have these things without being suicidal or suicidally reckless. So the method of difference leaves us without a clear solution.

3. *The method of concomitant variation.* What feature was present in Marilyn's life to a greater degree than it is in others? What feature can be seen to intensify in her as her death drew nearer? What intensified in other such stars as Presley and Cobain as their lives were ending?

Drugs. More drugs and more doctors writing more prescriptions. The necessity of the famous to perform; to provide, perhaps lavishly, for their dependents; the pressure to perform, which may eventually require pills to get up, pills to get down, pills to get awake, pills to get to sleep; the increasing feeling that nobody cares about them, that everyone wants to use them. Marilyn's most famous quote is "I'm so tired of being treated like a *thing.*" They grow increasingly careless of their lives because they are increasingly miserable. At the lowest point in their sad journey, hardly any difference exists between suicide and accidental overdose.

So we find the cause by Mill's third method. Although this example and its treatment might seem unscientific, not all serious thought, nor indeed even all logical thought, *must* be scientific and objective. The realm of the human and subjective is real and important, too, and well worth some logical analysis.[4]

AIDS   In 1986 there was some controversy about whether AIDS was a serious threat not only to homosexuals and injected-drug abusers but to heterosexuals as well. Among those who sounded an alarm to heterosexuals was then Surgeon General C. Everett Coop, who compared AIDS to the Black Plague that swept Europe in the fourteenth century, killing a third of the population.

In 1988 a director of the Los Angeles City/County AIDS Task Force, Neil Schram, in two persuasive articles in the *Los Angeles Times,* argued that the situation with AIDS was far worse for heterosexuals than society seemed willing to face up to. He brought several arguments to bear on this issue, basing his main conclusions on statistics compiled by the Centers for Disease Control: "The [Public Health Service] forecasts an exponential growth of AIDS due to heterosexual contact from 1100 cases this year to 7000 in 1991. . . ." He goes on to say: "In the same week that the PHS projections were made, the weekly AIDS report by

---

4. More information (and speculation) about Marilyn Monroe's death may be found in: Mailer, Norman, *Marilyn* (New York: Warner Paperback Library, 1975). Noguchi, Thomas T., *Coroner* (New York: Pocket Books, 1983). Spoto, Donald, *Marilyn Monroe: The Biography* (New York, HarperCollins, 1993). Summers, Anthony, *Goddess* (New York: New American Library, 1986).

the Centers for Disease Control showed that the number of cases due to hetero-sexual spread have risen for the first time from 1 percent to 2 percent. . . .”

Schram calls for less moralizing about homosexuality and more compassion, urges more funding for treatment and research on AIDS, and recommends edu-cating people to the fact that AIDS is not a "gay-only" disease.

In February 1987 Suzanne Fields, in an article for the *New York Times,* dis-puted the idea that heterosexuals are as much at risk as homosexuals. Her central argument is that the statistics used by such alarmists do not show that heterosex-uals are as much at risk as homosexuals.

AIDS Is Not a Serious Problem for All[5]
by Suzanne Fields and the *New York Times*

Suzanne Fields is a columnist for *The Washington Times.* In Part I of the following viewpoint, she argues that there is a campaign to frighten heterosexuals into identifying with the high risk AIDS groups by misrepresenting transmission statistics. *The New York Times* has frequently stated that society's extreme fear of AIDS is just that, fear. In Part II of the following viewpoint, a *Times* editorial contends that while there are legitimate reasons for concern about AIDS, exaggeration creates false fears.

As you read, consider the following questions:

1. What evidence does Fields cite to prove that old statistics have been skewed to show an increase of AIDS among heterosexuals?

2. Why do the *Times* editors believe that for the foreseeable future AIDS will stay confined to the known high risk groups?

3. What, in the opinion of the *Times* editors, might be gained by special interest groups in exaggerating the fears of heterosexual transmission?

I

Has AIDS become a disease for all of us?

The campaign to make heterosexuals think so continues—a campaign to frighten them into a closer identification with homosexuals and intravenous drug users, the high-risk groups for AIDS. It seems to be based on the presumption that such identification will heighten compassion, increase the federal money available to researchers, and speed a cure.

---

5. "AIDS Alarms, and False Alarms," 4 February 1987. Copyright © 1987 by The New York Times Company. Reprinted by permission of the *New York Times* and the author.

It's a strange strategy of irrationality, pushed by the very people who should be applying reason to a cruel and heart-breaking enigma.

Misreading the Facts

Columnist Ellen Goodman, for example, thinks of AIDS as an Equal Opportunity Infector. "What does it take," she asks, "to realize that a deadly virus doesn't discriminate on the basis of race, sex, or sexual orientation?"

Such a formulation might be an amusing twisting of semantics, except that it sadly misreads the facts. She arrives at her notion when she receives a sorrowful letter from a mother who discovers that her "dean's list" daughter has tested positive for the AIDS virus. (As terrific as making the dean's list is, it carries with it no immunity to any known disease, so far as anyone now knows.)

"I admit that I skimmed this letter looking for clues," Miss Goodman writes. "Was her daughter a drug user? Did she have a bisexual lover? Had she received blood? But there were no hints and so I was unable to separate my own family from hers into a safety zone."

I don't know what kind of hints would have satisfied Miss Goodman, but surely a mother of a college student is among the last ones on Earth to be conversant with the evidence of the risks and dangers of a daughter's secret life. Short of knowing details about her daughter's male friends, the nature of her sexual acts, whether, on the whim of a single moment, she ever pushed a polluted needle into her body, a mother knows very little. . . .

Rearranged Statistics

The facts about AIDS are sad enough without varnishing them with misrepresentation. A national tragedy of broken young lives needs no embellishment; we need no participation of heterosexuals to make us grieve for homosexuals victims.

What we have is not new evidence, but rearranged statistics.

Until [August 1986]. . . , the federal Centers for Disease Control reported that heterosexuals made up a fairly constant 2 percent of the diagnosed cases of AIDS. The statisticians now say that AIDS has risen to 4 percent among heterosexuals. The rise owes more to an "altered category" than to altered percentages.

Of the 862 heterosexuals who have been diagnosed as having AIDS, 483— or more than half—were born in Haiti or in central and east Africa. Haitians once were classified as a separate high-risk group for AIDS, but researchers decided that it unfairly stigmatized them. Haitians were moved into the heterosexual category. The decision was political, not medical.

There's "strong evidence," says Dr. Harold Jaffe, chief of the epidemiology branch of CDC, that AIDS is transmitted among Haitians heterosexually.

Statistics Need Better Understanding

That may be, but an understanding of the statistics is important. Certain studies indicate that one person in 20 has been exposed to AIDS in Haiti, compared to one in 10,000 in the United States. That is a big difference for people occupying the same category.

Only 379 heterosexuals born in this country have AIDS, less than 2 percent of the 22,792 diagnosed cases. Dr. Jaffe says he does not expect a pattern of heterosexual transmissions such as those observed in Haiti and central Africa to occur in the United States. He can speak with some confidence: the 2 percent figure—it's 1.6 percent, to be more precise—has varied almost imperceptibly over the months.

"The majority of cases will continue to be homosexual men, drug abusers, and, to a lesser degree, transfusion cases," he told *The New York Times*. Dr. Jaffe says the chances of infection for a heterosexual not having sex with any risk-group members are extremely low.

Misleading numbers of heterosexual cases have also been derived from the Army, which reported one study in which 15 out of 41 cases of AIDS were said to come through heterosexual contact. You don't have to be an expert to question these statistics, though many experts do, too. Would a homosexual or a drug addict recruit lie to an officer about a past that would get him kicked out of the army instantly?

What Women Should Really Know

A tiny handful of AIDS cases suggests sexual transmission from woman to man, but no such cases have been absolutely verified, and some researchers, noting that AIDS is transmitted sexually through penetration, say without equivocation that women cannot transmit the disease to men.

The statistics tell women plainly not to engage in sexual relations with men who are bisexuals, intravenous drug users, hemophiliacs, or liars. This means women are well advised to look out for themselves. (What else is new?) A woman should know, very well, who sleeps in her bed; keep the list a short one; and until she knows who she might be falling in love with, make it a peck rather than a passionate kiss.

AIDS Does Discriminate

Misguided liberals, with their penchant for applying compassion to problems crying out for reason and hard thinking, aren't the only purveyors of misinformation and panic about AIDS. Some conservatives, for their own ideological reasons, have added to the din. AIDS is a horrific affliction for society, even for those of us who are not at risk, but it is not an Equal Opportunity Infector. If there were ever a disease that discriminates on the basis of race, sex, and sexual orientation, AIDS is the one.

II

- The Surgeon General recently compared AIDS to the Black Death, a plague that killed a third of Europe's population in the 14th century.

- The Los Angeles Times warns, "It will not be long before the pattern the disease has followed among gays repeats itself among straights."

- The columnist Ellen Goodman predicts, "As—not if but as—AIDS spreads through the population, 'no' will become a much more common answer to sex."

These dramatic alarms are well meant. They may one day be genuinely alarming. Yesterday's proposal by the Federal Centers for Disease Control to test more widely for AIDS could help assess the pattern of the epidemic more exactly. But in the meantime, fears that it is spreading into the heterosexual population are just that, fears.

There is no clear evidence that AIDS in the United States has yet spread beyond the known risk groups, notably homosexuals and drug addicts. There is some reason to suppose it will stay confined to these groups for the foreseeable future.

Why has the truth disappeared so far from view? Perhaps because the chief interpreters of the data want them to reflect their own messages.

Public health experts see a unique chance to reduce all sexually transmitted diseases.

Medical researchers demand $1 billion in new Federal spending against AIDS, hoping to refurbish their laboratories.

Government epidemiologists, seeking to protect homosexuals and drug addicts, fear the Reagan Administration may acquire the notion that these are the only people at risk.

Moralists see a heaven-sent chance to preach fire, brimstone and restricted sex. Homosexuals have no desire to carry the stigma of AIDS alone.

With so many experts dramatizing the epidemic, it's little wonder that those who depend on their advice are coming to believe that AIDS is already as rampant as influenza.

Legitimate Concerns

True, there are solid reasons to fear that AIDS may one day break out of current risk groups into the general population. It can be transmitted heterosexually. In Central Africa, AIDS is already widespread and affects men and women equally. But Central Africa may suffer from special factors, like widespread medical use of unclean needles.

In New York, homosexuals and intravenous drug addicts are still the main groups at risk for AIDS. Some 91 percent of AIDS cases come from those two groups. A constant 2 to 3 percent of cases are "heterosexual contact"—the partners of addicts and bisexual men. If AIDS were spreading further, there would be a sharp rise in the "no known risk" category. But this continues to remain below 1 percent. The city believes most of its 65 such cases are members of risk groups but deny it.

Five years or more pass between contracting the virus and coming down with AIDS. So what counts in forecasting is not overt cases but infection with the virus. Of New York blood donors who tested positive for AIDS virus in 1985, 90 percent had previous homosexual or drug experience, or a partner who did. The same is true of virus-positive military recruits who sought counseling in New York. Neither blood donors nor recruits are wholly representative, but these figures do not prove that AIDS is spreading into the general population. If anything, they indicate that the risk groups will be much the same in five years as at present.

AIDS Is Grim Enough

Since AIDS might spread, people should learn how to protect themselves by using condoms and avoiding anal sex. But it would be folly to distract attention from the most likely source of spread, intravenous drug abusers. Homosexuals in major cities have admirably set up self-help groups and informed their communities; homosexuals elsewhere may still need education about AIDS. Meanwhile, the Reagan Administration remains consumed by irrelevant and prurient debate over whether to preach abstinence to schoolchildren.

Homosexuals and drug addicts have borne the brunt of a terrible disease that merits, and now generally receives, the fullest attention of medical research. Hysteria about AIDS may squeeze out a few extra research dollars, but at a terrible cost in false fears. AIDS is grim enough without exaggeration.

Until August 1986 the Centers for Disease Control (CDC) reported that heterosexuals made up a fairly constant 2 percent of diagnosed cases, but now (then 1986) they say it's 4 percent. Of the 862 heterosexuals with AIDS, 483 were born in Haiti or Africa; they were once considered a separate high-risk group, but researchers moved them into the "heterosexual" category; then some doctors said that was "strong evidence" that Haitians transmitted AIDS heterosexually.

But "other studies" showed that 1 Haitian in 20 has been exposed to AIDS, compared with 1 in 10,000 in the United States!

So only 379 heterosexuals "born in the United States" had AIDS in 1986, less than 2 percent of the 22,792 cases diagnosed, so "straight" people are *not* at any serious risk, Fields concludes.

Let's again ask our list of questions:

1. Was the sample really random? Probably so. (Randomness is not the problem.)

2. Was the survey targeted to the right population? Not when the high-risk Haitians and others were added to the "heterosexual-transmission" category. This would be like counting a recently arrived boatload of nuns from Portugal in the population from which we sample for "unmarried and sexually nonactive women," say, or counting a group of recent immigrants, all of whom already have AIDS.

3. Were questions phrased in a neutral way? It would be interesting to know. Were such questions as "Are you gay?" or "Do you share needles?" included?

4. Were the pollsters unbiased? They were working for the government, but did they have some agenda? It seems likely that Fields was right about the "altered category"—an action well meaning but, to a degree, dishonest. How was the poll taken? Probably from hospital and doctors' records. One can imagine such records being falsified because of the stigma attached to AIDS—people might not tell the truth.

5. How large was the sample? If it looked only at medical records, then it missed nonhospitalized members of the population and made "estimates."

6. Does the survey tell us about medians, means, and so on? For answers to these questions, we would need to inquire into the statistical methods of the Census Bureau or the CDC. But it is worth noting that, in partial vindication of Fields, more recent tabulations of AIDS cases include a new, separate category of transmission: persons born in Caribbean or African countries, now living in the United States. Newer government data also indicate, however, that by the end of June 1994 the cumulative total of AIDS cases in the United States had reached almost 402,000—of whom about 5700 have been children. Total deaths from AIDS have been about 243,500.

Furthermore, the percentage of cases arising from heterosexual contact has been growing, in what Schram would doubtless consider an alarming rate, from 16.2 percent in 1993 to 18.2 percent in 1994, according to the CDC.

For more information about AIDS and about their research methods, contact the National AIDS Clearinghouse (800)362-0071. For up-to-date information about the disease, call (800)342-2437.

Exercise 7.5   A. CDC statistics show that for 1991 total, cumulative AIDS cases in the exposure category of "heterosexual contact" were 3367 (an increase of 568 cases since 1990), which represents 8 percent of total AIDS cases. Do these figures bear out Schram's predictions or Fields's? For more statistics on AIDS, go to

www.cdc.gov/hiv/stats/exposure.htm

B. Consider these two opposing views: The death penalty discriminates against blacks; the death penalty does not discriminate against blacks.

In an 1988 article in *Criminal Justice Ethics,* Anthony Amsterdam argued persuasively that the death penalty in Georgia discriminates against blacks. His argument was based on statistics from a University of Iowa study: "Although less than 40 percent of Georgia homicide cases involve white victims, in 87 percent of the cases in which a death sentence is imposed, the victim is white."

What's more, he argues that the statistics showed that "22 percent of black defendants who kill white victims are sentenced to death; 8 percent of white defendants who kill white victims are sentenced to death; 1 percent of black defendants who kill black victims are sentenced to death; 3 percent of white defendants who kill black victims are sentenced to death."

In 1989 Laurence Johnson published an article in *Human Events* that contradicted Amsterdam's argument. He argued that the statistics did not prove that the death penalty discriminated against blacks. His statistics (from the *U.S. Bureau of Justice Statistics*) refer not to Georgia alone, but to the entire United States. His source, he says, "lists 10,499 single-victim, single-offender homicides. Some 3246 of these more than 10,000 murders are white, non-Hispanic and 1218 were white, Hispanic; 805 of these listed in the 'white' category were of unknown ethnicity and 4966 of the 10,499 killers were black."

He concludes that the black and Hispanic murderers far outnumber the white, non-Hispanic ones. So, he argues, although "less than 40 percent of homicides are committed by whites, more than half of the death sentences, and more than half of the executions have been allocated to white prisoners."

Does it seem to you that the statistics support one side of this controversy over the other?

Consider these statistics from the Bureau of Justice: Of persons under sentence of death in 1999, 1948 were white, 1514 were black, 28 were Native American, 24 were Asian, and 13 were classified as "other race." Tables 7.1 and 7.2 list more statistics about race of victims and offenders. From these statistics can you conclude anything about the issue of whether the death penalty discriminates against blacks?

For more information on the death penalty go to

www.usdoj.gov/bjs/homicide.htm

Table 7.1 Homicide Type by Race, 1976–99

| | | Victims | | | Offenders | |
	White	Black	Other	White	Black	Other
All homicides	51.2%	46.6%	2.2%	46.5%	51.5%	2.0%

Source: Bureau of Justice Statistics.

Table 7.2 Race of Defendants Executed since 1976

Defendant Race	Number Executed	Percent of Total Executed
Black	256	36
Hispanic	50	7
White	403	55
Native American and Asian	13	2
Persons Executed for Interracial Murders:		
White Defendant/Black Victim	11	
Black Defendant/White Victim	163	

Source: Death Penalty Information Center.

 *CHAPTER EIGHT*

Critical Analysis

The hopes of Frege, Russell, and the early Wittgenstein—that modern logic could provide us with a perfect language, solve all philosophical problems, and finally leave behind the imprecision and ambiguity of ordinary language—are no longer common, even among logicians. One reason was that Wittgenstein and some other philosophers, including Gilbert Ryle (1900–1976) and J. L. Austin (1911–1960) at Oxford, came to believe that it is ordinary language, rather than the ideal language of symbolic logic, that is the bedrock of philosophy. They doubted the power of symbolic logic to show us the structure of reality. This school of thought has been distrustful of symbolic logic's ways of dealing with ordinary language.

Another reason was Quine's argument that we have no reliable, noncircular way of making the distinction between analytic statements and factual statements. This argument, if taken seriously, casts serious doubt on logical truth and there-fore on the logician's rules of deduction, tautologies, and so on. Quine believed that logical truths are really factual and that logic is just another part of empirical science.

These issues, though challenging, have not deterred logicians from their orig-inal task—the critical analysis of arguments—to which this book is devoted.

8.1 Procedure

The point of all the technical material in this book is the logical analysis of real arguments about real issues. Keeping in mind that slashing through the under-growth in this way is necessarily both art and science and that different analysts may proceed differently, we can still attain a surprising amount of clarification—and even agreement—by approaching argumentative material in a systematic way. I recommend the following guidelines:

1. Read the essay carefully.

2. State the main conclusion, paraphrasing but maintaining the original meaning.

3. State the premises, arranging them into extended arguments or into several short arguments, each of which supports the main conclusion directly. Provide suppressed premises.

4. Challenge dubious premises and check for fallacies.

5. Separate deductive and inductive arguments. Symbolize the deductive arguments as syllogisms or deductive proofs. Check their validity with Venn diagrams, truth tables, or by the rules of deduction.

6. Evaluate inductive arguments by the methods that apply to analogical arguments, inductive generalizations, and the like.

7. Compose some brief critical remarks summarizing your analysis.

What's important is not so much *this* procedure but *some* procedure that employs most of the techniques of standard elementary logic. You should proceed in the way that makes the most sense to you. This procedure has the virtue of including most of the analytic strategies in this book.

Another point: As useful as a list of fallacies can be, an approach that was limited to a kind of slapdash application of the fallacies would remain essentially negative. A knowledge of the syllogism and of deductive proofs makes possible a much richer appreciation of the logical structure of an essay, showing up its hidden virtues as well as its faults.

In Section 8.2, I use my recommended procedure to analyze several examples of essays on various controversial issues.

8.2 Examples

Example 1 In our first example, Michael Kinsley argues that, since it is unthinkable to execute a financially rich celebrity like O. J. Simpson, even if he were guilty, perhaps we shouldn't execute financially poor murderers, either.

Bracketed numbers in the article indicate where I believe that fallacies occur. In the list on page 302, I identify each fallacy and briefly comment.

What Americans Won't Do[1]

by Michael Kinsley

They will never execute O. J. Simpson. They will never strap O. J. down in the gas chamber, seal the door, and drop the poison pellets (California's chosen method). Even putting it in these terms proves the point. It is unimaginable. We will not allow it—"we" being the same American citizenry that supports capital punishment by a wide margin in every poll, the same [1] citizenry to which politicians promise ever more executions for an ever greater variety of crimes.

Simpson, of course, is innocent until proven guilty. He may be telling the truth when he says, through his lawyer, that he was at home two miles away when his ex-wife and her male friend were murdered. Furthermore, as a rich man, he is entitled to the [2] true blessing of American justice—which isn't a fair trial but an unfair trial. Top criminal lawyers don't get $500 an hour or more [3] to supply justice no better than a run-of-the-mill public defender. Even if he's guilty, he may get off, or get off lightly.

But O. J.'s real guarantee against capital punishment is his celebrity, not his wealth. Imagine that the scenario we've all had running through our head actually happened: that O. J. Simpson drove his Ford Bronco over to his ex-wife's town house, donned a pair of gloves, confronted her and a man he at least thought was her boyfriend, inflicted "multiple sharp force injuries and stab wounds" (the coroner's report) on both and slit her throat to boot. Two deaths. Premeditated. Gruesome. No obvious complicating or mitigating circumstances.

Is that the kind of thing advocates of the death penalty have in mind when they say that some crimes are deserving of the ultimate sanction? Undoubtedly yes. Would society be able to impose it on O. J. Simpson? Undoubtedly no.

Why not? Because O. J. Simpson's celebrity means that for most Americans he is a flesh-and-blood human being. We comfortably call him "O. J.," even though we've never met him, because in our mind he's a friend. Even if convicted of murder, he'll never be an abstract symbol of evil like the typical death-penalty customer with three names—Robert Alton Harris, Rickey Ray Rector, John Wayne Gacy et al. For once, in the competition of humanization between the murderer and his victims, the murderer would have an unbeatable edge.

O. J. Simpson is not just a famous former football star. Through his sports commentaries, his Hertz Rent-a-Car commercials and his movie roles, he has created a persona: manly and likeable, the

1. *Source:* Michael Kinsley, "What Americans Won't Do," *Time,* 27 June 1994, 80. © 1994 Time Inc., reprinted by permission.

classic good-guy jock. Whatever actually happened last week, we now know that this persona was not entirely accurate. Good guys don't beat their wives until the police have to be called, as apparently happened more than once in the past.

But however much our image of O. J. Simpson may have to be revised, his celebrity will continue to protect him. This is only partly because the impression of O. J.'s likability—stamped into our brain by hundreds or even thousands of media moments over the years—will never be completely destroyed, even by the most compelling of contrary facts. More important is that likable or unlikable, O. J. Simpson is and always will be a *real person* in other people's mind. And all but the most hardened death-penalty enthusiasts will quaver at the thought of this real person—O. J. Simpson—[4] gasping for breath as the cyanide begins to do its fatal work.

So if it comes to the crunch, people will be understanding and compassionate. They will look for excuses: a troubled childhood, uncontrollable rage, the pressures of his high-powered winner's life. They will stress his remorse. They will point to his orphaned children. They will say the whole thing's a complex tragedy. They will argue for mercy. They will, in short, become liberals—at least for this one case.

As a [5] liberal softy, I oppose the death penalty, but I'm not a sentimentalist about it. There are many other circumstances in which the state sanctions the death of its citizens for policy purposes. The decision to go to war is the most obvious example, but even the less dramatic decision to build a [6] major tunnel or bridge contains the statistical probability of deaths in the process. We live with it. Furthermore, a quick and relatively painless end strikes me as preferable to echoing decades in the typical, miserable state prison with no hope of parole—the death-penalty opponents' favorite alternative. (Of course, most of those who actually face the choice disagree with me about this.)

But, as retired Supreme Court Justice Lewis Powell belatedly concluded after a career of upholding death sentences, the death penalty cannot be administered fairly. Nothing illustrates that better than the thought experiment of trying to imagine O. J. Simpson in the gas chamber. It's just not going to happen, no matter what he may have done. And rightly so. After all, this is a guy we've shared beers with—at least in our mind.

So, does that mean we should perhaps spare some human empathy even for the low-powered losers who are the usual murderers in our society? Is their tragedy, perhaps, also complex? Does their remorse count for anything? Should we hesitate to demand death for death in their cases?

[7] Heck, no. what are you—soft on crime?

The main conclusion is

We ought not to execute financially poor murderers.

The premises fall into several arguments:

ARGUMENT (A)

O. J. is rich.

The rich can afford top lawyers.

Those who can afford top lawyers can get an unfair advantage (a "better supply of justice" than what the poor must settle for).

Those so advantaged may get off or get off lightly, even if guilty.

O. J. may get off or get off lightly (because of his unfair advantage).

We write this as a deductive proof (the meaning of the letters should be evident):

(1) R

(2) $R \supset T$

(3) $T \supset U$

(4) $U \supset O$ /∴ O

(5) T 2, 1   MP

(6) U 3, 5   MP

(7) O 4, 6   MP

ARGUMENT (B)

O. J. is a celebrity.

Celebrities are "real people" to us.

Executing a real person is unthinkable.

Executing O. J. is unthinkable—even though the crime is premeditated, gruesome, without any mitigating circumstances, and so on.

We can treat this as a sorites:

All O are C.		*No R are E.* *(No real people are executable).*
All C are R.	and	*All O are R.*
All O are R.		*No O are E.*

and diagram it:

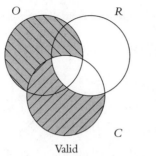
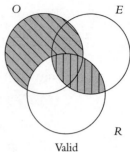

We can also treat it as a deductive proof:

(1) C

(2) C ⊃ R

(3) R ⊃ ~E   /∴ ~E

(4) R   2, 1   MP

(5) ~E   3, 4   MP

ARGUMENT (C)

The crime of which O. J. is accused is premeditated, gruesome, and so on.

One who commits such a crime is someone whom death penalty advocates consider deserving of the death penalty.

Whoever deserves the death penalty will get it, unless we have compassion, find excuses, and so on.

O. J. will not be executed, even if he's guilty.

We will have compassion, find excuses, and so on.

This should be treated as a deductive proof:

(1) G

(2) G ⊃ D

(3) D ⊃ (~C ⊃ E)

(4) ~E   /∴ C

(5) D   2, 1   MP

(6) ~C ⊃ E   3, 5   MP

(7) ~(~C)   6, 4   MT

(8) C   7   DN

It is tempting to question the third premise, but let's wait until we have examined the remaining argument.

ARGUMENT (D)

Because he's "real to us," we will find enough excuses and feelings of compassion to save O. J.

"And rightly so" means: We ought to find enough excuses and so on to save O. J.

If we ought to find enough excuses to save O. J., we ought to do the same for ordinary murderers, too.

We ought to find enough excuses to save ordinary murderers.

The first premise may be left aside, which will leave us

(1) F

(2) F ⊃ S   /∴ S

(3) S   2, 1   MP

ARGUMENT (E)

The state often sanctions the death of its citizens. If so, it's not so unusual. ("We live with it.")

If life without parole is worse, then the death penalty is not so cruel.

The death penalty is not so cruel and unusual. (Kinsley says he's not a sentimentalist about it, meaning he's not moved much by "liberal softy" reasons.)

We treat this as a deductive proof:

(1) S

(2) S ⊃ ~U

(3) L

(4) L ⊃ ~C   /∴ ~C · ~U

(5) ~C   4, 5   MP

(6) ~U   2, 1   MP

(7) ~C · ~U   5, 6   Conj

ARGUMENT (F)

O. J. won't be executed, no matter what he may have done.

Other, poorer murderers do get executed.

If some murderers are executed and some are not, the death penalty cannot be administered fairly.

The death penalty cannot be administered fairly.

This is not valid but just a reprise of Argument (D).

The only argument in this essay that might be considered *inductive* is the decision to build a "major tunnel or bridge [which] contains the stastical probability of deaths," but we will treat this as a fallacy.

Now let's look for fallacies:

1. "citizenry to which politicians promise ever more executions": This might be a *pooh-pooh,* suggesting that capital punishment is a kind of entertainment demanded by a shallow public.

2. "true blessing of American justice—unfair trial": This is a *question-begging epithet,* suggesting that justice can be bought.

3. "to supply justice no better than": This presumes that the outcomes of trials depend upon the cost of the lawyers, which is a *false cause.*

4. "gasping for breath": This is an *appeal to pity;* Kinsley continues in this way in the following paragraph.

5. "liberal softy . . . but . . . not a sentimentalist": Kinsley says human feelings (compassion and the like) are *not* his reason for opposing the death penalty but its "unfairness," but he says that these reasons are the right ones for opposing O. J.'s execution. He is just being a bit too arch, here. Are human feelings irrelevant? Can he only feel passion for an abstract principle of fairness? There is too much "strain" here because Kinsley wants to have his cake and eat it, too.

6. "major tunnel": This is a *false analogy* with executions.

7. "Heck, no . . . soft on crime?": This amounts to a *straw-man sophistry.* There are more and stronger arguments for the death penalty; for example, retribution and deterrance are standard arguments.

Next let's challenge the premises in arguments (A)–(F): In (A), it is not necessarily true that people who can afford "top lawyers" can get a "better supply of justice" than others. It is arguable that a defendant could get a "better" defense from a local, lower-powered attorney than from a "superstar." The other premises seem to be true.

In (B), it could be objected that celebrities are *not* real but larger than life and mythical *and* that it is not at all unthinkable to execute a "real person." That might be a media circus and not unprecedented. Many celebrities have been savaged by the media, from Socrates on.

In (C), the third premise, to the effect that *only* excuses and compassion and such can enable one to avoid execution, is surely false. There are other actions that one might take—bribing jurors or threatening them, the judge, or prosecutors. One might count on the race, gender, or age of jurors. One might pray. And so on. The fourth premise is not at all obvious and depends upon (weak, invalid) argument (B). (As it turned out, the prosecutors in this case decided early on *not* to seek the death penalty—not necessarily for Kinsley's reasons.)

In (D), it is not true that we ought to find enough excuses, compassion, and so on to save O.J. if he is guilty. This premise begs the whole question. If we ought to save O.J., even if he is guilty, then it would follow that we ought not to execute *any* murderer. The phrase "and rightly so" presumes that we think it's wrong to execute O.J. An advocate of the death penalty would not necessarily think that. "Let him off because he's my buddy" is hardly a good or moral reason, but it might be the *real* reason we except someone, and it it not logically inconsistent with the general advocacy of executions.

In (E), executing a murderer is not on the same moral level as sending citizens off to war. We intend to kill the murderer; we do not intend to kill the soldier, whom we train, equip with weapons, and so on.

In (F), we can easily think of circumstances in which O.J. would be executed—if he had bombed a federal building, say, killing 168 people.

Critical summary: Kinsley's main conclusion is that we shouldn't execute anybody. His main argument is that if we don't execute O.J., and we won't, then we shouldn't execute anybody. This is not a valid argument. For if we should but don't, that doesn't prove we shouldn't execute anyone else.

Kinsley argues that we won't. For one thing, O.J. is rich and can afford top lawyers who will give him an advantage and get him off or at least get him off lightly. But it would seem that some cases are too airtight for even the best lawyers to make the difference. Even top lawyers sometimes lose.

Kinsley argues that O.J. is a celebrity and celebrities are "real people" to us, and executing a real person is unthinkable. But it's not. Imagine Larry King brutally strangling Howard Stern, or vice versa. Isn't it as easy to imagine the guilty one being executed? Two "unthinkable" events are hardly more difficult to think than one.

Kinsley goes on to argue that since we won't execute O.J., even if he's guilty, we will come up with (what Kinsley strangely seems to consider phony) excuses and compassionate feelings. But it is not inconceivable that other reasons or causes could save O.J. For example, he could bribe a juror, or media coverage could make a fair trial impossible.

Kinsley outsmarts himself when he generously allows that the death penalty is not so cruel or unusual and that he's not squeamish about executing folks, likening it to having workers get killed building bridges and tunnels, which is ridiculous. Accepting deaths is *not* analogous to killing people, even deserving people. Kinsley is being ironic. He doesn't *mean* this, which is clear from his next argument.

What's really wrong with the death penalty is that it cannot be administered fairly. Kinsley's reasoning is that O. J. is a real person who won't be executed, guilty or not, and if we won't execute O. J., we ought not to execute anyone else. Realizing that this is invalid reasoning, he is driven to add, to "it's [the execution] not going to happen," the phrase "and rightly so" —thus begging the question. Certainly, if we ought not to execute (a guilty) O. J., it follows that we ought not to execute anyone else. But from "we won't" it's a long way to "we *ought* not." Maybe we "ought" to execute O. J. "if he's guilty," whether we in fact do so or not.

Example 2   Our second example is an editorial about the impact of the Comprehensive Test Ban Treaty on U.S. Security.

Editorial from the *Tampa Tribune*[2]

Whether it will be Democrats or Republicans who win the most political points from the rejection of the test ban treaty is of little consequence. Of lasting importance is the impact on U.S. security and world stability, and a ratified treaty would seriously threaten both.

It could not, as President Clinton promised, "end nuclear testing forever," any more than the international pact of 1928 to outlaw war did anything more than give the aggressors, Germany and Japan, a running start in World War II.

The treaty banning explosion of nuclear devices would be difficult to monitor and, as long as China and Russia hold veto power in the U.N. Security Council, impossible to enforce.

Already the United States has a no-test policy, as do France and Great Britain. But as nuclear weapons grow old and unreliable, it will likely be necessary sometime in the future to either test or forsake the time-proved policy of nuclear deterrence.

If the United States allows itself to weaken, its allies will feel more vulnerable and may well launch a new arms race as they build their own nuclear umbrellas or the equivalent in biological or chemical weapons.

---

2. *Source:* Editorial, *Tampa (Fla.) Tribune,* 18 October 1999. Editorial reprinted with permission from the *Tampa Tribune.*

One foolish argument made by U.S. proponents of the treaty is that it would freeze U.S. weapons superiority: We have the best weapons now, and if testing is stopped, potential enemies can never catch up. Those who believe all nations will be content to be inferior to U.S. power forever are as childishly hopeful as those who earlier this century thought they had banned war.

The reason war cannot be banned, says Baker Spring of the Heritage Foundation, is that "if war were truly outlawed, the means ultimately needed to enforce such a provision would be war itself."

What a no-test treaty would do is not make the world safer, but give the United States the illusion of safety, and politicians a cause to boast, while threats would continue to grow, as they always do.

"If we don't do the right thing," Clinton says, "other nations won't either."

That is correct, but it is also true that even if the United States does what Clinton thinks is right, which is to weaken our nuclear arsenal, other nations won't automatically weaken theirs. As Spring points out, the treaty will disarm and weaken only those states that honor it.

It would be wonderful if the ultimate goal of the treaty, world nuclear disarmament, were possible. It would also be marvelous if Tampa police could forgo handguns.

Unfortunately, neither is advisable.

The main conclusion is

The ratification of the Comprehensive Test Ban Treaty (CTBT) would threaten U.S. security and world stability.

The five premises (along with the arguments tying them to the main conclusion) are as follows:

(1)   *The CTBT cannot end nuclear testing.*

supp → *If the CTBT cannot end nuclear testing, it threatens U.S. security.*

          ∴ *The CTBT threatens U.S. security.*

We symbolize it next:

~E

If ~E, then T

∴ *T*

and then construct a truth table:

E	T	~E	~E ⊃ T	/∴ T
T	*T*	*F*	*F T T*	*T*
T	*F*	*F*	*F T F*	*F*
F	*T*	*T*	*T T T*	*T*
F	*F*	*T*	*T F F*	*F*

No row states T T F, so it is valid. Also, no row states

~E	~E ⊃ T	/∴ T
T	*T*	*F*

so it is valid.

> (2)   *The CTBT would be hard to monitor and impossible to enforce.*
>
> supp → *If the CTBT cannot be monitored and enforced, it will threaten U.S. security.*
>
> ∴ *The CTBT threatens U.S. security.*

The symbolism is

$H \cdot I$

$(H \cdot I) \supset T$

∴ T

and the truth table is

H	I	T	H · I	(H · I) ⊃ T	/∴ T
T	*T*	*T*	*T*	*T T*	*T*
T	*T*	*F*	*T*	*F F*	*F*
T	*F*	*T*	*F*	*T T*	*T*
T	*F*	*F*	*F*	*F F*	*F*
F	*T*	*T*	*F*	*T T*	*T*
F	*T*	*F*	*F*	*T F*	*F*
F	*F*	*T*	*F*	*T T*	*T*
F	*F*	*F*	*F*	*T F*	*F*

No row states

H · I	(H · I) ⊃ T	/∴ T
T	*T*	*F*

so it is valid. We can also show it as a deductive proof:

(1) $H \cdot I$

(2) $(H \cdot I) \supset T$ /∴ T

(3) T 2, 1   MP

(3)   *We will someday have to test or forsake our policy of deterrence.*

supp → *If we have to test or forsake our policy of deterrence, this will threaten U.S. security.*

∴ *The CTBT threatens U.S. security.*

We can treat this as a deductive proof:

(1) *(T v F)*

(2) *(T v F) ⊃ W   / ∴ W*

(3) *W   2, 1   MP*

(4) *If the CTBT freezes U.S. weapons superiority, other countries will not be content to be inferior.*

If other countries will not be content to be inferior, this will threaten U.S. security.

∴ *If the CTBT did freeze U.S. superiority, this would threaten U.S. security.*

This is proved as follows:

(1) *F ⊃ O*

(2) *O ⊃ T   / ∴ F ⊃ T*

(3) *F ⊃ T   2, 1   HS*

(5) *If war were banned, this ban could be enforced only by war itself.*

This paradoxical premise seems in this context to mean, or to imply, that

If the CTBT were ratified, it could be enforced only by nuclear weapons.

Neither statement seems quite true. The *threat* of war or of nuclear attack might be enough to stop agression.

Here are some minor points to Clinton's claim:

(1) *If we don't do the right thing, other nations won't either.*

The author replies:

If we do (what Clinton thinks is) the right thing, other nations won't, anyway.

(2) *The CTBT will disarm and weaken only those who honor it.*

(3) *World nuclear disarmament, like police forgoing handguns, is impossible and even inadvisable.*

These statements are so cynical that they hardly warrant development into arguments. They disparage all treaties and indeed all honor and trust among people and have the childish ring of "rules are for sissies." One might argue that such an attitude is hardly less threatening than nuclear weapons to security and stability.

Example 3   Our third example is Senator Jesse Helms's (R–N.C.) opinion that the Antiballistic Missle (ABM) Treaty should be rejected.

Amend the ABM Treaty? No, Scrap It[3]
by Jesse Helms

Under pressure from the Pentagon and congressional conservatives, President Clinton reluctantly decided to request $6.6 billion over six years in his new budget for missile-defense research. And Defense Secretary William Cohen announced yesterday that the administration wants permission from Russia to renegotiate the Antiballistic Missile Treaty.

But administration officials have made it clear that unless the Russians are willing to give that permission, they have no intention of actually deploying a nationwide missile defense system. Why? Because the administration believes that any such deployment would violate the ABM Treaty. And, as National Security Adviser Samuel Berger affirmed in a speech just last week, "We remain strongly committed to the 1972 Anti–Ballistic Missile Treaty [as] a cornerstone of our security."

What that means is that in Mr. Berger's view, deploying even the most limited missile defense would require getting permission from Russia to revise the ABM Treaty. Consider that for a moment: The Clinton administration wants to negotiate permission from Russia over whether the U.S. can protect itself from ballistic missile attack by North Korea.

The ABM Treaty is the root of our problems. So long as it is a "cornerstone" of U.S. security policy, as Mr. Berger says, we will never be able to deploy a nationwide missile defense that will provide real security for the American people.

We do not need to renegotiate the ABM Treaty to build and deploy national missile defense. We can do it today. The ABM Treaty is dead. It died when our treaty partner, the Soviet Union, ceased to exist. But rather than move swiftly to declare the treaty dead, and to build and deploy a national missile defense, the Clinton administration is attempting to resuscitate the ABM Treaty with new protocols to apply its terms to Russia and all the other nuclear states that were once part of the Soviet Union.

---

3. *Source:* Jesse Helms, "Amend the ABM Treaty? No, Scrap It," *Wall Street Journal,* 22 January 1999.

The world has changed a great deal since the ABM Treaty was first ratified 27 years ago. The U.S. faces new and very different threats today—threats which are growing daily. China has 19 intercontinental ballistic missiles [ICBMs], 13 of which are aimed at the U.S. As recently as 1997 a senior Chinese official issued a veiled nuclear threat, warning that the U.S. would never come to the defense of Taiwan, because we Americans "care more about Los Angeles than we do Taipei."

Saddam Hussein is doggedly pursuing nuclear, chemical and biological weapons and the long-range missiles to deliver them, and the will of the international community to confront and disarm him is crumbling. Iran, which is also developing a nuclear capability, just tested a new missile—built with Russian, Chinese and North Korean technology—which can strike Israel and Turkey, a NATO ally. And, according to the Rumsfeld Commission, Iran "has acquired and is seeking advanced missile components that can be combined to produce ballistic missiles with sufficient range to strike the United States." If Iran succeeds, the commission warns, it will be capable of striking all the way to St. Paul, Minn.

North Korea's unstable communist regime is forging ahead with its nuclear weapons program, and test-fired a missile over Japan last August which is capable of striking both Alaska and Hawaii. And Pyongyang is close to testing a new missile, the TD-2, which could allow it to strike the continental U.S.

America is today vulnerable to ballistic missile attack by unstable outlaw regimes, and that missile threat will increase dramatically in the early years of the 21st century. What are we doing today, in this waning year of the 20th century, to defend ourselves against these emerging threats? Practically nothing.

When the Senate votes on the new protocols expanding the ABM Treaty to Russia and other post-Soviet states, we will in fact be voting on the ABM Treaty itself. For the first time in 27 years, the Senate will have a chance to re-examine the wisdom of that dangerous treaty. If I succeed, we will defeat the ABM Treaty, toss it into the dustbin of history and thereby clear the way to build a national missile defense.

The Clinton administration wants to avoid that at all costs. So the president has delayed sending the new protocols to the Senate for approval. But Mr. Clinton does not have a choice—he is required by law to submit the ABM protocols to the Senate. On May 14, 1997, Mr. Clinton agreed to explicit, legally binding language that he submit the protocols, a condition that I required during the ratification of another treaty, the Conventional Forces in Europe Flank Document. It has been 618 days since Mr. Clinton made that commitment under law. I am going to hold him to it.

Today I am setting a deadline for the president to submit the ABM protocols to the Senate. I expect them to arrive by June 1. In the meantime, I will begin ratification hearings on the treaty shortly, so that the Foreign Relations Committee will be ready to vote and report the treaty to the full Senate by June 1. I say to the president: Let your administration make its case for the ABM Treaty, we will make our case against it, and let the Senate vote. If I have my way, the Senate this year will clear the way for the deployment of national missile defense.

Not until the administration has submitted the ABM protocols and the Kyoto global-warming treaty, and the Senate has completed its consideration of them, will the Foreign Relations Committee turn its attention to other treaties on the president's agenda.

Mr. Clinton cannot demand quick action on treaties he wants us to consider, and at the same time hold hostage other treaties he is afraid we will reject. The president must submit all of them, or we will consider none of them.

U.S. Senator Jesse Helms is the [former] chairman of the Senate Foreign Relations Committee.

The main conclusion is

> *The U.S. Senate should not ratify the ABM Treaty.*

The premises are the following:

> *The ABM (an early version of the CTBT) is dead since the Soviet Union ceased to exist.*
>
> *If so, we need not renegotiate it.*
>
> *As long as the treaty is a cornerstone of U.S. security policy, we cannnot deploy a missle defense.*

supp → *We should deploy a missle defense system.*

> ∴ *We should not maintain (ratify) the treaty.*

According to Helms, we face threats:

> *China has nineteen ICBMs.*
>
> *China has threatened us ("Los Angeles . . . Taipei").*
>
> *Iraq (S. Hussein) is pursuing nuclear, chemical, and biological weapons.*

Iran just tested a new missle; if Iran succeeds, the missle can strike as far as St. Paul.

North Korea is building nuclear weapons, threatening Alaska, Hawaii, and the continental United States.

America is vulnerable to outlaw regimes' missles.

America is doing "practically nothing" to defend itself.

supp → <u>*If we face these threats, we should not ratify the treaty.*</u>

∴ *We should not ratify the treaty.*

The final few paragraphs are not strictly arguments against the ABM Treaty.

Example 4 Our fourth example to be analyzed is Madeleine Albright's speech supporting the Comprehensive Test Ban Treaty (CTBT).

**Remarks at Commemorative Event
for the Comprehensive Test Ban Treaty[4]**
by Madeleine K. Albright

Secretary Albright: Thank you, General McInenry. I want to thank all of you who have been determined and tenacious supporters of a Comprehensive Test Ban Treaty— some of you for a very long time.

The Association of the Bar of the City of New York has a distinguished record of support for the CTBT, the NPT, and other major arms control agreements. We all know that the New York Bar sets painfully high standards. So it is a real honor to be here with you today.

Business Executives for National Security (BENS) played an invaluable role in ratifying the Chemical Weapons Convention. And every day BENS promotes the idea that diplomacy—in this case, arms control—is America's first line of defense.

This week, we mark two significant anniversaries in the long and distinguished history of the quest for a comprehensive test ban. Three years ago tomorrow, President Clinton became the first world leader to sign the CTBT. And thirty-six years ago tomorrow, just seven weeks after it was signed by President Kennedy, the Limited Test Ban Treaty was ratified by the Senate.

---

4. *Source:* Madeleine K. Albright, speech given at the Association of the City Bar, New York, 23 September 1999. Released by the Office of the Spokesman, U.S. Department of State.

Lest we forget, the first Test Ban Treaty helped us all breathe easier—quite literally. No longer did we have to fear the appearance of fallout in our food and water, or its effects in outer space. And the eighty Senators who voted to approve it did so in the hope that they were taking a first step toward a total ban on explosive testing.

Today, we have the ability to maintain a safe and reliable nuclear deterrent without nuclear tests. We have the technical capability we need to monitor other nations' nuclear programs.

We have the expertise gained from more than a thousand tests of our own. We have—with thanks to Senator Exon and others—a seven-year old U.S. moratorium on explosive testing.

We have dangerous possibilities for proliferation that make it more important than ever to put explosive testing out of bounds for good. We have a strong set of international norms against proliferation, backed by global public opinion. We have the signatures of 153 nations on the Comprehensive Test Ban Treaty.

And we have the support of distinguished military and civilian officials; of all the President's Cabinet; of leaders in both parties, and of the private sector.

We have, in short, everything we ought to need to make this a simple, non-partisan, non-controversial vote. We need this Treaty now. Not because we believe, naively, that signatures on a piece of paper can, by themselves, end the threat of nuclear attack. But because we have understood, rationally, that part of our fight against proliferation is building the strongest legal framework we can.

As most of you know, the CTBT cannot enter into force until it has been ratified by the United States and 43 other nations with nuclear power or research reactors. The Treaty specifies that, if the Treaty has not entered into force three years after it was opened for signature, those states that have ratified it may hold a conference and take measures to accelerate the Treaty's entry into force. Two weeks from now, the first—and we hope the last—such conference will be held in Vienna.

The United States, given our leadership on arms control, and our important interests, should have been in the forefront of these discussions. But because we have not ratified the Treaty, our strong delegation—which John Holum will lead—will be confined to the position of observer.

This is not right. Those critics who claim that this Treaty harms our interests would leave the United States outside one of the most important non-proliferation discussions of our time—certainly not a position we ought to be in.

They have failed to explain how our security can be damaged by asking others to end explosive testing, as we have already done, and to accept intrusive monitoring as well. And they have forgotten that, as I said on its conclusion in 1996, this is "a Treaty sought by ordinary people everywhere and . . . the power of that universal wish could not be denied."

Americans, and people around the world, do not want to live in a world in which nuclear testing is business as usual. They do not want to make it easy or acceptable for nuclear weapons to spread further. And they have encouraged their governments to take on the global monitoring and on-site inspections that will allow us, under the CTBT, to see that the Treaty is observed.

Today I urge the Senate to join the 45 states which have ratified the Treaty, and the 82 percent of Americans who so strongly support it. I pledge my strongest efforts, and those of this Administration, toward ratification—and I thank this audience for all that you have done, and all that you will do, to that same end.

The main conclusion is

> *The U.S. Senate should ratify the Comprehensive Test Ban Treaty*

and the premises are

> *The first test ban treaty eased our fears of fallout.*
>
> *The first test ban treaty gave hope of a total ban.*
> _____
>
> ∴ *The CTBT will probably ease our fears and give us hope, too.*

This is an inductive argument, hard to judge. Albright is arguing that if the Senate ratified it back then, then today's Senate should be even more motivated to sign it because of these other present-day reasons. The CTBT should be ratified if these points are true:

> *Today we can maintain a deterrant force without testing.*
>
> *We can monitor tests in other nations.*
>
> *We have the experience of 1000 tests.*
>
> *We have dangers of proliferation.*
>
> *We have international norms and global public opinion against proliferation.*
>
> *We have 153 signatures and support of world leaders for the CTBT.*
>
> *If we don't ratify it within three years, the signers may accelerate it into force.*
>
> *If that happens, we will be left out of important talks.*

This would be wrong.

U.S. security cannot be damaged by our asking other nations to end testing.

The people of the world want the CTBT, not testing and proliferation, and have encouraged their governments to monitor.

So the U.S. Senate should ratify the CTBT.

The first three premises mean to show that if the first ABM Treaty was signed, and if we breathed easier then, we should ratify the CTBT today since now we have so many more good reasons to ban testing:

We can now monitor so much more effectively.

We can maintain a deterrent force without testing ourselves.

We can lean on what we have already learned from our own testing.

Global and international attitudes favor the CTBT.

World leaders support the CTBT.

Furthermore, Albright argues that

If the United States does not ratify the CTBT, other signers (with nuclear force of their own) will "accelerate" it into law themselves.

If this happens, the United States will be left out of the decision making.

This is wrong.

We cannot be damaged by ratifying the CTBT (which only asks others to stop testing).

World opinion favors the CTBT.

Example 5 Our last example is an editorial arguing in favor of animal research.

Animals Play Vital Part in Easing Human Suffering[5]

Our View: Celebrities can protest, but they can't change the fact that animal research saves human lives

Today, as animal-rights activists and their celebrity salespeople attend the World Animal Congress near the nation's capital, AIDS victims plan a vigil.

---

5. *Source:* Editorial, *USA TODAY,* 20 June 1996. Copyright 1996, USA TODAY. Reprinted with permission.

Their purpose is to expose Hollywood's trendsetters and those who follow their lead to an awful truth: Animal rights and finding a cure for AIDS don't mix. By necessity, one excludes the other.

In fact, that's the simple truth about animal rights and medical research in general.

Treatments for everything from polio to menopause have required animal-based research and products. And future treatments for everything from cancer to spinal cord injuries to Alzheimer's will, too.

Researchers should practice the three Rs: reduce the number of animals used, refine tests to limit any pain, and replace animals whenever possible. Federal animal-welfare laws encourage such steps, which have cut in half the use of animals over two decades. But what scientists can't do is satisfy the extreme demands of such groups as People for the Ethical Treatment of Animals to use no animals in critical medical fields.

It's simple. People need to know the treatments they and their children receive are safe and effective. And no computer model or petri dish culture can fully mimic the complexity of a living creature. The stark choice is between animal testing first or making humans the guinea pigs.

The Nazis in World War II did the latter. They barred animal tests and experimented on Jews, Gypsies and Slavs instead. A shocked world afterward made it a matter of international law that animal testing precede any human trials. When it comes to protection, people come first.

But in their attacks on research, animal-rights groups have turned that table of values upside down to devastating effect. In 1992, for example, they destroyed years of research on a treatment for cryptosporidium. The diarrhea-causing bacteria is lethal to people with AIDS, and a 1993 outbreak in Milwaukee took 100 lives.

The Justice Department found more than 300 such acts of animal-rights terrorism from 1977 to mid-1993. The acts forced research centers to spend 10% to 20% more on security, adding millions in expense while interrupting vital projects.

Meanwhile, animal rightists, abetted by celebrities such as Alec Baldwin and k.d. lang, among others, attract millions of dollars a year to thwart animal-based research.

The AIDS protesters are letting the stars know their support of animal rights carries a steep price: human life.

The main conclusion is

Medical science must use animal research

and the premise is

Treatments for polio and other diseases etc. have required animal research.

∴ *Future treatments will require animal research.*

This is an inductive argument. An obvious question is whether, at some point, computer simulation might be so improved as to make animal research unnecessary; that is, the likelihood of advances in computer simulation weakens the argument.

> *We want to be sure medical treatments are safe.*
>
> supp → *This requires medical research.*
>
> supp → *Medical research must involve computer simulation, animal research, or "human guinea pigs."*
>
> • *No computer can mimic the complexity of living creatures.*
>
> *So we can't use computers alone.*
>
> *So medical research must use animals or "human guinea pigs."*
>
> supp → *It is wrong to use "human guinea pigs."*
>
> ∴ *We must use animal research.*

Exercise 8.2   A. The following essays and speeches—taken from newspapers, magazines, and the Internet—are concerned with some of the most serious issues of our time. Critically analyze them, using the procedure outlined in Section 8.1.

The first two exercises are about the failed July 2000 Middle East peace talks at Camp David.

Statement by Prime Minister Barak on His Return from the Camp David Summit[6]

Fifteen days ago, I set out from Jerusalem, the heart of the Jewish people, on a mission of peace in Camp David.

In the name of millions of citizens raising their eyes in hope and in prayer, I embarked to try and complete the task begun by the late Menachem

---

6. *Source:* www.mfa.gov.il/mfa/go.asp?MFAHOhnuO (3 July 2000). © 1999 by the State of Israel. (Translated from Hebrew; translator not known.)

Begin, and for which the late Yitzhak Rabin gave his life. In your name, I set out to bring peace and hope to our children and to put an end to the 100-year-old conflict between us and our Palestinian neighbors.

I embarked to try and strengthen Jerusalem, our capital, to enlarge and buttress it for generations to come with a firm Jewish majority.

I embarked to try and ensure that a majority of the settlers in Judea and Samaria would for the first time live under Israeli sovereignty. I embarked in the knowledge that there cannot be peace at any price, but also that there cannot be peace without paying a price—a painful, difficult and heartbreaking price.

Today I return from Camp David, and can look into the millions of eyes and say with regret: We have not yet succeeded. We did not succeed because we did not find a partner prepared to make decisions on all issues. We did not succeed because our Palestinian neighbors have not yet internalized the fact that in order to achieve peace, each side has to give up some of their dreams; to give, not only to demand.

I look into the millions of eyes in whose name we embarked on this mission, and say: We did everything we could. We turned every stone, we exhausted every possibility to bring an end to the conflict and a secure future for Israel. And we continue to hope.

Today the entire world knows that Israel desires peace. Today the entire world knows that we conducted negotiations willingly and honestly.

I wish to thank my colleagues, Ministers Amnon Lipkin-Shahak, Shlomo Ben-Ami and Dan Meridor, and all the members of the delegation, for the days and nights of difficult deliberations undertaken with a weighty sense of responsibilty for the future of Israel, for their joint efforts, for the friendship they displayed.

We conducted difficult negotiations; we were prepared to pay a heavy price. But we knew that on three things we could not compromise: the security of Israel, the sacred values of Israel, and the unity of the Israeli people. Let every Israeli and every neighbor know that there are things that are not negotiable. And if, God forbid, we will be faced with a choice of conceding or fighting for them, the choice will be clear to each and every one of us.

I, too, am disappointed today, as are many Israelis. I truly lament the loss of a tremendous opportunity which was so near, yet remains still far. In the name of the millions of eyes still gazing with hope and prayer, I promise not to despair, not to tire, not to cease to pursue peace.

To my brothers, the pioneering settlers in Judea, Samaria and Gaza, to our brothers in the Jordan Valley, to all of you I say today: My heart is with you in your pain. Your suffering is part of the path to the redemption of the land of Israel.

Throughout most of my life I fought alongside my brothers for the security of Israel. I will not let anyone harm it or weaken it.

To our neighbors, the Palestinians, I say today: We do not seek conflict. But if any of you should dare to put us to the test, we will stand together, strong and determined, convinced in the justness of our cause in the face of any challenge, and we shall triumph.

The road to peace is strewn with ups and downs, achievements and crises. We may still face difficult moments. But the hope of peace has not been extinguished—and it will come. Until then, we will stand united, in knowledge of our strength and the justness of our cause, ready to extend our hand in peace. Sure of our strength, we shall stride forward, with the prayer of generations in our hearts: "The Lord shall give strength to His people, the Lord shall bless His people with peace."

On the Brink of Disaster: The Crisis of the Peace-Process[7]

The king is naked. In spite of assurances and flowery declarations, the Israeli government, by its refusal to implement the signed agreements and to carry out its commitments under the Oslo–Wye–Sharm interim accords, has resolutely plunged the whole peace-process into a most dangerous crisis.

The components of this crisis are well identified. Besides the continuation of settlement activities, land confiscations and house demolitions, all of the *"unilateral measures liable to prejudice the outcome of final status negotiations,"* and as such contrary to both the spirit and the letter of the signed agreements, the Israeli government has demonstrated a manifest disrespect for both the substance and the time-line of implementation of the accords. It has refused to implement the third phase or the second redeployment, refusing to evacuate Palestinian populated areas in the vicinity of Jerusalem and Bethlehem, and insisting on withdrawal from discontinued unpopulated areas. It is also rejecting the very principle of the third redeployment, in an attempt to link it to final-status negotiations, and it still refuses to allow the operation of the Northern route "Safe Passage" between the West Bank and the Gaza Strip.

On the track of final-status negotiations, six months have been wasted in procrastination. The Israeli negotiating team has been reciting the well-known Israeli official positions in defiance of international legality and universally recognized principles: repeating the Israeli demand to annex half of the occupied territory, reaffirming the Israeli refusal to dismantle illegal

---

7. *Source:* Palestine National Authority. From www.pna.net/on_the_brink_of_disaster (31 July 2000).

settlements, pledging to perpetuate the illegal annexation of occupied East-Jerusalem, vowing not to recognize the right of return of Palestinian refugees. It has then, in view of the "persistent gap" between the positions of the parties, asked to do away with the agreed upon time-table, and engage in an open-ended process, where the goodwill (or lack of goodwill) of the occupant becomes the sole dynamic (or regressive) factor.

The PLO, the PNA and the Palestinian people as a whole, who have chosen Peace as a historical, strategic option, reject adamantly these attempts to empty the peace-process of its substance, and to impose a diktat on the Palestinian negotiators.

We have said it over and over again: only a resolute intervention of the international community, of the American sponsors of the negotiations, of the European Union, of the Arab, Islamic and Non-Aligned countries, and of all peace-loving forces in the world, can now salvage this gravely damaged peace-process. Only the forceful introduction of the parameters of justice and international legality can put this process back on the track of achieving a just, mutually acceptable and therefore lasting peace, paving the way to the historical reconciliation between the two peoples, and opening the door to a comprehensive regional peace. And we seize this occasion to greet, as the PLO Central Council did a few days ago, the Israeli Peace forces who work and struggle for the same objectives. They must be aware that their courageous action helps keep hope alive in the hearts of our people.

To rescue the peace-process from the abyss into which Israeli rejection has driven it, the Palestinian leadership has put forward the following proposals:

1. The remaining phases of redeployment should be immediately implemented, within a defined short-run time-schedule.

2. The remaining elements of the Interim agreements should be implemented at once, through consultation and sharing.

3. The Framework agreement should be concluded in due time, or be skipped altogether as an intermediary stage.

4. The deadline of September 13th 2000 to reach a Permanent-Status agreement should be maintained and respected.

5. The Government of Israel must recognize the binding character of UN resolutions 242 and 338, as well as other relevant international instruments, in particular Resolution 194 (1948) of the General Assembly, which provides for the Palestinian refugees right of return.

6. Unilateral measures, and in particular settlement activities, must be stopped at once.

Failure to move in this direction will bring the whole region on the brink of disaster, and will frustrate the hopes our peoples have formed to get out of the cycle of violence, war and confrontation, and to redirect their efforts towards development, prosperity and cooperation.

It may be that the Israeli Prime Minister's failure to honour his own solemn commitments stems from his domestic political problems. It does not make it more acceptable. But the attempt to regain popularity by stepping up military aggression against the people and State of Lebanon can only make things worse. Israeli state terrorism in Lebanon, and the criminal attacks on Lebanese civilian populations, besides causing a spectacular regression in the prospect of Israeli–Syrian and Israeli–Lebanese negotiations, will only reinforce the idea, among all the peoples of the region, that Peace with Israel is a lure, while convincing the Israeli people that violence remains the basis of Israel's relationship to the rest of the area.

B. The following is an anti-abortion argument.

Abortion[8]

Women Should Have Freedom of Choice (Abortion)

- All choices should not be legal or protected as a right. Humans have free will and therefore possess the ability to choose and control their actions. Law determines which choices, among all the possible, are legal, and which are not. Thus the decision to murder is, and always will be, one's choice, albeit an illegal and immoral one. To the extent that some choices or actions are wrong, either inherently or because they infringe upon the rights of others, they should be prohibited.

   The choice to abort is inherently wrong and infringes upon the rights of the preborn child; thus, this choice should be prohibited.

- All choices are not justifiable. To murder someone is the murderer's choice, to rape someone is the rapist's choice, to rob someone is the robber's choice, to enslave someone is the enslaver's choice, to aid and abet a crime is the aider and abettor's choice, ad nauseam. Thus, the choice must be defined.

---

8. *Source:* The American Life League at wysiwyg://124/http://www.all.org/issues/main.htm (2 January 2000). Used with permission.

For abortion, the choice is whether or not to kill an innocent preborn baby. Killing the innocent preborn cannot be justified. Thus, abortion is not a justifiable choice.

- "Pro-choice" really means "anything goes." Allowing choices without regard for human life, basic morality or personal responsibility is a recipe for anarchy. Saying "anything goes" regarding the killing of innocent preborn children is what "pro-choice" really means.

- "Freedom of Choice" means the Freedom to Kill.

What About the Hard Cases—Rape, Incest or the Life of the Mother? Shouldn't Abortion Be Allowed under These Circumstances?

RAPE AND INCEST

- I see no reason why incest often is coupled with rape in discussions of abortion, except for the fact that both arouse in most people an emotion of revulsion which proponents of abortion seek to divert from parties who are guilty to individuals who are innocent—the nameless unborn.

- Allowing preborn capital punishment for cases of rape punishes the innocent child more severely than the guilty rapist. An "innocent bystander" (at the time of assault not yet conceived!) is given a greater sentence than the perpetrator of the crime.

- Allowing abortion for cases of rape or incest effectively blames the preborn for another's (i.e., the father) crime. Killing a preborn because his or her father is a rapist is no more justifiable than killing the rapist's mother or father (perhaps even less so, in that, plausibly, a parent could have in some way influenced, caused or contributed to the son's actions. The preborn child has not yet been created; no causal influence and therefore culpability, is possible). The perpetrator alone should be punished; punishing the preborn makes him or her a scapegoat and the second victim.

- The circumstances of a preborn child's conception should not modify, let alone negate, his or her right to life. In other words, the preborn baby has a right to life regardless of the circumstances under which he or she was conceived.

- If we were to consider two infants, one conceived through marital intercourse, the other through forcible rape, would we say that one person was "more human" than the other?

- Two wrongs do not make a right. A second wrong makes a bad situation worse.

- Regardless of the father's identity, the woman is still the mother. The baby is still her child.

- The "hard cases" represent perhaps only 1 percent of all abortions. Yet we hear about them all the time. To be equitable, there are no doubt "easy cases" which can be brought up against the pro-abortionist. What about abortion performed for sex selection, or under duress, or without full disclosure of fact, or without parental consent or notification? Or abortion for birth control? Or abortion in the last month of pregnancy? Or how about abortions performed on the basis of coin flips, tea leaves, horoscopes, etc.? As upsetting or outlandish as some of these scenarios sound, all are possible. All are legally permissible. And such "easy cases" are no doubt much more prevalent than the oft cited "hard cases."

- If a rape/incest exception were allowed: How would we differentiate between the rape victim and an abortion-minded liar? Making a woman "prove" she was raped, not to convict her attacker, but to get an abortion, would be disastrous. Surely some women desiring an abortion would feign rape (the plaintiff in Roe v. Wade, Norma McCorvey, recently admitted to lying about being raped). This would cause great damage to the true victims of rape who already risk character assassination by the judicial system.

- Rape or incest engenders sympathy, and rightly so, for the victim. However, sympathy and concern should be confined to helping and healing the victim; caring for her and the innocent life within her. Caring for the victim cannot justify killing innocent life whether or not the woman, now a mother, desires an abortion. Murder is not a solution, even if the mother at such a distraught time believes it is.

- While abortion may seem to some like the best course of action for a mother after being assaulted, there is growing evidence that abortion harms the victim physically, psychologically and spiritually in the long term.

- In rape or incest, promotion of "therapeutic abortion" is derived from an assumption one could refer to as "murder-as-therapy." However, even if an abortion could provide the assault victim temporary relief there is no evidence to support the tenet that abortion provides long term benefits. The unfortunate woman and her sexuality is instead victimized twice. Any negative effects—physical, psychological or spiritual—arising from the abortion can only compound pre-existing problems. Also, destroyed are the potentially positive benefits for the mother which may arise from unselfishly preserving the life of her child. And, of course, one cannot forget the tragedy and injustice of abortion in regard to the preborn child.

- Our abhorrence towards incest (or rape) engenders sympathy for the victim, and rightly so. However, our sympathy and concern for the victim should not cloud our judgment on what is right or wrong. Also, the preborn baby equally deserves our sympathy and concern, especially under such unfortunate circumstances.

- We must deal with a tragedy in an appropriate manner. A negative event should be handled with a positive response. Killing a preborn baby is not, and never can be, a positive response to any situation. Also, we must be clear as to what is negative in the case of an incest victim becoming pregnant; obviously, the act (or acts) of incest is what is to be deplored. In contrast, conception, regardless of the precursory circumstances, is not negative: it is the creation of a new, unique and precious human being.

LIFE OF THE MOTHER

- In the event that the mother's life is threatened, we must remember that there are two patients involved. Every possible effort must be made to save both.

- There are virtually no conditions that threaten the mother's life in which abortion is a medically recognized treatment. In some conditions (e.g., an ectopic pregnancy or a cancerous uterus) a treatment may be required which indirectly kills the preborn. But in such cases, the treatment does not legally or morally qualify as an abortion. When removing a cancerous uterus, the intent is to save the mother, every effort to save the child should still be made. Thus even if the child dies, the treatment is still fully justified. The death of the child was never INTENDED. In contrast, for an abortion the intent is always the same: to kill the preborn child.

- Quote from Dr. Alan Guttmacher, pro-abortionist and former head of Planned Parenthood, in 1967: "Today it is possible for almost any patient to be brought through pregnancy alive, unless she suffers from a fatal illness such as cancer or leukemia, and if so, abortion would be unlikely to prolong, much less save life."

C. The following article is testimony on stem cell research.

Testimony of Kevin Wm. Wildes, S. J., Ph.D.[9]

Let me begin by thanking the Commission for undertaking its important work in the area of human embryonic stem cell research. As a Georgetown University faculty member, it is an honor to welcome you to Georgetown University, which was founded, in part, to foster dialogue between religious faiths and civil society on important matters.

In my brief testimony I would like to identify two important, though different, areas of profound moral concern of the Roman Catholic community regarding stem cell research using human embryos: the source of the stem cells used in the research and issues of social justice.

The Roman Catholic Bishops of the United States have made known their opposition to stem cell research, opposition that is based on the need to destroy human embryos in order to conduct this type of research.[1] Because the Bishops work from an assumption that the human embryo should be treated as a human person, destruction of the embryo to conduct research is morally problematic. If one begins with this assumption, then many of our commonly held views on research ethics come into play. Research ethics are grounded in an understanding of respect for persons that views the consent of the research subject as essential to the moral appropriateness of the research itself. Furthermore, any research that is undertaken should minimize the risks and harms to research subjects. In research involving human stem cells, consent cannot be obtained, and it is certain that harm will come to the embryos because they must be destroyed so that the research might take place.

The use of embryos in stem cell research, whether they be "spare" embryos or embryos created for research, presents a moral roadblock to that research, because the use of the embryos involves the destruction of human life for the sake of the research itself. Although the status of the embryo is clear in hierarchical statements about the embryo, this is a far-from-settled matter in our society, which is deeply divided over the moral standing of early human life. As Glenn McGee and Arthur Caplan have noted, "Embryonic and germ cell status is not a scientific matter. There is neither consensus nor fact from which to deduce the social meaning of different embryonic or fetal tissue."[2]

Another possibility for obtaining stem cells for research is to develop them from fetal tissue. However, if the tissue comes from an aborted fetus, this, of course, leads to an immediate problem in the Roman Catholic tradition, because such a situation puts the research and the researcher in a

---

9. *Source:* National Bioethics Advisory Commission, June 2000.

compromised position. Here we have traditionally used the language of cooperation or complicity with evil to describe such situations. Since abortion is viewed as the destruction of human life, one cannot "profit" from evil or immoral actions. Indeed, this has been the position held on the use of fetal tissue in other types of experimentation. As an alternative, fetal tissue from spontaneous abortions could be used as a source for stem cell research. However, I am led to think that such tissues have not proven to be good sources for this type of research.

This latter point leads me to make clear something that may be too easily lost. That is, I do not think one can argue that there is, in Roman Catholic thought, opposition to stem cell research itself. The crucial moral issues and stumbling blocks are the problems of the derivation of the stem cells used in the research itself. That is, the destruction of embryos or the use of fetal tissue from abortion are the key moral problems. If you think that embryos should be treated as human persons, then it makes sense to argue that they should not be destroyed for purposes of research. However, if there were a way to conduct stem cell research without destroying human life, either embryonic or fetal, I do not think the Roman Catholic tradition would have a principled opposition to such research. Indeed, Richard Doerflinger closed his testimony before this Commission by saying: "This commission should urge the National Institutes of Health to devote its funds to stem-cell techniques and other promising avenues of research that in no way depend upon such killing."[3]

It is important to point out, however, that there is no single Roman Catholic "position" on this topic or many moral topics. Like many issues in Catholic moral thought, there has been a long line of reflection on the moral standing of early human life.[4] It is hard to see how one can speak of human personhood in the totipotent stage. Within the Roman Catholic tradition, how one views the status of the early embryo is often tied to one's views about authority within the Church. The assumptions made about authority shape the arguments, positions, and premises one holds.

The second area of moral concern that comes from the Roman Catholic tradition is the concern that questions involving morality cannot be asked in isolation. Rather, such questions must be situated in the larger context of society and its just organization. That is, if we were to proceed with stem cell research, what type of review and oversight would be in place (in the way that we now review the use of human subjects in research and experimentation)?[5] In addition, if one thinks with a Roman Catholic imagination, age must also ask about the questions of justice in devoting resources, especially national resources, to such research when there are so many other basic medical and health needs that are unmet. Issues of social and distributive justice are not easy to discuss in American society.

Nonetheless, I would argue that the Roman Catholic tradition would say that such questions must be included in any discussion about how we organize our medical research and delivery.

Notes

1. Doerflinger, R., "Destructive Stem-Cell Research on Human Embryos," *Origins* 18 (1999): 770–773.

2. McGee, G., and Caplan, A., "What's in the Dish?" *Hastings Center Report* 29 (1999): 36–38.

3. Doerflinger, 773.

4. See, for example, Donceel, J., "Immediate and Delayed Hominization," *Theological Studies* 31 (1970): 76–105; Shannon, T. A., and Walter, A. B., "Reflections on the Moral Status of the Pre-Embryo," *Theological Studies* 51 (1990): 603–626; and Cahill, L., "The Embryo and the Fetus: New Moral Contexts," *Theological Studies* 54 (1993): 124–142.

5. Tauer, C. A., "Private Ethics Boards and Public Debate," *Hastings Center Report* 29 (1999): 43–45.

D. The following is a statement about the execution of Timothy McVeigh, convicted of bombing a federal building in Oklahoma City.

Attorney General Statement on the Execution of Timothy McVeigh[10]

Washington, D.C. Attorney General John Ashcroft today issued the following statement regarding the execution of Timothy McVeigh:

- "Our system of justice requires basic fairness, even-handedness and dispassionate evaluation of the evidence and the facts. These fundamental requirements are essential to protecting the Constitutional rights of every citizen and to sustaining public confidence in the administration of justice. It is my responsibility as Attorney General to promote and protect the integrity of our system of justice.

- "The ultimate sentence in the federal system of justice is the death penalty. The last death penalty imposed by the federal courts under the federal law occurred in 1963. The United States Congress and the

10. *Source:* From http://www.usdoj.gov/opa/pr/2001/May/218ag.htm (1 July 2001).

President of the United States reinstated the death penalty by law in the 1980s and expanded capital sentencing in 1994 for 60 new and existing federal offenses, including the most violent and brutal crimes imaginable.

- "Before the death penalty can be imposed, a special hearing is required to determine whether a sentence of death is justified in the particular case. Following a conviction for a major crime eligible for the death penalty, a jury must determine whether a sentence of death is justified, based on evidence and arguments presented by each side and instructions from the court.

- "On June 2, 1997, a federal district court jury convicted Timothy McVeigh of bombing the Alfred P. Murrah Building in Oklahoma City, Oklahoma. That bombing took place on April 19, 1995. His savage crime was the largest terrorist attack within the United States in our history, killing 168 innocent people, including 19 children, injuring hundreds more, and shattering the lives of thousands of Americans.

- "On June 13, 1997, a jury recommended that Timothy McVeigh be sentenced to death for his crime, and that sentence was imposed by a federal judge on August 14, 1997. McVeigh's convictions were affirmed on direct appeal and his post-conviction challenges have been rejected by the courts, including the United States Supreme Court. The Bureau of Prisons, which has been granted discretion by the district court over the imposition of the sentence, scheduled McVeigh's execution for May 16, 2001.

- "Yesterday, I was notified that documents in the McVeigh case which should have been provided to his defense attorneys during the discovery phase of the trial, were not given to Justice Department prosecutors by the FBI.

- "In most criminal cases, these FBI documents would not be required to be given to defense counsel during the discovery process. However, in the McVeigh case, the government agreed to go beyond the documentation required between prosecution and defense teams. While the FBI provided volumes of documents in this case, it is now clear that the FBI failed to comply fully with that discovery agreement that was reached in 1996. Today I have asked the Inspector General of the Justice Department to investigate fully the FBI's belated delivery of documents and other evidence created during this investigation.

- "When Justice Department prosecutors received the documents from the FBI, they notified District Court trial judge, Richard Matsch, and Timothy McVeigh's defense lawyers. These FBI documents were delivered to defense attorneys yesterday. The FBI is continuing to review its files to ensure full compliance with the court's discovery requirements.

- "Career attorneys at the Department of Justice are confident that these documents do not create any reasonable doubt about McVeigh's guilt nor do they contradict his admission of guilt for the crime.

- "Over the past twenty-four hours, I have carefully considered the facts of this situation. Timothy McVeigh, by his own admission, is guilty of an act of terrorism that stole life from 168 innocent Americans and these documents do not contradict the jury's verdict in the case.

- "However, I believe the Attorney General has a more important duty than the prosecution of any single case, as painful as that may be to our nation. It is my responsibility to promote the sanctity of the rule of law and justice. It is my responsibility and duty to protect the integrity of our system of justice.

- "Therefore, I have decided to postpone the execution of Timothy McVeigh for one month from this day, so that the execution would occur on June 11th in order to allow his attorneys adequate time to review these documents and to take any action they deem appropriate in that interval.

- "I know many Americans will question why the execution of someone who is clearly guilty of such a heinous crime should be delayed. I understand that victims and victims' family members await justice.

- "But if any questions or doubts remain about this case, it would cast a permanent cloud over justice—diminishing its value and questioning its integrity. For those victims and for our nation, I want justice to be carried out fairly. And I want a criminal justice system that has the full faith and confidence of the American people."

E. The following paper was contributed by one of my students.

Violence without Consequences[11]
by Jeff Bradley

Our society is becoming more and more violent with each passing generation. With the advent of televised violence, we are exposed to this behavior more frequently than ever before. The film and television industry produces violence without showing the consequences of this kind of behavior.

---

11. *Source:* Reprinted with permission, Jeff A. Bradley.

Over the past fifty years, television has become the foremost entertainment medium in every household. Since violence seems to sell, it has become quite prevalent in many television programs and films. Film producers thrive on society's apparent need to see violence. They tend to make much money from society's desire to see this barbaric carnage, but they don't take the time to realize the impact of what they are doing.

One obvious consequence is that people see violence in a movie and then mimic it in real life. An example of how a movie can inspire real-life violence was the 1981 assassination attempt on President Ronald Reagan. In the years preceding this violent act, John Hinckley, Jr., became obsessed with the movie *Taxi Driver*. The movie stars Robert DeNiro as Travis Bickle, a mentally unstable Vietnam War veteran who is unable to establish a normal relationship with anybody and thus becomes a loner. His lack of social skills alienates him from society, and he begins to imitate social interaction with himself as displayed in the well-known scene in front of the mirror when he says, "Are you talkin' to me? Well, I'm the only one here." Bickle makes an assassination attempt on a hypocritical senator who advocates cleaning up immorality on the streets. Earlier in the movie, Bickle witnesses this same senator adding to the filth by hiring a prostitute. Bickle also attempts to rescue an underage runaway girl by killing all the pimps and gangsters associated with her, whom he believes have forced her into prostitution.

Hinckley became so infatuated with this movie that he tried to portray the main character, Travis Bickle, in real life. He dressed like him, lived like him, and proceeded to play out the role. He tried to shoot Reagan, imitating Bickle's actions in the movie. Furthermore, he became obsessed with Jodie Foster who played the young girl forced into becoming a prostitute. Hinckley would write numerous letters professing his love for her and how he was going to "rescue" her.

This movie, as with most nowadays, displays scenes of graphic violence. One thing that is almost never shown in a movie is the reality or result of the violent act. In *Taxi Driver*, Bickle pulls out a gun and shoots people, and that's the end of it. The movie doesn't show how this may affect the families or loved ones of the people he kills. The movie just displays these people as bad guys who need to be terminated. It doesn't show a parent crying for their dead son or daughter. It doesn't show the impact that the death will have on everyone who knew the victim. The message here is that if someone commits a violent act, there will be no consequences. This is the message being taught to our children.

In the essay "Violent Reaction," written by Richard Lacayo, he asks a 15-year-old boy what kind of movie he prefers. The answer the boy gives is really quite shocking. The boy says, "I liked the part in *Pulp Fiction* where the guy points a gun and says a prayer from the Bible and then kills everybody. You hear the gun go *brrr.* It's cool." This child thinks it's "cool" to kill another human being. He thinks it's cool because that is the message being given to him from the movie. This is just one example of what televised violence is teaching our kids. They are being taught about the violent acts themselves but not the consequences of those actions. In a *Time* magazine forum, Senator Bill Bradley talks about violence on television and expresses it perfectly when he says, "It creates a sense of unreality about the finality, pain, suffering and inhumanity of brutal violence."

The American Psychological Association has established that there are very clear effects of watching all of this violence on TV. There is an increased tendency to act more aggressively toward other people; people become less sensitive to the pain and suffering of others; and people are more fearful of the world they live in. By watching movies like *Taxi Driver,* a person is seeing aggressive and violent behavior, but what they aren't seeing is that it's not normal. What they are also seeing is that this violent behavior goes unpunished. As a matter of fact, the character in the movie, Travis Bickle, goes on this killing spree and then gets praised for his actions. Rewarding this kind of behavior is not only bad, but it is going to teach a person that it's good to take a human life. Watching this kind of movie may very well cause a person to become more aggressive in real life. In the case of John Hinckley, it did.

[People] can also become so desensitized at seeing such behavior that will be less likely to understand the realization of violence if they were to see it in real life. Seeing all this violence can also make people more fearful of society. Children may learn from watching these kinds of movies that society is a violent place and will live in constant anxiety about what may happen to them in the real world.

Overall, what we are being taught by the "boob tube" is that there are no consequences to acting violent. One message that is being conveyed through this televised violence, which we often do not notice, is that violence is the answer to solve most problems. I strongly believe that violence is never the answer. We can never call ourselves civilized if we continue to allow this violent behavior to be taught to our children. On a final note, going back to Richard Lacayo's essay, he asked another 16-year-old his opinion on TV violence, and the boy simply stated, "Sure, the violence influences kids. But nobody can do anything about it." Yes, we can do something about it![12]

---

12. Works Cited: *Taxi Driver,* Dir. Martin Scorsese, Perf. Robert DeNiro and Jodie Foster, Columbia, 1976. Sachs, Andrea, and Susanne Washburn, "Tough Talk on Entertainment," *Time,* 12 June 1995, 32. Lacayo, Richard, "Violent Reaction," *Time,* 12 June 1995, 24.

F. The following is an article about abortion and moral behavior.

Editorial from the *Christian Science Monitor*[13]

One of the saddest aspects of the assassination of Dr. John Britton of the Pensacola, FL, Ladies Center this month is the alleged assassin's use of religion to justify such acts. John Barrett, his escort was also killed.

Paul Hill, a former minister who was indicted on two counts of first-degree murder on Tuesday, is part of an extremist group of Roman Catholics and Protestants who advocate a "new theology" of "justifiable homicide" as a way of stopping abortion. Politicians (including President Clinton and his staff) and judges who are pro-choice are considered legitimate targets to be hunted "as vermin."

Hill Is No John Brown

Sadly, this group and other sympathizers in the anti–abortion movement compare Mr. Hill to John Brown, the fiery anti-slavery Kansan whose martyrdom at Harper's Ferry in 1860 helped touch off the Civil War. These groups feel a cultural civil war is shaping over abortion.

Most sensible people know that using immoral means—murder—in search of moral ends is antithetical to the message preached by nearly all Christians. Rather than being a "new theology," this seems more a failure of theology—one conforming the views of those already based against religion, while under-cutting the earnest, often intelligent concern of those good people who feel, on moral grounds, that abortion is wrong.

Churches and religions in America are vital in maintaining a civil society, as author Stephen Carter has noted in his book "The Culture of Disbelief." They exist separately from the state and provide ground on which to inform as well as to disagree. Yet hate rhetoric and acts of terror in the name of religion will not enrich that ground but will impoverish it. While so far "only" two doctors have been murdered in recent years, and by a small group, the climate for such violence is already too prevalent. It is ironic that the very kinds of breakdown in civil society and moral discourse that Dr. Carter also laments in his book may itself feed a theology of hate and extremism—stopping abortion "by any means necessary." Such an attitude will bring not a healthy resolution, but polarization and strife.

---

13. *Source:* This editorial first appeared in the *Christian Science Monitor* on August 11, 1994, and is reproduced with permission. Copyright 1994 the *Christian Science Monitor.* All rights reserved. Online at csmonitor.com.

Of course, a civil war over abortion is what some would like. Even so, Hill is not an heir to John Brown's legacy. Brown was a zealot, but Harper's Ferry was an effort to liberate slaves, not assassinate pro-slavery politicians. Hill, by contrast allegedly waited in the bushes, shot three people in cold blood, and ran away.

Add to this that Brown had support among some of the finest intellects of the day, including Theodore Parker and Ralph Waldo Emerson. Today, no significant thinkers we know of argue to end abortion via homicide. Most anti-abortionists abhor the idea.

For some, the question is simply how to protect doctors. This is hardly enough. A sector of society believes life begins at conception and that 1.5 million unborn are murdered each year. Others feel that the opportunity to choose an abortion during the first trimester is a matter of reproductive rights.

It is possible to wholeheartedly adhere at an individual level to the moral and spiritual teachings of the Bible, yet also support, at this time and at a constitutional and public level, a woman's right to choose. There is an inner logic to scriptural teachings of purity, moral behavior, and family that, were they accepted through education and understanding, would make abortions largely unnecessary. We advocate this stand.

However, we also recognize that many in society are not yet ready to accept the authority or implications of such teaching. Roe v. Wade was an affirmative step for women's rights, but it also was a recognition of enormous changes brought by modernization in America—secularization, urbanization, the breakdown of traditional community and family, and of the many women who, despite all strictures, felt they had to endure unsafe and demeaning procedures rather than have a child.

Yet many wonder whether Roe has removed a moral questioning of abortion, making it simply another form of birth control. It must not be seen this way. At this point, we can't imagine a return to a federal ban. The problems that lead women to seek abortion remain unresolved.

Dangerous Divides

To avoid dangerous divides, more awareness of deeply felt views is needed. Killing people in a "holy war" and in the name of God doesn't forward this cause.

The self-discipline that promotes purity and moral behavior is the same self-discipline that prevents murder. As this newspaper said at the time of the Roe v. Wade decision, nothing "can ever take the place of the discipline and self-control that come from an understanding of man's relationship to his divine source, and from love and respect for good, pure, and noble in one's self and in one's neighbor."

APPENDIX ONE

Dialectic and Debate

Dialectic

Disagreement can result in an angry, irrational quarrel; in violence; in war. It can express itself in discussion and civilized argumentation—what the ancient Greeks called **dialectic,** the art of reasoned conversation.

The first employment of dialectic is attributed to the philosophers Parmenides (born ca. 515 B.C.) and his student Zeno of Elea (ca. 490–430 B.C.), who undertook to show that motion is impossible. One of Zeno's famous arguments (called **paradoxes**) went roughly this way:

Suppose motion is possible. A runner who tries to get from *A* to *B* (see the following diagram)

$$A \quad F \quad E \quad D \qquad C \qquad\qquad B$$

must first get to *C,* the midpoint of *AB.* And to get to *C* he must pass though *D,* the midpoint of *AC,* and so on ad infinitum. So the runner must complete an infinite series of tasks before he can get to *B.* This is impossible. So the premise that motion is possible cannot be true.

Such an argument is also called a ***reductio ad absurdum***—if a statement leads to an absurd conclusion, it cannot be true. If the assumption that motion is possible leads to the absurd conclusion that the runner completes an infinite series of tasks, then motion is impossible—no matter how things appear.

Socrates (ca. 469–399 B.C.) used a similar conversational–argumentative technique, which he imparted to his student Plato (ca. 427–347 B.C.), who called it the "queen of the sciences" and held it in the highest esteem. For Plato, dialectic was the distinguishing feature of the education of the philosopher-king and the highest of all the arts. Its noblest employment, Plato believed, was the dialectical approach, through the realm of Ideas, to the supreme logos (from which the word *logic* derives), the Idea of the Good.

So in Plato's Academy, dialectic had a place of honor. Plato's student Aristotle (ca. 384–322 B.C.) believed it to be less reliable than what he called *scientific demonstration,* because dialectic proceeds from uncertain premises. Still, he believed it to be useful in argumentation and inquiry and ventured to give it its first clear definition: "Dialectical arguments are those that reason from premises generally accepted to the contradiction of a given thesis." Dialectical problems, he said, "include questions in regard to which reasonings conflict (the difficulty being whether so-and-so is so or not, there being convincing arguments for both views)" (Aristotle, *On Sophistical Refutations*).

During the Dark Ages, dialectic—and, indeed, education—nearly died out. In the Middle Ages, however, it was revised as "disputation" and was conducted by means of syllogistic arguments (the subject of Chapter 4). A **thesis,** or statement, was presented and argued for, and then an opposing **antithesis;** and back and forth the argument went. Great practitioners of this formal dialectic were Peter Abelard (1079–1142) and St. Thomas Aquinas (ca. 1225–1274), whose *Summa Theologica* became the intellectual foundation of Roman Catholicism. The most famous of Aquinas's arguments were his five proofs of the existence of God, of which the fifth went (again, roughly):

The world shows evidence of design.

Design implies a designer.

Therefore, the world must have a designer (whom we call God).

Immanuel Kant (1724–1804), in his great work *The Critique of Pure Reason,* argued that some ideas, which he called *transcendental,* are beyond the scope of human experience and give rise to contradictions in which reason runs up against itself and can get no further. For example, with the idea of God as a first cause of everything, we get the following contradiction:

THESIS	ANTITHESIS
There must be a first cause because we cannot conceive of an infinite series of causes.	There cannot be a first cause because we cannot conceive of a cause without a cause.

Kant's argumentation was more complicated than this, but the idea is plain: Pure reason can get nowhere when it reaches beyond the world of human experience. Then another German philosopher, G. W. Hegel (1770–1831), argued that, far from stopping reason, this conflict of thesis and antithesis is essential to thought itself and, furthermore, to history. The dialectic does not come to a halt with the conflict of thesis and antithesis but necessarily moves on to a **synthesis** that somehow both preserves and overcomes the contradiction. This synthesis then becomes a thesis that again calls forth its opposite, and these are taken up into a new synthesis, and on and on. As a simple example of this dialectical movement, Hegel mentions Being as a thesis, Non-Being as its antithesis, and Becoming as their synthesis.

As bizarre and complex as Hegel's philosophy was, it inspired the dialectical materialism of Karl Marx (1818–1883), which in the twentieth century became the official philosophy of three-fourths of the world's population. Although it is now in decline, especially in Eastern Europe and what was once the Soviet Union, Marxism has powerfully influenced world history.

Debate

Logic-class debate topics should be fairly loose: Moral issues, factual disputes, policy decisions—all can be debated. Topics of all kinds can be found on the Internet.

Following are some guidelines and some general advice on the logic-class debate, in case your class is interested in engaging in a little structured argumentation. An example of an evaluation form is also provided (Figure A.1). Evaluation forms should be distributed to the class/audience at the beginning of the debate.

Preparation   Your biggest help when preparing for a debate is your librarian. With his or her help, you should accumulate enough facts and arguments to occupy your five-minute presentation, but prepare some more. If you are prepared, your five minutes will fly by. If you are not prepared, it will seem like an eternity.

Write your points on index cards and arrange them in the order in which you plan to present them. All information should include the source—for example, *Newsweek* or the *New York Times*. Do your share of the library research, which is a valuable skill in itself.

Plan with your partner what points you each will make. Anticipate objections and counterarguments and write your rejoinders on your index cards. During the rebuttal phase, pay close attention to what your opponents actually say and make notes. Finally, be brief, be clear, and be courteous.

Procedure   The logic-class debate lasts fifty minutes and proceeds as follows (each speaker gets five minutes per turn):

CONSTRUCTIVE PHASE	REBUTTAL PHASE
First affirmative	First negative
First negative	First affirmative
Second affirmative	Second negative
Second negative	Second affirmative

Debate Evaluation

Topic: _____

Date: _____

Clarity—Research—Arguments
(max. 5 points in each space below)

Constructive Phase

First affirmative
Name
Comments: _____ _____ _____

Second affirmative
Name
Comments: _____ _____ _____

First negative
Name
Comments: _____ _____ _____

Second negative
Name
Comments: _____ _____ _____

Rebuttal Phase

First negative
Name
Comments: _____ _____ _____

First affirmative
Name
Comments: _____ _____ _____

Second negative
Name
Comments: _____ _____ _____

Second affirmative
Name
Comments   _____ _____ _____

Figure A.1   Debate Evaluation Form

Questions from class should last ten minutes.

Evaluation   The categories that need to be evaluated are:

- *Clarity:* Did you understand what was said? Could you follow the arguments?
- *Research and preparation:* Did the speaker cite his or her sources? Were they reliable sources? Was the speaker ready when his or her turn came, or was he or she flustered and disorganized?
- *Arguments:* Did you catch any fallacies or sophistries, any invalid arguments? Were the arguments forceful and logical, or were they poorly thought-out and half-baked?
- *Rebuttal:* Did the speaker respond directly to the arguments of the other side? Were his or her responses clear and persuasive?

Points should be taken off for long-windedness, rudeness, or losing one's temper.

 *APPENDIX TWO*

Puzzles

Constructing arguments is a matter of saying *what* you think about some topic and *why* you think it. The better and clearer your argument, the more persuasive you will be.

Suppose you are given the following puzzle: You get up early, while it's still dark (the light bulb in your bedroom is burned out, let's say). You reach into your bureau drawer for socks. You know that five red socks and seven black socks are in the drawer, but you can't see which is which. What is the least number of socks you must take out to make sure of getting at least two that match?

Hmm, you say, let's see, five red socks . . . if I get seven socks I'm sure to get at least two black ones, even if I get all the red ones. But if I got only six, I'd still be sure to get at least two that match. If I got one, then another, those two might not match, but, aha! If I got *three* socks, two of them would have to match!

That's how we figure out things, by a sort of feeling around mentally in the dark. It's a sometimes clumsy, trial-and-error, intuitive process. But if you want to explain your answer to someone, you must construct an argument. The answer to the puzzle is the conclusion, and your reasons—brief, clear, and neat—are your premises.

So first you express the conclusion as a clear statement: To make sure of getting a matching pair, I must take out at least three socks.

Why?

If I get only two, they might not match. But if they didn't, the third one would certainly match one of them.

So you write the whole argument in clarified form:

If I get only two socks, they might not match.

If I get three, at least two of them *must* match.

So, to ensure getting a matching pair, I must take out at least three socks.

Hitting upon the right answer, then, is not enough. You must be able to say *why* it's the right answer. Leave out inessentials and irrelevancies and try to be persuasive by being clear and logical. Different people might of course approach the problem differently; but the point is to say what you think and why and to do so as briefly and clearly as possible.

· *Exercises:* Construct clear, sample arguments in clarified form in response to the following puzzles.

1. Three women, Anson, Brown, and Carter, work in a certain bank and hold the positions of cashier, manager, and teller (not necessarily in that order). The teller was an only child, and she earns the least. Carter, who is married to Brown's brother, earns more than the cashier. What position does each woman fill?

2. Four men, one of whom committed a murder, gave the following statements to the police when questioned:

   Al: Bill did it.
   Bill: Dave did it.
   Chuck: I didn't do it.
   Dave: Bill lied when he said I did it.

   If only *one* of these statement is true, who did it?

3. If a bicyclist's speed up a certain hill is 2 mph and his speed down the hill is 6 mph, what will be his average speed up the hill and back down?

4. A man and a woman are walking down the street. A man across the street shouts and runs toward them and is hit and killed by a truck. The first man bursts into tears. "Did you know that man?" the woman asks. He replies: "Brothers and sisters I have none, but this man's father was my father's son." What relation were the two men? Why?

5. A woman bought some chickens at a total cost of $60. She kept fifteen of them for her own use and sold the rest for $54, making a profit of 10 cents on each. How many chickens did she buy?

6. Smith sold a horse to Jones for $10. Then he changed his mind and bought it back for $20. Then Jones offered him $30, and he sold it to him again. But then he changed his mind again and bought it back for $40. Who lost money, and how much did he lose?

7. The Parks family includes Mr. and Mrs. Parks and their two children. Their neighbor, Wilbur Sludge (a gossip), says the following things about them:

   Bill and Ethel are blood relatives.
   Tom is older than Bill.
   Velma is younger than Tom.
   Velma is older than Ethel.

If only *two* of these statements are true, what is the full name of each member of the Parks family?

8. If each letter below represents a different digit, what does the *M* stand for?

$$
\begin{array}{r}
B\,C\,D\,E\,F\,A \\
\times\ M \\
\hline
A\,B\,C\,D\,E\,F
\end{array}
$$

9. On a certain island, there are two tribes—Liars and Truth-tellers. The Liars always lie, and the Truth-tellers always tell the truth. An explorer encounters three natives and asks the first man whether he's a Liar. He mumbles something unintelligible. The second man says, "He said he was not a Liar." The third man says, "The first native is a Liar." How many Liars are there among these three natives?

10. A jailer brings three prisoners to his office. All three are intelligent, but one is blind and one has only one eye; the other can see normally. The jailer tells them that he has three white hats and two red hats and then he puts one hat on each man's head in such a way that none can see his own hat. Then the jailer offers the one with normal vision his freedom if he can tell the color of the hat on his own head. The prisoner admits he can't tell. The jailer then makes the man with one eye the same offer, but he can't tell either. The jailer then politely asks the blind prisoner if he can tell the color of his own hat. To his surprise, the blind man tells him. How?

11. Three baskets are labeled "Apples," "Oranges," and "Apples and Oranges." None of the labels is correct. You cannot see into the baskets. By reaching into *one* basket and taking out one piece of fruit, you can discover what is in each basket. How?

12. Ames, Baker, and Clodd are accountant, cashier, and clerk (not necessarily in that order) in the Fosnik Department Store.

If Clodd is the cashier, Baker is the clerk.
If Clodd is the clerk, Baker is the accountant.
If Baker is not the cashier, Ames is the clerk.
If Ames is the accountant, Clodd is the clerk.

What job does each person hold?

13. The personnel director has decided that the company needs more than one of three employees: "We need Baker and, if we need Ames, then we need Clodd, if and only if we need either Baker or Ames and don't need Clodd." Whom does the company need?

14. Five female cheerleaders and five male members of the Mean Nasty gang must cross a lake. There is a canoe that will hold only three people. For obvi-

ous reasons the girls don't want to be in any situation in which they are out–numbered by Mean Nasties. How can everybody get across?

15. The explorer on the island with the Liars and the Truth-tellers comes to a fork in the road. He knows only one of the two branches will take him to the village. One native is present who will answer just one question with a yes or no. What question should the explorer ask to find out the right road to the village?

16. A certain businesswoman started a business with $20,000 and increased her wealth by 50 percent every three years. How much did she have at the end of eighteen years?

17. A doctor found a fifty-dollar bill on the street. He paid his dental bill with it, and the dentist then paid her legal bill with it, and then the lawyer paid his medical bill with it. When the doctor got the fifty-dollar bill back, he discovered it was counterfeit. It had been used to pay $150 worth of debts. Who lost money and how much?

18. Abe and Bruce together can build a garage in twenty-four days. If Abe can only work two-thirds as much Bruce, how long would it take each of them to do the job alone?

19. When Amy, Betty, and Cheryl eat out, each orders either beef or pork. If Amy orders beef, Betty orders pork. Either Amy or Cheryl orders beef, but not both. Betty and Cheryl do not both order pork. Who could have ordered beef yesterday and pork today?

20. Ames, Blake, and Chaney live in New York, Chicago, and Los Angeles (not necessarily in that order). They happen to be passengers on a bus on which there are a vampire, a werewolf, and a madman, who are also named Ames, Blake, and Chaney (not necessarily in that order). We also know these facts:

Chaney lives in Los Angles.
Ames never studied algebra.
Ames beat the werewolf at tennis.
The passenger whose name is the same as the madman's lives in New York.
The madman lives in Chicago.
The madman's nearest neighbor, one of the passengers, is a mathematician.

Who is the vampire?

21. Five space scientists and five murderous aliens are trapped on a small desert planet. Then they find a tiny spacecraft that will carry any three of them at one time. How can the scientists (using only the small craft they have found) get the aliens to the mother ship without having any situation in which aliens outnumber scientists? One of the scientists and one of the aliens can drive the spacecraft.

Answers to Selected Exercises

Chapter 1   **Exercise 1.1**

1. *It amounts to a tax cut for everyone.*

   ∴ *The new flat tax is a good idea.*

4. *He (the mayor) cannot distance himself from her (Mrs. Jones).*

   She is engulfed in a terrible scandal.

   ∴ *Mrs. Jones is a serious liability for her husband, the mayor.*

8. Already in standard form

Exercise 1.2

1. Already in standard form; deductive

4. Already in standard form; deductive

8. Already in standard form; inductive

12. Already in standard form; deductive

16. Already in standard form; deductive

20. Already in standard form; deductive

24. Already in standard form; deductive

Exercise 1.3(A)

> *A computer cannot mimic the complexity of life.*
>
> ∴ *Medical research can't get by on computer simulation.*
>
> ∴ *Medical research must use living creatures.*
>
> *We cannot use human beings as guinea pigs.*
>
> supp → *We must use either animals or human beings.*
>
> <u>*We must protect humans before animals.*</u>
>
> ∴ *Medical research must use animals.*

Exercise 1.4

> *Argument: Debris was found along its path.*
>
> <u>*Scraps of tire were found on the runway.*</u>
>
> ∴ *The plane must have been in the process of breaking up during its brief flight.*

Possible explanations: (1) objects being sucked into the engines on takeoff; (2) last-minute repairs. There is no clear example of innuendo.

Chapter 2   **Exercise 2.1(A)**

   1. Factual   4. Valuational   8. Verbal

Exercise 2.1(C)

   1. *Conclusion:* Assisted suicide should not be legal.

   Premise: It is wrong to help someone take his or her life.

Exercise 2.1(D)

Suppressed premise: Whatever is wrong should not be legal.

Exercise 2.2(A)

   1. No argument

   4. *You should not trust everyone . . .*

   <u>*They're just making a fool of you.*</u>

   ∴ *You should learn to think for yourself.*

Exercise 2.2(B)

We must not allow the war crimes to continue.

Without U.S. leadership they will continue.

∴ *We must be involved.*

We're committed to NATO.

∴ *We must meet that responsibility by getting involved.*

Exercise 2.3(A)

1. Expressive   4. Informative   8. Directive

12. Directive/   16. Ceremonial   20. Directive
    ceremonial

24. Directive   28. Ceremonial   32. Directive

36. Informative   40. Informative

Chapter 3 **Exercise 3.1**

1. "respond with overwhelming force" and "heavily armed" vs. "keeping the peace"

4. "murder is wrong" vs. "we should take the life" (which the argurer says in the first premise is murder)

Exercise 3.2(A)

1. Equivocation

2. Division

Exercise 3.2(B)

1. Composition   4. Equivocation   8. Composition

12. Accent   16. Amphiboly   20. Amphiboly

24. Equivocation   28. Division   32. Composition

36. Equivocation   40. Division   44. Amphiboly/accent

48. Accent   52. Division   56. Division

60. Amphiboly   64. Amphiboly   68. Division

72. Division   76. Accent/amphiboly   80. Hypostatization

84. Hypostatization 88. Equivocation   92. Amphiboly

96. Division   100. Equivocation   104. Division

108. Equivocation

Exercise 3.3(A)

1. Lexical	4. Technical	8. Persuasive
12. Ostensive	16. Technical/stipulative	20. Lexical
24. Lexical	28. Persuasive	32. Ostensive
36. Technical	40. Lexical	44. Lexical
48. Lexical	52. Technical	56. Lexical
60. Ostensive	64. Ostensive	68. Lexical/persuasive
72. Stipulative		

Exercise 3.3(B)

1. A male human child

4. Vertebrate with gills that lives in water

8. Extreme tiredness

12. Inflammation of the gums

16. An eating utensil with a small, shallow bowl on a handle

20. A living organism able to move

24. A volume made up of pages fastened along one edge and enclosed between protective covers

28. Creative writing

32. Coldest season of the year

36. Person who serves in the army

40. A board game played by two people, with the object of immobolizing the opponent's king

44. Water that condenses from atmospheric vapor that falls to Earth as drops

Exercise 3.3(C)

1. Negative definition	4. Too broad	8. Too narrow
12. Verbose	16. Too broad	20. Negative
24. Too broad	28. Too broad	32. Too narrow
36. Too broad and too narrow	40. Too narrow	44. Too broad
48. Too broad		

Exercise 3.4(A)

Grisham ad: false cause; magazine cover: complex question

Exercise 3.4(B)

1. Hasty generalization	4. False analogy
8. Black or white fallacy	12. Complex question
16. False analogy	20. Hasty generalization
24. Special pleading	28. Black or white fallacy
32. Question-begging epithet	36. Special pleading
40. Special pleading	44. Gambler's fallacy
48. Gambler's fallacy	52. Sweeping generalization
56. Sweeping generalization	60. Begging the question
64. Question-begging epithet	68. Special pleading
72. Sweeping generalization	76. Special pleading
80. Hasty generalization	84. Hasty generalization
88. Hasty generalization	92. Begging the question
96. False analogy	100. Complex question
104. Complex question	108. Hasty generalization
112. Special pleading	116. Black or white fallacy
120. Special pleading	124. Hasty generalization
128. Black or white fallacy	132. Special pleading
136. Begging the question	140. Complex question
144. Complex question	148. Complex question
152. Complex question	

Exercise 3.5(A)

1. Appeal to force	4. Abusive *ad hominem*
8. Appeal to ignorance	12. Circumstantial *ad hominem*
16. Abusive *ad hominem*	20. Appeal to authority
24. Appeal to authority	28. Circumstantial *ad hominem*
32. Circumstantial *ad hominem*	36. Mob appeal
40. Circumstantial *ad hominem*	44. Appeal to authority

48. Mob appeal/appeal to force

52. Genetic fallacy

56. Circumstantial *ad hominem*

60. Genetic fallacy

64. Mob appeal

68. Snob appeal

72. Appeal to force

76. Appeal to authority

80. Appeal to force

84. Circumstantial *ad hominem*

88. Mob appeal

92. Appeal to authority

96. Abusive *ad hominem*

100. Abusive *ad hominem*/poisoning the well

104. Snob appeal

108. Genetic fallacy

112. Mob appeal

116. Irrelevant thesis

120. Appeal to force

124. Appeal to authority

128. Appeal to authority

132. Poisoning the well

136. Snob appeal

140. Appeal to ignorance

144. Irrelevant thesis

148. Snob appeal/appeal to authority

152. Snob appeal

Exercise 3.6(A)

1. Pooh-pooh

4. Trivial objection

8. Exceptions that prove the rule

12. Hedging

16. Shifting ground

20. Red herring

24. Shifting ground

28. Trivial objection

32. Trivial objection

36. Red herring

40. Hedging

44. Shifting the burden of proof

48. Pooh-pooh

52. Shifting the burden of proof

56. Shifting ground

60. Shifting ground/hedging

64. Hedging

68. Red herring

Chapter 4   **Exercise 4.1**

1. A: universal and affirmative

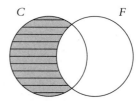

4. O: particular and negative

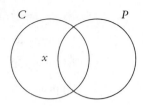

8. I: particular and affirmative

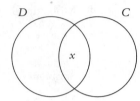

12. E: universal and negative

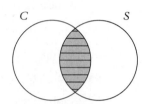

16. A: universal and affirmative

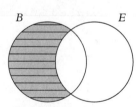

20. I: particular and affirmative

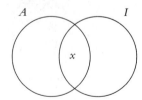

24. A: universal and affirmative

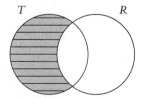

28. E: universal and negative

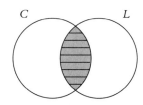

Exercise 4.2(A)

1. All people identical to Socrates are philosophers.

   All *S* are *P.*

4. All people are people who love lovers.

   All *P* are *L.*

8. All past events are prologue events.

   All *P* are *R.*

12. All women are fickle people.

    All *W* are *F.*

16. All people who deserve the fair must be brave.

    All *D* are *B.*

20. Some dogs are not vicious animals.

    Some *D* are not *V.*

24. All candy is fattening.

    All *C* is *F.*

28. No place is a place like home.

    No *P* is *L.*

32. No time when you are down and out is a time when people know you.

    No *T* is *K.*

36. No person is a person who likes a sore loser.

    No *P* is *L.*

40. No time of making many books is a time that has an end.

    No *M* is *E.*

44. All smoke occasions are fire times.

    All *S* are *F.*

48. All persons who are really beautiful are persons whose behavior is beautiful (good, not ugly).

   All *R* are *B*.

52. All lifetimes are passing-shadow times.

   All *L* are *S*.

56. All times are times when the poor are with you.

   All *T* are *P*.

60. All people who understand must be children.

   All *U* are *C*.

64. All people who are identical to John Wayne are patriotic people.

   All *J* are *P*.

68. Some stock traders are dishonest people.

   Some *S* are *D*.

72. All times I get a raise are times my insurance goes up.

   All *R* are *I*.

76. All people identical to Plato are philosophers.

   All *P* are *F*.

80. No woman is indecisive

   No *W* is *I*.

84. No person is one who skates as well as Katarina Witt.

   No *S* is *P*.

88. All eligible people must be veterans.

   All *E* are *V*.

92. No person is a person who likes a smart aleck.

   No *P* is *L*.

96. Some southerners are not bigoted people.

   Some *S* are *N*.

100. All people who can interview the Ayatollah must be identical to Ted Koppel.

   All *P* are *K*.

Exercise 4.3(A)

1. (1) I is true.

O is undecided.

A is undecided.

(4) E is false.

I is true.

A is true.

2. (1) I is false.

O is undecided.

A is false.

(4) E is false.

I is not determined.

O is false.

Exercise 4.3(B)

	SECOND STATEMENT	THIRD STATEMENT
1.	False	True
4.	False	Undetermined
8.	False	Undetermined
12.	False	Undetermined
16.	False	Undetermined
20.	False	Undetermined

Exercise 4.3(C)

	SECOND STATEMENT	THIRD STATEMENT
1.	Undetermined	Undetermined
4.	False	Undetermined
8.	False	Undetermined
12.	False	Undetermined
16.	False	Undetermined
20.	False	Undetermined

Exercise 4.4(A)

	SECOND STATEMENT	THIRD STATEMENT	FOURTH STATEMENT
1.	True	True	False
4.	True	True	False
8.	Undecided	Undecided	True
12.	False	True	True
16.	False	False	True
20.	False	True	True

Exercise 4.5

1. *No F are D.*

    All C are F.

    ∴ *All C are D.*   *EAA-1; not valid*

5. *No M are V.*

    All P are M.

    ∴ *No P are V.*   *EAE-1; valid*

10. *No B are M.*

    All P are B.

    ∴ *No P are M.*   *EAE-1; valid*

15. *All B are P.*

    All F are B.

    ∴ *All F are P.*   *AAA-1; valid*

20. *All S are I.*

    Some A are S.

    ∴ *Some A are I.*   *AII-1; valid*

25. *All S are R.*

    Some S are not A.

    ∴ *Some A are not R.*   *AOO-2; valid*

Exercise 4.6(B)

1. *All C are R.*

    All M are C.

    ∴ *All M are R.*   *AAA-1*

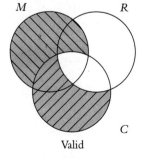

Valid

5. *No P are S.*

   Some C are not P.

   ∴ *Some C are not S.*   EOO-1

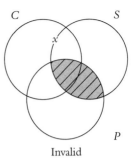

Invalid

10. *All C are R.*

    No D are R.

    ∴ *No D are C.*   AEE-2

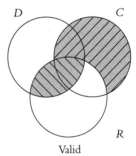

Valid

15. *Some A are G.*

    All M are G.

    ∴ *Some A are not M.*   EAO-2

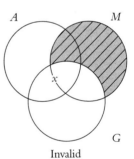

Invalid

20. *All T are E.*

    Some C are not T.

    ∴ *Some C are not E.*   AOO-1

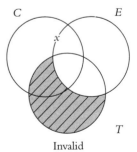

Invalid

25. *No P are E.*

   Some C are P.

   ∴ *Some C are not E.*   *EIO-1*

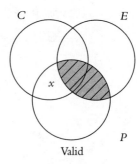

Valid

Exercise 4.7

5. *No C are D.*

   No W are D.

   ∴ *Some W are C.*   *Breaks rule 5.*

10. *No C are P.*

   Some D are not C.

   ∴ *Some D are not P.*   *Breaks rule 4.*

15. *All M are V.*

   All P are V.

   ∴ *No P are M.*   *Breaks rule 2.*

20. *All T are D.*

   Some C are T.

   ∴ *Some C are D.*   *Breaks no rule.*

Exercise 4.8(A)

The ← indicates the suppressed premise or suppressed conclusion.

1. *All V are M.* ←

   All D are V.

   ∴ *All D are M.*

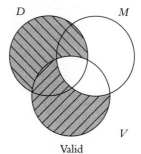

Valid

10. *All N are S.* ← *(N stands for nonbearded persons.)*

    All K are N.

    ∴ *All K are S.*

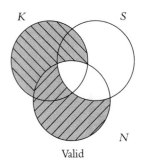

Valid

20. *All G are E.*

    All S are G.

    ∴ *All S are E.* ←

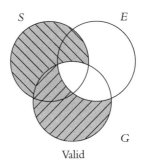

Valid

30. *All I are U.*

    All P are I.

    ∴ *All P are U.* ←

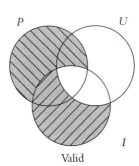

Valid

40. *No R are E.*

    All J are R.

    ∴ *No J are E.* ←

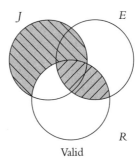

Valid

50. *No N are S.*

    All J are S.

    ∴ *No J are N.* ←

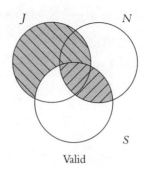

Valid

Exercise 4.8(B)

1. *No P are H.*

    All T are H.

    All L are T.

    ∴ *No P are L.*

    No P are H.

    All T are H.

    ∴ *No P are T.*

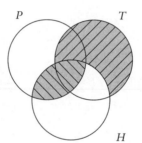

    No P are T.

    All L are T.

    ∴ *No P are L.*

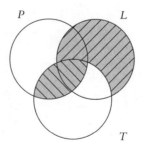

10. *All H are N.*

    Some I are H.

    All N are T.

    ∴ *Some I are T.*

All H are N.

Some I are H.

∴ *Some I are N.*

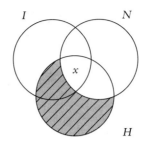

Some I are N.

All N are T.

∴ *Some I are T.*

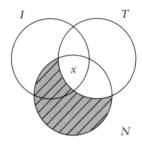

Exercise 4.10(B)

The main conclusion is

We should not keep Elian Gonzalez in the United States.

The first argument is

All children should be with their parents.

The standard form, using the parameter "persons," is

All children are people who should be with their parents

and symbolized: All *C* are *P*. The premise

Elian Gonzalez is a child

is, in standard form,

All people who are Elian Gonzalez are people who are children

and symbolized: All *E* are *C*. The conclusion is

∴ *All people who are Elian Gonzalez are people who should be with their parents.*

Symbolized, this is: All *E* are *P*.

We test this with a Venn diagram:

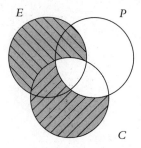

When the two premises are diagrammed, the conclusion comes out diagrammed as well. So this argument is valid. In ordinary English,

Elian Gonzalez should be with his parents (his father).

The next argument, in standard form with parameter "cases," is

All cases of a child being taken . . . are cases of kidnapping

and symbolized: All *T* are *K*.

All cases of kidnapping are cases we do not want for our own children

is symbolized: All *K* are *N*.

All cases of Elian-kept-in-the-United-States are cases of a child being taken . . .

is symbolized: All *E* are *T*.

All cases we do not want for our own children are cases we should not want for Elian

is symbolized: All *N* are *S*. The conclusion

∴ *All cases of Elian-kept-in-the-United-States are cases we should not want for Elian*

is symbolized: All *E* are *S*.

We can treat this argument as a sorites with four premises:

All T are K.

All K are N.

All E are T.

All N are S.

∴ *All E are S.*

All T are K.

All K are N.

∴ *All T are N.*

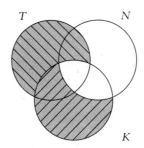

Then,

All T are N.

All E are T.

∴ *All E are N.*

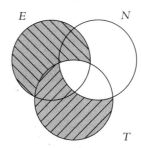

Finally

All E are N.

All N are S.

∴ *All E are S. (We should not want Elian
       kept in the United States.)*

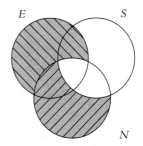

These arguments are obviously valid.

We could of course question the truth of any or all of the premises: Should all children be with their parents? Is keeping Elian in the United States equivalent to kidnapping?

Chapter 5 **Exercise 5.1(A)**

  1. P 4. $C \vee B$

  8. $\sim A$ 12. $\sim(R \vee G)$

16. $J \vee \sim S$ 20. $P \cdot B \cdot E \cdot O \cdot C \cdot [(T \cdot J) \vee (I \cdot H)]$

Exercise 5.1(B)

  1. True   4. True   8. True

Exercise 5.1(C)

1. False   3. False

Exercise 5.1(D)

1. True   4. False   8. False

Exercise 5.1(E)

1. False   4. True

Exercise 5.2(A)

1. $M \supset D$

    M $/\therefore D$

M	D	M ⊃ D	M	/∴ D
T	T	T	T	T
T	F	F	T	F
F	T	T	F	T
F	F	T	F	F

This argument is valid—no row shows true premises and a false conclusion.

4. $O \lor R$

    O $/\therefore \sim R$

O	R	O v R	O	/∴ ~R
T	T	T	T	F
T	F	T	T	T
F	T	T	F	F
F	F	F	F	T

There is a row with true premises and a false conclusion, so the argument is invalid.

8. $M \supset L$

    $\sim$ $/\therefore \sim L$

M	L	M ⊃ L	~M	/∴ ~L
T	T	T	F	F
T	F	F	F	T
F	T	T	T	F
F	F	T	T	T

There is a row with true premises and a false conclusion, so the argument is invalid.

12. $\sim R \supset S$

    $S \supset C$

    $C \supset \sim M$ $/\therefore \sim R \supset \sim M$

R	S	C	M	~R ⊃ S	S ⊃ C	C ⊃ ~M	/∴ ~R ⊃ ~M
T	T	T	T	T	T	F	T
T	T	T	F	T	T	T	T
T	T	F	T	T	F	T	T
T	T	F	F	T	F	T	T
T	F	T	T	T	T	F	T
T	F	T	F	T	T	T	T
T	F	F	T	T	T	T	T
T	F	F	F	T	T	T	T
F	T	T	T	T	T	F	F
F	T	T	F	T	T	T	T
F	T	F	T	T	F	T	F
F	T	F	F	T	F	T	T
F	T	T	T	F	T	F	F
F	F	T	F	F	T	T	T
F	F	F	T	F	T	T	F
F	F	F	F	F	T	T	T

This argument is valid. There are no rows in which the premises are all true and the conclusion false.

Exercise 5.2(B)

4.

p	q	p v q	~q	/∴ p
T	T	T	F	T
T	F	T	T	T
F	T	T	F	F
F	F	F	T	F

There is no row where premises are all true and the conclusion false, so the argument is valid.

8.

p	q	/∴ p · q
T	T	T
T	F	F
F	T	F
F	F	F

Here the guide columns and the two premise columns are the same —no row shows T T F, so the argument is valid.

12.

p	q	p v q	~p	/∴ q
T	T	T	F	T
T	F	T	F	F
F	T	T	T	T
F	F	F	T	F

There is no row with premises true and the conclusion false, so the argument is valid.

Exercise 5.2(C)

1. $K \vee \sim K$

   $K \supset D$

   $\sim K \supset I$ $/\therefore D \vee I$

   Response: Either Tom knew or he didn't. If he did, he intended to fix it. If he didn't know, his subordinates hadn't told him. So either he intended to fix it or he hadn't been informed about it.

5. $O \vee W$

   $O \supset S$

   $W \supset M$ $/\therefore S \vee M$

   Response: Either you can open it now or wait until Christmas. If you open it now, you'll be delighted and the torture of suspense will be over. If you wait, you can savor the anticipation. So either you will be delighted or you can savor the anticipation.

10. $F \vee \sim F$

    $F \supset H$

    $\sim F \supset S$ $/\therefore H \vee S$

    Response: Either I'll feed the stray dog or I won't. If I don't, it won't hang around. If I do, it won't starve. So either it won't hang around or it won't starve.

12. $\sim R \supset C$

    $R \supset P$

    $R \vee \sim R$ $/\therefore C \vee P$

    Response: If he resigns, he won't be crucified by the press. If he doesn't resign, he will be presumed innocent. So either he won't be crucified or he will be presumed innocent.

16. $D \vee C$

    $D \supset \sim O$

    $C \supset B$ $/\therefore \sim O \vee B$

    Response: If evolution is dropped, students' knowledge of science will suffer. If creationism is added, students will be confused. So either students' knowledge of science will suffer or they will be confused.

20. $D \supset C$

$\sim D \supset W$

$D \vee \sim D$ $/ \therefore W \vee C$

Response: If we divorce, we won't suffer. If we don't divorce, the children won't suffer. So either we won't suffer or the children won't suffer.

Exercise 5.3(A)

1. 1, 2   MP   4. 1, 2   MP   8. 2, 1   MP
   3   Add   3   Add

Exercise 5.3(B)

4. (1) $(A \vee B) \supset C$

   (2) $(C \vee D) \supset E$

   (3) $D \vee A$

   (4) $\sim D$ $/ \therefore E$

   (5) A 3, 4   DS

   (6) $A \vee B$ 5   Add

   (7) C 1, 6   MP

   (8) $C \vee D$ 7   Add

   (9) E 2, 8   MP

8. (1) $A \supset B$

   (2) $C \supset D$

   (3) $A \vee C$ $/ \therefore (A \cdot B) \vee (C \cdot D)$

   (4) $A \supset (A \cdot B)$ 1   Abs

   (5) $C \supset (C \cdot D)$ 2   Abs

   (6) $[A \supset (A \cdot B)] \cdot [C \supset (C \cdot D)]$ 4, 5   Add

   (7) $(A \cdot B) \vee (C \cdot D)$ 6, 3   CD

Exercise 5.3(C)

1. (1) $\sim R \supset \sim S$

   (2) $S \vee M$

   (3) $\sim R$ $/ \therefore M$

   (4) $\sim S$ 1, 3   MP

   (5) M 2, 4   DS

10. (1) $S \vee T$

   (2) $S \supset G$

   (3) $T \supset R$

   (4) $\sim S$ $/ \therefore T \cdot R$

   (5) $T \supset (T \cdot R)$ 3   Abs

   (6) T 1, 4   DS

   (7) $T \cdot R$ 5, 6   MP

20. (1) $B \supset O$

   (2) $O \supset P$

   (3) $P \supset L$

   (4) $L \supset S$ $/ \therefore B \supset (L \cdot S)$

   (5) $B \supset P$ 1, 2   MP

   (6) $B \supset L$ 5, 3   HS

   (7) $L \supset (L \cdot S)$ 4   Abs

   (8) $B \supset (L \cdot S)$ 6, 7   HS

Exercise 5.3(E)

1.	2 Impl	4.	1 Simp	8.	2 DM
	1, 3 HS		4, 2 Add		3 Imp
			5, 2 Conj		1, 4 HS

Exercise 5.3(F)

1. (1) $\sim A \vee B$

   (2) A $/ \therefore B$

   (3) $\sim\sim A$ 2   DN

   (4) B 1, 3   DS

4. (1) $(A \vee B) \supset C$

   (2) $C \supset D$

   (3) $\sim D$ $/ \therefore \sim B$

   (4) $\sim C$ 2, 3   MT

   (5) $\sim(A \vee B)$ 1, 4   MT

   (6) $\sim A \cdot \sim B$ 5   DM

(7) ~B · ~A   6   Com

(8) ~B   7   Simp

8. (1) (A · B) ⊃ C

   (2) ~C

   (3) B   /∴ ~A

   (4) ~(A · B)   1, 2   MT

   (5) ~A v ~B   4   Dm

   (6) ~B v ~A   5   Com

   (7) ~~B   3   DN

   (8) ~A   6, 7   DS

Exercise 5.3(G)

1. (1) W v C

   (2) N ⊃ ~C

   (3) N   /∴ W

   (4) ~C   2, 3   MP

   (5) C v W   1   Com

   (6) W   5, 4   DS

10. (1) (B · C) ⊃ F

    (2) (F ⊃ T) · (T ⊃ P)

    (3) ~R (B · C)

    (4) ~R   /∴ C · P

    (5) B · C   3, 4   MP

    (6) F   1, 5   MP

    (7) F ⊃ T   2   Simp

    (8) (T ⊃ P) · (F ⊃ T)   2   Com

    (9) T ⊃ P   8   Simp

    (10) T   7, 6   MP

    (11) P   9, 10   MP

    (12) C · B   5   Com

    (13) C   12   Simp

    (14) C · P   13, 11   Conj

20. (1) $W \vee P$

   (2) $W \vee N$

   (3) $[W \vee (P \cdot N)] \supset L$

   (4) $L \supset {\sim}K$ /∴ ${\sim}K$

   (5) $(W \vee P) \cdot (W \vee N)$ 1, 2   Conj

   (6) $W \vee (P \cdot N)$ 5   Dist

   (7) L 3, 6   MP

   (8) ${\sim}K$ 4, 7   MP

Exercise 5.4(A)

1. (1) $P \supset D$

   (2) $L \supset P$ /∴ P

P	D	L		$P \supset D$		$L \supset P$		/∴ P
T	**T**	**T**		**T**		**T**		**F** *Invalid*

10. (1) $N \supset (E \cdot F)$

   (2) $F \supset (S \cdot B)$ /∴ $(E \supset {\sim}F)$

N	E	F	S	B		$N \supset (E \cdot F)$		$F \supset (S \cdot B)$		/∴$E \supset {\sim}F$
T	**T**	**T**	**T**	**T**		**T T T**		**T T T**		**T F**
						T		**T**		**F** *Invalid*

Exercise 5.4(B)

1. (1) $N \supset F$

   (2) $D \supset {\sim}T$

   (3) N /∴ $T \vee {\sim}F$

N	F	D	T		/∴ $T \vee {\sim}F$
					F F
	T		**F**		**F**

N	F	D	T		$N \supset F$		$D \supset {\sim}T$		N		/∴ $T \vee {\sim}F$
T	**T**	**T**	**F**		**T T**		**T T**				**F F**
					T		**T**		**T**		**F** *Invalid*

10. (1) $N \vee C$

   (2) $N \supset K$

   (3) $C \supset (P \vee T)$

   (4) $O \cdot {\sim}L$ /∴ N

N C K P T O L	N v C	N ⊃ K	C ⊃ (P v T)	O · ~L	/∴ N
F T T T T T F	F T	F T	T T T	T T	
			T		
	T	T	T	T	F

Invalid

20. (1) $R \supset P$

(2) $V \supset G$ /∴ $G \lor P$

R P V G	R ⊃ P	V ⊃ G	/∴ G v P	
F F F F	F F	F F	F F	
	T	T	F	*Invalid*

Chapter 6   **Exercise 6.1**

1. $(\exists x)\,(Sx \cdot Px)$

5. $(x)\,(Wx \supset {\sim}Sx)$

10. ${\sim}(\exists t)\ Lt\ \ or\ \ {\sim}(\exists x)\,(Tx \cdot Lx)$

15. $(x)\,(Lx \supset Hx)$

20. $(x)\,(Vx \supset Px)$

25. $(x)\,(Px \supset Rx)$

35. $(\exists x)\,(Hx \cdot Gx)$

45. $(\exists x)\,(Cx \cdot {\sim}Wx)$

Exercise 6.2

1. $(x)\,(Dx \supset {\sim}Rx)$

   $(x)\,(Jx \supset Dx)$ /∴ $(x)\,(Jx \supset {\sim}Rx)$

   $Da \supset {\sim}Ra$ 1   UI

   $Ja \supset Da$ 2   UI

   $Ja \supset {\sim}Ra$ 4, 3   HS

   $(x)\,(Jx \supset {\sim}Rx)$ 5   UG

10. $(x)\,(Hx \supset Lx)$

    $(\exists x)\,(Px \cdot Hx)$ /∴ $(\exists x)\,(Px \cdot Lx)$

    $Ha \supset La$ 1   UI

    $Pa \cdot Ha$ 2   EI

    $Ha \cdot Pa$ 4   Com

    Ha 5   Simp

La	3, 6	MP
Pa	4	Simp
Pa · La	8, 7	Add
(∃x) (*Px · Lx*)	9	EG

Exercise 6.3

1.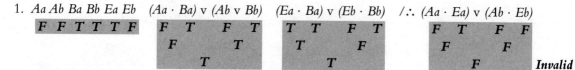

Analogous argument: Some dogs are fine pets, some cats are fine pets; so some dogs are cats.

10. (x) (*Dx* ⊃ *Hx*)

(x) (*Gx* ⊃ *Hx*)   / ∴ (x) (*Gx* ⊃ *Dx*)

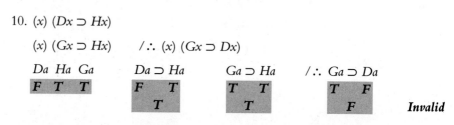

Analogous argument: All dogs have hair; all gerbils have hair; so all gerbils are dogs.

Chapter 7   **Exercise 7.1(A)**

1. Strengthens

4. Weakens

Exercise 7.1(B)

2. Weakens

4. Weakens

6. Weakens

Exercise 7.2

1. Coffee; method of agreement

4. Doing the homework after every class; method of concomitant variation

8. Type A; method of agreement

Exercise 7.4

2. Zero (only six sides to a die)

6. $\frac{4}{5}$

12. 30 percent

20. 35 to 1 against

4. $\frac{8}{52}$ = .15 (leaving out jokers)

8. 1 out of 52 (jokers removed)

16. $\frac{1}{12}$

Glossary/Index